THE CONGRESS PARTY OF INDIA:
THE DYNAMICS
OF ONE-PARTY DEMOCRACY

THE CONGRESS PARTY OF

THE DYNAMICS OF
ONE-PARTY DEMOCRACY

BY STANLEY A. KOCHANEK

PRINCETON, NEW JERSEY
PRINCETON UNIVERSITY PRESS
1968

To my parents

acknowledgments

The most important contribution to the work which eventually turned into this book came from the hundreds of Congressmen at all levels of the party who, in their homes and in their offices, at party conferences and in railroad compartments going to and from, gave so unstintingly of their time, spoke so candidly, and extended their hospitality so courteously to a total stranger. It is impossible to acknowledge their contributions individually, but that is perhaps true of some of the most important influences in any undertaking.

I am deeply grateful to the late Rajendra Prasad for permission to consult his private papers. They have contributed a great deal to my understanding of the Congress. In this connection I wish particularly to thank Mr. V. Verma, Secretary of the Rajendra Prasad Granthavali Trust for his assistance in helping me to sort through the papers and locate the materials relevant to my study. I am grateful to the family of Dr. B. Pattabhi Sitaramayya for permitting me to consult his unpublished autobiography and private papers, and I am similarly indebted to the family of Pandit Ravi Shankar Shukla, former Chief Minister of Madhya Pradesh, for permission to consult Pandit Shukla's private papers.

During my two trips to India I received an enormous amount of cooperation from various organs of the Congress Party. The A.I.C.C. office in New Delhi was always receptive to my requests, and the membership data in Chapter XIV could never have been collected without the active assistance of the Bombay, West Bengal, Gujarat, and Maharashtra P.C.C.s. Although I received a great deal of help from the entire A.I.C.C. secretariat, my thanks go particularly to Mr. Sadiq Ali, General Secretary; Mr. Chuni Lal Sharma and his staff of the press information section; Kumari Swadesh Suri and Mr. A. M. Zaidi of the Congress Party library; Mr. R. D. Dubey of the Organization Department; and Mrs. Mukul Benerjee. I wish to thank the Congress Party for permission to reproduce a copy of the latest party constitution and several tables dealing with the 1967 elections.

Among the Congress Party leaders in Parliament I am most deeply indebted to the late Prime Minister Jawaharlal Nehru for granting me permission to consult the minutes of the C.P.P. Party Executive and General Body. I also wish to thank Dr. Ram Subhag Singh, former secretary of the Congress Party in Parliament, and Mr. K. C. Saxena, office secretary of the C.P.P. Unfortunately, I cannot acknowledge individually the help I received from the multitude of Congress Members of Parliament who not only permitted me to interview them at length but who also provided me freely with detailed data about themselves and their personal views of Indian politics.

This book would not have been produced without the generous support which I have received from various organizations. I am first of all deeply grateful to the U.S.E.F.I. and to its former director, Olive I. Reddick, for the support provided during my first trip to India from 1959 to 1961. I also wish to thank Dr. Tara Chand and the Indian Council of World Affairs for providing their facilities during this stay. I am equally indebted to the American Institute of Indian Studies, whose grant in 1967 allowed me to review my earlier observations in the light of the situation surrounding and following the Fourth General Elections. Finally, I wish to acknowledge the financial support of the Central Research Fund of the Pennsylvania State University, which enabled me to pursue my research at various libraries in the United States.

In researching various parts of this book I received a great deal of help from several of my graduate assistants and students at the Pennsylvania State University, including Howard Becker, John Dawson, George Payette, Richard Rhone, and Prakash Kapil. I wish to thank particularly Mark

Acknowledgments

Sirkan for his efforts in collecting the data on state Congress ministers.

In the course of my studies of the Congress I have profited greatly from the large number of detailed monographs on various aspects of Congress party development at the state and local level, as well as from the thought-provoking work of Myron Weiner and W. H. Morris-Jones. I have acknowledged specific debts in footnotes, but their impact on my thinking has been more difficult to assess, much less express.

I wish to thank Norman Palmer of the University of Pennsylvania for reading parts of the manuscript in an early form. I also want to thank my colleagues at the Pennsylvania State University, Henry Albinski and Bernard Hennessy, for reading the entire manuscript and providing helpful comments. Finally, I am particularly grateful to Myron Weiner for his stimulating critique of an earlier version of the manuscript. The final responsibility for all shortcomings, of course, must be my own.

I wish to thank Ralph Meyer of Lafayette College for permitting me to use portions of his data on U.P. Ministers; Leo Rose, Assistant Editor of *Asian Survey*, for permission to use material which appeared in slightly different form in that journal; Mrs. Ruth P. Madara and her associates at the University of Pennsylvania library for their assistance over quite a few years; and the University of Chicago Press for permitting me to see the galleys of Weiner's *Party Building in a New Nation*.

Though her total contribution is impossible to assess, there is little doubt that the burden of the editorial work was borne by my wife Pat, whose skill, patience, and hard work have contributed substantially to the preparation of the book.

I also wish to thank the editors of Princeton University Press for permitting me to withhold the final chapter of this book until late in the final stages of production.

Finally, I thank Ashok Kumar Butani for his painstaking efforts in the final editorial stages of production.

A word in connection with spelling is necessary. In cases

Acknowledgments

where alternative spellings are possible, the version accepted
was that which seemed to represent the broadest consensus.
No doubt, however, there will be those who feel that the
choice in some cases was unfortunate. To them I can only
respond that, so long as the transliteration problem in regard
to Indian names remains in flux, there is bound to be disagreement. I should also mention that, in extended discussions of the activities of certain well-known and outstanding
Congress personalities, I have referred to them at times, according to Indian custom, by their familiar names, such as
Morarji for Morarji Desai, Pattabhi for Dr. B. Pattabhi
Sitaramayya, and so on.

S. K.

New Delhi
January 1968

contents

Contents

LIST OF TABLES

List Of Tables

List Of Tables

APPENDICES

xv

THE CONGRESS PARTY OF INDIA:
THE DYNAMICS
OF ONE-PARTY DEMOCRACY

introduction

The emergence of a wide variety of one-party regimes in Asia and Africa in the wake of decolonization has rendered the concept of dominant one-party systems far too simple, if not meaningless.[1] Thus, for example, to classify India as a dominant one-party system during the first two decades of independence tells very little about the nature of the dominant party or about the Indian political system. An alternate approach to dealing with one-party systems would be to focus more attention on the nature of the dominant party. The study of such factors as the locus of power within the dominant party, party-government relations, inner party structures, and the social base from which the party derives its leadership and support would provide a more comprehensive understanding of the particular one-party regime under investigation and of the nature of the political system itself.

The Indian National Congress has been one of the most successful of the nationalist movements of Asia and Africa and yet has received surprisingly little attention from scholars. It is clear, however, that the stable, effective, and democratic government which India has enjoyed during the past two decades can to a very large extent be traced to the success of the Congress in adapting itself to the task of governing. Its effectiveness has not rested, as some have argued,[2] merely on the charisma of Nehru; the durability of the Congress is attributable rather to its well-exercised abil-

[1] A. R. Zolberg, *Creating Political Order: The Party-States of West Africa* (Chicago: Rand-McNally & Co., 1966), pp. 2-3; W. H. Morris-Jones, "Dominance and Dissent," *Government and Opposition*, I, 4 (July-Sept. 1966), 451-454.

[2] H. Tinker, *India and Pakistan: A Political Analysis* (New York: Frederick A. Praeger, 1962), p. 103.

ity to adapt pragmatically to change, its highly developed skill in managing internal conflict, and its evolution of a decision-making process designed to aggregate the demands of a highly differentiated following.

Although the Congress enjoyed two full decades of dominance in post-independence India, the Congress was not, and did not function as, a monolith. In fact, the Congress leadership was acutely aware of the need to develop and observe procedures which would permit—and ensure—the democratic functioning of the party in itself and as a responsible element in the society at large. Though the leadership did indeed dominate the decision-making levels of the party, methods were elaborated and multiplied whereby a highly diversified mass membership could be consulted on policy and organizational issues through the All-India Congress Committee (A.I.C.C.) and Annual Sessions. Moreover, although its formal structure suggests a highly centralized or oligarchic model, in practice the Congress has in the past twenty years undergone a gradual but marked process of decentralization from which has emerged a system of interdependence between center and state, and between state and district, Congress party units. Finally, although the dominance of the Congress in Indian political life tended to reduce the level of inter-party rivalry for power, the same overwhelming dominance gave rise simultaneously within the Congress to intra-party factionalism as a powerful source of internal conflict, criticism, and change. Development of factionalism at all levels of the party thus functioned to ensure a circulation of elites and a constantly more diversified recruitment which went far to rescue the Congress from stagnation. But it also had a disintegrative effect in creating circumstances under which Congressmen failed to become sufficiently aware of external threats, and thereby jeopardized continued Congress control and stability.[3]

[3] P. Brass, *Factional Politics in an Indian State: The Congress Party in Uttar Pradesh* (Berkeley: University of California Press, 1965), pp. 232-243.

Introduction

With the exception of certain changes providing for the development of a more elaborate field organization below the district level and for broadening the composition of the various Congress committees at each party level, the basic configuration of the Congress organization has undergone little modification since independence. Before the transfer of power, the Congress was functioning more or less as a parallel government with an organization extending into almost every part of India. The Congress machine acquired this configuration in 1920 under Mohandas K. Gandhi, who believed that a mass organization commanding the loyalty of the Indian people could challenge even the power of the British raj. Beginning at the village level and extending up through the district and provincial levels, the field structure of the Congress conformed to the British administrative apparatus with one exception: the Congress provinces were organized along linguistic lines to facilitate communication with the masses. Today a similar system prevails. The Congress organization parallels the Indian administrative organization from the highest national level down to the lowest level of panchayati raj.

FIELD ORGANIZATION
OF THE CONGRESS PARTY*

Pradesh Congress Committee (P.C.C.)
Delegates from each province
↑
District/City Congress Committee (D.C.C.)
↑
Block/Ward Congress Committees
Area comprising a population of 60,000
Coterminus with the Development Block
↑
Committees subordinate to the Block are
determined by the Pradesh Congress Committee
↑
MEMBERSHIP
PRIMARY　　　　　　　　　*ACTIVE*

* For details of the field organization of the Congress, see Appendix II.

xxi

Introduction

Uniting and directing this vast Congress organization in pre-independence days was a pyramidal national decision-making structure. At the base was the Annual Session of the Congress, attended by delegates from each province. Next came the A.I.C.C., a small representative body chosen from among the provincial delegates and regarded as the unofficial parliament of India. At the apex of the Congress pyramid was the Working Committee, a small executive sub-committee of the A.I.C.C. that functioned as the cabinet of the movement. Finally, as titular head of the organization and symbol of Indian unity stood the President of the Congress.

NATIONAL DECISION-MAKING
STRUCTURE OF THE CONGRESS PARTY*

President of the Congress
elected by the delegates
for a two-year term
↑
Working Committee (W.C.)
Congress President and twenty members:
7 elected by the A.I.C.C.
13 appointed by the President
↑
All-India Congress Committee (A.I.C.C.)
⅛ of the delegates of each province
elected by the delegates of that province
↑
Annual Congress Session
President, Ex-Presidents
and all delegates
(all members of the Pradesh
Congress Committees are delegates)

At first the President was chosen annually by an ad hoc committee appointed to organize the yearly meeting of the Congress sessions. After 1934 he was elected directly by the provincial delegates. Direct election of the Congress President was introduced when Gandhi decided, after a decade of experience with civil disobedience campaigns, that it was necessary to have centralization of leadership. He therefore

* For details of the national decision-making structure, see Appendix I.

arranged for a popularly elected President empowered to choose his own Working Committee, which until that time had been considered to be an elective body. In point of fact, however, Gandhi himself continued to select both the Congress President and his Working Committee. Only in 1960 did intermittent pressure for the reintroduction of the principle of an elected Working Committee bear any fruit. Even then the results were equivocal.

With the formation of the Interim Government, the creation of Congress ministries in the states, and the granting of complete independence in August 1947, the role of the Indian National Congress as a parallel government became a matter of history. Although, somewhat misleadingly, the parallel structure was retained, the role of the party organization underwent a transformation. During this process of change and adaptation the most delicate problems facing the Congress arose from the need to determine the appropriate relationship between party and government. As this relationship evolved over the years, it was accompanied by far-reaching modifications in the functioning of the party executive. No less important were the changes which took place in party recruitment as the Congress attempted to broaden its social base in a political system based on mass franchise.

The evolution of party-government relations and the transformation of inner party structure passed through three phases. The first, a period of transition which lasted from 1946 to 1951, was marked by conflict between party and government and by disorder and confusion at the executive level of the party organization as the Congress sought to adapt a nationalist movement to a political party. A transitional phase such as this is always critical, for as Huntington has observed: "Usually an organization is created to perform one particular function. When that function is no longer needed, the organization faces a major crisis. It either finds a new function or reconciles itself to a lingering death."[4] Its

[4] S. P. Huntington, "Political Development and Political Decay," *World Politics*, XXVII (April 1965), 398.

ability to adapt itself to governing after a history of agitation showed that the Congress had initiated the necessary process of change and development.

The period of transition came to an end with Nehru's assumption of the Congress presidency in 1951, the year which marked the beginning of a period of centralization and convergence. As Congress President and Prime Minister, Nehru succeeded so well in restoring harmony between party and government that it was possible after 1954 for him to turn over the day-to-day work of the party to a series of Congress Presidents chosen with his approval and responsible to him. During this period Nehru was in many ways the supreme arbiter of party, government, and all-India affairs. Yet he also devoted himself to the crucial task of developing a complex role for the Working Committee, which under his guidance came to perform the functions of party-government coordination, center-state coordination, and conflict resolution.

If the period of convergence was one in which the government dominated the party and the center dominated the states, the period of divergence which followed saw the development of a certain equilibrium of power between party and government, center and states. The Congress presidency acquired a status and authority it had not enjoyed for some time; the party gained greater autonomy; and a fragmentation of decision-making replaced the more centralized system of the previous decade.[5] The Congress felt the full impact of these changes at the time of the Fourth General Elections in 1967.

Neither the development of effective party-government relations nor the evolution of coordinating, arbitrating, and mediating structures and procedures, however, could have ensured a position of dominance for the Congress during the first two decades of the post-independence period without certain other important developments. There has been a constant trend toward broadening the social base of the

[5] M. Brecher, *Nehru's Mantle: The Politics of Succession in India* (New York: Frederick A. Praeger, 1966).

Introduction

party. As the sources of Congress support have diversified, new elements have been absorbed into the leadership. The resulting diversity of Congress leadership and the party's ability to aggregate the demands of a highly differentiated base have been an indispensable source of Congress strength.

The present analysis of these post-independence developments in the Congress falls into three parts. Part I deals with the relationship between the national party and the national government, using as its focus the relationship between the Prime Minister and the Congress President. It attempts to show how the Prime Minister subordinated the mass organization to the needs of the new function of the party as government, what the role of the Congress President was during the period of centralization and convergence, and what changes developed during the period of divergence as the Congress presidency gained new status and authority. Part II explores the changing role of the Working Committee of the Congress. It deals with the changes in the composition of the party executive, its behavior and decision-making style, its relationship to the national government, the state governments, and the state parties, and its role in candidate selection. Part III examines the sources of Congress recruitment and the nature of the leadership elite in party and government. Altogether this analysis, it is hoped, provides a comprehensive view of the dynamics of one-party democracy in India.

PART I

THE PRIME MINISTER AND THE CONGRESS PRESIDENT

THE PERIOD OF TRANSITION:
1946-1951

Until independence the locus of power in the Indian National Congress clearly rested with the Congress President and his Working Committee. With the formation of the Interim Government, however, the Congress was faced with the critical problem of determining how the Congress movement could be adapted to its dual role in the new republic. Specifically, what was to be the relation between the Congress in its new function as ruling party and the Congress in its other function as mass organization? In the process of evolving a workable relationship between the two, the Congress was confronted by demands from the mass movement for direct control of the parliamentary leadership and the government policy-making process. Resisting the extremes of these demands, the Congress leadership has nevertheless over the years established a pattern of interaction which, while permitting the party organization to influence broad government policy, does not prejudice the essential responsibility of the parliamentary wing to the electorate as a whole rather than to the party alone.

The present distribution of power in the Congress evolved through three major phases, each distinguished by the way in which the Congress President and his Working Committee interacted with the Prime Minister and his Cabinet. The first phase, extending from 1946 to 1951, was a period of conflict and transition. The office of Congress President was held by four men, two of whom, having attempted to challenge the supremacy of the parliamentary wing, were forced to resign. The second phase, which may be characterized as the period

3

in consultation with the Congress President and the Working Committee. By contrast, Nehru, Vallabhbhai Patel, and other senior Congressmen in the government consented only to keep the Congress President and the Working Committee informed of events. The party executive, they argued, should play a role in shaping long-range goals, but the government could not be expected to consult the party organization on the whole range of immediate and specific problems confronting it at any one time. Party-government discord over procedural questions was accompanied and exacerbated by a series of clashes over substantive issues brought about by partition. These wide-ranging differences embittered Kripalani's relations with his colleagues in the government.

The first clash between Kripalani and his Congress colleagues in the government occurred shortly after Kripalani's election at Meerut in November 1946. Without consulting the new Congress President, the members of the Interim Government had agreed to a proposal by British Prime Minister Attlee to send a delegation to London to attempt to break the deadlock between the Congress and the Muslim League positions on the Cabinet Mission proposals. Although he was informed of the decision before the delegates left for London, Kripalani resented the government's failure to consult him or the Working Committee on the decision itself.[3] This incident was but the forerunner of many other disagreements which, accentuated by personality factors, eventually embittered the relationship between Kripalani and his former colleagues.

Gradually the Interim Government members became equally disillusioned with Kripalani. Even more, they were becoming skeptical of the idea that the organization could play a role in shaping policy while the Congress was in power. One early source of friction arose from the problem of maintaining the secrecy of deliberations. Delicate negotiations with the British and the Muslim League demanded almost abso-

[3] P. Sitaramayya, "Autobiography," an unpublished manuscript, p. 8.

6

lute secrecy. Concerning this problem Nehru wrote to Kripalani: "There are many matters which some of us have been discussing among ourselves for days past. There was no reference in the Press because we could keep our secrets." However, the secrecy which surrounded small inner circle discussions evidently did not hold true for the Working Committee as a whole. Despite continued warnings, the Interim Government members found that their remarks in the Working Committee were being leaked to the press. Therefore, Nehru concluded his note to Kripalani by informing the Congress President that he and his government colleagues would have to be very careful about what they said in the Working Committee. If there was anything which they did not want to make public, it would have to be discussed on a private basis and only with certain individuals, not in the committee at large.[4] If the leaks *still* continued even under such stringent conditions, Nehru warned, it would be impossible to discuss any matter of importance with the members of the Working Committee.[5]

On the eve of independence, after eight months of such experience in attempting to coordinate decision-making procedures between the party and the Interim Government, Nehru decided to set down his views on patterns of coordination in the future. He drafted a top secret memorandum for circulation only to Kripalani, Patel, Rajendra Prasad, C. Rajagopalachari, and Gandhi—a procedure which illustrates quite vividly the power distribution existing in the Congress. In the note Nehru informed his colleagues that, once the transfer of power took place, the government would be faced with many important decisions and, in such matters as finance, economics, and defense, the issues could not easily be discussed in the Working Committee. Papers dealing with these affairs would be secret. Unimpeded day-to-day decisions

[4] The process laid down here by Nehru, of continuing informal consultations among senior Congress leaders, was to become the most important means of coordinating party-government relations.

[5] Unpublished Prasad Papers, Letter J. Nehru to J. B. Kripalani, May 2, 1947.

would have to be made, and the government would require the latitude to shape policies and act freely within the ambit of the general policy laid down by the Congress. Moreover, in the cabinet system of government, Nehru observed, the Prime Minister had a special role to play in giving direction and coordination to the activities of the government. In sum, the role of the party would have to be limited.

> My purpose in drawing attention to all these matters that will have to be decided soon is to inform you of the problems before us. It is hardly possible for the Working Committee to consider them in any detail or to give us directions in regard to all of them. The point is that the Committee should realize what the Government will be faced with and should lay down a general policy as to how it should function with or without reference to it. A continued reference, is of course, impossible. Normally, a Party executive lays down the broadest lines of policy and leaves it to the Government to work it out.[6]

Nehru's memorandum was dated July 15. Published proceedings of the Working Committee meeting which began four days later make no reference to the memorandum itself. But several minor issues mentioned specifically in the memorandum were not only discussed but formed the basis of several resolutions. Therefore, Nehru's memorandum must have been on the agenda.[7]

During the course of debate, the basic approach of the memorandum also received its initial test. The committee was discussing a rather innocuous condolence resolution in honor of Aung San and the members of the Burmese Interim Government who had been murdered by a group of terrorists. In the course of the discussion, Nehru informed his fellow committee members that, as Prime Minister, he had authorized the use of Indian troops then present in Burma

---

[6] Unpublished Prasad Papers, J. Nehru, *Note for the Congress President*, July 15, 1947.

[7] *Congress Bulletin*, No. 5, Nov. 1947, p. 3.

to help the Burmese government maintain order. This announcement set off what promised to be a more detailed debate. Nehru, however, intervened. Informing the Working Committee that the use of Indian troops was the responsibility of the government, he refused to permit the committee to express an opinion on the matter.[8]

Kripalani, alarmed by this expression of Nehru's views, voiced his concern to Gandhi, who suggested that he raise the issue directly with the Prime Minister. At first Kripalani was hesitant. Then, upon hearing a news release announcing that Nehru had informed Indonesia that India would give all possible aid to the Indonesian freedom struggle, he was stung into action, for he had interpreted the announcement as implying the possible use of Indian troops. From Kripalani's point of view, a decision on such an important issue should not have been announced independently by the Prime Minister; it should have been raised first in the Working Committee.[9]

Kripalani's interpretation of the statement was bewildering to Nehru, who took immediate steps to clarify the matter with the Congress President. The policy of the Indian Cabinet, he wrote Kripalani, was to withdraw all Indian troops from abroad. The troops that remained in Burma, though requested by the Burmese government, were to be used largely to protect Indian nationals and Indian property. They would not be employed against the Burmese people. As for Indonesia, there was, he explained, no question of sending Indian troops to the spot; the statement had been simply an expression of moral support for the Indonesian freedom struggle.[10]

After independence the friction between Kripalani and the Congress government became still more acute. The irritants which had been largely procedural developed into substantial

[8] Unpublished Prasad Papers, Letter J. B. Kripalani to J. Nehru, July 25, 1947.

[9] *Ibid.*

[10] Unpublished Prasad Papers, Letter J. Nehru to J. B. Kripalani, July 25, 1947.

substantive differences. Kripalani, as a Sindhi, had been deeply affected by partition. He opposed the government's policy toward Pakistan and advocated instead rapidly staged preparations for war. In the meantime, he wanted an immediate economic blockade of Kashmir, a complete break in economic relations with Pakistan, and a rejection of the recently concluded financial agreements. He also advocated strong policy measures regarding evacuee property and opposed the standstill agreements with the Nizam of Hyderabad.[11] Because of his wide-ranging differences with the government on these subjects, Kripalani decided to resign. Before taking action, however, he consulted Gandhi, who advised him to remain until the upheavals caused by partition could be overcome and conditions in the country stabilized.

Gandhi knew that Kripalani had lost the confidence of his colleagues in the government and agreed that he would eventually have to step down. He made this clear in a letter to Patel dated August 26. "None of you has a high opinion of him. If his seniors have no confidence in him it seems best that he should be allowed to go."[12] By November 1947, Kripalani felt conditions were stable enough to permit him to push for his resignation again, and, after he had consulted Gandhi once more, he decided on placing an irrevocable resignation before the next A.I.C.C. meeting. In his final speech to the A.I.C.C. delegates, he outlined his conception of the proper relation between party and government.

> How is the Congress to give to the Government its active and enlightened co-operation unless its highest executive or at least its popularly chosen head is taken into full confidence on important matters that affect the nation? If there is no free and full co-operation between the Governments and the Congress organisation the result is misunderstand-

[11] Unpublished Prasad Papers, Letter J. B. Kripalani to R. Prasad, Dec. 21, 1947.

[12] M. K. Gandhi, *Letters to Sardar Vallabhbhai Patel* (Ahmedabad: Navajivan Publishing House, 1957), p. 221.

ing and confusion, such as is prevalent to-day in the ranks of the Congress and in the minds of the people. Nor can the Congress serve as a living and effective link between the Government and the people unless the leadership in the Government and in the Congress work in closest harmony. It is the party which is in constant touch with the people in villages and in towns and reflects changes in their will and temper. It is the party from which the Government of the day derives its power. Any action which weakens the organisation of the party or lowers its prestige in the eyes of the people must sooner or later undermine the position of the Government. . . .

In the same speech Kripalani also enumerated some of the factors which had led to his resignation.

While no one disputes the necessity of a close and harmonious co-operation between the Government and the Congress Executive, the difficulty is how to achieve it. The need for this co-operation is recognized in theory but I find it missing in practice. It may be due to the fact that all of us are not united on basic policies. Or it may be that this co-operation is lacking because I who happen to be President of the organisation do not enjoy the confidence of my colleagues in the Central Cabinet.[13]

Despite his disagreements with the Congress leadership, Kripalani was invited by his successor to join the Working Committee. Later he was offered the governorship of Bihar. Refusing both posts, he told his colleagues that he wished to be free of official duties in order to express publicly his disagreements with government policy.[14] Later he became the leader of a group of Gandhian dissidents who eventually seceded from the parent Congress organization.

Kripalani, as the first post-independence Congress President, had envisioned a dominant decision-making role for

[13] *Congress Bulletin*, No. 6, Dec. 1947, pp. 11-12.
[14] Unpublished Prasad Papers, Letter J. B. Kripalani to R. Prasad, Dec. 21, 1947.

the party organization. He failed to recognize the significance of the formation of the Interim Government and the shift in the locus of power implicit in the decision of the old High Command of the Congress to join that government. The uniqueness of the new role of the Congress as government left Kripalani with no clear boundaries setting the limits of his office. Acting on his own assumption that the Congress organization and its President would be playing the supreme role, Kripalani came into conflict with the leaders of the new government. Having lost the battle, Kripalani had no choice but to resign. In doing so, he established a precedent for the supremacy of the Congress government over the mass organization.

The selection of Kripalani's successor was complicated by the inability of the big three of the Congress—Nehru, Patel, and Gandhi—to agree on a single candidate. Gandhi, wishing to head off the threat of a Socialist secession from the Congress, recommended Narendra Dev, a Congress Socialist, as Kripalani's successor, but Patel's anti-Socialist bias caused him to reject the proposal. Although Nehru agreed with Gandhi's choice, he felt compelled to cooperate with Patel in finding a man who, first and foremost, could be counted upon to reduce party-government friction. He therefore joined Patel in asking one of their ministerial colleagues, Dr. Rajendra Prasad, to become Congress President. Following the offer, Prasad consulted with Gandhi, who opposed the idea. Prasad, as was his custom, bowed to the Mahatma's wishes and promised to withdraw. Yet, after further discussions with Nehru and Patel, Prasad was persuaded to change his mind again. In effect, he acceded to the wishes of the *new* Congress leadership. "Gandhi," concluded Louis Fischer, Gandhi's biographer, "had been defeated by the Congress machine and by the key men in the Government.[15] Essentially, by the end of 1947, Gandhi had withdrawn into the

[15] L. Fischer, *The Life of Mahatma Gandhi* (Bombay: Bharatiya Vidya Bhavan, 1951), II, 238-239.

12

background of party leadership. The Congress was in the hands of his successors.

For the second time in his life Prasad had been called upon to fill a vacuum in the Congress at a time of crisis. Prasad was the most Gandhian of the Congress giants. He was highly respected in the organization, and, because of his long association with the Parliamentary Board, he had a great deal of personal influence among party members. Since he belonged to the inner circle of decision-makers and had acquired an understanding of governmental problems through his position as Food Minister, there was little likelihood of a clash developing between the organization and the government. His selection was welcomed in Congress circles,[16] and it was expected that he would add renewed dignity and vigor to the office.

At first, there were suggestions that Prasad should remain in the government, perhaps as Minister without Portfolio. But Gandhi objected, and Prasad himself felt that the presidency required his undivided attention.[17] Moreover, the leadership felt that it was essential to keep the two functions separate. "The policy has always been," Prasad once wrote, "not to mix up the office of the government with that of our Congress organization."[18] Therefore, he resigned as Food Minister, although he still retained his position as President of the Constituent Assembly.

Prasad's tenure as Congress President was short. It was essentially an interim arrangement designed to meet the immediate challenge to the government posed by Kripalani's resignation. Yet during this period of about a year, three major events took place: Gandhi was assassinated; the Congress Socialists left the party; and friction between Nehru and Patel caused a realignment of forces within the Congress, the reverberations of which were felt when the time came to

[16] *Hindustan Times* (New Delhi), Nov. 18, 1947.
[17] *Ibid.*
[18] Unpublished Prasad Papers, Letter R. Prasad to R. A. Kidwai, June 4, 1948.

select the President for the Jaipur Session of the Congress in 1948.

Despite their own increasingly divergent opinions on party and government policies, both Nehru and Patel encouraged Prasad to remain as President in order to ensure the continuance of the party-government harmony which had subsisted during his tenure; but Prasad insisted that his health would no longer permit him to shoulder the burdens of the office.[19] When Prasad remained firm in his decision, Nehru and Patel, for the first time deprived of the mediating influence of Gandhi, were unable to agree on a candidate to replace him. Therefore, they decided to remain neutral and permit an open contest, a rarity at that point in Congress history. As a result, the stage was set for a struggle among the junior leaders of the party.

Although the contestants for the post of President in 1948 were sharply divided on ideological, sectional, and organizational goals, the issue most debated was the distribution of power in the Congress. The orthodox Gandhians decided to place their hopes in either Shankarrao Deo, then General Secretary of the Congress, or Dr. P. C. Ghosh, former Chief Minister of Bengal. The right wing decided upon the venerable Purshottamdas Tandon, Speaker of the Uttar Pradesh Legislative Assembly. A fourth candidate was Dr. Pattabhi Sitaramayya, a South Indian who felt that he alone carried the mantle of Gandhi. Finally, to complete the list, Kripalani decided late in the campaign to contend for the post from which he had resigned less than a year before. With his entry, the relationship between the party and the government once more became a critical issue.

The Gandhians, led by Deo and P. C. Ghosh, were deeply concerned about the state of the Congress organization and its ability to carry out Gandhi's expectations. "We who may be called juniors," Deo wrote Prasad, "are really very anxious

[19] Unpublished Prasad Papers, Letter R. Prasad to Dr. P. C. Ghosh, Oct. 1, 1948.

14

and worried about the future of the Congress." The Congress, he insisted, must not only live, but live vigorously in order to fulfill the task set by Gandhi. But conditions, he found, were most unfavorable; moreover, "yourself, Sardarji [Patel] and Panditji [Nehru] are not looking at the matter from the same viewpoint as ours."[20] In another letter to Prasad, Deo declared that Patel had also expressed his belief that the organization was in deplorable condition. Evidently he, too, did not know what steps should be taken to improve it.[21] Both Ghosh and Deo were willing to renounce their candidacy if the leadership would offer a solution to the problem of revitalizing the party.

Tandon was an orthodox Hindu from Uttar Pradesh who was not a member of the Working Committee or of the All-India Congress Committee and was, therefore, completely outside the circle from which Congress Presidents were normally chosen. He represented the conservative wing of the party. Because of his very strong views on communal problems, he was staunchly anti-Pakistan and had opposed partition. A firm supporter of Hindi as the national language, he opposed any attempt to change Hindu custom or tradition. Because of these views, which were diametrically opposed to those of the Prime Minister, Tandon had vigorous support from conservative groups in the Hindi-speaking states of North India, but little in the South.

The fourth candidate was Dr. Pattabhi Sitaramayya of Andhra. Ever since his selection by Gandhi to oppose Subhas Bose in 1939 and his subsequent defeat, he had been passed over for the post of Congress President. Pattabhi, feeling as he did that Gandhi's will had been thwarted in 1939, was passionately determined to become Congress President. Upon hearing of Prasad's desire to step down, he began immediately to seek support for his candidacy. On September 18, he wrote

[20] Unpublished Prasad Papers, Letter Shankarrao Deo to R. Prasad, Sept. 17, 1948.
[21] Unpublished Prasad Papers, Letter Shankarrao Deo to R. Prasad, Sept. 20, 1948.

letters to Nehru, Prasad, Patel, and Maulana Abul Kalam Azad asking for their endorsement.[22]

Invoking a kinship between Andhra and Bihar in his letter, Pattabhi asked Prasad for his active support. He admitted that he was not a member of the inner group, the existence of which he acknowledged, but of the second rank of leadership. He then pointed to his years of service and his devotion to the cause of independence: "It may be extravagant to expect that elder statesmen of the country will judge of the times and favor one of their own long trusted colleagues who, whatever his failings, has been a cent [*sic*] per cent Congressman and follower of Gandhiji's teachings without becoming actually a member of the inner group."[23]

In his reply of September 28, Prasad indicated that he was very sympathetic to Pattabhi's cause although Patel was pressing him to serve another term.

> I need hardly tell you that it will give me genuine pleasure if I could support you, not only because I owe it as a friend but because I think you should be given the responsibility. I do not look upon the Congress Presidentship particularly nowadays as a soft job. When we were fighting, everything was clear. We had to be prepared to suffer and when once that determination was there, nothing else mattered. Nowadays, however, the position has become very, very complicated and I feel that the work of the President of the Congress is much more difficult now because of the conflicting pulls in various directions. On supporting you I would therefore not be showing any kindness to you but really be putting on you a heavy burden.[24]

The response Pattabhi received from Pandit Nehru was not so favorable. Claiming, as he frequently did until the death of

[22] Sitaramayya, "Autobiography," p. 15.

[23] Unpublished Prasad Papers, Letter P. Sitaramayya to R. Prasad, Sept. 18, 1948.

[24] Unpublished Prasad Papers, Letter R. Prasad to P. Sitaramayya, Sept. 28, 1948.

Patel in December 1950, a lack of knowledge of organizational affairs, Nehru refused to endorse him outright.

> As for the Congress Presidentship, I must confess that I feel reluctant to take any step. Ever since I took office, I have done so little direct Congress work that I do not feel justified in giving any kind of a lead in such a matter.
> I would welcome you of course as the Congress President. But there appear to be several candidates, all of whom are our old colleagues. It was right and proper for Gandhiji to recommend one person. But much smaller folk are not in a position to do so and where there are several candidates in the field, it becomes even more difficult to support any one of them publicly. But as I have said above, I would welcome your election.[25]

If Nehru's response was noncommittal, Patel's response was to ignore the letter completely. As for Azad, although we have no copy of his reply, later events revealed his active support for his old friend Dr. Pattabhi.[26]

Acharya Kripalani was the most controversial entrant in the presidential contest. Although still popular among rank-and-file Congressmen, his chances of success were considered slight because of his resignation only a year before. Rajendra Prasad was particularly disturbed about how Kripalani's announcement of his candidacy would affect the party-government relationship. Therefore, in his role as Congress President and as a senior Congress leader, he wrote to Kripalani arguing that his presence in the race would create the impression that the party lacked confidence in the government. Prasad advised Kripalani to withdraw immediately.

> Your election can have only one of two interpretations. Either people may think that your views have been accepted by the bulk of the Congressmen in the country and you are re-instated to your old position because the

[25] Unpublished Prasad Papers, Letter J. Nehru to P. Sitaramayya, Sept. 22, 1948.
[26] Sitaramayya, "Autobiography," p. 15.

17

Congress repudiates the action of the All-India Congress Committee which accepted your resignation and in a way shows its want of confidence in the Government for the attitude it adopted toward you, or the other interpretation may be that there has been no change in the position at all but that you yourself have given up that attitude and are elected more or less after expressing your repentance at least by implication of what you did. I do not think either position is good. It is not in the interest of the country to do anything which might leave an impression that there is a difference between the Congress and the Ministry and the Congress has given a slap to the Ministry.[27]

Kripalani, left with little choice but to comply with Prasad's request, withdrew.

Meanwhile, reports appearing in the *Hindustan Times* to the effect that the High Command was pressing Prasad to retain the Congress presidency for another term in order to ensure cooperation and harmony between the Congress organization and the government[28] prompted Pattabhi to contact Dr. Prasad immediately to assure him of his own ability to cooperate and maintain a proper balance between the party and the government. "On the most vital occasions," he assured Prasad, "I shut up my mouth in the interest of such harmony and cooperation." On the failure of the Patiala Ministry, for example, he had said nothing, and on the retention of the Maharaja of Bilaspur as administrator, "I swallowed my feelings." In the legislature, he observed, he had never introduced an interpellation, had asked only a few supplementaries, and had even kept quiet in the Executive Committee of the Congress Party in Parliament. The issue of linguistic states was, he realized, the one item on which he has incurred the displeasure of Patel. Although the possibility of a Telugu-speaking Andhra had already been granted

[27] Unpublished Prasad Papers, Letter R. Prasad to J. B. Kripalani, Oct. 10, 1948.
[28] Sept. 23, 1948.

to him, Patel felt that Pattabhi had a tendency to belabor his advocacy. Pattabhi assured Prasad that he had no personal ambitions and that he had the solid backing of his province. In fact, he was quick to point out that the whole South was behind him. "This may be news to Sardarji [Patel] who was reported to have said that I could not get two members in my own province to support me."[29]

By October 1, three days before the closing of nominations, Prasad reached a decision. He announced officially that he would not be a candidate, and he addressed confidential letters to each of the other candidates asking them to step down to permit the unanimous election of Dr. Pattabhi. He had been persuaded that the sentiments of the South deserved consideration and had received assurances that Pattabhi was solidly backed by the South. The South having provided only four Presidents in the history of Congress, he felt that for this reason, primarily, Pattabhi should be the party's unanimous choice.[30]

Several days later, while brisk canvassing was being conducted throughout the country,[31] Prasad met with P. C. Ghosh, Shankarrao Deo, and Jugal Kishore, another General Secretary, to discuss the election.[32] It was decided that Patel's cooperation should be sought in order to secure an uncontested election, and, because of Prasad's poor health, Deo was delegated to discuss the issue with Patel. When Deo approached Patel, Patel was clearly annoyed. He agreed with Prasad's reasoning as far as Kripalani's candidacy was concerned and approved of Deo's and Ghosh's decisions to withdraw. However, he was upset at the thought of raising a North-South issue. Feeling that the South had little cause for complaint, he did not think the selection of a new Congress President should be decided on sectional grounds. He re-

[29] Unpublished Prasad Papers, Letter P. Sitaramayya to R. Prasad, Sept. 25, 1948.

[30] Unpublished Prasad Papers, Letter R. Prasad to Dr. P. C. Ghosh, Oct. 1, 1948.

[31] *Hindustan Times* (New Delhi), Oct. 9, 1948.

[32] *Hindustan Times* (New Delhi), Oct. 8, 1948.

fused to cooperate in bringing about an uncontested election, asserting that his relationship to Tandon was not so close that he could request him to withdraw. Lastly, Patel argued that his personal intervention would be contrary to an informal agreement with Nehru and Prasad according to which each of them had planned to remain neutral in this matter.[33]

On October 15, the last day for withdrawals, all candidates except Tandon and Pattabhi eliminated themselves from the race. There were reports that Tandon, ready and willing to withdraw, had been persuaded to maintain his candidacy by a member of the High Command.[34] In any event, Prasad's efforts to achieve an uncontested election failed, and the direct confrontation of Pattabhi and Tandon highlighted once more the issue of party-government relations which Prasad had hoped to avoid by persuading Kripalani to withdraw. Although Pattabhi had provided Congress leaders in the government with assurances that he could be trusted to cooperate in maintaining an amicable relationship between party and government, a victory by Tandon almost promised a challenge. Realizing the implications of the impending contest, Deo wrote to Prasad with a warning that "it would be the greatest calamity if . . . Pattabhi is not elected, not only personally to him but to the Congress as an organisation, because people will not take this contest as between two persons but between two ways of thinking and defeat of the one is not victory for the other personally, but success for the principles, policy and programme he stands for."[35]

Deo's warning notwithstanding, once the field had been narrowed down to two candidates, various forces in the Congress began to coalesce around one or the other. A contest of major proportions was in the making. Pattabhi, though personally a conservative, became the symbol of the progressive forces within the Congress. He was supported by the

[33] Unpublished Prasad Papers, Letter Shankarrao Deo to R. Prasad, Oct. 12, 1948.

[34] *Amrita Bazar Patrika* (Calcutta), Oct. 16, 1948.

[35] Unpublished Prasad Papers, Letter Shankarrao Deo to R. Prasad, Oct. 15, 1948.

Gandhian and leftist groups in the organization as well as by the leaders of the South. Tandon, on the other hand, was backed by the right wing of the Congress, by conservative industrialists like G. D. Birla, who financed his campaign,[36] and by the party bosses of the northern and western states.

The Congress High Command remained nominally uncommitted, but their influence was always present. Although Nehru remained neutral and was absent from the country during the actual struggle, his name was used freely by Pattabhi's backers, who claimed his moral support. Those who wished to believe Nehru preferred Pattabhi could also point to the fact that Pattabhi's campaign was headed by Rafi Ahmad Kidwai, a minister in Nehru's Cabinet and a close personal friend of the Prime Minister.[37] Pattabhi was also supported by Maulana Azad, Shankarrao Deo, and P. C. Ghosh, all of whom were close followers of the Prime Minister. Patel was publicly neutral, but privately he worked actively for Tandon.[38] During the canvassing, his secretary contacted all the key state Congress leaders and asked them to support Tandon.[39] Throughout the contest, however, Pattabhi's supporters attempted to maintain the myth of Patel's impartiality in order to neutralize his role as much as possible.[40]

When the election was over and the votes of the delegates to the Jaipur Session of the Congress were counted, Pattabhi emerged victorious by an unimpressive margin of 114 votes. He had received a total of 1,199 votes to Tandon's 1,085.[41] It was a narrow victory for the self-professed Nehruites. All major state delegations were split because of local factional

[36] Sitaramayya, "Autobiography," Ch. 34, p. 1. ·

[37] P. Sitaramayya, *Speeches Delivered by Dr. B. Pattabhi Sitaramayya: Governor, Madhya Pradesh* (Nagpur: Government Printers, Madhya Pradesh, 1956), p. 387.

[38] Satabhisha, *Rashtrapathi Dr. Pattabhi* (Madras: Jayeeya Jnana Mandir, 1948), p. 60.

[39] *Indian Nation* (Patna), March 3, 1950; Sitaramayya, "Autobiography," pp. 15, 20.

[40] *Hindustan Times* (New Delhi), Oct. 21, 1948; *The Statesman* (New Delhi), Oct. 23, 1948.

[41] *National Herald* (Lucknow), Jan. 2, 1949.

intrigues, but the distribution of votes by states is revealing. Of the twenty-three Congress provinces, Tandon received a majority in only nine: Berar, Bombay, Gujarat, Vindhya Pradesh, Karnatak, Mahakoshal, Orissa, Uttar Pradesh, and West Bengal. Thus, Tandon's support came, as was expected, largely from the Hindi-speaking states of the North and the industrial areas of the West. Karnatak, the only southern state to give Tandon a majority, divided its votes almost evenly and reflected the sharp local factional disputes in the state. On the other hand, except for scattered losses, Pattabhi received almost unanimous backing from the South. The 36 votes he lost in his home state of Andhra were cast by T. Prakasam and his followers, who were at the time engaged in a bitter factional feud with Pattabhi's group in that state. In the North, Pattabhi received 129 votes in Uttar Pradesh, Tandon's home state. These votes were cast largely by the Kripalani-Kidwai faction. Pattabhi lost heavily in West Bengal because of Tandon's strong anti-Pakistan stand. The continued resentment among Bengalis over Pattabhi's 1939 contest with Subhas Bose and the weakness of the sympathetic P. C. Ghosh faction in Bengal Congress politics also damaged Pattabhi's influence in West Bengal. Ghosh had been Chief Minister of Bengal until January 1948, but after that he had lost power in both the government and the organization. In the Punjab, on the other hand, Pattabhi was able to overcome Tandon's influence because he received strong support from the Praja Mandals in Pepsu. Equally important, Pattabhi profited from the anti-Hindi attitude of the Punjabis. His well-known stand on linguistic provinces received strong backing in the Punjab. Yet Pattabhi was also to carry the Hindi-speaking province of Bihar because of the moral support of Dr. Prasad and the Harijan leader Jagjivan Ram. Maharashtra supported Pattabhi almost unanimously owing to the efforts of Shankarrao Deo. In general, Pattabhi received the votes of the minority communities—Sikhs, Muslims, Christians, and Harijans—as well as strong support from the former princely states including Rajputana, the largest of them.

Although no one could know it at the time, Pattabhi's election to the Congress presidency in 1948 was only a preliminary to the major bout that was destined to take place in 1950. In the meantime, however, the immediate crisis was overcome, conflicts within the party were temporarily halted, and Pattabhi's two years in office helped to reinforce the relationship between the Congress President and the Prime Minister which had been more than implicit in the circumstances leading to Kripalani's resignation.

Fortunately, Pattabhi, who recognized the limitations of the office of Congress President, was also temperamentally equipped to play a passive role as the day-to-day administrator of the party machine. In his presidential address at the Jaipur Session of the Congress, he detailed his conception of the function of the party as a complement to that of the government:

A Government must govern and is therefore concerned with the problems of the day, and with the passions of the hour. Its work is concrete, its solutions must be immediate. The Congress has a wider jurisdiction and the more remote task of coordinating through a dispassionate criticism the achievements of the past, the endeavours of the present and the anticipation of the future. The Congress is really the Philosopher while the Government is the Politician. The latter has power and the former influence. Sometimes the influence which is moral overcomes power which is physical. Or shall we say, the Congress is like a benevolent and elderly mother-in-law and the Government is like a tactful and young daughter-in-law. All the power is in reality vested in the latter through the husband. Yet she attempts—not merely affects—to obey her parents-in-Law, while ultimately carrying out her own will.

*   *   *   *   *   *   *   *   *   *   *   *   *   *

The Congress is at once the "Thermometer" that measures the rise of "temperature" in its emotions and the "Barometer" that gauges the fall in pressure of its actions. Or shall we say, varying the simile, the Congress represents the tentacles of the body politic, probing public opinion in the land. It is sometimes described also as the brain-trust of Government which ought to supplement and sublimate the experiences of Ministers gathered by them in their tours and talks. Our ministers have to work under high pressure and tension, and are not able to take the all too desirable week-end holidays in which to think out the problems too knotty for quick or easy solution. Holidays are really meant for making possible high-level thinking during weekdays, and may not be grudged till sick leave is necessitated. That is why the Government of the day requires the aid of unencumbered thinking.[42]

Before relinquishing the Congress presidency at the end of his term of office, Pattabhi warned his successor that the conception of the Congress as a parallel government had ceased to be relevant. Both the legislative and executive functions of the nation, he declared, were now being performed by a popular government.

I congratulate myself on the success with which I have maintained the utmost cordiality of relations with the Ministers at the Centre and in the States. It would have been profoundly easy to put them to a strain, but it required both forbearance and charity on both sides to prevent any disturbance. To that extent, however, the critic may be in a position to question or even challenge the vigour, as well as the rigour of my administration and I am willing to let go the challenge unanswered.

There is much of routine in the discharge of the duties that fall to the lot of the Congress President which need

[42] Dr. B. P. Sitaramayya, *Presidential Address, The Indian National Congress, Fifty-fifth Session* (New Delhi: A.I.C.C., 1948), pp. 48-50.

not be dwelt upon and which cannot be even described categorically. . . . Suffice it to say that when I became President I only thought I was made the *Pathi* without a Rashtram which was quietly removed from it. But, later by an 'open dacoity' my whole title was taken away and made over to the President of the Republic. I am sincerely proud that if I have done nothing for the Republic I have at least supplied the title for its President. Let me conclude these light-hearted remarks with a serious quotation from the memoirs of the Duke of Windsor who made an observation wholly and equally applicable to me when he said of the Prince of Wales: *"Presidentship is a position of responsibility without authority, expectation without opportunity, prestige without power."*[43]

What a contrast, then, between Pattabhi and Kripalani, who, recognizing the same problem, had chosen not to adapt but to protest. Refusing to abide the shifting locus of power within the Congress, determined instead to implement his own conception of the role of the Congress President in independent India, Kripalani came into direct conflict with his senior colleagues in the government. His position became increasingly untenable and he resigned. The first great effort to preserve organizational supremacy failed.

Rajendra Prasad was selected to restore unity and harmony to a divided Congress. His role as President depended, not upon the office, but upon his own stature as a member of the Congress inner circle. His close personal relations with his colleagues in the government, his position as President of the Constituent Assembly, his prior governmental experience, and his personal temperament made him an ideal successor to Kripalani. Prasad knew how to exercise self-restraint. The factors which made him a good Congress President also made him an excellent choice as the first President of India—a post he held for the first twelve

[43] *Congress Bulletin*, No. 6, Sept.-Oct. 1950, pp. 216-217. Italics mine.

years of the Indian Republic. Unfortunately, during most of his tenure as Congress President, he was extremely ill and unable to play an active role as administrator of the party.

Even before his election as Congress President, Dr. Pattabhi had articulated publicly the changes that had taken place in the Congress movement. After the Interim Government had been in office for only eight months, he was asked to assess the relationship between the party and the government and replied: "There can be no doubt or dismay about the matter. The political centre of gravity shifted from the Congress to the Government House. The members of the Interim Government are naturally the first to hear about all new issues and proposed solutions to them with which they come to the Working Committee."[44] Pattabhi, who was satisfied if the Congress could in some way influence policy, did not, as President, stress the need for initiating or controlling it.

Thus, for a period of three years following the resignation of Kripalani in 1947, a spirit of uneasy accommodation prevailed between party and government. Just as Kripalani had lost his bid to retain organizational supremacy, so the party had ceased to be the center of decision-making in India, and the functions of the Congress President were increasingly confined to strictly organizational affairs, the locus of power having already shifted to the new Congress government. But the principle of supremacy had not yet been conceded. A group within the organization was determined to make another attempt to reverse the process. By 1950, as the end of Pattabhi's term as Congress President drew near, the time seemed ripe for the challenge.

[44] Dr. B. P. Sitaramayya, *Current History in Questions and Answers* (Calcutta: Automatic Printers Ltd., 1948), p. 357.

THE TURNING POINT:
1950-1951

The end of Pattabhi's term coincided with a crisis in the country and turmoil in the party. With renewed communal friction a mass of refugees fled from East Pakistan to West Bengal, and the enormity of the migration brought into question the wisdom of Nehru's policy toward Pakistan and the viability of India as a secular state. Since Patel had only reluctantly supported these aspects of Nehru's policy, such developments brought the Nehru-Patel relationship under renewed stress, and the resulting friction between the leaders was reflected in the party organization.[1] At the same time, within the organization itself, long-submerged tensions and disagreements over the Nehru government's foreign, domestic, and social policies and on the issue of party-government relations rose again to the surface. As in the Pattabhi-Tandon battle two years earlier, these dissensions within the party were reflected in an open contest for the Congress presidency.

As a result of the Congress organizational elections which had been held in the interim under the new Congress constitution, however, the circumstances surrounding the impending contest were significantly different. The intensity and bitterness of the campaign grew from a universal realization that the office bearers who were to be elected would play a decisive role in the party's machinery for selecting candidates for the forthcoming First General Elections under the

[1] M. Brecher, *Nehru: A Political Biography* (London: Oxford University Press, 1959), pp. 429-431.

27

new Constitution of free India.[2] In the acrimonious scramble to capture power in the state Congress organizations, it had already become clear that the Gandhians, the former Congress Socialists, and the various regional groups which had played such an important role in Pattabhi's election had been reduced to a dissident minority.[3] The old guard, having achieved victory at the state level, was determined to do the same at the national level, while the dissidents believed that maintaining key posts at the center provided their sole hope for survival. The ground was laid for the bitterest and most prolonged struggle in post-independence Congress history. Harmony within the organization and in party-government relations was restored only when the Congress presidency was taken over by the Prime Minister.

Although seven names were placed in nomination for President of the Nasik Session of the Congress, all but three—Purshottamdas Tandon, J. B. Kripalani, and Shankarrao Deo[4]—withdrew,[5] and only Tandon and Kripalani were significant contestants. The alignment of forces and the points at issue were identical to those of the previous election, but the situation in 1950 seemed graver because the prestige of both Nehru and Patel, whose relations had deteriorated in the intervening two years, was obviously committed to the outcome. The seriousness of their differences as reflected in organizational policy led Ramkrishna Dalmia, a leading industrialist and friend of Patel, to observe publicly that the two Congress leaders, "being divided" over the election of the Congress President, were "indulging in sectional politics" and "creating bitterness among themselves and the voters."[6]

[2] Indian National Congress, *Report of the General Secretaries, Jan. 1949–Sept. 1950* (New Delhi: A.I.C.C., 1950), pp. 80-82.

[3] *Hindustan Times* (New Delhi), June 6, 1950.

[4] Deo was never a serious contender. His major contribution was to emphasize, as he had in 1948, the policy issues which were inherent in the election.

[5] The other candidates were Nehru, N. G. Ranga, Seth Govind Das, and S. K. Patil.

[6] *Times of India* (Bombay), Aug. 23, 1950.

Tandon's presence in the race clearly demonstrated that the old guard of the Congress, already in control at the state level, was determined to capture the Congress presidency. Tandon himself disclosed that, while he had not personally sought the nomination, he had been persuaded by "friends" —presumably Patel—to run.[7] At the same time, though privately, Nehru had indicated to Tandon that he should not contest the election,[8] a fact which Tandon later publicly confirmed.[9] The reasons for Nehru's reluctance to endorse Tandon were perhaps suggested most succinctly by the *Hindustan Times*, a paper recognized as close to top Congress circles: "Pandit Nehru, it is well known, was not happy that his old friend Mr. Tandon should have stood for the Presidential election. On personal grounds he could not himself have chosen a more suitable candidate, but he was not sure that what is known as the Congress programme would prosper under the aegis of a person like Mr. Tandon."[10] Although Nehru did not openly announce his disapproval of Tandon's candidacy, his public statements constituted a veiled attack on Tandon's stance in regard to many vital questions facing the nation. For specific mention at a press conference in August, for instance, Nehru singled out the communal question as a "fundamental" issue. Assuring the competing factions that he did not want to interfere, he nevertheless made it clear that "the election of the next President of the Congress *vis-à-vis* this issue was important and the result . . . was bound to have its effects" on the Prime Minister as well as on the country.[11]

Tandon's opposition, led by Kidwai, suffered at first from a lack of coordination and then from the difficulty of finding a candidate strong enough to oppose him. As election time drew near, they sought unsuccessfully to persuade Pattabhi

[7] *National Herald* (Lucknow), Aug. 25, 1950.
[8] *The Indian Express* (New Delhi), Aug. 25, 1950.
[9] Letter P. D. Tandon to J. B. Kripalani, Jan. 20, 1951, *Hitavada* (Nagpur), May 16, 1951.
[10] Sept. 26, 1950.
[11] *Tribune* (Ambala), Aug. 27, 1950.

to run for re-election. But Pattabhi, somewhat disillusioned by his experience in the post he had coveted for so long, had already decided, in conjunction with a few of his close friends, to back the candidacy of Shankarrao Deo. In accepting this offer of support, Deo pledged as a matter of principle to remain in the race regardless of all future developments.[12] Kidwai evidently did not agree that persistence was sufficient to oppose successfully the power of the conservative old guard. Instead, he tried to draft Nehru for the presidency. On hearing of his nomination, the Prime Minister confided that "it had not struck me as a possibility that I might be Congress President again."[13] But in spite of pressures for him to accept the post, Nehru felt compelled to withdraw his name, probably because he feared the implications of an open conflict with Patel. In public, however, he confined himself to the position he had taken in 1946. He declared that it would not be proper to combine the office of Congress President with that of Prime Minister—a position he would not be able to defend indefinitely. Meanwhile, having failed to persuade either Nehru or Pattabhi to run, Kidwai and his followers selected Kripalani, whose popularity among Congressmen would enable him, they hoped, to put up a strong fight against the old guard.[14]

As in 1948, Kripalani's very presence in the race raised the crucial issue of party-government relations. As a part of his campaign it was essential for him to explain to his fellow Congressmen his relationship to the Congress High Command, especially in light of his 1947 resignation, and his attitude toward cooperation between the party and the government. In an effort to neutralize the effect of this issue, his supporters placed reports in the press which indicated that Kripalani had received basic guarantees of cooperation from the High Command. At one point the question was raised as to whether such assurances of cooperation had been re-

[12] Sitaramayya, "Autobiography," p. 14.
[13] *National Herald* (Lucknow), Aug. 13, 1950.
[14] Sitaramayya, "Autobiography," p. 13.

ceived from *both* Nehru and Patel.[15] This question was never fully answered. But Kripalani's supporters attempted to quiet some of the doubt about his standing with the High Command by circulating, in the last days of the campaign, a paper which purported to be the transcript of an interview between Nehru and Kripalani in which Nehru had indicated his approval of Kripalani's candidacy and dubbed Tandon a communalist.[16]

The press was also interested in ascertaining the relationship between the Prime Minister and the candidates for Congress President. The editor of *Harijan*, for example, demanded that either Nehru declare his preference for one of the candidates or the candidates state clearly their views in relation to those of the Prime Minister. Only upon reading this challenge did Tandon break his self-imposed silence. He informed the editor that he did not agree with the assumption upon which the editorial had been based. In the process he made it quite clear that he had no intention, if elected, of adopting a policy of blind obedience to the government. "While cherishing the desire to strengthen the hand of the Government and of its Prime Minister," he observed, "it is also our duty to place before the Government the opinions which we believe in with an honest heart and to press them for their acceptance."[17] Since it was already quite clear that Tandon and Nehru were poles apart on many issues facing the government, Tandon's declaration indicated that he had no intention of following Pattabhi's advice on the role of the Congress presidency.

Balloting took place on August 29, 1950. According to the results announced early in September, Tandon had received 1,306 votes; Kripalani, 1,052; and Deo, 202.[18] Un-

[15] Letter P. S. Patel to J. B. Kripalani, *Hitavada* (Nagpur), Aug. 25, 1950.

[16] Letter P. D. Tandon to J. B. Kripalani, Jan. 20, 1951, *Hitavada*, (Nagpur), May 16, 1951.

[17] *Tribune* (Ambala), Aug. 29, 1950; text, *National Herald* (Lucknow), Aug. 29, 1950.

[18] *Report of the General Secretaries, 1949-50*, p. 83.

31

fortunately, Kala Venkata Rao, the returning officer, deliberately mixed the ballot boxes to prevent the votes from being broken down by states. He announced only the total number of votes cast for each candidate.[19] Press reports, however, indicated that Tandon had received support from roughly the same areas which had backed him in 1948—the Hindi-speaking North and the West, particularly the states of Bombay, Gujarat, West Bengal, Madhya Pradesh, Uttar Pradesh, Bihar, Vindhya Pradesh, and Rajasthan. Kripalani, though fairly well supported in northern states like the Punjab, Uttar Pradesh, Bihar, Rajasthan, and Himachal Pradesh, received his strongest backing from the South. The bulk of Deo's votes came from his home state of Maharashtra.[20]

In the 1950 election there were 316 more voting delegates than in 1948. Tandon increased his total vote by 221 over 1948 levels, while Kripalani and Deo combined received only 95 more than Pattabhi had polled two years before. Thus, if previous voting patterns remained essentially the same, it could be argued that the bulk of the 221 extra votes for Tandon came largely from the 316 new delegates. It is probably for this reason that the dissidents charged that the dominant groups in the states had used bogus enrollment and fraudulent election practices in selecting delegates and demanded that the election, which had been very close, be reversed pending an investigation of their charges.

In view of Tandon's election to the presidency, Nehru decided to place before the Nasik Session a series of resolutions embodying the basic policies of his government in order to see whether the Congress was still committed to the "policies of old." These resolutions endorsed the foreign policy of the government—especially its relations with Pakistan—condemned communalism, reaffirmed the secular state concept, and approved the government's economic policy. All of them were passed by huge majorities. But, though Nehru was somewhat satisfied by the public vote of confi-

[19] *The Hindu* (Madras), Sept. 3, 1950.
[20] *Times of India* (Bombay), Aug. 31, 1950.

dence for his policies, he was still left with a disturbing suspicion that underneath there existed little real firm commitment to them. He was also troubled by "a feeling of different pulls in the country and different pulls and ideas in the Congress."[21]

The unity which the Indian press had acclaimed, along with Nehru's triumph, as the keynote of the Nasik Session, was not characteristic of the discussions over the composition of the party executive. Despite an invitation from Tandon himself, Nehru dramatized his disapproval of the outcome of the election by refusing at first to join the new Working Committee. A fresh crisis seemed to be brewing. Only after holding talks with his colleagues, Azad and Rajagopalachari, did Nehru finally agree to participate.[22] However, the ensuing deliberations ended in a dispute over whether or not to include Kidwai, who had been a member of successive Working Committees since 1946. Because of Kidwai's efforts to defeat Tandon in 1948 and again in 1950, he was unacceptable to the victors. Nehru did not press his advocacy of Kidwai over Tandon's opposition, and the discussions were called temporarily to a halt with only thirteen members selected. The remainder of the slate was finalized on October 16, probably without Nehru's participation.[23] When the names of the new Working Committee members were announced, it was clear that Tandon had dropped all the dissidents who had opposed him in order to make room for his own supporters and to create a committee which he felt was more representative of true Congress thinking in the states. The resulting Working Committee had a total of eight P.C.C. Presidents from the states of Assam, Bihar, Maharashtra, Bombay City, Mahakoshal, Madras, the Punjab, and West Bengal. The P.C.C. Presidents of Gujarat and Rajasthan were represented by individuals chosen in consultation with them. Orissa's P.C.C. President, though not a member of

---

[21] *Hindustan Times* (New Delhi), Aug. 22, 1951.
[22] *The Hindu* (Madras), Oct. 16, 1950.
[23] Text of Tandon's Resignation Speech, *Tribune* (Ambala), Sept. 8, 1951.

the committee, was made a permanent invitee. In the end, by contrast to previous Working Committee tradition, the Tandon Working Committee was dominated largely by party bosses, many of whom lacked the broader all-India outlook of the men they had replaced.

The election of Tandon placed the right wing of the Congress in complete control of the party organization and its decision-making organs. Yet, at the height of its power, the group lost the support of its major patron. On December 15, 1950, Sardar Vallabhbhai Patel died. With Patel's death, Nehru was forced to intervene more actively in party organizational affairs, which, until then, he had left largely to Patel. "Of course," he told his Parliamentary colleagues, "whenever major matters of policy were discussed in the Committee, Sardar Patel and I and our senior colleagues took part. But on the whole I kept away apart from an expression of opinions from time to time. . . . Apart from my preoccupations I did not feel it would be right for me to interfere in the Congress organization except when broad matters of policy were discussed in committee. . . . Either one interfered, and took some responsibility, or one did not interfere at all."[24] Yet, although Nehru had refrained from interfering very often, he admitted that he had been concerned about developments in the Congress for some time. What particularly concerned him was the impact of Congress disunity on the much-needed unity of India. He felt that the Congress represented the only foreseeable "cementing force." "Whether the Congress was good, bad or indifferent" was "another matter" altogether.[25] For almost a year after the death of Patel, therefore, Nehru attempted to restore unity to the Congress. His efforts necessitated the calling of four A.I.C.C. meetings—at Ahmedabad, Delhi, Bangalore, and again Delhi—and culminated in a full session of the Congress on the eve of the First General Elections. In the end,

[24] *Hindustan Times* (New Delhi), Aug. 22, 1951.
[25] *Ibid.*

Nehru scored a personal success, but he lost his bid to maintain complete Congress unity.

The principal immediate threat to the unity of the Congress was a confrontation between Tandon and his Working Committee and the Democratic Front, a group which had been organized by Kripalani following his failure to win the Congress presidency. The objective of the Front was to purify the Congress in order to enable it to carry out its traditional program, especially the goal of communal unity.[26] Considering the existence of such a group detrimental to organizational unity, Tandon brought the matter to the attention of the Working Committee early in November.[27] No action was taken until December 4, when the committee authorized the President to inform Kripalani of the Working Committee's desire that the Front be dissolved.[28] "The formation of such a group," Tandon informed Kripalani, "can only have a disruptive influence on the Congress organization and lead progressively to a weakening of it." He concluded by inviting Kripalani to meet with the Working Committee to discuss differences.[29]

Kripalani stated the Front's minimum demands in his reply to Tandon. He pointed out that the members of the Front, agreeing completely with the policies and programs of the Congress, did not wish to leave the organization. They had, however, committed themselves firmly to opposing conservative and reactionary elements. The Front had also been formed specifically to combat certain organizational malpractices. "In the last election," Kripalani observed, "methods were used to influence the voters that are highly repugnant.

[26] *The Hindu* (Madras), Nov. 3, 1950. In addition to communal unity, most of the membership of the Democratic Front also supported Nehru's economic, social, and foreign policy.

[27] *Congress Bulletin*, No. 7, Nov.-Dec. 1950, p. 246.

[28] *Congress Bulletin*, No. 1, Jan.-Feb. 1951, pp. 6-7.

[29] Letter P. D. Tandon to J. B. Kripalani, Dec. 7, 1950, *Hitavada* (Nagpur), May 16, 1951.

. . . The bribes of offices and other advantages were freely used by some of those in possession of the organization and the Government. Nay, in many cases administrative machinery was used to secure votes for the dominant group in the centre and the states. The Working Committee appointed an election-disputes subcommittee. Its records bear an eloquent, if damaging, evidence of what was done or attempted."[30] Kripalani demanded of Tandon a broad impartial inquiry into the last Congress election. He asked for an end to the partiality exhibited by the general secretaries of the Congress Secretariat. He also objected to what he called the partisan approach adopted by Tandon in the selection of his Working Committee.[31]

Despite an exchange of views, neither Tandon nor Kripalani was willing to make a meaningful concession at the time of the Ahmedabad meeting of the A.I.C.C., the first after Patel's death. Therefore, Nehru felt obliged to intervene in Congress affairs by introducing a unity resolution. The resolution, carefully phrased in conciliatory terms, pointed to the disruptive effects of intra-party groups and declared that the major problem in the country was a lack of unity.[32] The unity resolution was passed unanimously by the A.I.C.C.

When, shortly after its passage, the unity resolution was put to a test, it was clear that the unanimity had been purely superficial. The point at issue was the election of five members of the Central Election Committee (C.E.C.), the newly created body which would have the final say in selecting Congress candidates for the forthcoming First General Elections. Since many of the leaders of the Democratic Front had already been defeated at the state level, Kripalani and his supporters realized that they had to make the most of their remaining influence at the center in order to prevent all their members from being denied tickets for the General Elections by the majority group. Therefore, they worked behind the

[30] Letter J. B. Kripalani to P. D. Tandon, Dec. 10, 1950, *ibid.*
[31] *Ibid.*
[32] *Congress Bulletin*, No. 1, Jan.-Feb. 1951, pp. 16, 30-33.

scenes at Ahmedabad to achieve a mutually acceptable list of candidates for the C.E.C. which would contain as many neutrals or members of their own group as possible. In this way they sought to avoid an open confrontation on the floor of the A.I.C.C., which as a minority group they were sure to lose.[33] But the members of the Tandon group had no intention of making meaningful concessions or of relinquishing their recently won control over the party machine. The result was a deadlock which could not be resolved in the time available. Therefore, on the recommendation of Maulana Azad, who had been acting as an intermediary, the election was postponed.[34] This inconclusive skirmishing over seats on the C.E.C. demonstrated to Nehru that his first efforts to achieve unity had failed.

In a series of unity talks following the A.I.C.C. meeting at Ahmedabad, Nehru and Azad appealed for a dissolution of the Democratic Front. Kidwai and Kripalani, the leaders of the dissident group, replied that such a step could be taken only in consultation with their supporters.[35] They therefore scheduled a meeting of the Democratic Front to coincide with the next meeting of the A.I.C.C., which was to be held in Delhi in May. At this time Nehru and Azad met with the members of the Democratic Front to ask them to work for their goals within the Congress. Largely in deference to Nehru and Azad, the dissidents agreed to dissolve the Front, but they also made it clear that they remained concerned about the Working Committee's past hostility and by its refusal to take the initiative in purifying the Congress.[36] In return for their cooperation, it was reported, Nehru promised the leaders of the Front that he would secure adequate representation for them on the C.E.C.[37]

The Working Committee welcomed the news of the

[33] *Amrita Bazar Patrika* (Calcutta), Feb. 2, 1951.

[34] *Congress Bulletin*, No. 1, Jan.-Feb. 1951, p. 29.

[35] Letter J. B. Kripalani and R. A. Kidwai to J. Nehru, April 15, 1951, *Hitavada* (Nagpur), May 16, 1951.

[36] *Tribune* (Ambala), May 4, 1951.

[37] Brecher, *Nehru*, p. 433.

Front's dissolution.[38] That the old guard had no intention of relinquishing their control of the organization, however, became painfully clear once the A.I.C.C. assembled at Delhi to elect the members of the C.E.C. As soon as nominations were opened, S. K. Patil, party boss from Bombay and a representative of the majority group, proposed a list of five names, none of them drawn from the dissident group, for the five seats on the C.E.C. His proposal was immediately seconded by Seth Govind Das, a staunchly conservative Congressman from Madhya Pradesh and a strong supporter of Tandon. Thirteen other names were placed in nomination, but five of these nominees withdrew immediately. Normally, at this point, nominations would have been closed. But once again, as at Ahmedabad, Azad rose to inform the A.I.C.C. delegates that private talks regarding unity were in progress. He suggested that nominations remain open. Tandon agreed, and the A.I.C.C. passed on to the next items on the agenda.[39]

At a private meeting with Kidwai, Kripalani, and Azad that evening, Tandon offered both dissidents a seat on the C.E.C.[40] In view of the list of nominees Patil had submitted that morning, Kripalani doubted that either Azad or Tandon had the authority to make such an offer. Therefore, the offer was rejected and the unity talks collapsed. The next morning all the dissidents withdrew their names from nomination. Azad made one last attempt at reconciliation. He urged the A.I.C.C. delegates to consider that Patil had submitted his list as an individual and not on behalf of the Working Committee. It was essential to Congress unity, he argued, that Kidwai and Kripalani be brought into the C.E.C. This time, however, Azad's pleas went unheeded. Except for those nominated by Patil, all the remaining candidates withdrew. The majority group had achieved a major triumph.[41]

[38] *Congress Bulletin*, No. 3, May-June 1951, p. 80.
[39] *Ibid.*, p. 85.
[40] *The Hindu* (Madras), May 18, 1951.
[41] *Congress Bulletin*, No. 3, May-June 1951, p. 90.

The defeat of the dissidents led immediately to Kripalani's resignation from the Congress. In doing so, he charged that the Ahmedabad unity resolution had been flagrantly ignored by the majority group. In the state Congress organizations, he said, the dissidents were being systematically weeded out and urged not to return. Yet, when he had demanded an end to partisanship and the initiation of an impartial inquiry into the last organizational elections, he had been told in response that unity could be achieved only by dissolving the Democratic Front rather than by solving the problems which had led to its formation. Although he still agreed with the principles and programs of the party, Kripalani felt that the Congress was no longer an effective instrument for the implementation of those objectives. His "differences with the Congress President," the "condition of the country," and the "inability of the Congress to arrest the deterioration of that condition" were, he said, the main causes for his resignation.[42] One month after his resignation Kripalani and his followers joined with P. C. Ghosh to form the Kisan Mazdoor Praja Party (K.M.P.P.).

Although he agreed in essence and in substance with Kripalani's position, Kidwai refused to follow Kripalani's example. Unlike Kripalani, Ghosh, and some of the other dissident leaders, Kidwai was not completely isolated from power in the Congress. He was still a member of Nehru's Cabinet. Therefore, he felt he could achieve his objectives within the Congress. Instead of resigning, he placed his hope in the efforts of some Congressmen to convene a special session of the A.I.C.C. to discuss the issues which had been raised, continuously and futilely, by Kripalani. The question of unfair and undemocratic functioning of the Congress machine, he argued, had never been placed directly before the supreme body of the Congress, which was the A.I.C.C. He recalled that in past years the A.I.C.C. had been called into session repeatedly until serious internal conflicts had been resolved to the relative satisfaction of all disputants.

[42] *Hindustan Times* (New Delhi), May 18, 1951.

In 1922-1923, for example, it had taken four A.I.C.C. meetings to settle the controversy between the pro-changers and the no-changers. The Working Committee had been reconstituted three times before a final agreement had been reached. For this reason, Kidwai saw no inconsistency in calling another session of the A.I.C.C. only two months after the previous one had been adjourned.[43]

Hoping that "the issues which divide the old colleagues may be freely and fairly discussed and a solution found," Azad supported Kidwai's call for a special session of the A.I.C.C. It was his opinion that the dissidents were entitled to put their case before the most representative body of the party before leaving the organization.[44]

By mid-June, while a number of the dissidents who had already left the Congress were preparing to hold a special convention at Patna, the pressure for calling a special session of the A.I.C.C. became irresistible. Nehru met with key Congress leaders to insist that circumstances demanded the calling of a unity session,[45] and the Working Committee was forced to take a stand on the issue when a proposal was submitted in the form of a petition signed by twenty-nine A.I.C.C. members that a special meeting of the A.I.C.C. be convened to consider the rift in the Congress. Realizing that such a request could not be blocked, the Tandon-dominated majority group in the committee sought to de-emphasize the unity aspect of the proposed session by suggesting that a consideration of the Congress Election Manifesto also be placed on the agenda. As a legal rationalization for the peculiar nature of the unscheduled meeting, Tandon called attention to a provision of the Congress constitution which declared that the A.I.C.C. must devote at least four hours to unofficial resolutions. The Working Committee finally decided that the format of the special session would be drawn up so as to permit A.I.C.C. members to submit sug-

[43] *The Hindu* (Madras), May 18, 1951.
[44] *Amrita Bazar Patrika* (Calcutta), May 20, 1951.
[45] *Indian Nation* (Patna), June 12, 1951.

gestions on key topics such as party organization, the political and economic status of the country, and the Election Manifesto, although no actual resolutions on these topics would be acceptable.[46] The Working Committee managed to adjourn without having directly discussed either the unity problem or the Patna convention.[47]

As the delegates assembled in Bangalore for the third A.I.C.C. meeting in seven months and the most important since independence, rumors were circulating to the effect that Nehru would become *de jure* as well as *de facto* leader of the Congress organization. At the same time, a group of Members of Parliament was distributing among A.I.C.C. members a letter which called for the election of Nehru as President of the Congress in order to create a united Congress front for the forthcoming general elections.[48] The old guard remained aloof from these overtures, but, as at Nasik, Ahmedabad, and Delhi, they did not attempt to challenge Nehru's policies. In fact, they endorsed a special report which reviewed the entire stewardship of the Nehru government and affirmed the basic social, economic, and foreign policies for which the government stood. Throughout the meetings, however, the continuing concern of the old guard was to maintain control of the Congress machine. Thus, while Nehru worked to preserve Congress unity by keeping the door open for the return of those dissidents who had left the Congress, Tandon and his supporters preferred to exclude the renegades as a means of consolidating their own position in the party in time for the general elections.[49]

Discussion at the Working Committee meetings which preceded the Bangalore A.I.C.C. Session revolved around two issues: the problem of Congress unity in general and, in particular, the status of Kidwai. Since Kidwai had been elected to the Executive Committee of the party created at Patna by Kripalani, Ghosh, and other dissidents, the Work-

---

[46] *Congress Bulletin*, No. 3, May-June 1951, p. 96.
[47] *The Hindu* (Madras), June 13, 1951.
[48] *The Hindu* (Madras), July 12, 1951.
[49] *The Indian Express* (New Delhi), July 12, 1951.

ing Committee asked for his explanation. Kidwai indicated that he had attended the Patna convention only after he had been unsuccessful in attempting to have it postponed. He assured the committee that he had no immediate intention of resigning from the Congress. He hoped that the Bangalore Session would make such action unnecessary.[50]

Realizing, like Kidwai, that all previous unity resolutions and statements had been ineffectual platitudes, Nehru told the Working Committee that concrete organizational reform was essential. If the Congress expected to win the impending general election, he declared, people would have to be able to place confidence in the party machine as well as in its executive.[51] As early as Ahmedabad he had come to the conclusion that the "necessary" first step lay in "a reconstitution of the Congress Working Committee."[52] At Bangalore, therefore, he demanded a reconstitution not only of the Working Committee but also of the newly elected C.E.C.[53] At this suggestion Tandon and his Working Committee offered to resign altogether. Since Nehru did not want to create irreconcilable antagonisms within the Congress, he was forced once more to moderate his position.[54] Therefore, he confined himself to drafting a resolution inviting all who agreed with Congress policies and objectives to return to the fold and promising prompt and impartial inquiries into all charges of corruption where there existed a *prima facie* case. Compromise that it was, Nehru's resolution was far stronger than that which certain A.I.C.C. members had submitted for the Working Committee's approval: "The A.I.C.C. is of the opinion that ways and means should be devised to avert the impending rift in the Congress so that it may function as a consolidated and integrated body to tide over the national crisis." Although the Working Committee decided to give precedence to Nehru's resolution, it took the

[50] *The Statesman* (New Delhi), July 14, 1951.
[51] *Congress Bulletin*, No. 4, July-Aug. 1951, p. 123.
[52] *Hindustan Times* (New Delhi), Aug. 22, 1951.
[53] *The Hindu* (Madras), July 15, 1951.
[54] *The Hindu* (Madras), July 17, 1951.

unusual step of granting individual members permission to support the original resolution on the floor of the A.I.C.C. if they so chose.[55]

When the milder of the two resolutions was submitted to the A.I.C.C., it gave rise to a series of amendments reflecting a partisan approach to the problems facing the Congress. On the one hand, there were calls for immediate reconstitution of the Working Committee and the C.E.C. On the other hand, there was a demand for a vote of confidence in Tandon and a vote of censure against those who were attempting to disrupt the organization. The two positions seemed to be irreconcilable. But Nehru, still reaching for consensus, asked the A.I.C.C. to view the problem in a wider context. It was no less correct, he observed, for a majority to squeeze out a minority than for a minority to behave in a re-calcitrant manner. After further discussion the original resolution was withdrawn.[56] Thus, the floor was cleared for Nehru's resolution, which was passed unanimously.[57] The resolution was an excellent example of Nehru's consistently conciliatory approach. He placated the dissidents with promises of reform and investigation wherever there was "*prima facie* justification" for "charges of irregularity in the working of the organisation." He pacified Tandon's followers by declaring that "the Congress does not approve of the formation of groups within its fold." To those who had already left the party he proclaimed that "all those who agree with the general aim of the Congress" would "find a welcome place within its ranks."[58] Thus, the Bangalore Session of the A.I.C.C., which had opened with some expectation of fundamental changes in the leadership and administration of Congress affairs, culminated in little more than another resolution of compromise. Yet, as subsequent events were to reveal, a turning point had been reached.

[55] *Congress Bulletin*, No. 4, July-Aug. 1951, p. 124.
[56] *The Hindu* (Madras), July 16, 1951.
[57] *Congress Bulletin*, No. 4, July-Aug. 1951, pp. 132-133.
[58] *Ibid.*

Since Kidwai had counted on much more action from the Bangalore Session, he submitted to Prime Minister Nehru, immediately upon his return to Delhi, a letter of resignation from both the Congress and the Cabinet. He was joined in the gesture by his close friend and cabinet colleague, A. P. Jain. In a public statement announcing their decision, they made it very clear that they had resigned because they opposed the undemocratic manner in which the organization had been functioning.[59]

Nehru's response was to ask both to reconsider.[60] The following day Kidwai and Jain announced that they had decided not to resign from the Cabinet although they intimated that they still expected to be free to work in political opposition to the Congress. As if to demonstrate the extent of the freedom they expected to enjoy, they delivered a blistering attack on the undemocratic functioning of the party organization and an equally virulent attack on the Congress President. "Is there a parallel in the world," they asked, "where the executive head, i.e., President of an organization is the very antithesis of everything that the organization stands for? What is there in common between Shri Purshottamdas Tandon and the policies of the Congress—economic, communal, international and refugees? Even at this juncture when our ways parted, we wished and hoped that the working of the Congress should fall in line with its profession."[61]

The reaction of the old guard was immediate and sharp. Hearing of the Kidwai-Jain statement, several state Congress leaders and close supporters of Tandon, including Morarji Desai, D. P. Mishra, and S. K. Sinha, made anxious telephone calls to Delhi demanding assurances from the Prime Minister that the two Cabinet dissidents would not be given the political liberty they had arrogated to themselves.[62] Tandon himself had already announced bluntly that, if Kidwai and

[59] *National Herald* (Lucknow), July 19, 1951; *The Statesman* (New Delhi), Aug. 3, 1951.
[60] *Hindustan Times* (New Delhi), July 21, 1951.
[61] *The Statesman* (New Delhi), July 22, 1951.
[62] *The Statesman* (New Delhi), July 24, 1951.

Jain were to remain in the Cabinet, they "obviously" would not be in a position to carry on propaganda against the Congress. "I am very doubtful if the Prime Minister could have agreed to this arrangement," he said, "for this would create an impossible position." Furthermore, he reminded Nehru, "the Prime Minister and his Cabinet are responsible to the Congress and have to carry out policies laid down by the Congress from time to time." The Working Committee, he concluded, would naturally have to take note of this situation.[63] In this way the role of the Congress vis-à-vis the Cabinet became an active issue.

Pressures from his own supporters,[64] plus indications from Nehru that he would not have the political freedom he had expected, forced Kidwai to reconsider his earlier decision. On July 30, he submitted his second letter of resignation. This time it was accepted.[65]

Kidwai's resignation stung Nehru into action. On August 6, Nehru wrote to Tandon stating his decision to resign from the Working Committee and from the C.E.C. as well. In explanation he declared, "I am convinced that I do not fit into the Working Committee and am not in tune with it."[66] Nehru's letter came as a shock to Tandon, who believed that he and Nehru had worked harmoniously together with the exception of a few differences over organizational problems. In reply Tandon warned Nehru that his resignation was likely to create a permanent schism in the organization. Begging the Prime Minister not to precipitate

[63] *The Statesman* (New Delhi), July 23, 1951.

[64] M. Weiner, *Party Politics in India* (Princeton: Princeton University Press, 1957), p. 78.

[65] Letter J. Nehru to R. A. Kidwai, July 31, 1951, *The Statesman* (New Delhi), Aug. 3, 1951. Since Jain had never insisted on the far-reaching freedom of action that Kidwai had demanded, it was agreed that he would remain in the Cabinet. Letter J. Nehru to A. P. Jain, July 31, 1951, and A. P. Jain to J. Nehru, Aug. 1, 1951, *The Statesman* (New Delhi), Aug. 3, 1951.

[66] Letter J. Nehru to P. D. Tandon, Aug. 6, 1951, *The Statesman* (New Delhi), Sept. 11, 1951.

a crisis at that time, Tandon himself offered to resign if that would help bring about a solution.[67]

Nehru responded by assuring Tandon that he could not have thought more exhaustively about his action. "I have long been distressed," he wrote, "at the attitude of some persons which indicated that they wished to drive others from the Congress who did not fit in with their views or their general outlook." Nehru pointed out that he had been trying to achieve unity ever since the previous January, but his failure had become apparent to him at Bangalore. "This has distressed me greatly because I feel that the Congress is rapidly drifting away from its moorings and more and more the wrong kind of people, or rather people who have the wrong kind of ideas are gaining influence in it. It may, and probably will win elections. But in the process, it may also lose its soul."[68] Nehru's first step in preventing such a contingency was to resign from the Working Committee. He did not feel it was advisable for Tandon to resign because the gesture would have been misleading. "This is not a personal matter," he observed.[69]

The Working Committee met from August 11 to 13 in an atmosphere of urgency. Nehru attended the first session only long enough to explain his letter of resignation. He then withdrew, leaving the committee to debate the problem. Three alternatives were discussed: 1) that Nehru's resignation represented a lack of confidence on account of which the Working Committee as well as the Congress President should resign in order for Nehru to assume leadership; 2) that Nehru's resignation from the Working Committee should be placed before a special session of the A.I.C.C.; or 3) that the issues should be handled by Nehru and Tandon, since the Working Committee members were merely the nominees

[67] Letter P. D. Tandon to J. Nehru, Aug. 9, 1951, *The Statesman* (New Delhi), Sept. 11, 1951.
[68] Letter J. Nehru to P. D. Tandon, Aug. 9, 1951, *The Statesman* (New Delhi), Sept. 11, 1951.
[69] *Ibid.* By this time Azad, too, had resigned from the Working Committee. *The Statesman* (New Delhi), Aug. 12, 1951.

of the President.[70] While the Working Committee debated a course of action, B. C. Roy and Pandit Govind Ballabh Pant attempted to mediate the dispute. In their discussions with Nehru they explored the possibilities of a reconstitution of the Working Committee and the appointment of new general secretaries in consultation with him. Tandon, however, insisted that he would rather resign than reconstitute the Working Committee. He was reported to have said that, as head of the Congress, he did not intend to be "dictated" to by the Prime Minister whoever he might be. The mediators had also suggested that Nehru fill the existing two Working Committee vacancies with men of his own choosing.[71] But Nehru showed little interest in piecemeal solutions. "I am not interested in adjustments this way or that way—a majority or a minority," he declared. "That has not been my way and I have not functioned in groups throughout my Congress career."[72] In the end, the mediation efforts succeeded only in postponing the denouement, and the Working Committee adjourned after passing a resolution appealing to Nehru and Tandon to confer and find a solution. The President was also authorized to call another special session of the A.I.C.C., if necessary.

A week after Tandon had tried unsuccessfully to persuade Nehru to withdraw his resignation,[73] Nehru addressed the Congress Party in Parliament, setting forth his reasons for resigning and reviewing the events of the past year which had led to it. A motion of confidence in Nehru's leadership was introduced and passed. Most Congress Members of Parliament perceived the real conflict between the Prime Minister and the Congress President as one involving the relationship between the party organization and the Parliamentary Party and felt that the clash was almost inevitable because of the lack of clearly defined roles. Many felt that

[70] *The Hindu* (Madras), Aug. 12, 1951.
[71] *The Hindu* (Madras), Aug. 13, 1951; *The Indian Express* (New Delhi), Aug. 13, 1951.
[72] *Hindustan Times* (New Delhi), Aug. 22, 1951.
[73] *Congress Bulletin*, No. 5, Sept. 1951, pp. 162-163.

47

this expression of confidence would strengthen Nehru's hand at the emergency meeting of the A.I.C.C. which had just been called by Tandon. Tandon supporters, on the other hand, resented the action of the Parliamentary Party. In their opinion, confidence in Nehru's leadership had never been brought to issue. Moreover, they stressed the necessity for maintaining the authority of the Working Committee over the government in order to prevent dictatorship.[74]

Meanwhile Tandon, who was making a speaking tour of India, indicated that he was not in full agreement with Nehru on the nature of the issues involved in his debate with the Prime Minister. While Nehru tended to express the conflict in terms of policy,[75] Tandon translated it in terms of procedure. He declared at Kolhapur that no Chief Minister, not even a Prime Minister, could afford to ignore the resolutions of the Congress. It was, he maintained, the responsibility of the Congress government to follow mandates given by the party.[76] He also reiterated his interpretation of the power of the Congress President. Later at Gwalior, he told Congress workers what he had already said many times before: "It is the inherent right of the Congress President to constitute his Working Committee and I am going to exercise this right."[77] If necessary, he said, he was prepared to step down in favor of Nehru. But he promised to try to avoid a showdown.

As the Working Committee members assembled in Delhi on the eve of the fourth A.I.C.C. meeting in eight months, senior Congressmen were working desperately behind the scenes to avoid a showdown. Although Tandon personally continued to oppose any reconstitution of the Working Committee, it was understood that he would, as Congress President, implement a resolution in this regard if passed by the A.I.C.C. In order to bring this about to their advantage,

[74] *The Hindu* (Madras), Aug. 22, 1951; also Aug. 23, 1951.
[75] *The Hindu* (Madras), Aug. 28, 1951.
[76] *The Pioneer* (Lucknow), Aug. 23, 1951.
[77] *The Statesman* (New Delhi), Aug. 25, 1951.

some of Tandon's Uttar Pradesh colleagues proposed that the Working Committee place a resolution before the A.I.C.C. asking Nehru to withdraw his resignation, expressing confidence in Tandon, and requesting Tandon to reconstitute his Working Committee by the process of election within the A.I.C.C. Then, they reasoned, before the election, Nehru and Tandon could devise a mutually agreeable list of candidates for the A.I.C.C.'s acceptance.[78] When the Working Committee meeting finally took place, every member presented his resignation to Tandon,[79] believing evidently that in so doing they were strengthening Tandon's hand while, at the same time, enabling Nehru and Tandon to agree on the composition of a reconstituted committee. The next evening, however, Tandon called a press conference at which he announced his own resignation. He rejected as "dishonorable" any suggestion that his Working Committee could be reconstituted, even under the auspices of the A.I.C.C.[80] He revealed that his decision to resign had been "settled long ago" in his own mind. Since the Working Committee had resigned under pressure from the Prime Minister, he felt compelled to do the same. Nehru's resignation, on the other hand, he could not accept, because "Pandit Nehru is not an ordinary member of the Working Committee. He represents the nation more than any other individual today."[81] Shortly after the press conference, Tandon met with the Working Committee to inform them of his decision.[82]

Although Tandon had decided to step down gracefully, the extreme right-wing faction among his followers did not share his view of Nehru's indispensability. This segment, which was willing to form a strong anti-Nehru group within the party, was led by Pandit D. P. Mishra, Home Minister of Madhya Pradesh and formerly a devoted follower of

[78] *National Herald* (Lucknow), Aug. 28, 1951.
[79] *Congress Bulletin*, No. 5, Sept. 1951, p. 161.
[80] *Hindustan Times* (New Delhi), Sept. 8, 1951.
[81] *Tribune* (Ambala), Sept. 8, 1951.
[82] *Congress Bulletin*, No. 5, Sept. 1951, p. 162.

Patel.[83] As early as August 22, just after Nehru's resignation from the Working Committee and his vote of confidence from the Congress Party in Parliament, Mishra had issued a public statement denouncing Nehru's actions as dictatorial and declaring that, if Patel had been alive, he would have placed his support squarely behind Tandon.[84] Mishra felt that ever since the death of Patel a group very close to Nehru had begun a "sneaking vilification of Sardar Patel" while also carrying on a campaign against the Congress President simply because he had been supported by Patel.[85] In order to demonstrate beyond question his opposition to what was happening in the Congress organization, Mishra resigned from his post as Home Minister of Madhya Pradesh.[86] Explaining his actions in a speech before the state assembly, he lashed out at Nehru's policies and tactics. The Hindu Code Bill, he told the assembly, was being pushed by the Prime Minister in spite of strong objections. Unrealistic economic controls were being enforced, and India's foreign policy had led to disaster. The only honorable recourse left to India, he exclaimed, was to issue an ultimatum to Pakistan demanding that she ensure the safety of the Hindu population or face invasion and occupation by Indian troops.[87]

Mishra's condemnation of Nehru was received with hostility. Immediately following his speech in the Madhya Pradesh Assembly, the Congress members of the assembly passed a resolution expressing confidence in Nehru's leadership.[88] Outside the assembly some 100,000 people filled the streets for a demonstration at which Mishra's effigy was burned.[89] Although a popular reaction of this kind might

[83] It was Mishra whom the Working Committee had selected to fill the vacancy on the C.E.C. which had been created by Patel's death. *Congress Bulletin*, No. 1, Jan.-Feb. 1951, p. 13.

[84] *The Indian Express* (New Delhi), Aug. 23, 1951.

[85] Unpublished Shukla Papers, Letter D. P. Mishra to R. S. Shukla, Aug. 24, 1951.

[86] *Ibid.*

[87] *Amrita Bazar Patrika* (Calcutta), Aug. 30, 1951.

[88] *National Herald* (Lucknow), Aug. 30, 1951.

[89] *Hitavada* (Nagpur), Sept. 3, 1951.

have had an intimidating effect on other Congressmen with similar ideas, Mishra was unrelenting. After Tandon's resignation from the Congress presidency, Mishra resigned from the Congress Party altogether. Condemning the Nehru dictatorship once more, he warned: "A political murder of Rajrishi Tandon committed yesterday is a murder of democracy in the Congress. This is merely the beginning of the slaughter of democracy in India. The sin has been perpetrated merely with the narrow and selfish motive of winning the election with the help of Pt. Nehru."[90]

The bitterness which might have spread widely through the Congress as a consequence of the events leading to Tandon's resignation was almost completely neutralized by Tandon's decision to accept Nehru's invitation to join the new Working Committee. Mishra's revolt proved futile and the affair ended. After supporting communal candidates in the 1952 elections, Mishra decided to rejoin the Congress. He was able to regain a great deal of his lost power, but, because of his damaged relationship with the central leadership, he was condemned to exercise it for a long time behind the scenes.

Suggestions that Nehru take over the party leadership had been filling the air for weeks. At the time of the Bangalore Session, Nehru had opposed any such idea, but increasingly he left the door open. "I definitely think that it is a wrong thing practically and even otherwise, for the Prime Minister to be the Congress President," he declared. "But that being the general rule, I cannot say what necessity might compel one to do in special circumstances when a hiatus is created or something like that."[91]

By the time of the second Delhi A.I.C.C. meeting, having been faced with a series of major defections from the party, the resignation of two of his ministers, and a direct challenge to his leadership as Prime Minister by the newly resigned Congress President, Nehru had reached the point

90 *National Herald* (Lucknow), Sept. 10, 1951.
91 *The Hindu* (Madras), Aug. 29, 1951.

where "the compulsion of events" would lead him to agree to accept the *de jure* leadership of the party. On September 8, therefore, the A.I.C.C. accepted Tandon's resignation and elected Nehru to the Congress presidency by a vote of 295 to 4. Immediately upon his election Nehru announced that a special session of the Congress would be called within three weeks to ratify the decision of the A.I.C.C. and give a clear policy guide to the Congress.[92] In the interim Nehru attempted to restore unity to the party leadership. As a means of consolidating his position among those he had just defeated, he appointed Tandon to his Working Committee.[93] He then focused his attention on the dissidents. In his first public statement as Congress President, he invited all those who had seceded from the Congress to rejoin the party.[94] Kidwai, responding favorably, attempted unsuccessfully to have the K.M.P.P. dissolved.[95] Failing that, in October he announced that he and some of his followers had decided to rejoin the Congress as individuals.[96]

Meeting in Delhi from October 15 to 19, the Congress adopted a series of resolutions embodying Nehru's policies on economic problems, communalism, and foreign policy. The Session also ratified the decisions reached by the A.I.C.C. on organizational affairs.[97] The crisis had finally been overcome. Nehru emerged as the undisputed leader of the Congress.

Tandon's election had marked the beginning of the second great effort to restore organizational control over the government. After Patel's death, when differences within the party extended into the Cabinet, Tandon attempted to remind the Prime Minister that he held office only because the party organization supported him. It was Tandon, however, who was forced to resign. Tandon's resignation was the climac-

---

[92] *Hindustan Standard* (Calcutta), Sept. 8, 1951.
[93] *The National Herald* (Lucknow), Sept. 15, 1951.
[94] *Hindustan Times* (New Delhi), Sept. 15, 1951.
[95] *The Hindu* (Madras), Sept. 29, 1951.
[96] *The Hindu* (Madras), Oct. 5, 1951.
[97] *Congress Bulletin*, No. 6, Oct.–Nov. 1951, pp. 200-209.

tic and concluding act of this period of intermittent struggle between the Congress President and the Prime Minister. It confirmed the pre-eminent role of the Prime Minister and reinforced the boundaries of the office of Congress President, which had been revealed once more as limited strictly to organizational affairs with no special responsibility for policy-making. Once again it was evident that no Congress President could succeed in an attempt to hold the government responsible to the extra-parliamentary mass organization of the party. Moreover, in confirmation of the supremacy of the parliamentary wing, the Nehru government's program of social and economic reform was accepted by the party as a guideline for united Congress action. The period of transition had come to an end, and already the process of centralization and convergence which would characterize the developments of the next decade was under way.

THE PERIOD OF CENTRALIZATION
AND CONVERGENCE:
1951-1963

For three years following the Tandon resignation which closed the transitional phase, Nehru attempted to ensure party-government harmony by consolidating roles of Prime Minister and Congress President in his hands. Nehru provided the party organization with vigorous leadership in preparation for and during the First General Elections, but his post-election activities were concentrated on organizing and energizing the new government. As a result, Nehru had little time to devote to party organizational affairs. Therefore, day-to-day work was carried on by U. S. Malliah and Balvantrai Mehta, Nehru's two General Secretaries, who consulted him only on important matters. As time went on, it became apparent that Nehru's earlier assumption that a merging of the offices of Prime Minister and Congress President would result in a suppression of one of the functions had begun to prove correct. For this reason Nehru continued to look upon his dual role as a temporary situation forced upon him by extraordinary circumstances. The party, however, did not share his assessment of the matter.

The Congress constitution sub-committee, meeting shortly after the general elections to revise the party's Ahmedabad constitution, worked under the assumption that Nehru would remain Congress President for some time to come and therefore sought to formalize machinery which could aid him in his work. They recommended the creation of an office of Vice President with responsibility for the day-to-day administration of party affairs—a suggestion which had appeared in similar form prior to the formation of the Interim Government in 1946. However, when the Working Committee considered the report of the constitution sub-committee, the recommendation was deleted.[1] This led observers to conclude that Nehru had definitely decided to step down from the Congress presidency.[2]

Such was not the case, however. The issue of party-government relationships had been revived again. In the month-long interval between the Working Committee meeting in August and the Indore meeting of the A.I.C.C., a major debate had been developing between K. Hanumanthaiya, Chief Minister of the state of Mysore, and S. K. Patil, P.C.C. President in Bombay. Patil, angered when the Congress Ministry in Bombay imposed a new tax over the objections of the party organization, argued for the principle of organizational supremacy. Hanumanthaiya rejected Patil's contention and insisted that the distinction between organizational and parliamentary wings was no longer relevant. He felt that the two functions should be merged in order to create an undisputed parliamentary supremacy. He then attempted to press for the adoption of this principle by reintroducing the provision for a Congress Vice President which would enable the Prime Minister to continue as President without neglecting the organization. When Nehru intervened to ask that the amendment be withdrawn on the grounds that it had already been rejected by the Working Committee,[3] it seemed as if he had definitely decided not to continue as Congress President.

But at Indore the debate on the issue of party-government relations had been so intense that it was generally believed that Nehru would be forced to reconsider his stand against remaining Congress President for at least one more term. At the same time the Prime Minister was faced with strong

[1] *Congress Bulletin*, No. 3, April-Sept. 1952, p. 111.
[2] *Times of India* (Bombay), Aug. 11, 1952; *The Hindu* (Madras), Aug. 11, 1952.
[3] *Congress Bulletin*, No. 3, April-Sept. 1952, p. 130.

opposition from certain segments of the Congress who felt that it was not sound party policy for the same person to head both organization and government. It was for just this reason, in fact, that Tandon had resigned from Nehru's Working Committee less than a month before.[4] Yet Nehru was persuaded to accept another term as Congress President. In his acceptance speech before the Hyderabad Session of the Congress, Nehru referred sympathetically to Tandon's stand: "I agree entirely with those friends and comrades of ours who have objected to the high offices of Prime Minister and Congress President being held by one and the same person."[5] However, "hemmed in" as he was by "facts and circumstance," he "had no alternative but to accept." Therefore, he told the delegates, "I am here at your bidding. . . . And yet, I feel a little unhappy that I should have been chosen once again as Congress President. . . . I tried hard that this should not occur and pleaded with my comrades in the Congress to make some other choice, but their insistence and the circumstances were against me in this matter. I felt that for me to go on saying 'No', in spite of the advice of so many of my valued colleagues, would not be proper."[6]

As Nehru's second term as Congress President drew to a close in the fall of 1954, he was at the height of his personal popularity. India's role in Korea and Indo-China had given the country international recognition and prestige. On the domestic scene, the food crisis had been overcome, and the First Five Year Plan was on its way to fulfillment. However, since the mental and physical strain of the past three years as Congress President and Prime Minister had been considerable, Nehru wrote to the P.C.C. Presidents notifying them of his wish to be permitted to step down from both posts for a short time. He was also motivated by annoyance at constant press references to the question of "After Nehru who?" He argued that it was absurd to think that the fate

[4] *Hindustan Times* (New Delhi), Dec. 30, 1952.
[5] J. Nehru, *Presidential Address, The Indian National Congress, Fifty-eighth Session* (New Delhi: A.I.C.C., 1953), p. 1.
[6] *Ibid.*

of a great nation depended on any one individual. In the end, he left open his decision on the prime ministership, but he emphatically stated that he would not continue as President of the Congress.[7]

On the surface Nehru's tenure as Congress President was less turbulent than during the years immediately following independence, but the trend over which so much controversy had been generated under Kripalani and Tandon nevertheless continued. As a result, by the time Nehru stepped down from the post, a significant change in Congress attitudes had taken place. There had been created, as Frank Moraes observed, "a Congress habit of mind which has led the overwhelming bulk of the party to look to the prime minister and not to the president of the Congress for political guidance."[8]

The development of this attitude was due in no small part to Nehru's views on party-government relations. To Nehru the problem of party-government relations resolved itself into a choice between variations of two basic models: the British and the Communist. In the British model for party-government relations, as Nehru saw it, the party as government played the dominant decision-making role. In the Communist model, on the other hand, the party organization was supreme. India's place, Nehru believed, could be located somewhere between these two extremes, for in India, "It is basically the government policy and the implementation of that policy that affects the people. The Congress comes in not only in broadly effecting that policy or pushing it in this direction or that, but much more so in carrying the message of that policy to the people."[9]

Yet, for all its ability "to broadly effect" policy or "to push it in this direction or that," Nehru consistently held that

[7] Letter J. Nehru to Presidents of the P.C.C.s, Oct. 11, 1954, *Letters to the P.C.C. Presidents* (New Delhi: A.I.C.C., 1955), pp. 28-31.

[8] F. Moraes, *India Today* (New York: The Macmillan Co., 1960), p. 98.

[9] J. Nehru, "General Elections and the Congress," *A.I.C.C. Economic Review*, IX (May 1, 1957), 3-6.

the party organization could not expect the Prime Minister and his government to be directly responsible to the party executive. "The Prime Minister or a Chief Minister," he noted, "is the archstone which forms the basis of a democratic structure. Once he is chosen, he must have the full discretion left to him. If he does not command the confidence of the legislature, he may go." However, the Prime Minister's responsibility to the legislature did not extend to the party organization. Nehru considered it wholly unjustified to expect the Prime Minister to hold his post only so long as the party executive permitted him to remain in office. To do so, he argued, would reduce parliamentary democracy to a "mockery."[10]

Despite his fondness for envisioning the Indian model as a unique solution to the problem of party-government relations, Nehru frequently relied on examples drawn from the experience of the British Labour Party. Throughout its history the Labour Party has been subject to internal conflict over the respective roles of party and government. One of the most famous incidents, one with which Nehru was thoroughly familiar and which he cited frequently, was the Attlee-Laski controversy of 1945. Prime Minister Churchill had invited Attlee, leader of the Labour Party and soon to be Labour Prime Minister, to the Potsdam Conference, which was scheduled to take place following the polling in the 1945 General Elections but before the results could be determined and announced. Attlee accepted the invitation but encountered opposition from the party. In his role as Chairman of the Labour Party's National Executive Committee, Harold Laski attempted to intervene by insisting that Attlee could attend only as an "observer." "The Labor Party," Laski declared, "cannot be committed to any decision arrived at, for the three-Power Conference will be discussing matters which have not been debated either in the Party Executive or at meetings of the Parliamentary Labour

10 *Congress Bulletin*, No. 6, Aug. 1954, pp. 290-291.

Party."[11] Rejecting Laski's interpretation of the role of the party in decision-making, Attlee replied that, though the party executive had a right to be consulted, it could not challenge the actions and conduct of a Labour Prime Minister. In relating this incident to Congressmen, Nehru left little doubt that he supported Attlee's position wholeheartedly and that he, as Prime Minister of India, would also refuse to subordinate the parliamentary wing of the party to the mass organization.[12]

When, in the fall of 1954, Nehru relinquished the Congress presidency, the lessons he had learned during the Kripalani and Tandon crises, his three years as Congress President, and his conception of the role of the Prime Minister vis-à-vis the chief executive of the party conditioned the selection of Congress Presidents for the next decade. These ten years constituted the second phase of the period of centralization and convergence. In evaluating candidates for the presidency during this period, Nehru relied extensively on the recommendations of his chief advisers in the party, particularly Pandit G. B. Pant and Lal Bahadur Shastri. The acceptability of each candidate depended to a great extent on Nehru's assessment of the consensus of opinion in the party and on his reading of political conditions in the country. Political exigencies required that candidates be selected in light of such considerations as regional balance, minority representation, and the development of new young leaders. However, the single most important criterion for selecting Congress Presidents during this decade was prior government experience at the highest possible level. It was argued in support of this criterion that men who have held important executive posts in the government are capable of a much clearer understanding of the circumscribed role required of the leader of the party organization. U. N. Dhebar, for

[11] R. T. McKenzie, *British Political Parties* (New York: Frederick A. Praeger, 1963), p. 330. See also pp. 612-617 for an account of the more recent clash over unilateral disarmament.
[12] *Congress Bulletin*, No. 6, Aug. 1954, pp. 290-291.

example, displayed this kind of understanding when he declared: "In relation to the task before the Government, the special features of our Constitution make the Governments responsible to the Legislatures which consist of partymen as well as non-partymen. Congressmen have to appreciate that this necessarily results in placing some limitations upon the Government."[13] Largely because of their appreciation of such limitations, all Congress Presidents selected by Nehru after 1954, with the exception of Mrs. Gandhi, were former Chief Ministers.

Once Nehru's intent to resign from the Congress presidency was clear, the difficult search for a successor got under way. The difficulty in finding an acceptable candidate for the post lay in the fact that it was no longer the most coveted political prize in India. In fact, it was turned down by B. G. Kher, a senior Congressman who had formerly been the Chief Minister of Bombay. Finally Shastri, one of Nehru's most important advisers on party affairs, recommended U. N. Dhebar, Chief Minister of the small state of Saurashtra. Nehru, acting on Shastri's suggestion, asked Morarji Desai to contact his fellow Gujarati. Morarji did so, and early in October Dhebar indicated his willingness to accept the post. On Nehru's recommendation, the Working Committee endorsed Dhebar unanimously.[14]

Dhebar seemed to be the ideal candidate. In the first place, he had been Chief Minister of Saurashtra for seven years and was thus equipped to understand the problems of the governmental wing. Secondly, at age forty-nine, Dhebar was a member of the generation to whom the Congress leadership had eventually to pass if the party was to survive as a political force. Thirdly, he was a staunch advocate of constructive works, which, it was hoped, would provide opportunities for party members to function in useful social roles between elections rather than abandoning them to dissipate

[13] *Congress Bulletin*, No. 5, May 1958, p. 357.
[14] *Congress Bulletin*, No. 8, Oct.-Nov. 1954, pp. 352-353.

their energies and the reputation of the party in factional rivalries. Finally, his willingness to leave a high elective office to accept the post of party chief seemed to indicate that Dhebar was not merely seeking personal power and prestige.

Until the election of Dhebar, Congress Presidents had been drawn from the generation which had provided such outstanding leaders as Azad, Nehru, and Prasad. Secondary leaders like Kripalani, Pattabhi, and Tandon also belonged to this generation of Congressmen. For all their differences in prestige, there was among the members of this generation a relative parity in terms of age, party position, duration of leadership, provincial prominence, and personal sacrifice during the independence struggle. Years of close personal and party relationships had created a certain rapport which influenced all subsequent official relations among them. The fact that Dhebar, who was born in 1905 and joined the Congress movement only in 1936, belonged to an entirely new generation of Congress leaders meant that his relationship to the Prime Minister and the senior members of the High Command was of a completely different nature. In one of his first public speeches he acknowledged the pre-eminence of the older leaders:

> Having taken over, I am trying to do my best. It is a mistake to consider that there is a dual leadership in the country. India, for the last forty years, has been accustomed to think in terms of a single leadership and by the grace of God, we have been endowed with men who had borne the brunt out of consideration or service to the country singularly well. There is only one leader in India today and that is Pandit Jawaharlal Nehru. Whether he carries the mantle of Congress Presidentship on his shoulders or not, ultimately, the whole country looks to him for support and guidance.[15]

Thus, Dhebar accepted Nehru as supreme leader. But to say that he played a subordinate role is not to tell the full

[15] *The Hindu* (Madras), Jan. 20, 1955.

story of his relationship with the Prime Minister. Familiar with the pattern of the past ten years of Congress organizational history, Dhebar developed an approach to his new office which, in effect, sidestepped the issue of party-government relations. He felt, correctly, that Nehru wished to discuss problems with as wide a circle as possible. He also knew that Nehru would rarely refuse to discuss a topic once it was raised. Thus, it was Dhebar's custom to submit a broad and comprehensive agenda to the Working Committee. After Dhebar's election the number and scope of subjects considered by the Working Committee increased markedly. Nehru in turn facilitated cordial relationships by taking Dhebar into his confidence on key problems facing the government. The result was a series of interchanges between the government and the party which functioned successfully for four and a half years. Dhebar himself described the coordinating processes in this way:

> At the Central level a pattern of cooperation is slowly evolving. There are the routine meetings of the Working Committee once every two months; the meetings of the Presidents and PCCs once in every four months; and the meetings of the AICC once in every six months with its counterpart of informal discussions. Panditji takes his full share in these meetings despite his other commitments. We also occasionally invite the Ministers to join in the discussions. This process is supplemented by the frequent informal meetings between the Leaders. This has led to the creation of certain affinities without which no organisation can function. This pattern will one day, I hope, take a more concrete shape when the Working Committee, AICC and Presidents' Conference will be utilized to the full in developing corporate thinking and fashioning an organisational mind.[16]

The existence of such an elaborate consultative process did

[16] U. N. Dhebar, "Establishing effective contacts of the organisation and administration," *Congress Bulletin*, Nos. 3-4, March-April 1957, pp. 83-84.

not prevent occasional differences of opinion from arising between the Prime Minister and the Congress President. At such times Nehru's decision was final on governmental matters, while Dhebar was usually permitted to exercise his own judgment in organizational affairs.

During his first three years in office,[17] Dhebar concentrated on rebuilding an organization debilitated by years of neglect. He worked out a scheme intended to make the Congress machinery effective not only as a party organization but also as an aid to national economic development. This plan called for a decentralization of the organization with the creation of a new basic unit called the Mandal Congress Committee consisting of one member for each thousand inhabitants of an area with a population of 20,000. Concerning the organization of the Mandals, Dhebar said, "There is little to which, during my Presidential term, I have attached more importance."[18] Although these reorganization plans had been drawn up before the 1957 election, implementation was postponed to prevent the organization from being caught in a transitional phase during an election year. Following the Second General Elections when the scheme went into effect, Dhebar's extended first term came to a close. The leadership in general desired Dhebar to continue, for several reasons. For one thing, no suitable successor seemed to be available. But it was also believed that a second term would permit Dhebar to implement the organizational changes which he had drawn up.

Dhebar was not enthusiastic about undertaking a second term as Congress President;[19] he agreed to serve only after a personal appeal from Nehru,[20] and, when the term was only half over, he resigned. Ironically, although Dhebar had sought to strengthen the party by way of a scheme for decentraliza-

[17] Since Dhebar's term of office was due to expire in January 1957 on the eve of the Second General Elections, it was decided to extend his term for a year. *The Indian Express* (New Delhi), June 14, 1956.

[18] *Congress Bulletin*, No. 5, May 1958, p. 358.

[19] *The Statesman* (New Delhi), Oct. 2, 1957.

[20] *Times of India* (New Delhi), Oct. 24, 1958.

tion within the state Congress organizations, his frustration stemmed from the fact that a great deal of the power which had previously been associated with the center had devolved to leaders at the state level. Thus, toward the end of his tenure as Congress President, Dhebar warned of the dangers of bossism, entrenchment, and indiscipline.

Dhebar criticized bossism not only for preventing younger people from advancing into positions of responsibility but also for the growing sense of frustration among Congressmen in the party organization.[21] Many of the strong Chief Ministers who wished to ensure their own control of the state governments felt it was essential to maintain a firm grip on the corresponding party organization. Particular importance was attached to the offices of P.C.C. President, Executive Committee of the P.C.C., and Election Committee. Control was maintained directly, when the Chief Minister managed to get himself elected P.C.C. President in overt violation of Congress policy, or indirectly, when one of the Chief Minister's supporters was appointed to the post. Dhebar, however, insisted that all P.C.C. offices be truly elective and thus truly representative of the party organization.

An example of the difficulties Dhebar faced can be drawn from Bihar party politics. Following the 1957 elections, a bitter struggle took place in Bihar between the two rival groups for the chief ministership. S. K. Sinha emerged victorious by a narrow margin. Then followed a struggle in the organization for control of the party machine. When the two groups could not agree on a single candidate for the presidency of the P.C.C., a resolution was passed by the party office bearers requesting the Chief Minister to nominate the President. Dhebar objected violently to this procedure and made his views known to the Chief Minister of Bihar, who simply ignored him.[22]

In order to combat this trend toward bossism and en-

[21] *Ibid.*

[22] *The Searchlight* (Patna), Jan. 8, 1958; Feb. 6, 1958; Feb. 15, 1958; March 13, 1958.

trenchment, Dhebar suggested that no party officer be permitted to succeed himself, a proposal which was embodied in a resolution at the Hyderabad Session of the A.I.C.C. in the fall of 1958.[23] As a weapon against bossism the Hyderabad resolution was to prove useless. However, it was later to play an important role in the struggle for power after Nehru's death.

Dhebar's comments about bossism indicated that he was also dissatisfied with the predominance of government leaders in party matters. It was reported that he was annoyed even with Nehru and that, following the Nagpur Session of the Congress, he had written to the Prime Minister accusing him of being intolerant of party criticism.[24] In addition, Dhebar was unhappy about the tone of Congress administration in some of the states. The situation in the Punjab particularly distressed him. The Parliamentary Board, investigating some charges submitted by Punjab Congressmen, found that, although there was no firm basis for the charges of actual corruption, there were cases of "improprieties" in some of those relating to the Chief Minister as well as "certain procedural irregularities in administrative matters."[25] Finally, Dhebar was concerned about the growing lack of party discipline in states like Mysore, Orissa, Delhi, and the Punjab, where groupism was rampant. Thus Dhebar, having been responsible for the adoption of the Hyderabad resolution which limited the term of Congress office holders, set a good example by submitting—willingly—to its provisions.

Nehru shared some of Dhebar's disillusionment with the state of the Congress organization. At the end of April 1958, he told the members of the Congress Party in Parliament that he wished to relinquish the post of Prime Minister. The pressure of work, problems at home and abroad, the lack of unity within the country and the party, and the continued

[23] *Times of India* (New Delhi), Oct. 24, 1958.
[24] *New York Times*, Feb. 3, 1959.
[25] Indian National Congress, *Report of the General Secretaries, 1958* (New Delhi: A.I.C.C., 1959), pp. 28-29.

concern over "after Nehru who?" had contributed to his decision.[26] The audience, stunned, pleaded with Nehru to reconsider. Having administered his shock treatment, Nehru agreed to continue in office. Shortly thereafter, the A.I.C.C. met in Delhi to undergo self-examination. In the end, little changed.[27]

As the Congress assembled at Nagpur in January 1959, there was a great deal of speculation about the selection of Dhebar's successor. The consensus among leading Congressmen seemed to favor a candidate from the South. The development of a separatist movement in the area, the dissatisfaction over the national language question, and the fact that a southerner had not held the President's post since 1949 also helped to focus attention on the South as a source of presidential timber in 1959. The two most frequently mentioned possibilities were C. Subramaniam, Finance Minister of Madras, and S. Nijalingappa, who had just been ousted as Chief Minister of Mysore. Although Subramaniam was the favorite, K. Kamaraj, the Chief Minister of Madras, refused to part with him, arguing that the loss of his Finance Minister would reduce the effectiveness of the state's administration.[28] Nijalingappa, on the other hand, was reportedly blocked by Morarji Desai, a member of the Congress High Command, who felt that Nijalingappa's strong advocacy of linguistic states would cause him to favor his own state's claims to the bilingual district of Belgaum, which was an area of dispute between Mysore and Morarji's home state of Bombay.[29]

The only non-southerner mentioned for the post of Congress President in 1959 was S. K. Patil, a Central Minister and former party boss in the city of Bombay. Patil's role in

[26] Brecher, *Nehru: A Political Biography* (London: Oxford University Press, 1959), p. 504.
[27] *Congress Bulletin*, No. 5, May 1958, pp. 276-346.
[28] *Hindustan Times* (New Delhi), Jan. 6, 1959.
[29] Related to the author in New Delhi in 1960 by leading Congressmen.

the events leading up to the election reveals some of the inner maneuverings of the party leadership. On the eve of the Nagpur Session, rumors appeared in the press that Patil was being seriously considered for the presidency. In newspaper circles, however, it was generally agreed that Patil himself had set the speculations going in order to test party reactions.[30] Of the senior Cabinet Ministers at the time, he was undoubtedly in the weakest position, and he felt that by capturing an important post in the party he could enhance his chances as a possible successor to Nehru. However, Morarji Desai opposed his candidacy, and Patil was forced to abandon his scheme. He called a press conference to deny that he had ever been "in the race for the Congress Presidency."[31] He told reporters that he regretted that his name had been dragged into the competition and that his reported candidature had not found favor with his colleagues in the High Command. The whole incident, he noted, had been a source of embarrassment to himself and to his associates.

As the Nagpur discussions progressed, a "veritable conspiracy was hatched"[32] by G. B. Pant, Dhebar, and key southern leaders to elect Mrs. Indira Gandhi, Nehru's daughter, as Congress President.[33] Nehru first heard of the idea on the day before the end of the Nagpur Session. He expressed reservations but did not veto the proposal. "Nobody had mentioned it to me before," he later revealed, "and it came rather as a surprise. I gave a good deal of thought to this matter and I came to the conclusion that I should firmly keep apart from this business and not try to influence it in any way except rather generally and broadly to say that it had disadvantages." In the first place, he observed, the state of her health was not good, and, secondly, "normally speaking

[30] Related to the author in New Delhi in 1960 by Indian journalists covering the Congress Party.
[31] *Hindustan Times* (New Delhi), Jan. 9, 1959.
[32] *Hindustan Times* (New Delhi), March 23, 1959.
[33] *Times of India* (New Delhi), Feb. 8, 1959.

it is not a good thing for my daughter to come in as Congress President when I am Prime Minister."[34]

Mrs. Gandhi, too, was rather hesitant about the idea. After first agreeing, she changed her mind. But finally, after long consultations, she decided to accept the advice of her colleagues, Pant and Dhebar.[35] In the meantime, Sanjiva Reddy, K. Kamaraj, Nijalingappa, and K. P. M. Nair, the leaders of the four southern states, had issued a public statement supporting Mrs. Gandhi as the perfect successor to Dhebar.[36] Three other candidates were nominated, but all withdrew in favor of Mrs. Gandhi, who was elected unanimously.[37] It was similar support from state leaders that was to win her the prime ministership in 1966.

As Congress President, Mrs. Gandhi had several important advantages. As a woman, she could help attract more women to work actively for the Congress cause. Next, since she was only 42 years old, she would help create the impression of a newly evolving leadership in the Congress, encourage aspiring younger elements in the party, and serve as a hint to some of the old guard that perhaps they, too, should give way to new blood. Most important of all, as Nehru's daughter, she would give new prestige to an organization that was losing its glamour. It was also felt that she would be able to act with greater vigor than Dhebar had been able to muster and that she was perhaps the only candidate who could compete with her father on almost equal terms. Finally, some observers viewed her victory as a swing to the left, even though Nehru himself denied that his daughter's election could be given such an interpretation. Her election, he said, indicated neither a leftist nor a rightist swing, but rather a desire on the part of the sections of the Congress to get out of a rut by introducing a new, young leadership instead of the same old faces.[38]

[34] *Ibid.*
[35] *Ibid.*
[36] *Hindustan Times* (New Delhi), Jan. 13, 1959.
[37] *Congress Bulletin*, No. 1, Jan.-Feb. 1959, p. 10.
[38] *Times of India* (New Delhi), Feb. 8, 1959.

Mrs. Gandhi's term opened with a flare of enthusiasm. In her first public statement she called for the return of all former Congressmen who still believed in the Congress program. Later she demonstrated her firm commitment to this policy by appointing Sucheta Kripalani, a dissident who had returned to the Congress after passage of the Avadi resolution in 1955, to a post as one of her general secretaries. In the same initial statement Mrs. Gandhi also complained that the party was moving too slowly. The Congress, she said, had to strike a balance between the need for ideological cohesion and the necessity for prodding the diverse interests within the party to work together.[39] Later, she warned that she would deal firmly with party factional feuds in such states as Uttar Pradesh, Punjab, Andhra, Rajasthan, and Orissa.[40]

After a few months in office Mrs. Gandhi's enthusiasm began to subside. Like Dhebar, she discovered herself unable to bring about the revitalization of the Congress which she had promised. Her firm stand on party factionalism was undermined when, despite her intervention, a dispute in Uttar Pradesh exploded into the most serious party-government struggle at the state level since independence and the Orissa Congress was torn apart by an intra-party struggle for organizational control.

As Nehru's daughter, however, Mrs. Gandhi was able to exert much more influence on policy-making than her predecessor. She was credited with having played a major role in two important decisions: the ousting of the Communist government in Kerala and the bifurcation of Bombay. Despite her short term, it could probably be said that she was among the more vigorous Congress Presidents in post-independence India.

Mrs. Gandhi had been elected on an interim basis to complete the remaining ten months of U. N. Dhebar's two-year term. She had been in office only a few months when the issue of her future role arose. Although there were strong pres-

[39] *Hindustan Times* (New Delhi), Feb. 10, 1959.
[40] *Times of India* (New Delhi), Feb. 27, 1959.

sures for her to remain, she announced that she would not seek re-election.[41] The major reason for this decision was her poor health, and, in fact, she underwent surgery immediately upon leaving office. Other factors which played a role in her decision to step down were the uncomfortable situations created by her relationship to the Prime Minister and her inability to bring about the radical transformation of the Congress she desired. She was also disillusioned by a series of clashes with powerful state leaders over organizational matters and the issue of cooperative farming, a policy adopted by the Congress at the Nagpur Session. Nevertheless, she had established herself within the Congress as a figure to be reckoned with.

Once more the search for a new Congress President was under way. The same factors which had prompted the leadership to turn to the South earlier in the year now suggested the same recourse. In fact, with the formation of the Swantantra Party by C. Rajagopalachari as a reaction against the passage of the cooperative farming resolution, the political situation in the South had become even more delicate. Nijalingappa and Subramaniam were considered once again, but both were rejected for the same reasons as before. K. Hanumanthaiya of Mysore was also mentioned. But since he had long been out of favor with the High Command, he was considered unacceptable. Instability in the state of Kerala had prevented the emergence of any single leader. Gradually, attention focused on the young Chief Minister of the state of Andhra, Sanjiva Reddy. Reddy's record in his own area was promising. He had been able to unite the state Congress organization and bring strong government to Andhra after years of instability. His youth was in keeping with the desire of the central leadership to create a progressive, dynamic image for the organization. Moreover, a vigorous young man was needed to carry the burdensome responsibilities of the Third General Elections which would take place dur-

[41] *Hindustan Times* (New Delhi), Nov. 12, 1959.

ing his term. Finally, having served as Chief Minister and member of the State Cabinet for several years, Reddy could be counted on to understand the problem of party-government coordination.

The High Command asked Reddy to come to Delhi for talks. He arrived late in the evening on November 16. Immediately he met with Nehru, Pant, Mrs. Gandhi, Morarji, and Dhebar.[42] They offered him the job. Although he was reluctant to accept the office, he felt obliged to do so, largely because of the forthcoming elections.[43] "Any Congressman," he explained, "will have to accept any post of responsibility if he is asked to do it. No Congressman can run away from that."[44] The day after his talks with the High Command, nomination papers were filed in his behalf.[45] Four other nominations were received, but all withdrew before the close of nominations.[46] Reddy was declared unanimously elected.

Compared to his new associates at the center, Sanjiva Reddy was junior in age, status, and influence. He was, moreover, a hand-picked, captive candidate with a purely local orientation who had nevertheless, like others of his generation, become a master in group maneuvering and caste politics at the state level. After holding the Congress presidency for a year, he admitted that, until then, "My connections . . . had been mainly with the people of my own State of Andhra and except for occasional visits, I have had no vital contacts with the rest of India. This one year has helped to correct this imbalance, and has enabled me to view the local and regional problems from a national standpoint and appreciate their significance from a wider range."[47]

[42] *Hindustan Times* (New Delhi), Nov. 17, 1959.
[43] Told to the author during an interview with Mr. Reddy in New Delhi in 1960.
[44] *Hindustan Times* (New Delhi), Nov. 18, 1959.
[45] *Ibid.*
[46] *Hindustan Times* (New Delhi), Jan. 4, 1959.
[47] N. S. Reddy, *Presidential Address, The Indian National Congress, Sixty-sixth Session* (New Delhi: A.I.C.C., 1961), pp. 1-2.

Reddy had no illusions about the influence attached to his new role. As a former Chief Minister, he knew where the power really rested. He knew in advance where he would stand among the top leaders at the center and made quite clear his understanding of his position in his first public statement to his fellow Congressmen in Bangalore. This statement is an excellent summary of the role played by the Congress presidency in the early 1960's:

> I am fully aware that the Presidentship of the Indian National Congress does not now carry the same weight as it did before, during the days of the freedom struggle. During those halcyon days the Congress was a dynamic organisation, in opposition to the rule of one of the mightiest empires that the world had ever seen. It was, therefore, manned and led by the best brains in the country, and the finest patriot that the country could throw up usually became the President. But after the achievement of independence, the Government has become our own, and hence there has to be a division of all available talent in the country between the organisational wing of the party and its governmental wing. There should be no friction between these two wings, and both of them should function in a spirit of cooperative endeavour, in order to conduce to the best advantage of the nation.[48]

During Reddy's absence from Andhra, the stability that had existed in his home state since November 1956 broke down. Group rivalries developed into a serious conflict which Reddy had watched closely despite his distance from the scene. After his selection as Congress President, many had expected that his chief lieutenant, A. S. Raju, would become Chief Minister. Reddy himself, however, had objected to Raju. Finally, as a compromise candidate, all parties concerned managed to settle on D. Sanjivayya, a Harijan, who had been one of the youngest men ever to have achieved the

[48] N. S. Reddy, *Presidential Address, The Indian National Congress, Sixty-fifth Session* (New Delhi: A.I.C.C., 1960), pp. 1-2.

post of Chief Minister in India. Throughout Sanjivayya's term there were attempts to oust him. Repeatedly the High Command prevented them from succeeding. These group rivalries in Andhra hurt the Congress in the 1962 elections after which, in order to restore unity to the state Congress situation, the High Command allowed Reddy to resign. He returned to Andhra and resumed his former position as Chief Minister. Over Reddy's objections, Sanjivayya, who refused to join Reddy's Cabinet, was picked by Mrs. Gandhi and Shastri to fill out Reddy's term as Congress President.[49]

In the period from 1946 to 1963 the role of the Congress President evolved from that of the powerful symbol of national leadership to that of party chairman. As we have seen, this transformation was far from tranquil. In the early years especially, the uniqueness of the problem, the lack of clear-cut precedents, ideological splits, and leadership conflicts all combined to create severe stresses. Unity was restored to the Congress only when Nehru centralized the leadership of the party and the leadership of the government in his own hands. Nehru's position became so dominant that people began to ask, "After Nehru who?" Overwork and a desire to give less basis to the growing feeling that he was indispensable brought Nehru to a decision to give up the office of Congress President in 1954.

The very circumstances under which U. N. Dhebar, Mrs. Gandhi, Sanjiva Reddy, and D. Sanjivayya were selected prevented them from challenging the Prime Minister. By this time the Congress President was commonly described as functioning as no more than "a glorified office boy of the Congress central government headed by the Prime Minister."[50] And Sanjiva Reddy bitterly complained to a friend that as Congress President he was treated as "Mrs. Gandhi's chaprassi."[51]

[49] *New York Times*, June 7, 1962.
[50] Moreas, *India Today*, p. 98.
[51] M. Brecher, *Nehru's Mantle* (New York: Frederick A. Praeger, 1966), p. 131.

Prime Minister And Congress President

The supremacy of the Prime Minister was never more evident than during the decade comprising the period of centralization and convergence. During this period each candidate for Congress President had to receive Nehru's personal endorsement, and once in office the chief executive of the party lacked the stature to challenge the Prime Minister's authority. The Congress President became the chairman of the party responsible only for its day-to-day operation and exercising even that responsibility under the supervision of the Prime Minister and senior Congress leaders in the Cabinet. Yet the Nehru era no less than the period of transition had to come to an end, and, even before Nehru's final illness and death, the Congress was evolving into a new phase of development.

THE PERIOD OF DIVERGENCE:
1963-1967

The period of centralization and convergence marked the high point of the parliamentary wing's supremacy over the organization during the first two decades of independence. Yet, even toward the end of this phase, party-government relations had begun to change perceptibly. The process was accelerated by the introduction of the Kamaraj Plan, the election of Kamaraj as Congress President, and the death not only of Nehru but of his successor Shastri. By 1963 it was clear that something different in the way of party-government relations was in the offing. As it turned out, a period of divergence of power was at hand.

But some years after his defeat of Congress President Tandon, Prime Minister Nehru had decided that party-government relations had swung too far in the direction of parliamentary supremacy. As early as 1959, in fact, Nehru was writing to his colleagues:

> Many people say that the Congress has become some kind of camp follower of the Government. This is, I think, basically not true. It is inevitable that when leading personalities in the Congress and the Government are to a large extent the same, the direction of both should also be the same. But it has to be remembered that the push forward in regard to basic policies has come from the Congress organization, representing public urges, and the Government and the Planning Commission have followed these up and worked them out in detail.[1]

[1] Quoted in M. Brecher, *Nehru's Mantle* (New York: Frederick A. Praeger, 1966), p. 131.

Sensitive to these charges that the Congress organization had ceased to play a vital role in Indian political affairs, Nehru undertook to establish greater equilibrium between party and government. The instrument he selected was the Kamaraj Plan. This proposal, put forward by the Chief Minister of Madras, called for senior Congressmen in the parliamentary wing of the party to step down from office in order to devote full time to party organizational work. The genesis and appeal of the Kamaraj Plan must be viewed in the light of two significant earlier developments: The Chinese attack of October 1962 and the fluctuating electoral fortunes of the Congress.

The transformation of the Sino-Indian border dispute from a series of incursions and minor forays into a major military confrontation was one of the most important events in the post-independence history of India. It had a profound effect on both the Congress and the country. The confrontation with China underlined the failure of Nehru's China policy and weakened his position as Prime Minister and leader of the Congress. It also produced dramatic results throughout the country. At first the Congress and the nation were stunned. Then the initial reaction of shock and outrage turned into a sense of national purpose which found people ready to sacrifice whatever they might be called upon to give. However, once the immediate military threat had dissolved into seemingly interminable diplomatic maneuvering, the economic stresses of defense mobilization gnawed away the consensus. Rising prices, increased taxes, drastic financial measures calling for gold control and compulsory deposits, and continuation of the emergency declaration all aroused opposition; and, as if stringent policies were not enough to jeopardize the popularity of the Congress government, a renewal of factionalism within the party itself brought about still greater resentment.

To many, clear evidence of this resentment was apparent in the results of three important by-elections in May 1963, just seven months after the Chinese attack. The Congress

itself suffered a major psychological blow when Acharya
J. B. Kripalani, Dr. Ram Manohar Lohia, and M. R. Masani,
some of the government's bitterest critics, defeated three leading Congressmen in Amroha and Farrukhabad in Uttar
Pradesh and in Rajkot, an old Congress stronghold in Gujarat.
Although detailed studies of these by-elections have revealed
that factors other than government policy may have played
a much more important role, the opposition parties, the
press, and the Congress itself tended to perceive these defeats as a protest against government policy.[2] Immediately
there were demands from the party organization that the
Congress leadership call a special session of the A.I.C.C.
to discuss the reverses and their implications for the party.
The demands took the form of a rare petition signed by eighty
A.I.C.C. members. When the Working Committee met to
consider the petition, it decided against creating the impression of giving in to party pressures. Instead, a regular
meeting of the A.I.C.C. was scheduled for August. At this
time the impact of the by-elections would be discussed.[3]

Meanwhile, a dramatic and dynamic proposal to revitalize
and strengthen the Congress organization was being discussed among senior Congress leaders. Although Kamaraj
was publicly the author of the proposal which bore his
name, Brecher has argued that the idea in fact originated
with Biju Patnaik, the dynamic young Chief Minister of
Orissa.[4] It was Patnaik who persuaded Kamaraj to make the
formal proposal. Kamaraj was quite receptive to the idea,
possibly because ever since the 1962 elections he had been
deeply concerned about the growing strength of the Dravida
Munnetra Kazhagam (D.M.K.), a Tamil-oriented, anti-
northern party in Madras. By the middle of 1963 he had

[2] For an excellent analysis of the factors responsible for these defeats, see R. Kothari, "Three Bye-Elections," *The Economic Weekly*,
XVII (May 22, May 29, and June 19, 1965), 845-858, 893-902, 987-
1000.

[3] *Congress Bulletin*, Nos. 7-8, Aug. 1963, pp. 34, 63.

[4] Brecher, *Nehru's Mantle*, p. 16.

reached the conclusion that the only effective way of combating the D.M.K. was to resign from the chief ministership and devote his full energies to rebuilding completely the Congress organization in Madras. Once relieved of his duties, he believed that he could undertake an intensive and prolonged tour of the state down to the block level. His ultimate purpose was a revitalization of the party machine, necessitated, in his opinion, by the fact that Congressmen had become too preoccupied with positions of power at the parliamentary level.[5] By his example he hoped to demonstrate the importance of the party organization and, ultimately, to influence the behavior of his fellow Congressmen.

Patnaik and Kamaraj discussed the proposal with Nehru. At first, Nehru was hesitant. He asked Kamaraj whether there was not an approach that would be equally effective in strengthening the party organization without requiring ministers to resign from office.[6] However, after a meeting with Kamaraj at Hyderabad in May, Nehru was converted.[7] Characteristically, he then offered to be the first to resign. Insisting that such action would simply make matters worse, Kamaraj informed the Prime Minister that persistence in pressing such a suggestion would result in his withdrawing this particular proposal for revitalizing the party altogether.[8]

Thus, when the Working Committee assembled on the eve of the A.I.C.C. meeting which had been called to discuss the implications of the by-election defeats, Kamaraj was ready to submit his bold but simple proposal "that leading Congressmen who are in Government should voluntarily relinquish their ministerial posts and offer themselves for full-

[5] *The Hindu Weekly Review* (Madras), Oct. 7, 1963.

[6] *Congress Bulletin*, Nos. 7-9, July-Sept. 1964, p. 362.

[7] "India: After the Kamaraj Plan," *Round Table*, 54 (December 1963), 83.

[8] *Congress Bulletin*, Nos. 7-8, July-Aug. 1963, p. 37. This would not be the first time Nehru had offered to resign. He made similar gestures in 1951, 1954, and 1958.

time organizational work." Again Nehru offered to resign, but the Working Committee refused to entertain the notion. All Chief Ministers and Central Ministers also submitted their resignations. At this point the Working Committee was faced with the delicate problem of determining who should be chosen. Finally, the decision was left to Nehru.[9]

Between the adoption of the Kamaraj Plan by the Congress Working Committee on August 10 and its implementation two weeks later, when Nehru released his list of candidates for resignation, a critical session of the Indian Parliament took place. At that time the small but vocal cluster of opposition parties introduced, for the first time in the sixteen-year history of the Nehru government, a no-confidence motion. The acrimonious debate which followed lasted four days. While not supporting the motion as such, the Communist Party of India took the occasion to demand the immediate resignation of the two "reactionaries" in Nehru's cabinet, S. K. Patil and Morarji Desai.[10] Of all the opposition attacks in the course of the debate, however, none was more stinging than the indictment which came from Acharya Kripalani, who tellingly insisted that "the government should get out of the rut which Nehru admits he is in."[11] Nehru's response to these sharp attacks was an hour-long rambling speech totally lacking in spirit and vigor. Nevertheless, since the Congress enjoyed a large majority in Parliament, the motion was easily defeated by a vote of 346 to 61. Still, the critics had had their say.[12]

The defeat of the no-confidence motion came on August 22. The next day, when the Working Committee assembled to consider the problem of implementing the Kamaraj Plan, Nehru revealed that he was not yet able to present his recommendations. He was requested to submit them the next day.[13] On August 24, Nehru presented a list of twelve names

[9] *Ibid.*, pp. 12-14.
[10] *New York Times*, Aug. 20, 1963.
[11] *New York Times*, Aug. 23, 1963.
[12] *Ibid.*
[13] *Congress Bulletin*, Nos. 7-8, July-Aug. 1963, pp. 17-18.

which was described as including six "top-ranking" Central Ministers in addition to the Chief Ministers of six states. The Central Ministers, by no means of equal importance, turned out to be Morarji Desai, Jagjivan Ram, Lal Bahadur Shastri, S. K. Patil, B. Gopala Reddi, and K. L. Shrimali. The six Chief Ministers whose resignations were accepted were K. Kamaraj of Madras, B. Patnaik of Orissa, Bakshi Ghulam Mohammed of Jammu and Kashmir, Binodanand Jha of Bihar, C. B. Gupta of Uttar Pradesh, and B. A. Mandloi of Madhya Pradesh. Nehru explained that his selections had been influenced by two considerations. He had to take action "on such a scale as to be worthwhile," and yet he could not afford to disrupt the administration too drastically. Other resignations, he suggested, might be accepted at a later stage.[14] Meanwhile, the shake-up was dramatic enough to indicate that Nehru was not so deeply mired in habit as Kripalani's accusation had implied. Overnight Nehru had re-established his undisputed control over the Congress and had added a new dimension to the prestige of the organizational wing for the first time since independence.

Although the ulterior motives attributed to the Prime Minister in his implementation of the Kamaraj Plan detracted somewhat from the organizational wing's new image, Nehru repeatedly denied the cunning attributed to him. To the Congress Party in Parliament he declared that there was "no design" behind the reorganization. Nor was the plan intended to "get rid of anybody."[15] To his other critics in Parliament he insisted that the Kamaraj Plan, as strictly an organizational issue, had absolutely nothing to do with government policy or with the attack on that policy which had given rise to the no-confidence motion. Rather, he emphasized, the Kamaraj Plan had one objective, which was to strengthen the Congress Party organization so as to restore balance within the Congress between party and government. As he told the

[14] *Ibid.*, p. 23.
[15] *New York Times*, Aug. 30, 1963.

A.I.C.C., the Congress had two functions to perform, neither of which was more important than the other. Yet, "because too much importance had begun to be attached to a Minister's job rather than to a job in the Congress organisation, the balance was being upset. And this balance . . . had to be set right, by putting greater stress on the work of the Congress organisation. . . . By the resignation of top ranking Congressmen the people should realise the importance of the organisation."[16] Even if this were the case, however, many disagreed sharply with the position. It was argued that the Kamaraj Plan might result in back-seat driving by the party, which could weaken the administration and result in instability.[17] S. K. Patil perhaps stated this objection most forcefully when he said: "In a free country it was the Government and not the Party which was more important. After all, millions of people were not bothered whether the Congress had a good or bad secretary. They were concerned about their daily necessities for which the Government was directly responsible. Nothing, therefore, must be done which would weaken the Government or the Administration."[18]

To many inside and outside the Congress the Kamaraj Plan was also an indication that the Gandhian spirit was still alive within the Congress. J.P. Narayan, who welcomed the plan "as an act of renunciation," expressed the hope that the Congress leaders who resigned would not confine themselves to the task of rebuilding "the badly damaged edifice" of the Congress but would rather go to the people as a Lok Sevak Sangh in the Gandhian spirit of service. In the end, however, Narayan warned, what the plan accomplished would depend on the role of the Prime Minister, for "it is he who has largely been responsible for undermining the position of the organization." Under Nehru, declared Narayan, the feeling had grown that "the Congress President had been reduced

[16] *Congress Bulletin*, Nos. 7-8, July-Aug. 1963, pp. 42-43.
[17] *The Hindu Weekly Review* (Madras), Aug. 12, 1963.
[18] "Kamaraj Plan," *Indian Recorder and Digest*, IX (Sept.-Oct. 1963), 4.

to a position of a head clerk, and that no one counted unless he held high office."[19]

The renunciation theme also appeared in the Congress *Report of the General Secretaries*. The acceptance and implementation of the Kamaraj Plan, according to this official interpretation, was a demonstration that the Gandhian emphasis on self-abnegation still prevailed within the Congress and that, as a result of this new affirmation of that spirit, "people would begin to realize that the Congress had not lost its power to evoke the spirit of sacrifice and service in its members, however highly placed they may be, and that the so-called lust for power was only a myth, and that the Organization had not lost its importance."[20] A number of people were not convinced. And with good reason, as subsequent events were to indicate.

Nehru was in fact accused of having carried out a "bloodless purge" within the Cabinet.[21] The inclusion of two wholly obscure ministers—Gopala Reddi and Dr. Shrimali—admitted even by Nehru to stand "on a slightly different plane," created the impression that Nehru was using the Kamaraj Plan for his own ends. The removal of Morarji Desai, S. K. Patil, Jagjivan Ram, and Shastri had eliminated the most important potential successors to the prime ministership and had restored ideological balance to the Cabinet.[22] Openly questioning the Prime Minister's motives, S. K. Patil told a meeting in Calcutta, "I am not ridiculing the Plan," but, "if somebody uses it for his own purposes or uses it for getting rid of a minister whom he does not like, then I will say Mr. Kamaraj never intended this."[23] Morarji Desai, who did not at the time openly question Nehru's motives, later told Brecher that in retrospect, after the battle for succession, "it seemed . . . to have

[19] *The Hindu Weekly Review* (Madras), Sept. 2, 1963.
[20] Indian National Congress, *Report of the General Secretaries, Jan. 1962–Dec. 1963* (New Delhi: A.I.C.C., 1964), pp. 1, 3-4.
[21] *New York Times*, Sept. 4, 1963.
[22] S. Kochanek, "Post Nehru India: The Emergence of the New Leadership," *Asian Survey*, VI (May 1966), 291-292.
[23] "Kamaraj Plan," *Indian Recorder and Digest*, IX (Sept.-Oct. 1963), 4.

been motivated not only to get rid of him but also to pave the way for Mrs. Gandhi to the Prime Ministership," just as his father Motilal had passed on the Congress presidency to him in 1929.[24]

Whatever Nehru's motives in implementing the Kamaraj Plan and despite the plan's failure to accomplish its stated objectives, there is no doubt that the Kamaraj Plan had a profound effect on the Congress during the months which preceded Nehru's death. It added new vigor to the Congress presidency, gave new prestige to the Working Committee, and was ultimately to play a vital role in the succession.[25]

The first effect of the Kamaraj Plan was to destroy the old hierarchy of leadership within the Congress Ministry. Because of his seniority and his personal influence, Morarji Desai had clearly occupied a central position in this hierarchy. According to a survey of the Congress members of the Second Lok Sabha,[26] for example, it was discovered that 55.5 per cent of the members ranked Morarji as the third most important leader in the Congress after Nehru and Pandit G. B. Pant. With Pant's death, Morarji moved up to the number two position. Deprived of leverage and patronage in the Ministry, the focus of Desai and the other deposed leaders shifted of necessity to the party organization and the upcoming contest for the Congress presidency. For the first time in a decade and a half, some of the most prominent leaders in the Congress were showing an interest in the post. This sudden fascination with organizational affairs, however it may have conformed to the letter of the Kamaraj Plan, partook very little of its intended—or publicized—spirit.

Prior to the introduction of the Kamaraj Plan it had been assumed almost as a matter of course that Atulya Ghosh, party boss of West Bengal, would be named the next Con-

[24] Brecher, *Nehru's Mantle*, p. 14.
[25] *Ibid.*, p. 16.
[26] This survey was conducted by the author in New Delhi in 1960-1961.

gress President. Afterwards, however, things had changed.[27] Morarji Desai and Lal Bahadur Shastri, the most important of the recently resigned Cabinet members, became major candidates for the office. It looked as if a bitter and protracted contest was in the offing.

Instead, the issue was settled quickly and—apparently— easily at a Working Committee meeting on October 9. At this time, "unknown to Kamaraj," according to Brecher, "Atulya [Ghosh], who was sitting close to Nehru, leaned over and told the Prime Minister that he did not want the post and asked whether Kamaraj was acceptable: Nehru replied in the affirmative. Then, just as the meeting was coming to a close, Atulya asked the Congress President to request the group to stay on for a few minutes because he wished to propose, informally, a name for the next Congress President."[28] The proposal was accepted unanimously.[29]

Behind this deceptively simple resolution lay a scheme worked out by several major Congress figures from non-Hindi states at a conference held shortly before the Working Committee meeting of October 9. This conference has since been called the Tirupathi Conclave, and those who attended came to be known as the Syndicate. The purpose of the conclave was to retain control of the Congress presidency and especially to prevent the office from falling to Morarji Desai. The participants were Kamaraj, Sanjiva Reddy, and S. Nijalingappa of the South, and Atulya Ghosh of West Bengal. Although S. K. Patil was not present, he was privy to the decision, for Ghosh went directly from Tirupathi to Bombay to confer with him. Regarding the proceedings of the conclave, Sanjiva Reddy has given an account. At Tirupathi, according to Reddy, it was decided that Lal Bahadur Shastri should be chosen as the next Congress President. If Shastri should refuse, a contingency plan called for Kamaraj to be elected. Thus, when Shastri's fear of an open conflict with

---

[27] *The Indian Express* (New Delhi), Oct. 11, 1963.
[28] Brecher, *Nehru's Mantle*, p. 20.
[29] *Congress Bulletin*, Nos. 9-11, Sept.-Nov. 1963, p. 6.

Morarji lead him to decline the office, the name of Kamaraj was immediately proposed—and accepted.[30] This well-planned and swiftly executed maneuver evidently caught Morarji and his supporters off guard. Morarji told the Working Committee that he saw little point in considering the matter so early, but the consensus was clear.[31] Although no one clearly realized it at the time, the first battle for succession was over. And Morarji had lost it.

Not only did the coalition known as the Syndicate engineer the election of Kamaraj as Congress President, but, at the subsequent Bhubaneshwar Session of the Congress, it also managed to secure the election of a list of seven candidates to the Working Committee, thus blocking an attempt by C. B. Gupta, as one of Morarji Desai's supporters, to gain a seat on the Working Committee.[32] In the process of polling the delegates, the Syndicate's strength in the A.I.C.C. was strikingly demonstrated. Of the approximately 470 A.I.C.C. delegates present, the dominant group received a maximum of 347 votes cast for Mrs. Gandhi and a minimum of 268 votes cast for Mohanlal Sukhadia, Chief Minister of Rajasthan. The best that C. B. Gupta could muster was 160 votes, or 100 votes short of the least received by any of the Syndicate's candidates.[33] This is not to say that the newly elected members of the Working Committee all belonged to the Syndicate, but rather that members who were not acceptable to the Syndicate were kept out. The unity displayed by the Syndicate before and during the Bhubaneshwar Session continued to operate throughout the period of the first succession.

The implementation of the Kamaraj Plan and the subsequent election of Kamaraj as Congress President took on a totally new significance in January 1964 when Prime Minister Nehru suffered a stroke. By removing from office four

[30] *The Hindu Weekly Review* (Madras), Oct. 21, 1963.
[31] *The Hindu Weekly Review* (Madras), Oct. 28, 1963.
[32] *The Hindu Weekly Review* (Madras), Jan. 27, 1964.
[33] *Congress Bulletin*, Nos. 12, 1–2, Dec., Jan., Feb. 1963-1964, pp. 67, 114.

of the most likely candidates for succession, the Kamaraj Plan had already upset the seniority pattern in the Cabinet which might have been used to claim legitimacy for a successor. In addition, the Kamaraj Plan had enhanced the prestige and authority of the Congress presidency after a period of decline by bringing to the national scene in the person of Kamaraj himself a powerful figure equipped to deal with events.

Nehru's stroke intensified the behind-the-scenes maneuvering for succession. It was clear that the Prime Minister would be obliged to curb his activities and delegate a great deal of his authority and responsibility. As an interim arrangement Nehru's responsibilities as Prime Minister were divided between the two most important ministers remaining in the Cabinet: Home Minister G. L. Nanda and Finance Minister T. T. Krishnamachari. However, it was felt that Nehru would be forced to appoint a Deputy Prime Minister either on a *de facto* or on a *de jure* basis prior to the convening of Parliament early in February.[34] Naturally the selection of a Deputy Prime Minister would have important implications for the ultimate issue of succession. As a result, the right, left, and center of the Congress tried desperately to influence the Prime Minister's decision.

From the very beginning it was evident that Shastri was the man to stop. Shastri's recall was vigorously opposed by Krishna Menon, leader of the small but influential left wing of the Congress, who tried to convince the Prime Minister to appoint his daughter Mrs. Gandhi to the Cabinet.[35] The supporters of Morarji Desai, the major leader of the right wing of the Congress and Shastri's chief rival, felt that the recall of Shastri would be a clear indication that the Kamaraj Plan had been used deliberately to squeeze Morarji out of the Cabinet and prevent him from becoming Prime Minister. The primary support for Shastri came from the same coalition of leaders who had seen to Kamaraj's election as Congress Presi-

[34] *New York Times*, Jan. 9, 1964.
[35] *New York Times*, Jan. 23, 1964.

dent—Kamaraj himself, the other leaders of the South, S. K. Patil, and Atulya Ghosh.[36] The major figure behind the scene was Kamaraj. On the day before the decision to recall Shastri as Minister without Portfolio was announced, the Congress President had one of the longest conferences permitted to Nehru since his illness.[37]

Shastri's strength consisted of his recognized administrative abilities, his reputation as a compromiser and conciliator, his support from the Syndicate, and his acceptability to most segments of the party. To Kamaraj, it seemed that Shastri would be able to ensure stability during the transitional period that would follow Nehru's disability or death until the 1967 general election. To many, Nehru's recall of Shastri was a clear indication of his sympathies in regard to his ultimate successor. Yet the recall brought its own problems. The official announcement that Shastri would rejoin the Cabinet had to be postponed for ten days while Congress leaders sought to evolve a definition of his new role. Originally it was assumed that he would be given the title of Deputy Prime Minister. But the official announcement defined his position in rather vague terms. For this hedging there were two basic reasons. It prevented a too facile assumption that the succession problem had been resolved, and it met the objections of senior Cabinet members who refused to be subordinated to the Minister without Portfolio.[38] Even so, the very fact that Shastri had been recalled obviously placed him in a strategic position in the contest for succession and conferred upon him Nehru's blessing as an acceptable successor.

The necessity to answer the long-debated question of "After Nehru who?," had to be faced sooner than most people had anticipated. On May 27, 1964, only a few months after his stroke and shortly after Shastri's recall, Nehru suffered a final and fatal stroke. The moment of succession had

[36] *New York Times*, March 19, 1964.
[37] *New York Times*, Jan. 23, 1964.
[38] *New York Times*, Feb. 17, 1964.

arrived. Intensified maneuvering by the right, left, and center was renewed almost immediately. Within hours of Nehru's death, G. L. Nanda, the member of the Cabinet with most seniority, was designated to act as Prime Minister until the Congress Party in Parliament could meet to elect a successor.[39] It was argued that this tactic had been engineered by Kamaraj, who persuaded Radhakrishnan, President of India, to appoint an Interim Prime Minister until the final selection could be made.[40]

Because of his backing by the Syndicate, Shastri clearly had a majority in the Congress Party in Parliament—the Congress body formally responsible for electing the leader. However, members of the right and the left wings of the Congress schemed to head off his election. Those on the right felt that they could discourage Shastri by threatening an open contest. As a precedent, they pointed to his refusal a few months before to stand for the Congress presidency—a refusal which they attributed to his distaste for conflict. The strategy of the left wing of the Congress was to attempt to postpone the selection of a successor indefinitely, for, like the right wing, they believed that Shastri would prefer any alternative to an open contest. According to this strategy, Nanda would be retained as Interim Prime Minister in the hope that eventually support could be rallied in favor of Mrs. Gandhi.[41] However, both the right and the left had miscalculated. The stakes were higher and the circumstances had changed. Although preferring a unanimous election, Shastri's backers insisted that, if an open contest was unavoidable, the challenge had to be met.

Meanwhile, with the support of President Radhakrishnan, Kamaraj was working for a unanimous election.[42] Kamaraj had thrown his own support to Shastri, whom he had persuaded to fight if necessary, although it was reported that

[39] *New York Times*, May 28, 1964.
[40] *The Observer* (London), May 31, 1964.
[41] *New York Times*, May 31, 1964.
[42] *The Washington Post*, May 30, 1964.

he would also accept Nanda, the Interim Prime Minister, in case of a deadlock.[43] By Saturday, May 30, just three days after Nehru's death, Kamaraj appeared to have lined up 60 to 65 per cent of the Parliamentary Party to vote for Shastri, but he had not yet convinced Morarji that a contest was hopeless.[44]

In his role as Congress President, Kamaraj did not call for a meeting of the Working Committee until Saturday, May 30. At that time the Committee confined itself to passing a condolence resolution, then adjourned until the next day. On Sunday, May 31, the Working Committee met at Nehru's residence to consider the question of the election of a leader. This meeting lasted almost three hours. It was attended by thirty-seven Congressmen, including the important members of the Central Cabinet, the Chief Ministers of all the Indian states, and the elected leaders of the Congress Party in Parliament. Presiding over the meeting Kamaraj declared that "this was a time when the Congress should stand united" and make the selection of the new leader "a unanimous decision." Each Congressman present, with the exception of Mrs. Gandhi, expressed his views on the succession problem. It was finally decided to call a meeting of the Congress Party in Parliament for Tuesday, June 2, at 9:00 a.m., to elect a leader. In the interim, the Working Committee "authorized the Congress President to consult Chief Ministers, Working Committee members, office bearers of the Congress Party in Parliament and such Congress M.P.s whom he desires to consult and ascertain the consensus of opinion on the question of the choice of the Leader of the Congress Party in Parliament and tender his advice accordingly."[45]

Thus, with the Working Committee's decision to hold the election immediately, the left wing's hopes for postponement were dashed.[46] The right wing was so despondent that

[43] *The Observer* (London), May 31, 1964.
[44] *New York Times*, May 31, 1964.
[45] *Congress Bulletin*, Nos. 3-6, March-June 1964, p. 209.
[46] *New York Times*, June 1, 1964.

one of Morarji's followers was quoted as saying, "We've lost the fight."[47] The Desai supporters had hoped the election would be thrown into the Congress Party in Parliament without outside interference. Altogether, the pressures for unanimity were so great that all challengers were severely weakened.

For the next forty-eight hours, in an effort to fulfill his mandate to "tender his advice" on the "consensus of opinion" on the choice of a leader, Kamaraj carried out the most intensive consultations ever attempted in the Congress. He spoke privately with many of the 537 members of the Congress Party in Parliament, with the Chief Ministers of all the Indian states, and with the members of his Working Committee. Finally, by Monday evening, the night before the critical meeting of the Congress Party in Parliament, it was clear that he had accomplished his objective. The unanimous election of Shastri as the successor to Nehru was assured. After a half-hour talk with Kamaraj, Morarji announced that he would second Shastri's nomination at the meeting the next day.[48] It had taken less than a week to provide an answer to the long-standing question of "After Nehru who?"

What factors contributed to Shastri's victory? Despite the fact that he was a native of the Hindi heartland state of Uttar Pradesh, Shastri enjoyed backing from the leaders of the South and the non-Hindi-speaking states of West Bengal and Maharashtra. It was the same kind of solid support from the Syndicate which had played such an important role in electing Kamaraj President of the Congress and in determining the composition of his Working Committee at Bhubaneshwar. Yet the very unity of purpose which his supporters had displayed engendered just so much more bitterness on the part of Morarji Desai and his supporters. It was reported that "Mr. Desai was very bitter that his seniority and service should not be accorded their due rights. He was furious that the Congress leaders from Madras,

[47] *The Washington Post,* June 1, 1964.
[48] *New York Times,* June 2, 1964.

Andhra Pradesh, West Bengal, and Maharashtra had ma-
neuvered and ganged up against him. He thought that if the
'outsiders' did not intervene, he would have no difficulty in
getting elected by the Congress Parliamentary Party. With
his usual aggressive bluntness, Mr. Desai said all this and more
to the Congress President himself and to others."[49]

Morarji Desai had drawn his support from an extremely
diverse coalition of leftists, Harijans, and others—particularly state leaders, who were led to back him for a multitude
of personal reasons. Krishna Menon threw his support to
Morarji in expectation of obtaining the Foreign Ministry,
while B. Patnaik, former Chief Minister of Orissa and an
ally of Menon, worked for Morarji's election as a reward for
the latter's support during some financial difficulties which
Patnaik had encountered while he was Chief Minister and
Morarji Finance Minister at the center. Pratap Singh Kairon,
Chief Minister of Punjab, supported Morarji in the hope that
Morarji would support him as Nehru had against charges of
corruption, especially in light of the Das Report. Morarji's
home state of Gujarat gave him strong backing, as could
have been predicted after the coup by which his supporters
had gained control of the Gujarat ministry. At first Jagjivan
Ram, the Harijan leader, resentful that four or five leaders
had attempted to settle the succession issue without his
knowledge, was planning to support Morarji. But he also
saw that such a move would be ineffective.

The fact was that Morarji's major weakness proved crucial. He was unable to gain the support of the Hindi heartland states of Madhya Pradesh and Uttar Pradesh. In this
the wisdom of Kamaraj's strategy was borne out. Morarji
had the *personal* support of both C. B. Gupta, former Chief
Minister of Uttar Pradesh, and D. P. Mishra, Chief Minister
of Madhya Pradesh. But neither Gupta nor Mishra could
afford to risk the possibility of revolt among the rank and
file if he publicly backed a Gujarati against Shastri, a Hindi-
speaker and one of the leading political figures of Uttar

[49] *The Hindu Weekly Review* (Madras), June 8, 1964.

Pradesh. The defection of the Mishra and Gupta forces turned the tide and made contest a futile gesture.

The role played by Kamaraj in securing the unanimous election of Shastri gave rise to a great deal of speculation concerning the crucial problem of the relationship between the Congress President and the Prime Minister, a problem which had all but disappeared under Nehru. With the passing of Nehru, many feared a return to the conflict which had marked the early years of the post-independence period of the Congress and had resulted in the resignation first of Kripalani and later of Tandon. It was also feared that there would be some attempt to subordinate the parliamentary wing of the party to the dictates of the mass organization. However, Kamaraj and Shastri were able to establish a workable distinction in roles. Although in the months following Nehru's death, Kamaraj spoke out on several issues with a boldness and an air of autonomy uncharacteristic of most recent Congress Presidents, his behavior was indicative, not of revolt, but of the new spirit of debate and criticism which marked all organs of the Congress.

Kamaraj's statements on domestic issues, such as planning and language policy, and even his comments on foreign affairs indicated considerable freedom of action. In his first Presidential Address at Durgapur, for instance, Kamaraj suggested a scaling down of the size of the Fourth Plan because "any inflationary pressures arising out of large investments would again have its severe impact on the poorer and weaker sections of society."[50] These remarks caused such a flurry of activity in government circles that a special meeting of the Planning Commission was called to reconsider the size of the plan.[51] No immediate changes were made, but the debate continued. When the final size of the plan was announced at approximately the figure first mentioned, it was

[50] *The Hindu Weekly Review* (Madras), Jan. 9, 1965.
[51] *The Economic Weekly*, XVII (Jan. 16, 1965), 77.

92

well above the limit Kamaraj had suggested.[52] Although this incident suggests the extent of Kamaraj's influence, it does not necessarily indicate conflict between the Prime Minister and the President of the Congress. As one observer close to Kamaraj suggested, Shastri had also personally preferred a smaller plan but had given way to demands from members of both wings of the party for the larger commitment which had been anticipated while Nehru was still alive.[53]

It is also interesting to note that Kamaraj felt free, at the height of the national language controversy early in 1965, to make a statement indicating some annoyance with central government language policy.[54] Later, in the midst of the Rann of Kutch incident, he delivered a speech in Madras attacking the United States for its silence on the alleged use of American weapons by the Pakistani forces and praising the Soviet Union for its friendship with India.[55] It would be difficult to imagine the Congress Presidents of the previous decade taking such strong positions independently.

While it is impossible not to recognize that Kamaraj added new stature and authority to the Congress presidency, played an influential role in policy-making, and enjoyed considerable autonomy in organizational affairs, it is also clear that his position was in many ways subordinate to that of the Prime Minister. Several important factors influenced his relationship with the Prime Minister. In the first place, it is interesting to note a certain parallel between Kamaraj and Rajendra Prasad, the two major personalities (with the exception of Nehru) to have held the office of Congress President during the period under consideration. Like Prasad before him, Kamaraj enjoyed an independent political reputation yet felt compelled to play a restrained role. As a southerner, Kamaraj was unlikely to see himself in the position of pretender to the prime ministership. Moreover, his

---

[52] *The Hindu Weekly Review* (Madras), Aug. 16, 1965.
[53] *The Hindu Weekly Review* (Madras), Jan. 25, 1965.
[54] *The Economic Weekly*, XVII (Feb. 1965), 152.
[55] *New York Times*, May 13, 1965.

conception of collective leadership, like Nehru's and Prasad's, incorporated the belief that the party had no right to interfere in the day-to-day decisions of the government.[56] Secondly, because Kamaraj came to the Congress presidency after ten years as Chief Minister of Madras, he was in a position to appreciate the limitations which ministerial responsibility place on the parliamentary wing of a governing party. As Chief Minister, he had earned a reputation not only for maintaining high standards of administration but also for harmony between the party organization and the government.[57] Finally, Kamaraj was at a disadvantage just as any Congress President would be, for, once Shastri had established himself firmly in office, the power and patronage at his command placed him in a clearly dominant position. In fact, almost immediately upon his election, Shastri demonstrated his independence by constituting his Cabinet with little outside help. Later, appointing a new Minister of External Affairs without consulting Kamaraj, he responded to questioning with the declaration that "this is the prerogative of the Prime Minister."[58]

Soon the maneuvering over the re-election of Kamaraj as Congress President was to increase the strength of Shastri's position, for the Prime Minister played a dominant role in attempting to assure Kamaraj's re-election. Shastri insisted that Kamaraj remain Congress President in order to ensure continued cooperation between party and government. "Lal Bahadur Shastri," it was reported, "told the Working Committee in unmistakable terms that he needed the continued co-operation of Mr. Kamaraj as Congress President." From this it was deduced that he was "bluntly suggesting that he cannot place the same confidence in others."[59]

The almost certain re-election of Kamaraj, however, was complicated by the existence of a resolution adopted in 1958

[56] Brecher, *Nehru's Mantle*, p. 133.
[57] *The Hindu Weekly Review* (Madras), Aug. 19, 1963.
[58] Brecher, *Nehru's Mantle*, pp. 107-108.
[59] *The Hindu Weekly Review* (Madras), Aug. 2, 1965.

at the Hyderabad Session of the A.I.C.C. This resolution, passed at the insistence of the then Congress President U. N. Dhebar, placed a one-term limit on office holding in the party. At the time, Dhebar had argued that a ban was essential in order to curb the growing tendency toward bossism in the states.[60] In order to circumvent the restrictions of the Hyderabad resolution, a new resolution was submitted to the A.I.C.C. meeting at Bangalore in July 1965. The new resolution was designed to secure for the Working Committee discretionary authority in applying the Hyderabad resolution.

The case for the Working Committee was presented to the A.I.C.C. by Defense Minister Y. B. Chavan. Chavan argued that the restriction on office holding incorporated into the Hyderabad resolution was intended not to be permanent but to meet the political situation at the time of its passage. If the Congress had wished to make the ban permanent, he observed, then certainly the principle would have been incorporated into the party constitution. Chavan went on to say that the present proposal did not alter the substance of the Hyderabad resolution. It was designed merely to add a certain flexibility by granting the Working Committee authority to permit exceptions when deemed necessary.[61]

This vigorous defense was not a formal gesture. Morarji Desai, as a member of the Working Committee, had first opposed the modification of the Hyderabad resolution in the Working Committee itself. Outnumbered there, he had taken the rare step of carrying his disagreement to the floor of the A.I.C.C. In the Hyderabad resolution he had found a principle that could be asserted without directly attacking the Prime Minister and yet offering a possible means of breaking up the Shastri-Kamaraj leadership. "It is an unusual thing that I am doing," he conceded before the A.I.C.C., "but this is a crisis of conscience for me."[62] He then assailed the substance of the proposal by insisting that "I do not think any-

[60] *The Times of India* (New Delhi), Oct. 24, 1958.
[61] *The Hindu Weekly Review* (Madras), Aug. 2, 1965.
[62] *New York Times*, July 26, 1965.

95

thing has happened in the country to make an exception in the case of anyone." Moreover, at any time, making "an exception to one person however high he may be is a negation of democracy." And yet, he charged, all indications pointed to the fact that the Working Committee was seeking a change in the Hyderabad resolution "in order to enable Mr. Kamaraj to have another term of office."[63]

In the end, Morarji did not press for a vote. Instead, he sat silent while Shastri announced that he had asked Morarji not to press his objection. Behind Morarji's silence was the knowledge of an informal tally of A.I.C.C. delegates indicating that the Shastri-Kamaraj coalition commanded a clear majority of 400 to Morarji's 50.[64] Thus failed the first post-Nehru attempt to challenge the Prime Minister by gaining control of the Congress presidency.[65]

Shastri's triumph at Bangalore was one of the first signs of his emergence as a leader in his own right. But the real test of his leadership did not come until a few months later when, in the midst of the most serious clash between India and Pakistan since the war over Kashmir in 1947, he reacted decisively, dramatically, and yet judiciously. Suddenly he appeared in newspaper editorials as "the strong man of India," and wherever he traveled—to Bombay, Calcutta, Jaipur, or Gauhati—he was cheered by crowds as large and enthusiastic as any attracted in earlier times by Nehru or Gandhi.[66] India discovered that its preoccupation with the banyan tree metaphor had been unproductively obsessive. Yet, tragically, Shastri's triumph was short-lived. At Tashkent, within hours of signing a declaration restoring peace and normalizing relations between India and Pakistan, an agreement ironically

[63] *The Hindu Weekly Review* (Madras), Aug. 2, 1965.

[64] *Ibid.*

[65] Ironically, the Indo-Pakistan War made the Bangalore resolution unnecessary, for all Congress organizational elections were postponed and Kamaraj remained Congress President until after the 1967 General Elections.

[66] J. A. Lukas, "Nehru's 'Munshi' Comes out of Nehru's Shadow," *New York Times Magazine* (Nov. 28, 1965), p. 166.

made domestically palatable by his earlier firmness, Shastri succumbed to a heart attack. For the second time in less than two years India was faced with the problem of succession.

Finding a successor to Shastri proved much more difficult than answering the earlier "After Nehru who?" question. Several factors contributed to the difficulty. In the first place, Kamaraj's position was not as strong as it had been nineteen months before. Shastri's emergence as a leader in his own right and the South Indian language riots had tarnished Kamaraj's image somewhat. Second, the shocking unexpectedness of Shastri's death, by contrast to the months preceding Nehru's death, caught the entire Congress leadership unprepared. Third, the Syndicate, having lost its cohesion, acted indecisively. Fourth, largely as a consequence of the first three factors, there was no candidate able to command the widespread support Shastri had enjoyed. Finally, the pressures for unanimity were not so great as they had been in 1964.[67] In fact, especially in view of Morarji's lingering bitterness, there was a feeling that an open contest would be a healthy thing. In the meantime, using as a model the procedures followed after Nehru's death, the senior member of the Cabinet, G. L. Nanda, was appointed Interim Prime Minister pending the election of a new leader.[68]

The Working Committee met on January 14, 1966, to consider the issue of a successor to Shastri. But, unlike the similar meeting some twenty months before, no consensus was forthcoming. The "politics of unanimity" had given way to the "politics of overt conflict."[69] The Working Committee had set January 19 as the date for the election of a new leader and had assigned a committee consisting of Kamaraj, Morarji Desai, Nanda, and Jagjivan Ram the task of attempting to gain unanimous approval of a successor to Shastri. This com-

---

[67] J. A. Lukas, "Political Python of India," *New York Times Magazine* (Feb. 20, 1966), p. 27.

[68] *New York Times*, Jan. 11, 1966.

[69] Brecher, *Nehru's Mantle*, p. 205.

mittee never met.[70] By the weekend (Shastri had died on Tuesday) strong pressures had begun to build up behind Mrs. Gandhi. All but three Chief Ministers had indicated their support for her election as Prime Minister.[71] Kamaraj, in a grand alliance with the state leaders, had built up such massive forces for the election of Mrs. Gandhi that even the Syndicate had no choice but to go along.[72] Nevertheless, Morarji Desai insisted on the necessity for an open contest.

In the ensuing contest between Morarji Desai and Mrs. Gandhi, the Congress Party in Parliament, by an overwhelming majority of 355 to 169, elected Mrs. Indira Gandhi the third Prime Minister of independent India. As in the case of Shastri's election, the dominant coalition consisted of the four southern states plus the non-Hindi-speaking states of West Bengal and Maharashtra rallying about a candidate from Uttar Pradesh. Morarji's support had come largely from his home state of Gujarat, augmented by minority factions in Uttar Pradesh and Bihar and a handful of dissidents in other states.[73] That Mrs. Gandhi owed her election to the Congress President and a coalition of Chief Ministers was one more indication of the new trend toward divergence within the Congress.

Mrs. Gandhi's election as Prime Minister was viewed by many as an interim arrangement designed to fill the gap until the 1967 General Elections. It was felt that Mrs. Gandhi would enhance the electoral appeal of the party by enabling the Congress to continue to capitalize on the Nehru name. Yet almost from the beginning of her term as Prime Minister of India, it was evident that Mrs. Gandhi was not going to be the puppet some senior Congress leaders had expected. In the very process of Cabinet formation she attempted to remove G. L. Nanda, one of the old guard, from his strategic position as Home Minister. When Nanda demanded the post of Deputy Prime Minister as a reward for relinquishing the

[70] *Ibid.*, p. 206.
[71] *New York Times*, Jan. 16, 1966.
[72] Brecher, *Nehru's Mantle*, pp. 209-211.
[73] *New York Times*, Jan. 20, 1966.

Home portfolio, Mrs. Gandhi backed down.[74] Nonetheless, while preserving an appearance of continuity by making only slight alterations in Shastri's Cabinet, Mrs. Gandhi managed to institute changes that were quite significant. Jagjivan Ram was brought back to the Cabinet; Manubhai Shah was promoted to Cabinet rank; and Asoka Mehta, G. S. Pathak, and Fakhruddin Ali Ahmed were brought into the new Cabinet. Modest though the changes were, the effect was to add new blood in sufficient quantity to make observers recall that Shastri had retained the Nehru Cabinet "virtually unchanged" in 1964. As a result, concluded Brecher, though Mrs. Gandhi's action might not have been "drastic" enough for everyone, "yet a 'new look' had come to the summit of India's Government."[75]

It was this "new look" which upset Kamaraj, to whose eyes there appeared to be emerging around Mrs. Gandhi an entirely too influential young clique. The move to drop Nanda, for example, had been instigated by this group, which consisted of Y. B. Chavan, C. Subramaniam, and Asoka Mehta.[76] Speaking theoretically, however, Kamaraj still took the position that the formation of the Cabinet was the responsibility of the new leader.[77] Nor did he relinquish this position in the confusion which marked the Cabinet reshuffle almost a year later. At this time, when Nanda was forced to resign in the wake of the riots against cow slaughter, Kamaraj resisted strong pressures from state leaders and senior Congressmen to intervene in order to block Chavan's appointment as Home Minister. Again he insisted that it was the Prime Minister's business to select her ministers and to allocate portfolios.[78] Thus, in the early months of Mrs. Gandhi's term, Kamaraj worked harmoniously with the Prime Minister even when he was not in complete agreement with her.

In policy areas as well, Kamaraj and Mrs. Gandhi coop-

[74] *Hindustan Times* (New Delhi), Jan. 24, 1966.
[75] Brecher, *Nehru's Mantle*, p. 225.
[76] *The Hindu Weekly Review* (Madras), July 11, 1966.
[77] *Hindustan Times* (New Delhi), Jan. 21, 1966.
[78] *Hindustan Times* (New Delhi), Nov. 12, 1966.

erated closely at first. They moved rapidly and decisively to settle the Punjab problem by pressing for the immediate creation of a Punjabi Suba. They also worked together in developing a policy toward the Nagas. Moreover, even though Kamaraj disagreed with the Prime Minister's decision to change the government's fertilizer policy so as to permit foreign majority participation in the fertilizer industry, extensive consultation prevented Mrs. Gandhi's action from seeming peremptory.[79] Thus, for the first few months of Mrs. Gandhi's term in office, the inevitable differences in outlook did not prevent the Congress President and the Prime Minister from acting in harmony with one another.

However, honeymoons are notoriously short-lived. A major rift had developed by the summer of 1966. At this time, in consultation with her young policy advisers in the government, but without consulting the Congress President or the Working Committee, Mrs. Gandhi decided to devaluate the Indian rupee. The Prime Minister insisted, as Nehru had argued at the outset of his own tenure as Prime Minister, that prior discussion of certain delicate issues was imprudent. Only complete secrecy of deliberations could have prevented adverse economic repercussions. Therefore, Kamaraj was informed of the government's decision before it was publicly announced, but he was not invited to participate in the making of the decision. It is reported that he remained silent during the stormy Working Committee meeting at which the devaluation decision was finally discussed, but it was also known that he had in traditional Congress fashion expressed his displeasure to the Prime Minister in a long private meeting.[80]

Although attempts were made to patch up their differences, friction between Mrs. Gandhi and Kamaraj continued long enough to become reflected in the process of candidate selection for the 1967 elections. The Prime Minister and the

[79] *The Hindu Weekly Review* (Madras), July 11, 1967.

[80] R. Kothari, "India: The Congress System on Trial," *Asian Survey*, VII, 2 (February 1967), 87-88; also *The Hindu Weekly Review* (Madras), Aug. 1, 1966.

Congress President were unable to agree on a common list of names to support for election to the C.E.C., and the results of the ensuing election led Kothari to conclude that "with the election of D. P. Misra, Sadiq and Gupta and the defeat or discomfiture of Malaviya, S. N. Misra . . . and Sukhadia, the Prime Minister appeared to be no longer a prisoner of Kamaraj and looked forward to an equal partnership with the Congress President at least until the election results were out."[81]

The rift between the Prime Minister and the Congress President had resulted from Mrs. Gandhi's attempt to move boldly and vigorously during the early phases of her tenure as Prime Minister. It also derived from the fact that her style differed so markedly from the slow consensus-building approach of Shastri. Her predilection for independent action also clashed with Kamaraj's concept of collective leadership. Such a lack of prior consultation could only lead to a reduction of the influence of the Working Committee.

Mrs. Gandhi's freedom of action, however, did not last very long. Shortly after the devaluation decision her government was confronted by a paralyzing series of events. First, the government was taken aback by the bitter criticism heaped upon its economic policies by both the Congress Party in Parliament and the Parliament. Next, its plans for economic improvement were counteracted when the monsoon failed for the second year in a row, creating severe food shortages and rampant inflation. Finally, a wave of violence swept the country. Government workers demonstrated to obtain higher pay; students rebelled against the dismal conditions prevalent in Indian universities; violence erupted in Andhra over the location of a new steel plant under the Fourth Plan; and rioting took place outside Parliament over demands that the government take action to prevent cow slaughter. The government was clearly shaken by this wave of violence, and to many it seemed that law and order had broken down. At this point, Mrs. Gandhi made

[81] R. Kothari, "India: The Congress System on Trial," p. 89.

things even worse by acting indecisively in her attempt to reshuffle the Indian Cabinet after Nanda's resignation. However, once the new Cabinet had been installed, the government moved to meet the most pressing threats to stability. In cooperation with the new Home Minister Y. B. Chavan, the Prime Minister was able to bring a satisfactory conclusion to the political fasts over cow slaughter and the Punjab border demarcation. In addition, the Prime Minister took action to restore coordination between party and government. The Working Committee was consulted in the government's negotiations with Punjab leaders, and, when Mrs. Gandhi was asked about the nature of these consultations, she replied that "on important things we consult important members of the Working Committee."[82]

Despite the government's ability to recover control and the resumption of party-government coordination, many observers believed as the general elections approached that a change in government was almost inevitable. Such conjectures seemed to be supported by the fact that the process of candidate selection revealed divided leadership at the center. Mrs. Gandhi's fate as Prime Minister depended on the results of an election more unpredictable than any since independence. But whatever the electoral fortunes of the Congress as such, her re-election would also depend on the ability of those who opposed her leadership to agree on a successor. The process of divergence had already led to open conflict, and to some it seemed that disintegration was the obvious next step.

Thus, the period of divergence from 1963 to 1967 was characterized by a weakening of centralized power and by the development of factionalism within the Congress elite. The death first of Nehru and then of Shastri left the national leadership of the party in the hands of a group of leaders of relatively equal status and authority who drew their support from different institutional bases of power. The object of contention among them was the prime ministership,

[82] *The Hindu Weekly Review* (Madras), Jan. 16, 1967.

and their inability to reach a consensus resulted in an open contest from which Mrs. Gandhi emerged victorious. Although many Congress leaders, even her supporters, viewed her election as an interim arrangement, Mrs. Gandhi consciously sought to use the power, prestige, and authority of the prime ministership to consolidate her leadership of party and government. The rapidly approaching elections, the deterioration of economic and political conditions at home, and the deliberate attempt by senior Congressmen to maintain a check on her, however, functioned to contain her aspirations. Owing to her relatively short time in office, no less than because of her indecisiveness, Mrs. Gandhi was not able to consolidate her leadership sufficiently to prevent a challenge to her continued control of the prime ministership from seeming inevitable. Nevertheless, her position was—if not invulnerable—strong, for the developments of the first two decades of independence had made the prime ministership the locus of power in the Congress, a position of dominance achieved by way of a series of complex interactions between successive prime ministers and Congress presidents. There were essentially three phases to the process.

The first phase from 1946 to 1951 was a period of transition and conflict. Nehru and his senior colleagues in the Working Committee decided to join the new Interim Government instead of exercising supervisory power from the organizational wing. With this decision the Congress presidency became the focal point of conflict between the new government and two Congress Presidents who insisted futilely that the government could act only with the explicit approval of the Congress President and the party executive. Both were forced to resign, for senior leaders in the government as well as the Prime Minister held to the theory that the parliamentary system requires that the Prime Minister enjoy a special position leaving him unfettered to conduct the affairs of government without constant reference to the party. Such a philosophy required that the party establish only the broadest outlines of policy within which the government was free to act as it saw fit. By 1951 this issue was essentially settled. None of the assaults on parliamentary prerogatives that were yet to occur would be launched as vigorously and pursued as implacably, whatever the precise relationship of the incumbents of the Congress presidency and the prime ministership.

A second phase in the development of party-government relations was the period of centralization and convergence which lasted from 1951 until about 1963. At first, coordination was ensured by Nehru's decision to hold the office of Congress President along with the prime ministership. By 1954 the parliamentary wing's autonomy no longer seemed threatened. Coordination seemed sufficiently assured for the Congress presidency to be functionally separate once more. For the next decade a series of junior leaders—Dhebar from 1954 to 1959, Mrs. Gandhi from 1959 to 1960, Sanjiva Reddy from 1960 to 1962, and D. Sanjivayya from 1962 to 1964 —selected with the approval of the Prime Minister headed the Congress organization. Although several of these Congress Presidents were frustrated by the limitations of the office during this period of convergence and centralization, they lacked the seniority, the status, and the authority to challenge the Prime Minister. Nehru had become the supreme arbiter of party and government, leaving to successive Presidents the responsibility for the day-to-day work of maintaining the party machine.

That the Congress organization needed a full-time President to carry out the broad supervision of the party machine was fully demonstrated during the period of centralization and convergence. The Congress at the time of independence was urgently in need of organizational reform, but these reforms were first delayed because of the conflict marking the period of transition, then suspended during Nehru's tenure as Congress President. Only under Dhebar were there any serious studies of the Congress organization carried out, and then the Congress was shocked to discover that the party did not exist as a coherent organization below the district level.

To remedy this situation Dhebar began to rebuild the party at these long-neglected lower levels. By 1959 pressures at the top had also generated demands for the total reorganization of the Congress. Soon debates over what to do about the Congress organization were dominating party meetings. Clearly the party organization had begun to come to life after a period of only partly involuntary dormancy.

The Kamaraj Plan, the election of Kamaraj as Congress President, and the first and second successions gave further impetus to the resurgent importance of the organization. A multi-centered leadership began to develop, and a period of divergence was at hand. As a result, the Congress President acquired a new status and authority reinforced by the succession process which made the Prime Ministers for a time dependent on the support of others in the party organization. During Shastri's tenure as Prime Minister, relations with the Congress President were harmonious. To a very large extent this harmony can be attributed to Shastri's style of consensus leadership. Yet a number of factors conspired to make Shastri and the Congress President co-equals for only a very brief period. For one thing, Kamaraj found his power declining from his high point as kingmaker, while Shastri could be confident that he continued to be the choice of both country and party and that Kamaraj had "neither the pretension nor ambition to occupy the centre of the stage."[83] But most important perhaps was the fact that the enormous power, prestige, and patronage enjoyed by the Prime Minister placed him in an unmistakable position of dominance over the Congress President.

Mrs. Gandhi's relations with Kamaraj demonstrated anew that the Prime Minister would seek to establish independence and develop a position of leadership in her own right. Mrs. Gandhi, seeking advice predominantly from a group of young advisers in the government, attempted to ignore her senior colleagues in the party. The result was a major rift between the Congress President and the Prime Minister, a rift

[83] Brecher, *Nehru's Mantle*, p. 132.

which did not, however, take the extreme form of rupture which had characterized the earlier conflict between Nehru and Tandon. As it happened, the dissension at the top of the Congress pyramid made Kamaraj a natural ally of Mrs. Gandhi against Morarji Desai, thus forcing them to play down their differences as much as possible, while looking to the election as an opportunity to obviate the necessity for such uncomfortable collaboration.

The power, prestige, and patronage of the Prime Minister has developed over the years to the point that Congressmen look to the Prime Minister, and not to the Congress President for leadership. Whatever authority remains in the office of Congress President depends largely on the stature of the person chosen to fill it. But the process of selection, heavily dependent on the wishes of the Prime Minister, leaves the strongest Congress President at least psychologically in the position of vassal to lord. Therefore, despite its resurgence in recent years, the Congress presidency has regained only a negligible portion of the power and prestige lost during the last two decades.

Although traditionally and *de jure* nominated by any ten delegates to the Annual Sessions and elected by a majority of the delegates, the Congress President was *de facto* from 1951 to 1963 the appointee of the recognized leader of the party—the Prime Minister. Just as Gandhi had designated Congress Presidents in the years from 1920 to 1947, so Nehru reinstated this procedure in 1951. Throughout, however, the elective principle has never been eliminated. There are several reasons for this. In the first place, it is a concession to past tradition. At the Annual Sessions of the Congress the President is still treated to an elephant ride, a procession through town, garlanding, and other special gestures. Secondly, a strong feeling on the part of many Congressmen—and many Indians—for demonstrations of unanimity even in the midst of conflict seems to be involved in holding elections even where the candidate is unopposed. This feeling is partly a demonstration of the traditional consensus approach and partly a psychological carry-over from pre-independence days when demonstrations of unity were an important part of the united front maintained at all times toward the British.

A third reason for the retention of the elective principle is that it gives the party membership a feeling of participation. This was especially true when the Congress President had the power to appoint his entire Working Committee. At that time demands for an elected Working Committee were usually answered by the proposition that the Working Committee operated on the basis of collective responsibility which could be achieved best by permitting a popularly elected President to appoint a homogenous Working Committee. The recently adopted constitutional amendment which provides for an elective element in the Working Committee was also a concession to the demands for greater participation.

Finally, though the elective principle may remain dormant so long as there is a single recognized leadership, it can become an extremely valuable method of resolving conflicts when the leadership itself is unable to agree on a single candidate. Following Gandhi's death, it was used by Nehru and Patel to select a leader for the organization. More recently, the resort to an open vote for settling leadership disputes was demonstrated at the time of the struggle over Kamaraj's re-election to a second term as Congress President, when the Hyderabad resolution had to be amended by an open vote in the A.I.C.C. Thus, it seems that during periods of transition and leadership change the Congress President may play an important role in bringing about the selection of a leader of the parliamentary wing smoothly and efficiently, much as the Prime Minister does in the selection of a Congress President. Between such periods of transition, however, the Prime Minister is the *de facto* leader of both party and government.

PART II

THE WORKING COMMITTEE

THE COMPOSITION OF THE
WORKING COMMITTEE

The evolution of an effective pattern of party-government relations as reflected in the changing relationship between the Prime Minister and the Congress President was accompanied by a similar process of change in the structure and functions of the party executive, the Working Committee. By the end of the period of transition, the Working Committee had come to perform essentially four functions. First, as a sub-committee of the A.I.C.C., it was "the highest executive authority of the Congress" and had the power "to carry into effect the policy and programme laid down by the Congress and by the A.I.C.C." In practice, if not in theory, this meant that the Working Committee was the chief policy-maker for the organization. It played the dominant role in initiating the policy which would subsequently be ratified by the A.I.C.C. and the Annual Sessions. Second, the Working Committee was the chief executive of the party with power both over individual members and over sub-units in the organization. It was responsible for framing rules for the working of the organization and, in the performance of this function, superintended, directed, and controlled all Pradesh Congress Committees and took disciplinary action against committees or individuals in the Congress. Third, the Working Committee was charged with coordinating party-government relations in the states by means of a sub-committee called the Parliamentary Board. Finally, through a second sub-committee called the Central Election Committee (C.E.C.), the Working Committee played a significant role

111

in the selection of candidates for the national and state legislatures.[1]

Before independence the Working Committee had acted primarily as the chief policy-maker for the movement and as the chief executive of the organization. The role of coordinating party-government relations in the states was performed only for the brief period marking the 1937-1939 Congress ministries. With the transfer of power, it was inevitable that the performance of these three traditional functions should undergo major modifications. In addition, the Working Committee found it necessary to replace the system in which *ad hoc* committees created by the A.I.C.C. had been charged with selecting candidates by a Central Election Committee, which was established in 1948 in time to select candidates for the First General Elections. These modifications of the role of the Working Committee in post-independence India, evolving through three stages roughly parallel to those which marked the relations between the Congress President and the Prime Minister, aided materially in the transformation of the Congress from an independence movement to a governing political party and contributed to its dominance during the first two decades following the transfer of power.

The traditional policy-making function of the Working Committee underwent the most radical transformation in the post-independence period as a result of the creation of a Congress government at the center alongside the Congress ministries which had existed in most of the states for the past two decades. The relationship of the Working Committee to both levels of government had to be developed and stabilized. Before independence the Working Committee had functioned as the Cabinet of the movement, and, so long as independence was the goal, the Working Committee was clearly the locus of power in the Congress. Even during the 1937-1939

[1] M. V. Ramana Rao, *Development of the Congress Constitution* (New Delhi: A.I.C.C., 1958), pp. 220-223.

Congress ministries, most of the national leaders of the Congress had remained in the organizational wing from which they exercised broad supervision over the Congress governments. But with the final transfer of power and the emergence of the Congress as a dominant party, the national leaders undertook the responsibility of leading the new central government. As a result, the traditional, unchallenged decision-making role of the Working Committee suffered eclipse. A new role for the Working Committee had to be evolved.

The development of a new policy-making role for the Working Committee centered particularly on its relationship to the new central government. The evolution of this relationship passed through several phases—a process of change best illustrated by the Working Committee's contribution to several significant decisions made during each of the three phases of development. In the course of these changes, Congress leaders found it necessary to address themselves to several important questions. How were the policies of two separate institutions with their own lines of authority and control to be harmonized and coordinated? Could the Working Committee issue policy directives to the government? How much freedom and flexibility was the government to have in interpreting and timing its implementations of Working Committee resolutions? Did a parliamentary system based on certain principles of representation place any restrictions on the role of the party executive and mass organization?

The relationship of the Working Committee to the state governments raised even more important issues concerning the degree to which the Congress, as a centralized party within a federal system, should continue to formulate all-India policies for the guidance of the state Congress ministries. Again, the changing nature of the Working Committee's role is best illustrated by observing the decision-making process followed in formulating significant all-India policies. How centralized could decision-making be in the face of a rapid devolution of power to the states? What role were party channels to play in coordinating center-state relations? To what degree could party channels alone be used in determining all-India policy?

The determination of the policy-making role of the Working Committee was not the only organizational problem faced by the Congress. Even after independence, despite some defections, the Congress continued to expand its base of support until it excluded very few sectors of Indian society. Because of this openness, the party tended to comprehend the diversity of India itself. Yet, while such diversity helped in sustaining the Congress in a position of dominance, it also created major obstacles to the maintenance of party unity and solidarity. Under such stresses the Congress, exemplifying traditional Indian values of compromise, conciliation, and consensus, developed a complex system of conflict resolution employing its role as chief executive of the party, coordinator of party-government relations, and final authority for the selection of candidates. Empowered as chief executive of the party to supervise and direct the activities of the state parties, the Working Committee attempted to develop membership criteria, ensure systematic enrollment of members, provide for fair organizational elections despite widespread group conflict, and, most important of all, act as a final arbitrator and court of appeals in cases of malfunctioning state machinery. In its role as coordinator of party-government relations the Working Committee acted through the Parliamentary Board to set down policy guidelines for party-government coordination and to arbitrate conflicts between groups competing for power. Finally, through the Central Election Committee, the Working Committee became a vital link between party and government by performing the difficult task of allocating seats and thus providing various conflicting groups and interests with access to power.

The Working Committee's ability to perform its many functions has to a large extent been determined by its composition, behavior, and decision-making style. The composition of the Working Committee alone has been the subject of a great deal of debate and conflict. The most significant question in dispute has been the degree to which the committee should remain autonomous with respect to the parliamentary wing of the party. This issue has been debated in various forms for the past two decades. Yet to a very large extent it has been settled for some time in practice. An analysis of continuity and change in the Working Committee since independence demonstrates that the debate over the autonomy of the Working Committee has indeed become a dead issue. Dominated by a hard core of leaders drawn largely from the parliamentary wing, the Working Committee has developed a process of consensus building and a style of operating which has enabled it to carry out its major functions in such a way as to contribute substantially to the stability and effectiveness of the Congress in the first two decades of the post-independence period. Nevertheless, for some time after the transfer of power, the creation of the new role of the party as government aroused serious and justifiable concern about the composition and autonomy of the Working Committee.

The composition of the Working Committee passed through three stages of development. During the period of transition from 1946 to 1951, the struggle over the composition of the Working Committee took the form of attempts by the mass organization to impose formal requisites for Working Committee membership designed to preserve the committee's autonomy from the parliamentary wing. The period of centralization and convergence brought dispute over the composition of the Working Committee to a halt. During this period a clear pattern of Working Committee membership was evolved, as can be seen by analyzing committee membership since independence. A third phase developed toward the end of Nehru's life when organization pressure for an elected element in the Working Committee finally succeeded. However, the reforms have up to now had little real effect on the composition of the Working Committee.

Throughout the period of transition the Congress mass organization, bereft of its agitational function and uncertain of the fate of its constructive works function, tended to visualize the new role of party as government as strictly subordinate to the dictates of the mass movement to which it was responsible. At the same time there was a desire to protect the mass organization from the taint of identification with constituted authority. Such an attitude was largely anachronistic, an emotional set acquired during the struggle as a nationalist movement against the British raj and persisting as a distrust of anyone exercising power. Thus, to organization-oriented Congressmen, those colleagues accepting positions of power were considered to have sacrificed something of their influence rather than to have gained prerogatives in party leadership.

For all these reasons the mass organization resisted what it perceived as attempts by the parliamentary leadership to encroach upon the autonomy of the party and sought to impose a series of formal requisites for Working Committee membership. The first was an attempt to prevent any members of the Congress government from holding seats on the Working Committee. The second, something of a retreat from earlier rigidity, involved repeated efforts to impose a limitation on the number of members of the parliamentary wing in the Working Committee. Finally, there was a demand by the party for a larger and more representative Working Committee. The failure of the organization to restrict the parliamentary leadership's role on the Working Committee led to the domination of the Working Committee by a hard core of leaders drawn predominantly from the parliamentary wing.

The question whether members of the government should retain seats on the Working Committee arose with the formation of the Interim Government. The Working Committee was itself seriously divided on the issue, and even those who agreed in principle to dual membership thought it desirable to prevent the government members from dominating the party executive by limiting the number of ministers who would be permitted to retain Working Committee seats. Because of this absence of consensus, it was decided to submit the issue directly to the A.I.C.C. for settlement. Working Committee members were to be free to express their personal opinions frankly and openly before the A.I.C.C.[2]

At the A.I.C.C. meeting late in September 1946, G. B. Pant, Chief Minister of Uttar Pradesh and an important member of the Working Committee, asked the Committee to permit him to move a resolution in his personal capacity. Pant, as an old Swarajist, was probably one of the most experienced parliamentarians in the Congress. He had been Chief Minister of Uttar Pradesh from 1937 to 1939 and again after the 1945-1946 elections. He had been forced to deal with the problem of coordinating party and government at the state level, and his experience had led him to fear the development of divergence at the center. Therefore, his resolution stated that "no one will be debarred from the membership of the Working Committee or any other body of the Congress on account of his holding office in the Interim Government." The Working Committee approved Pant's unusual request. Later, supporting his resolution in the A.I.C.C., Pant warned delegates that, if members of the Interim Government were debarred from the Working Committee, the importance of the committee would diminish and a serious rift would open between the Congress leaders in the party and those in the government.[3]

The debate on the Pant resolution revealed that the members of the Working Committee were about equally divided. Among those in opposition was Maulana Azad, the only member of the Congress inner circle who had not joined the Interim Government. Azad cautioned the A.I.C.C. that "to identify the highest executive of the Congress organization struggling to achieve freedom with the Interim Government

[2] *Congress Bulletin*, No. 6, Sept. 1946, pp. 18-19.
[3] *Hindustan Times* (New Delhi), Sept. 24, 1946.

or any provincial government would create a dangerous illusion among the people that freedom had already been achieved."[4] Of the sixteen A.I.C.C. members who spoke to the resolution, the majority also opposed it. Most of the amendments proposed to the resolution represented attempts to impose some limit on the proportion of the Interim Government members who would be permitted to sit on the Working Committee. In the end, however, all amendments were rejected.[5] After two days of debate, despite the strong opposition, the Pant resolution was passed by a vote of 135 to 80.[6]

By adopting the Pant resolution, the A.I.C.C. had established what would become one of the most important methods of coordinating party and government activities. Clashes such as those foreseen by G. B. Pant occurred during the term of the next Congress President and intermittently for some time thereafter. But the resolution permitting dual membership prevented the conflict between the party and the government from becoming irreconcilable, and the decision still ranks high among the more significant organizational decisions in Congress history.

Despite the passage of the Pant resolution, the battle over ministerial encroachment was not over. It had only shifted to a second front. The reluctance with which the party had accepted Pant's proposal was demonstrated by continued efforts to limit the proportion of ministers on the Working Committee. In fact, as early as the A.I.C.C. debate, many delegates had insisted that no more than one-third of the Working Committee should be composed of ministers. Formal restrictions were rejected at the time, but Acharya Kripalani, the first post-independence Congress President, announced that he felt morally and personally constrained to limit the number of ministerial members on his Working Committee to one-third of its membership.[7] Yet Kripalani's gesture

---

[4] *Ibid.*   [5] *Ibid.*

[6] *Hindustan Times* (New Delhi), Sept. 25, 1946.

[7] *Congress Bulletin*, No. 1, Jan. 1947, pp. 33-34.

was soon to be nullified. With the reconstitution of the Indian Cabinet following the transfer of power, more than half of his Working Committee received posts in the government,[8] a situation Kripalani found intolerable. There is little doubt that it played a role in his subsequent decision to resign from the Congress presidency.

In forming his Working Committee, Kripalani's successor, Dr. Rajendra Prasad, tried to lessen the resentment in the party organization over what was considered to be growing parliamentary control over the mass organization. He realized, however, that, if the Working Committee was to remain an effective body, it had to contain Congress leaders of stature, most of whom had chosen to serve in the government. As a result, despite Prasad's efforts, seven of the fifteen members of his Working Committee were ministers.

The distrust of government domination of the Working Committee expressed by Kripalani and the desire to ensure organizational control of the party executive continued to be widely shared by the rank and file in the Congress. So widely shared was it that, when the A.I.C.C. met next at Bombay to consider the first post-independence reorganization of the party, the delegates succeeded in imposing, over the objections of the Working Committee, a limitation on ministerial membership on the Working Committee. This restriction, according to which ministers were to constitute no more than one-third of the total membership, was embodied not merely in a resolution but in an amendment to the new Congress constitution.[9]

Not satisfied with this accomplishment, the organization leaders next demanded that the Working Committee be enlarged. The arguments for expansion, which had been mooted since 1945, were primarily geographic. In a Working Committee of only fifteen, many of the twenty-one Congress provinces had gone permanently without representation. It

[8] *Congress Bulletin*, No. 6, Dec. 1947, p. 12.
[9] *Congress Bulletin*, No. 1, July 1948, pp. 12-13; *Hindustan Times* (New Delhi), April 26, 1948.

was argued that the size of the Working Committee should therefore be expanded to at least twenty-one members and preferably more. The assumption implicit in this demand was that the Congress P.C.C.s rather than the newly established Congress ministries in the states would benefit by the increased representation.[10] Both a sub-committee of the Working Committee and the Working Committee itself insisted that the size of the party executive should remain unaltered. But when a proposal to retain the status quo was presented to the A.I.C.C. at Bombay, it received strong and embittered criticism from the floor. The delegates proceeded to move several amendments to the official resolution submitted by the Working Committee. Each amendment was designed to permit a larger party executive, and one of them, which proposed to increase the Working Committee membership to twenty-five, was defeated by a margin of only fourteen votes. In view of the temper of the delegates and the closeness of the vote, the Working Committee agreed to revise its proposal. Henceforth the Working Committee was to have twenty members.[11]

In a sense, the changes made in the size and composition of the Working Committee marked the end of an era. Ever since 1920, the Working Committee had consisted of a small, tightly knit elite which acted as the directorate of a vast revolutionary movement. With the introduction of the new Congress constitution in 1948, the Working Committee's role underwent the first alteration intended to adapt it to meet effectively the demands of the post-independence era. Yet, ironically, the immediate impact of these changes designed to strengthen the committee was to weaken it still further. Broader representation meant that men of lesser stature now found a place on the committee, while the limitations on ministerial appointments kept many important Congress leaders

[10] S. K. Patil, *The Indian National Congress: A Case for its Reorganisation* (Aundh: Aundh Publishing Trust, 1945), p. 37.

[11] When the 1948 Congress Constitution was revised at Ahmedabad in 1951, the Working Committee was expanded to 21 members.

outside the committee. The result was a party executive staffed by men who enjoyed little real power or prestige in the Congress as a whole.

The one-third rule placed organizational leaders in a majority on the Working Committee for a brief and ineffectual period. It is not coincidental that the peak of organizational influence on the Working Committee was reached during the stormy term of Purshottamdas Tandon's presidency of the Congress. Nor is it surprising that the high point of party-government conflict was reached at the same time. Tandon's Working Committee was composed largely of party bosses from the major states, many of whom opposed the social and economic policies of the Nehru government. Thus, while Kripalani's challenge to the parliamentary leadership focused largely on the role of the Congress President, the Tandon-Nehru conflict was broader in scope. It involved the members of the party executive as well. While Tandon considered his Working Committee truly representative of Congress thinking in the states, Nehru did not. Furthermore, Nehru was "convinced" that he himself did not fit into Tandon's Working Committee. As he put it, he was "not in tune with it."[12] In the end, when Tandon and his Working Committee attempted to call the tune for the parliamentary wing, they were forced to resign under pressure from the Prime Minister, who then became Congress President.

Under Nehru's leadership the composition of the Working Committee underwent a significant alteration as he set about adjusting its functions to the requirements of independence and the beginning of planned economic development. The resulting pattern of membership continued substantially unchanged for the next decade and a half.

The process of change under Nehru was facilitated after the First General Elections, at the Indore Session of the A.I.C.C., when the Congress President was given complete freedom to select his Working Committee. The one-third

[12] Letter J. Nehru to P. D. Tandon, Aug. 6, 1951, *The Statesman* (New Delhi), Sept. 11, 1951.

rule was dropped.[13] As a result, the organizational element, which in Tandon's Working Committee had been represented by P.C.C. Presidents, was replaced by a strong ministerial element drawing not only upon central Cabinet Ministers but also upon important Chief Ministers in the states—an indication that Chief Ministers were emerging as powerful figures within the Congress Party. Moreover, by liberally invoking an old Congress tradition of inviting important non-members to Working Committee meetings, Nehru was able to expand the circle of discussion to include those Chief Ministers not formally appointed to membership. In this way organizational dominance was superseded by ministerial dominance, and the Working Committee became a means of coordinating all-India Congress policy informally at the non-official party level. From this point on, there was no significant divergence between party policy resolutions and government action. Yet, while it facilitated efforts to centralize decision-making during the period of convergence, the process of recognizing the Chief Ministers as powerful in their own right also laid the ground for the later divergence of power, when the central leadership would become more dependent upon the Chief Ministers.

The extent to which failure befell the organization's attempt to forestall encroachment by the parliamentary wing may be seen not only in the backfiring of institutional reforms but also in the composition of successive Working Committees since independence. Although the Working Committee is the highest organ of the mass organization, it is so thoroughly infiltrated by the parliamentary wing that it has no separate and vital existence apart from it. The predominant role of the parliamentary leadership within the Working Committee is evident from the composition of the sixteen successive Working Committees over the past twenty years. Although some ninety Congressmen served on the Working Committee during these two decades, twenty-nine

---

[13] Rao, *Development of the Congress Constitution*, p. 136.

served only one term, eighteen served for two, thirteen for three, and only thirty for four or more terms. Thus, only one-third of the ninety members of the Working Committee served for any significantly continuous period. Since continuity of membership on the Working Committee is clearly a major index of leadership influence and status, it is revealing to compare the characteristics of this long-term group with those of the shorter-term members of the Working Committee. Such a comparison in fact reveals that the parliamentary wing has contributed the overwhelming majority of the influential hard-core members.

Of the thirty hard-core leaders who served at least four terms during the post-independence period, only nine were still members of the Working Committee as of January 1967. These nine, the inner circle of the Working Committee at that time, included five members of the Indian Cabinet: the Prime Minister Mrs. Indira Gandhi, S. K. Patil, Sanjiva Reddy, Y. B. Chavan, Jagjivan Ram. Morarji Desai was an important long-term member of the central Cabinet until his resignation in 1963 in accordance with the implementation of the Kamaraj Plan. The remaining three were K. Kamaraj, Congress President and former Chief Minister of Madras; S. Nijalingappa, Chief Minister of Mysore; and Sadiq Ali, a Muslim and long-time General Secretary of the Congress. Of the twenty-one other four-term members of the Working Committee, thirteen were dead by early 1967, three were no longer members of the Congress, two attended meetings of the Working Committee by invitation although not officially members of the party executive, and the remainder had suffered political eclipse. Most of the deceased long-term members of the Working Committee, it should be noted, were prominent figures in the nationalist movement who had made up the hard core of the Congress executive during the late forties and most of the fifties. Such were Nehru, Vallabhbhai Patel, Rajendra Prasad, Maulana Azad, G. B. Pant, B. C. Roy, Rafi Ahmad Kidwai, and Lal Bahadur

Shastri. C. Rajagopalachari, the last of the great figures of the Gandhian era, had become one of the leaders of the Swatantra Party.

To the roster of important members of the Working Committee must be added seven others who have served fewer than four terms for various reasons—some because of their youth, others because of peculiar situations in their home states. This group includes G. L. Nanda, former Home Minister; D. Sanjivayya, former President of the Congress; Dr. Ram Subhag Singh; B. Patnaik, former Chief Minister of Orissa; Atulya Ghosh, political boss of Bengal; Darbara Singh, Sikh leader in the Punjab; and M. L. Sukhadia, Chief Minister of Rajasthan. Thus, of the ninety Congressmen who served on the Working Committee at one time or another from 1946 to 1967, the hard core consisted of no more than thirty-seven leaders.

The existence of an inner circle in the Working Committee is no recent development. During pre-independence years the party executive exhibited an even greater continuity. In fact, during the Gandhian era from 1920 to 1946, over half of its members served throughout.[14] That this hard core constituted a recognized inner circle has been confirmed by Dr. Pattabhi Sitaramayya. Although he was a Working Committee member for at least half of the twenty-five years preceding independence, he acknowledged the existence of an "inner group" to which he did not belong.[15] What is new about the inner circle, however, is that it is drawn from the parliamentary leadership.

The dominance of the parliamentary leadership is demonstrated by the fact that thirty of the thirty-seven long-term members of the Working Committee, or 81 per cent, had served during the major portion of the past twenty years as members of the central Cabinet or as Chief Ministers. Of these, seventeen, or 46 per cent, had been members of the Indian Cabinet, while thirteen, or 35 per cent, had headed

[14] Patil, *The Indian National Congress*, p. 34.
[15] Unpublished Prasad Papers, Letter P. Sitaramayya to R. Prasad, Sept. 18, 1948.

the governments of their respective states. The Chief Ministers who have been members of the Working Committee were usually those whose authority in their home state was firmly established. They tended to be the more powerful state leaders. By contrast, the organizational wing of the Congress contributed seven, or only 19 per cent, of the long-term members of the Working Committee. Four of these had been General Secretaries who typically bear responsibility for day-to-day administration of party affairs and lack independent political stature. The only truly powerful organizational representative on the Working Committee was Atulya Ghosh, political boss of West Bengal, a man who had never held a ministerial portfolio at the center or in his home state although he had been a Member of Parliament since 1952.

Among the fifty-three shorter-term members of the Working Committee the pattern is strikingly different, for thirty-five of these members, or 66 per cent, were drawn from the organizational wing. There were three sources of organizational representation. Party executives, including two early Presidents of the Congress and fourteen P.C.C. Presidents, constituted the largest organizational category. Party administrators ranked next; twelve of the shorter-term members of the Working Committee were General Secretaries. Finally, a number of old party workers, largely Gandhians and Congress Socialists, served more or less briefly on the committee. Many of these organizational representatives served only one term. Thus, while there was a high turnover among organizational representatives, particularly P.C.C. Presidents, Chief Ministers tended to serve on the Working Committee for many years at a stretch. Organizational leadership is less significant as a determinant of Working Committee membership and influence than prominence in the parliamentary wing.

The remaining eighteen members of the Working Committee since independence ought to be accounted for, but they are difficult to classify. Half of these were women. The Congress traditionally has ensured that women are represented at the highest levels of the party. Yet the restrictive role normally assigned to women in Indian society has prevented all but a few from reaching prominence in political life. Thus, most women appointed to the Working Committee, lacking any real political stature, tended to serve for only one term or two at most. Those women who have served on the Working Committee for long periods of time, such as Indira Gandhi and Sucheta Kripalani, have eventually been absorbed into the parliamentary wing. The other nine members of the post-independence Working Committee fit into no one category.

In this way, in terms of formal membership, the Working Committee came to be dominated by the leaders of the parliamentary wing at the center and in the states. As a result, there has been a tendency for the policies of the Congress government and the pronouncements of the party not to diverge very widely. In addition, since the Working Committee has traditionally provided policy leadership in the form of official resolutions for the more broadly based party organs—the A.I.C.C. and the Annual Sessions—the ability of the mass organization to act independently of the leadership has been kept within limits.

This is not to say that the A.I.C.C. and the Annual Sessions are merely rubber stamps or without influence. Even though the more broadly based organs of the mass membership have seldom succeeded in modifying or defeating official Working Committee resolutions, their criticisms have not been ignored. The A.I.C.C. and the Annual Sessions have acted as sounding boards of party sentiment and as communications links between the leadership and the mass membership. They also retain a certain latent power, for Working Committee resolutions must be approved and the leadership may lead only so long as it is united. When the leadership is divided, the A.I.C.C. and the Annual Sessions tend to be energized and mobilized by the competing leadership factions. The emergence of parliamentary domination during the period of convergence, then, was not the product of an attempt to concentrate unchallenged power in the hands of the government. It grew out of the necessity to develop new sets of relationships by which the government could take into account the views of the mass organization without depriving itself of the freedom of action to consider the views of the parliamentary membership to which it was ultimately responsible.

Toward the end of the Nehru era, however, there developed a revolt within the party as a result of growing resentment over the alleged domination of the Working Committee by a small oligarchy drawn from the parliamentary wing. The revolt took the form of a determined attack on the total existing structure of the party, but it concentrated in particular upon a demand that the Working Committee become more representative of the party by including some members elected by the A.I.C.C. Demands of this nature had plagued Congress for decades. From the time of its creation until 1934, the Working Committee had been elected by the A.I.C.C. By that time, however, Gandhi's experience with conducting civil disobedience campaigns had convinced him that the Congress needed to be shaped into a more effective instrument for non-violent action. His reorganization resulted in substituting for an elected Working Committee a party executive appointed by the Congress President. In the reorganization of the Congress which followed independence, however, the A.I.C.C. pressed for a return to the elected Working Committee. Meeting at Bombay in 1948, the A.I.C.C. demanded that the new Congress constitution make provision, if not for a committee chosen wholly by the A.I.C.C., at least for an elective element within the Working Committee. These proposals were dropped only after Maulana Azad made a plea that the A.I.C.C. consider the possible consequences of such a procedure. He warned the A.I.C.C. that an elected Working Committee would have a disruptive effect on the Congress organization. He insisted that an appointed Working Committee was essential in order to guarantee harmony and prevent the development of groups within the

Congress executive.[16] Although the Bombay A.I.C.C. finally accepted Azad's plea, the demands for an elected element in the Working Committee continued intermittently for over a decade. They were finally met in 1960 at Raipur, when the A.I.C.C. adopted a proposal to elect a third of the committee.

The Raipur resolution was one more attempt to re-assert organizational influence on the Working Committee. It grew out of an increasing dissatisfaction with the functioning of the Congress. This dissatisfaction was intensified by the belief that the Working Committee had become dominated by a loose-knit "dictatorship" of half a dozen leaders drawn from the parliamentary wing. The demands which led most immediately to the Raipur resolution had first come in the form of an unofficial resolution at the Delhi meeting of the A.I.C.C. in May of 1959.[17] In the ensuing debate, Nehru told the party that no one was really fully satisfied with the party's constitution or with its functioning. He suggested that the mover, K. Hanumanthaiya, join his colleagues in preparing a draft of suggested changes in the constitution. Ironically, this modest commission gave rise to a series of reform suggestions drafted not only by Hanumanthaiya[18] but also by the Congress Party in Parliament[19] and by Humayun Kabir,[20] a member of the central Cabinet.

Late in 1959, Hanumanthaiya submitted his report. It called for a reconstitution of the Working Committee so as to include just eighteen members distributed according to the following formula: (1) the leader of the Congress Party in Parliament; (2) two leaders of the Congress parties in the state legislatures chosen by the leaders of the respective legis-

[16] *Congress Bulletin*, No. 1, July 1948, pp. 1-3; *Hindustan Times* (New Delhi), April 26, 1948.

[17] *Congress Bulletin*, Nos. 4-5, April-May 1959, p. 280.

[18] K. Hanumanthaiya, *Report on the Congress Constitution* (New Delhi: A.I.C.C., 1960).

[19] *Report of the Committee of the Congress Party in Parliament* (New Delhi: A.I.C.C., 1960).

[20] H. Kabir, "Reorganization of the Congress," *Hindustan Times* (New Delhi), May 29, 1960.

lative parties (the positions would be rotated); (3) the chairman and secretaries of the A.I.C.C.; (4) three P.C.C. Presidents chosen from among themselves by the P.C.C. Presidents as a group (these positions would also be rotated); and (5) six members elected by the A.I.C.C.[21] On December 30, 1959, the Working Committee appointed a special sub-committee to consider this and other organizational suggestions.

The sub-committee rejected Hanumanthaiya's recommendations on several grounds. First, the series of elections demanded by Hanumanthaiya would mean a long delay in forming the Working Committee. Second, the suggestions assumed that the offices of Prime Minister and Congress President would be merged, thus inhibiting the potential for conflict inherent in dual leaderships, and the committee rejected this proposition. Third, though admitting the possible advantage of a partially elected Working Committee, the sub-committee argued that, since the Working Committee remained the one stabilizing factor in the whole Congress organization, the Congress President should have a committee of his own choosing capable of functioning collectively like a cabinet.[22]

Meeting on the eve of the Poona Session of the A.I.C.C., the Working Committee endorsed the sub-committee's recommendations that the Congress executive remain a nominated body,[23] but no formal resolutions were placed before the A.I.C.C. Instead, a simple list of proposals was presented. This was a rare occurrence in Congress history. As the first day of the A.I.C.C. meeting wore on, a parade of frustrated, bitter speakers came to the rostrum. Most of them focused their attention on the demand for an elected Working Committee or at least a Working Committee with an elective element. At this point Nehru intervened to oppose

[21] Hanumanthaiya, *Report on the Congress Constitution*, pp. 31-32.
[22] U. N. Dhebar *et al.*, *Report of the Reorganisation Committee* (New Delhi: A.I.C.C., 1960), pp. 5-6.
[23] *Hindustan Times* (New Delhi), June 4, 1960.

the idea of an elected Working Committee on the grounds that it would create tensions within the party executive. The Working Committee, he said, functioned under the principle of joint responsibility. Only nomination could make such a system workable, for, if members were elected, they would "owe their loyalty to the pulls of the group that elected them." Nevertheless, Nehru promised somewhat vaguely that he would request the Working Committee to reconsider the demands for an elective element.[24]

The next day, when the proposal to permit the election of one-third of the Working Committee was put to a vote in the A.I.C.C., it was defeated 78 to 148. Under normal circumstances this would have been the end of the matter. But in this case the circumstances were far from normal. During the polling Jawaharlal Nehru descended dramatically from the dais to stand among the delegates supporting the electoral principle.[25] Later, explaining his action during a press conference, Nehru reported that in listening to the debate he had observed the fervor of the speakers in favor of an elective element and had decided, after some thought, that it would be wrong to oppose it. Therefore, he had suggested to Dhebar, as chairman of the sub-committee which had just finished reviewing the proposal negatively, and to Congress President Sanjiva Reddy that perhaps the concession should be granted after all. Dhebar agreed to consult the other members of the Working Committee.[26] At the time, it was clear that the rest of the Working Committee feared the consequences of a change and were hesitant to grant the concession.[27] Yet, in the end, Nehru's will prevailed. When the Working Committee met again in July, it reversed its previous stand by adopting the provision for an elective element consisting of a third of the committee's membership.[28] Three

[24] *Hindustan Times* (New Delhi), June 5, 1960.
[25] *The Statesman* (New Delhi), June 6, 1960; *Times of India* (New Delhi), June 6, 1960.
[26] *Hindustan Standard* (Calcutta), June 25, 1960.
[27] *The Statesman* (New Delhi), June 6, 1960.
[28] *Hindustan Times* (New Delhi), July 29, 1960.

months later at the Raipur Session of the A.I.C.C., a constitutional amendment embodying the electoral principle
was passed.[29]

So far two elections have been held under the Raipur
amendment, one at Bhavnagar in 1961 and the other two
years later at Bhubaneshwar. In both cases it was clear that
the Working Committee had no intention of submitting to
the unpredictability of a spontaneous election. In both cases,
while the formalities of an open election were adhered to,
the delegates were in fact presented with a slate of officially
recommended candidates. At Bhavnagar, for example, twelve
candidates were nominated for the seven elective seats on
the Working Committee. But the A.I.C.C. delegates were
made to understand by vigorous canvassing of Chief Ministers and Central Ministers that the official list consisted of
Mrs. Gandhi; Y. B. Chavan, Chief Minister of Maharashtra;
H. K. Mahtab, Chief Minister of Orissa; Darbara Singh,
President of the Punjab P.C.C.; two of the General Secretaries of the Congress, Sadiq Ali and G. Rajagopalan; and
Dr. Syed Mahmud, an old Congress Muslim from Bihar, the
only person on the list who was not already a member of
the Working Committee. The remaining five candidates, the
"non-official" nominees, were Dr. Ram Subhag Singh, a popular back-bencher and Secretary of the Congress Party in
Parliament; K. Hanumanthaiya, a major supporter of the
reforms under which he was seeking election; V. B. Raju of
Andhra; Seth Govind Das; and Shah Mohammad Umair,
another Bihar Muslim who had been placed in the race to
try to attract votes which otherwise were expected to go to
Syed Mahmud.

Canvassing for the Working Committee election was brisk
and lasted through half the night. Despite the tremendous
pressures brought to bear on the A.I.C.C. delegates and to
the surprise of many, one non-official candidate emerged victorious. The upset occurred with the defeat of Dr. Syed
Mahmud and the election of Dr. Ram Subhag Singh. The

---

[29] *The Statesman* (New Delhi), Oct. 30, 1960.

threat of Ram Subhag's candidacy, ironically, had probably been the reason for Syed Mahmud's inclusion on the official slate of candidates. As a senior Congressman and fellow Bihari, it was expected that he might attract votes away from Ram Subhag, an outspoken critic in the Congress Parliamentary Party, whose presence on the Working Committee was not desired by the leadership. At the time, Ram Subhag Singh's victory was considered to be an impressive triumph for the proponents of reform through the elective element.[30] The sense of triumph, however, was premature. At Bhubaneshwar two years later, every candidate on the "official list" drawn up by the Syndicate was elected without difficulty.[31] In fact, the success of the officially endorsed candidates at Bhubaneshwar demonstrated once again the impressive strength of the group which had already managed to elect K. Kamaraj to the Congress presidency.[32]

In short, the introduction of an elective element has thus far diluted the strength of the ministerial element of the Working Committee no more than any of the other attempts at reform, for except in the case of Ram Subhag Singh, who was very shortly co-opted into the leadership circle, every candidate elected to the Working Committee was already a member of the party executive. The attempt to limit the number of ministers on the committee was abandoned. The decision to permit dual membership legitimized existing ministerial control. The effect of increasing the size of the committee was essentially neutral in that it did little to change the decision-making process. Moreover, later experience

[30] *Congress Bulletin*, Nos. 1-2, Dec.-Jan. 1960-1961, pp. 68-69; *The Statesman* (New Delhi), Jan. 7, 1961.

[31] *The Hindu Weekly Review* (Madras), Jan. 27, 1964; *Congress Bulletin*, Nos. 12, 1-2, Dec.-Jan.-Feb. 1963-1964, pp. 67, 114.

[32] During the course of the year G. Rajagopalan, one of the elected members of the Working Committee, died. His successor was elected at the Durgapur Session of the Congress in January 1965. Despite Kamaraj's public denial that there existed an "official" candidate, Darbara Singh, the man who purportedly enjoyed this designation, easily defeated all other candidates. *Congress Bulletin*, Nos. 1-3, Jan.-March 1965, pp. 69-70.

was to show that a small, tightly controlled body was not suited to perform the functions of the Working Committee after independence. The Working Committee therefore came to consist of an inner and an outer core of leaders whose influence within the committee differed considerably. The fact that the inner core has been drawn primarily from the parliamentary wing of the party has facilitated the role of the Working Committee in coordinating party-government relations and in the performance of its other functions.[33]

[33] At the Hyderabad Session of the Congress in January 1968, which took place after this book went to print, the leadership again succeeded in electing an official list of candidates as the elective element in the new Working Committee.

THE WORKING COMMITTEE:
BEHAVIOR AND STYLE

Although the composition of the Working Committee has changed in response to post-independence developments, there is a great deal about Working Committee behavior and style which reflects pre-independence practice. The Working Committee still operates according to a code of informality, secrecy, and collective responsibility which characterized its behavior when it served as the cabinet of the movement. In addition, since even disagreements within the Working Committee have only infrequently been aired in open discussion in the A.I.C.C. or at the Annual Sessions, little is known about the details of Working Committee deliberations. The *Congress Bulletin*, the official record of Congress activities, publishes only the agenda of items considered by the Working Committee, the ultimate disposition of each item, and, in the case of important decisions, the text of the resolution embodying the decision. It does not contain a detailed account of Working Committee deliberations. Working Committee procedures also provide opportunities for discussing issues which never appear on the agenda and which therefore are never mentioned in the *Congress Bulletin*. Although a brief summary of Working Committee debate is kept by the A.I.C.C. office for purposes of official reference in cases of disputes, these records remain unpublished and inaccessible to outsiders. At times, a summary of Working Committee proceedings is circulated to members with certain passages marked "not for publication." Such passages do not appear in the *Congress Bulletin*. They are intended for the information of Working Committee members only. Nevertheless, some understanding of Working Committee behavior and style can be obtained by supplementing official material with data gleaned from a wide variety of unofficial sources. From this material it is possible to make some headway in reconstructing the nature of Working Committee deliberations, the process of consensus building, and the distribution of Working Committee time according to its major functions.

The Prime Minister plays an important role in determining the agenda for the Working Committee, which is prepared by the Congress President and his General Secretaries in consultation with the Prime Minister. The agenda is usually heavily dependent on political conditions in the country, for Working Committee procedures provide for a review of activities between meetings. On most issues of importance special notes are prepared and circulated for the members to study in advance. During Nehru's presidency, some question was raised regarding the utility of these notes. For example, there were complaints that Working Committee agendas and notes were distributed too late to permit careful consideration by members prior to meeting. It was suggested that such material could not be useful unless circulated more promptly.[1] Notes dealing with party organizational matters are prepared by the Congress President and General Secretaries, while notes on important elements of government policy are drawn up by the Prime Minister or the Cabinet Minister whose ministry is involved. In the case of foreign policy issues all draft resolutions considered by the Working Committee are prepared by the External Affairs Minister or the Prime Minister. Thus, it turns out that, in the preparation of both the agenda and the background policy notes, the Working Committee is heavily dependent upon its ministerial members.

With the many functions the Working Committee must perform and the limited time at its disposal, it is evident that only the broadest issues can be considered in the course of any one meeting and then only after a great deal of spadework

---

[1] *Congress Bulletin*, No. 5, June-July 1954, pp. 227-228.

has been performed outside. Since the Congress does not have a very elaborate secretariat and since the secretariat that does exist is kept busy coping with party organizational affairs, almost all the basic work on policy issues is carried out by the ministerial element, especially by the Cabinet Ministers on the Working Committee. Thus, the ministerial element is able to come to Working Committee meetings particularly well fortified with the knowledge and insight drawn from innumerable formal and informal consultations within the government and between the central government and the states. The result is that, by the time the Working Committee as a whole can meet to consider a policy issue, the structure and the content of the subsequent resolution are often almost predetermined. Changes in the resolution are made largely in anticipation of the political impact of the resolution on different groups in the party and in the country as a whole.

The Working Committee meets periodically throughout the year and, as in the determination of the content of the Working Committee agenda, the duration of its meetings and the interval between them are to a large extent dependent upon political conditions within the country. In the early years of transition immediately following independence, for instance, the frequency of Working Committee meetings fluctuated widely. But when Nehru became Congress President, the Working Committee met regularly from seven to nine times a year. During the presidency of U. N. Dhebar from 1955 to 1958, there was established a comprehensive pattern for party meetings, in which the Working Committee met six times a year, the A.I.C.C. twice, and the Annual Sessions once.[2] This pattern continued until the 1960's when, faced with the Kamaraj Plan and the end of the Nehru era, the Working Committee met much more frequently. However, the Working Committee has never met frequently enough or long enough to deal comprehensively or in detail with all major policy issues.

[2] *Congress Bulletin*, Nos. 3-4, March-April 1957, pp. 83-84.

Behavior And Style

Working Committee meetings normally extend over a period of only two to three days, and each day is broken down into a morning and an afternoon session. When business is pressing and time is short, the Working Committee may also hold an evening session. The Working Committee usually sits two or three hours at each session, though at times a session may last less than two hours or more rarely for as long as five. Generally, the longer sessions tend to precede meetings of the A.I.C.C. and the Annual Sessions at which time broad policy resolutions are discussed. These policy resolutions usually ratify previous government actions and decisions, and the number of members and invitees in attendance at these meetings is quite high.

The role of invitees to Working Committee meetings has been greatly expanded since 1951 when Nehru's presidency began. In an effort to broaden the range of consultation and coordination within the Working Committee, Nehru liberally invoked the Congress tradition of bringing important leaders to Working Committee meetings as special invitees. During his term as President the number of invitees averaged about eleven per meeting, while more recently the range has been from nine to sixteen. At times the influx of invitees has almost doubled the attendance at Working Committee meetings. Thus, it was not unprecedented when the session at which a successor to Nehru was under discussion turned out to have thirty-seven Congress leaders in attendance. There were forty-four Congress leaders in attendance when Shastri's successor was being considered.[3]

In recent years nearly all of these special invitees have been Chief Ministers or Central Ministers. On special occasions such as the succession meetings the leaders of the Executive Committee of the Congress Party in Parliament may attend. Yet the habitual special invitees differ significantly from the regular ministerial members of the Working Committee. Whereas formal membership on the Working Committee is based on such factors as personal stature, minority leader-

[3] *Congress Bulletin*, Nos. 3-6, March-June 1964.

ship, and regional balance, most invitees attend in consequence of a very specific political role. Thus, while influential Chief Ministers are likely to become members of the Working Committee, all others attend only as invitees. The changes brought about by the Kamaraj Plan provide an excellent illustration of this point. Despite his resignation as Chief Minister of Madras, Kamaraj continued to be a member of the Working Committee. Three other Chief Ministers who resigned in accordance with the Kamaraj Plan—Binodanand Jha, B. A. Mandloi, and C. B. Gupta—had been frequent invitees to the Working Committee while in office. After stepping down, they were no longer invited to attend Working Committee meetings, but their successors, previously not in attendance, became regular invitees.

The invitee category has also been used to give important Congress leaders a part in Working Committee proceedings when unusual circumstances warrant it. For example, in an attempt to encourage older Congressmen to make way for younger leaders, Nehru refused to accept an appointive seat on the Working Committee during the last few years of his life. Instead, he attended every meeting as a special invitee. The problem of maintaining geographic distribution has also been surmounted by the invitee system. Lal Bahadur Shastri and G. L. Nanda remained in the invitee category for over a decade because of the large number of senior Gujarat and Uttar Pradesh leaders who were already on the Working Committee. In this way the special invitee procedure enables the Working Committee when necessary to expand its membership to include all institutional and other interests in the Congress.

Working Committee discussions are based on the agenda, on the previously prepared notes, and on draft resolutions. The order of discussion is normally as follows: (1) general discussion of an agenda item, note, or draft resolution; (2) discussion and review of the scope and phrasing of the draft resolution; (3) scrutiny of the final draft resolution; and (4) passage of the resolution. By tradition, Working Committee resolutions are extremely long and detailed. This discursive-ness arises from the necessity to establish a consensus as well as from the traditional educative purpose of Congress resolu-tions. Thus a resolution always includes a great deal of sup-plementary detail designed to place the operative part of the resolution in perspective and to ensure that different points of view are taken into account. Each resolution, part and product of a continuous process of coordination, has three major functions: to create a favorable public image of Con-gress policy, to provide policy guidance to the rank and file, and to set forth clearly the basic substance of Congress policy.

The way in which the Working Committee follows pro-cedures designed to obtain consensus may be seen by exam-ining the process which led to the adoption of the resolution to establish a planning commission in 1950. The idea of a planning commission was not new. As early as 1946, the In-terim Government had set up an Advisory Planning Board. In February 1948, Nehru had told Parliament that the gov-ernment wanted to create a planning commission, but the dislocations ensuing from the transfer of power had delayed concrete action.[4] The idea languished until the end of 1949, when the development of almost chaotic conditions in the Indian economy clearly demanded some definite action on the part of the government.[5]

The decision to create a planning commission came in January 1950 in the form of a Working Committee resolu-tion. The agenda for the meeting from which the resolution emerged had called for a consideration of two documents dealing with economic policy: the Sarvodaya Economic Plan and a note prepared by Shankarrao Deo, a General Secre-tary who was closely associated with the Gandhian wing of the party. Attending the meeting as special invitees were Khandubhai Desai and G. L. Nanda, two important Congress

[4] *Indian Nation* (Patna), Feb. 19, 1948; A. H. Hanson, *The Process of Planning* (London: Oxford University Press, 1966), pp. 27-49.

[5] M. Brecher, *Nehru: A Political Biography* (London: Oxford University Press, 1959), pp. 514-515.

labor leaders.[6] The Working Committee began its deliberations by discussing Deo's note on Congress economic policy. This note contained a severe indictment of government policy, which it characterized as vacillating, weak, and indecisive. It warned of the possibility of grave social disorders unless definite steps were taken to improve economic conditions. To avert this danger, the note called for a Gandhian program based on austerity and a planned economy.[7]

Following the first round of discussion on Deo's note, G. L. Nanda was asked to prepare a draft resolution embodying the sense of the meeting. In the resulting document[8] Nanda called attention to the fact that the Congress in the past had committed itself to planning. He also stressed the importance of planning in the modern world. The draft resolution embraced past Congress resolutions on economic policy, Congress election manifestos, and the pronouncements of Gandhi and other Congress leaders, all hailed as giving economic content to the word "freedom." There is little doubt that the introductory paragraphs of the draft resolution were designed so that Gandhians could be convinced that the policy of the proposed planning board would be acceptably Gandhian in nature without preventing the Congress socialists from reconciling it with their image of Nehru's economic policy or the right wing from identifying it with the economic views of Patel and Rajendra Prasad. Thus, context was given to the operative part of the resolution which called for the immediate creation of a planning commission by the government. Despite this strategy, when Nanda's draft resolution was submitted to the Working Committee in the second phase of the procedure, several changes had to be made before a consensus was achieved.

[6] Nanda later became the first Minister of Planning in the central government; *Congress Bulletin*, No. 1, Jan.-Feb. 1950, p. 9.

[7] Unpublished Prasad Papers, Shankarrao Deo, "Note on Economic Policy," prepared for the Working Committee, Jan. 15, 1950.

[8] Unpublished Prasad Papers, G. L. Nanda, "Draft Resolution on the Formation of a Planning Commission," prepared for the Working Committee.

During the debate on the draft resolution two major points of contention developed, the first over the objectives of planning, and the second over the planning commission's role in the governmental system. The disagreements in regard to the objectives of planning centered on certain particularly controversial passages, especially one which called for a "proper balance between rural and urban economy and equitable exchange relations between agricultural and non-agricultural products,"[9] and one which envisioned as part of the principles to be realized through planning, "the progressive elimination of a social, political and economic exploitation and inequality, the motive of private gain in economic activity or organization of society and the anti-social concentration of wealth and means of production."[10] The debate over the second passage is representative of Working Committee procedure during the second phase of discussion. As was evident from a note later submitted by Nanda, there was pressure from the right-wing members of the Working Committee to drop the passage on the grounds that such broad objectives could create enough anxiety within the business community to alienate it from the Congress. Others pointed out that the silence resulting from simple deletion was no substitute for a policy of actively seeking the realization that businessmen, too, would have to make some sacrifices to the national welfare.[11] In the end, both passages were deleted.[12]

The discussion also resulted in the addition of several sections to the draft resolution. The additions, in contrast to the general principles of economic planning which formed the bulk of the original resolution, contained provisions for the immediate improvement of specific economic conditions. They called for a speedy elimination of luxury goods, acquisi-

[9] *Ibid.*
[10] *Ibid.*
[11] Unpublished Prasad Papers, G. L. Nanda, "Special Note to the Working Committee," Jan. 19, 1950.
[12] Unpublished Prasad Papers, G. L. Nanda, "Corrected Final Draft Resolution."

tion of capital equipment necessary for increasing production, maximized production of essential primary goods, and accelerated progress on irrigation projects.[13]

The second major debate developed over the issue of the role of the planning commission. A majority of the Working Committee envisioned the planning commission as strictly an advisory body to be charged with making recommendations to the Cabinet. However, Nanda, who was to become the first Minister for Planning, took serious issue with this view of the planning commission's role. He argued that a planning commission required some form of executive authority without which planning would be so ineffectual that the idea of planning itself would soon become discredited. "A plan is not a body of recommendations of a reporting committee which may be accepted or rejected in part," he declared. "The part which will be rejected may be found by the Planning Commission to dislocate the entire structure of its creation, rendering the Commission incapable of taking further responsibility."[14] Although the Working Committee did not endorse Nanda's views, the relationship between the planning commission and the Cabinet was left to the government to work out.

The third stage, or final scrutiny of the draft resolution, resulted in two sets of changes, each largely a matter of phrasing and emphasis, yet designed to give the government greater flexibility in implementing the resolution and to ensure that the resolution in no way implied a criticism of existing governmental policy. For example, the final version no longer insisted that a planning commission be established "as soon as possible." The timing was left to the government. Instead of stating that the planning commission "will" have the following "terms of reference," the final draft was made to read that the planning commission "should" have the following "duties." Instead of referring to "the steady worsening of the situation for want of coordinated thought and action in

[13] *Congress Bulletin*, No. 1, Jan.-Feb. 1950, p. 12.
[14] Nanda, "Note to the Working Committee," Jan. 19, 1950.

the economic sphere," the resolution was changed to read "the steady worsening of the economic situation in India and the world." And finally, instead of referring to "acute economic difficulties," the resolution in its final form referred simply to "economic difficulties."[15] When the process of scrutiny was completed, the draft resolution was officially and unanimously adopted. A consensus had been achieved, and the negative political impact of the resolution was neutralized by significant changes in tone and phraseology.

The format of Working Committee discussions normally provides an opportunity for each member more or less guardedly, according to temperament, seniority, and status, to express his views. Within the general format, however, there may be variations. Under U. N. Dhebar, for instance, junior members of the committee were usually called upon to express their ideas first. Only after all other members of the Committee had addressed themselves to a subject did Dhebar call upon Prime Minister Nehru. Yet, whatever the variations in the pattern of discussion from Congress President to Congress President, it is customary for a senior member of the Working Committee to summarize the consensus of the meeting once the discussion is over. Votes are seldom taken. In essentials the internal procedures of the Working Committee have changed very little since the pre-independence days when, according to Dr. Pattabhi Sitaramayya, "generally while each member expressed his view, there was hardly any such thing as voting, conclusions being always registered by some elderly member summarizing the debate."[16]

Still there are occasions when consensus is lacking. At such times, the Working Committee may avail itself of one of three alternatives: the decision of the senior leaders may be accepted; further consideration of the issue may be postponed; or a full vote in the A.I.C.C. may be permitted. Thus, under

[15] Nanda, "Corrected Final Draft Resolution": For the text of the resolution passed by the Working Committee, see *Congress Bulletin*, No. 1, Jan.-Feb. 1950, pp. 9-12.
[16] Sitaramayya, "Autobiography," Ch. 16, p. 116.

the first alternative, issues relating to government policy are likely to be settled by a simple declaration on the part of the Prime Minister. If the issue involves organizational policy, the Congress President may be granted the final word. On other questions which indicate a complete lack of consensus, the Working Committee may postpone the issue for further consideration. During the 1950's, members of the Working Committee could recall only two such cases. One involved the issue of ceilings on income and the other concerned price floors for agricultural commodities. The third alternative open to the Working Committee in the absence of a consensus is to permit a free vote in the A.I.C.C. Yet to do so requires a consensus of a kind, for only the committee as a whole can make the decision to set the matter before the A.I.C.C. In this manner the Working Committee is collectively responsible for its decision, and its members are not permitted to air their differences before the larger body.

At times, however, conflict within the Working Committee does spill over into the A.I.C.C., especially when the committee is divided along group lines. A major example of this total breakdown of collective responsibility occurred during the Nehru-Tandon controversy in 1950. A more recent example involved Morarji Desai's open break with the party executive over attempts to give the Working Committee discretionary power in interpreting the one-term ban on office holding at the Bangalore Session of the A.I.C.C. in August 1965 and in his open dissent on the Working Committee's decision on Punjabi Suba.[17] It was fear that such dissension would become more frequent and more severe which for a long time frustrated attempts to introduce an elective element into the Working Committee. Many Congress leaders argued that collective responsibility could function only in an appointive committee where members were responsible solely to the Congress President who appointed them, while elected members would probably feel no hesitation in taking their

[17] *The Hindu Weekly Review* (Madras), Aug. 2, 1965.

case before the A.I.C.C., the body which would have elected them to committee membership and to which they would presumably feel responsible. Thus, it was argued, the introduction of an elective element would destroy the old harmony of the Working Committee.[18] The hesitation to permit open votes in the A.I.C.C. on issues on which the Working Committee lacked a consensus was based on the same principle. The fear was that splits within the Working Committee would be accentuated as leaders favoring different positions attempted to mobilize A.I.C.C. delegates in support of opposing positions. In those rare instances when the Working Committee has resorted to the free vote approach, the issues involved have tended to be organizational rather than policy issues. In 1946, for instance, the Pant resolution was placed before the A.I.C.C. for an open vote.[19] More recently, in Poona the A.I.C.C. was asked to decide on the desirability of permitting an elective element on the Working Committee.[20] The ability of the Working Committee to appeal to the more broadly based A.I.C.C. to break a deadlock gives the A.I.C.C. an important latent function.

Although it is customary to think of the Working Committee as a body whose main function is decision-making, an analysis of eight years of Working Committee agendas drawn from two widely separated four-year periods indicates the changing role of the Working Committee. Each period represents a different phase of post-independence Congress development. The first, extending from 1951 to 1954, was a period of adaptation and change during which Nehru, as Congress President, sought to mold the Working Committee to the new requirements of Indian development and reconstruction. The second period, from 1960 to 1964, was remarkable for its relative stability. By this time the Working Committee's role was regarded as clearly established; its procedures had been regularized; and yet the similarity of agenda items indicates minimal, though important, changes

[18] See Ch. V, pp. 127-132.   [19] See Ch. V, pp. 117-118.
[20] See Ch. V, pp. 129-130.

The Working Committee

in priorities from one period to the other. During the eight years comprising these two periods, the Working Committee was convened 53 times for a total of 131 separate sessions, which considered 625 individual agenda items. Of these agenda items, 171 may be classified as pertaining to routine or procedural matters requiring little discussion. (See Table VI-1.) Thus, of the 625 agenda items, only 454 may be considered substantive in nature—262 during the 1951-1954 period and 192 during the 1960-1964 period.

TABLE VI-1

DISTRIBUTION OF WORKING COMMITTEE
AGENDA ITEMS

Type of Agenda Item	1951-1954		1960-1964		Total	
	No.	%	No.	%	No.	%
Substantive items						
Organizational	102	38.93	84	43.75	186	40.96
Policy	120	45.80	59	30.72	179	39.42
(Domestic)	*(88)*	*(33.58)*	*(43)*	*(22.39)*	*(131)*	*(28.85)*
(International)	*(32)*	*(12.20)*	*(16)*	*(8.33)*	*(48)*	*(10.57)*
Non-Policy	40	15.26	49	25.52	89	19.60
(Elections)	*(17)*	*(6.48)*	*(27)*	*(14.06)*	*(44)*	*(9.69)*
(Parliamentary)	*(15)*	*(5.72)*	*(4)*	*(2.08)*	*(19)*	*(4.18)*
(Other)	*(8)*	*(3.05)*	*(18)*	*(9.37)*	*(26)*	*(5.72)*
Total substantive items	262	76.70	192	67.85	454	72.64
Routine Procedure items	80	23.30	91	32.15	171	27.36
Total	342	100.00	283	100.00	625	100.00

Note: In each of the two periods selected for analysis, Working Committee meetings were broken down into morning, afternoon, and evening sessions. These sessions became the basic unit of analysis. In the 1951-1954 period the Working Committee met 26 times in 68 separate sessions while from 1960 to 1964 it met 27 times for 63 sessions. Nehru was Congress President during the first period, and the second period covered the terms of Sanjiva Reddy, D. Sanjivayya, and the first few months of the term of K. Kamaraj. The agendas used for the study are contained in the *Congress Bulletin* 1951-1954 and 1960-1964.

146

When the substantive agenda items are broken down, they illustrate approximately how the Working Committee distributes its time among its major functions. It would appear from the data in the table that the Working Committee's function as chief executive of the party consumes the largest portion of its attention. Some 41 per cent of the substantive items during the eight years considered were devoted to organizational issues. The second largest category (39 per cent) was related to the Working Committee's decision-making function. As might be expected, most of the policy items concerned domestic issues. The remaining 20 per cent of the substantive agenda items concerned elections, parliamentary matters, unofficial resolutions, and various items of a general nature. Quantitatively, then, it would appear that the Working Committee's decision-making function ranks slightly below its function as chief executive of the party, while its coordinating and electoral functions fall well behind the first two. That coordinating and electoral functions did not constitute a larger percentage of agenda items is undoubtedly attributable to the fact that the Working Committee is called upon to deal only with broad policy in these areas. The details are handled by the Parliamentary Board and the Central Election Committee.

The distribution of agenda items from one period to the other shows some interesting contrasts. For instance, during Nehru's presidency the Working Committee discussed policy issues far more frequently than after he had given up the post. While Nehru was Congress President, 46 per cent of the agenda items were of a policy nature. This pattern clearly reflects Nehru's concern for party-government coordination. It was his habit to submit resolutions summarizing government policy for ratification by the Working Committee and the A.I.C.C. While the major emphasis was on domestic policy, foreign policy issues were mentioned somewhat more frequently than during the second four-year period. During the 1960-1964 period, only 31 per cent of the agenda items were devoted to policy issues, a decline of some 15 per cent.

By the early 1960's the coordination problem at the center had been solved, and the Working Committee was more deeply involved in performing its other functions. The increase in agenda items relating to elections, parliamentary matters, and unofficial resolutions during the later period (26 per cent as compared to only 15 per cent during Nehru's presidency) can be attributed in large measure to the fact that the 1962 general elections took place during this period.

Perhaps the most interesting point which emerges from a comparison of the two periods is the fact that the Working Committee's role as chief executive of the party increased by 5 per cent while policy-making showed a drop of 15 per cent. This change may be attributed to several factors. In the first place, since the issue of party-government coordination had been a major factor in Nehru's decision to become Congress President, he went out of his way to avoid further friction by giving the organization a sense of participation in the policy process. Second, while Nehru was never personally interested in the details of party organizational affairs, he believed that the Congress should spell out its policy clearly. Thus, to a large extent, the shift reflects the greater emphasis which was placed on the rebuilding of the party organization after Nehru stepped down. Nehru's successor to the Congress presidency, devoting full time to party organizational affairs, attempted to strengthen the mass organization in the face of increased disruption caused by the development of major intra-party factionalism in the states. For all these reasons the chief executive function of the Working Committee received greater emphasis in the second period than in the first.

Although an examination of agenda items reveals that the Working Committee has discussed a fairly broad range of domestic policy issues, it also reveals that the Working Committee does not involve itself with the full range of issues faced by the Congress Party as government. During the eight years under consideration the policy issues which most occupied the Working Committee's attention were, in order of frequency: language policy, general economic policy, planning, communal problems, and social policy. Insofar as two of these major substantive issues—planning and language —fall into areas over which the states have a major responsibility, the frequency with which these items appear on the agenda goes far toward indicating the importance of the Working Committee's function as a coordinating body between the center and the states. During neither the later nor the earlier period did such issues as defense policy, important elements of financial policy, or budget policy appear on the agenda.

It seems clear, then, that a purely quantitative analysis of Working Committee agenda items discloses important information about the functions of the Working Committee and its changing role over the past two decades. This is the picture that emerges: the Working Committee considers only a limited range of broad, long-term policy issues; it is deeply involved in the problems of center-state coordination; in recent years it has become increasingly concerned with organizational affairs; although the details of party-government coordination in the states and selection of candidates are handled by two sub-committees—the Parliamentary Board and the Central Election Committee—the Working Committee does deal with some of the broad policy issues in these areas. Each of these functions of the Working Committee will be explored in greater detail in later chapters.

A quantitative analysis of Working Committee agenda items does not, however, tell the whole story of the role of the Working Committee. There are two major reasons for this. First, not all Working Committee business calls for a formal decision. Second, many issues are never actually considered in the Working Committee itself. The Working Committee agenda provides two occasions for free and open discussion on issues not formally identified on the agenda. The first opportunity occurs during the opening remarks by the Congress President. Among his comments the President may include any points he chooses, and the committee may discuss them. Usually these remarks take the form of a review of political events since the last meeting. In this sense, the procedure in the Working Committee is similar to that practiced in the A.I.C.C. where the President gives a brief summary of developments between A.I.C.C. sessions. The second occasion for spontaneous discussion presents itself at the close of deliberations when the Prime Minister summarizes his observations on subjects of his own choosing. When Nehru was Prime Minister, these remarks most frequently consisted of a general review of international affairs. Insofar as the Prime Minister's remarks referred to foreign policy, however, they were not subject to debate. Although the Working Committee was kept informed on foreign policy, it was not permitted to attempt to make decisions on foreign policy matters.[21] Since Nehru's death, foreign policy seems to have remained in the hands of the Prime Minister and the External Affairs Minister. For example, at the Durgapur Session of the Congress following Nehru's death, the Working Committee requested Sardar Swaran Singh, External Affairs Minister, to prepare the draft resolution on international affairs.[22] As Prime Minister, Shastri continued Nehru's practice of briefing the Working Committee on foreign policy developments. Thus, at one meeting of the Working Committee, the *Congress Bulletin* reported that "The Prime Minister, Shri Lal Bahadur Shastri, apprised the Committee of the latest developments in the Rann of Kutch, Nagaland, and Manipur. Shri Shastri also informed the members of the latest position in Vietnam."[23]

The provision for free and open discussion on issues not formally identified on the agenda thus provides state leaders with significant opportunities to express informally their views on national policy. This political feedback mechanism enables central Cabinet members to modify their policies in light of these informal criticisms, thereby facilitating coordination

[21] See Ch. I, pp. 8-10.
[22] *Congress Bulletin*, Nos. 1-3, Jan.-May 1965, p. 3.
[23] *Congress Bulletin*, Nos. 4-6, April-June 1965, p. 140.

and providing state leaders with a means of indirectly influencing policy.

At the same time, many important issues are never formally discussed in the Working Committee, but the convening of a Working Committee meeting provides an opportunity for important informal contacts among leaders. Coordination in the Congress over the past two decades has been a continuous process, and important members of the Working Committee are constantly consulted on major issues. The process of informal consultation can perhaps best be illustrated by the way the central leadership handled the issue of the Bengal-Bihar border adjustments at the time of states reorganization. The Bengal-Bihar border dispute was one of the most difficult problems that had faced the States Reorganization Commission (S.R.C.).[24] The dispute had a long history. As early as 1948, the West Bengal government had submitted a memorandum to the Constituent Assembly claiming some 16,000 square miles of Bihar territory. Later, during the S.R.C. hearings, the government of West Bengal, reducing its claim somewhat, demanded 11,840 square miles containing 5.7 million people, while the West Bengal P.C.C. claimed 13,950 square miles and 6.7 million people. The S.R.C., while recognizing a claim, had recommended a transfer of only 3,812 square miles and 1.7 million people.[25] These claims involved two districts in Bihar: Manbhum and Purnea. The Manbhum district was divided into two subdivisions, each of which had been treated as a separate administrative unit. The first, Dhanbad, had a population of 732,000 of whom 65 per cent were Hindi-speakers. The second unit, Purulia, with a population of 1,548,000, had the largest concentration of Bengali-speaking people outside Bengal. The S.R.C. recommended that Purulia, with the exception of a small sub-division known as Chas thana, be

[24] Ministry of Home Affairs, *Report of the States Reorganization Commission* (New Delhi: Government of India, 1955), p. 172; hereafter referred to as the S.R.C. Report.
[25] *Ibid.*, p. 182.

transferred to Bengal. The Purnea district area was more complex and involved administrative rather than linguistic considerations. Because of partition and the integration of princely states, parts of northern Bengal were not geographically contiguous with the rest of the state. The Bengalis demanded a corridor which would permit them to integrate the new areas more completely. The S.R.C. accepted this claim and proposed that portions of Kishanganj, a sub-division east of the Mahananda River, extending down to and including the national highway in that area of the Purnea district, be transferred to Bengal. Because parts of this area were predominantly Muslim and therefore deeply concerned about the disadvantages of becoming part of Bengal, the Commission suggested that the Bengal government give special guarantees to the Muslims concerning the protection of Urdu as a minority language. Bengal was also asked to promise not to settle East Pakistan refugees in the area.[26]

On January 15, 1956, the evening before the release of the Home Ministry communiqué on states reorganization, a meeting was held in Delhi between delegates from Bihar and Bengal and a four-man Working Committee sub-committee on states reorganization. Bengal was represented by Chief Minister B. C. Roy and by P.C.C. President Atulya Ghosh. S. K. Sinha, Chief Minister of Bihar, and Finance Minister A. N. Sinha represented Bihar. During the meeting Congress President U. N. Dhebar succeeded in persuading Roy and Ghosh to concede about 600 square miles of the territory that had been granted to Bengal under the S.R.C. recommendations.[27] This area, located in the Purulia sub-district, contained the coal reserves and waterworks of the Tata iron and steel factory at Jamshedpur in Bihar. The concession was announced as part of the January 16 Home Ministry communiqué on states reorganization. Later reports indicated that

[26] *Ibid.*, pp. 177-181.
[27] Congress Party in Parliament, Unpublished Minutes of the Executive Committee, Aug. 8, 1956.

B. C. Roy's visit to New Delhi had actually prevented an even greater reduction in the area to be transferred from Bihar to Bengal.[28]

The possibility that parts of Bihar would have to be transferred to Bengal and the concession to Bihar of part of the territory which had been awarded to Bengal by the S.R.C. produced agitation in both states. In Bengal, demonstrations and hartals were successful in stirring up opposition to the concession. In Bihar, conditions were so explosive that Chief Minister Sinha requested permission to resign. The ground for his resignation, he told the Prime Minister and the Congress President, was that the transfer of territory would disrupt the economy of the state and result in widespread unrest.[29]

At this juncture B. C. Roy and S. K. Sinha came forward with a startling proposal that Bihar and Bengal merge into one state. The initial response throughout the country was so highly favorable that there was even talk of creating Dakshina Pradesh composed of the three southern states of Madras, Mysore, and Kerala. Since the proposal to federate was made at the height of the Bombay disturbances, it provided some support to those pressing for the continuance of a bilingual formula for Bombay. The new spirit, however, was short-lived. Despite the fact that the Bihar legislature had already approved the merger proposal, strong opposition in Bengal prevented any further action.

The withdrawal of the Bihar-Bengal merger proposal forced a return to the January 16 decision to transfer some 3,000 square miles from Bihar to Bengal. A bill entitled the West Bengal–Bihar Transfer of Territories Act was introduced into the Lok Sabha in mid-July and referred to a joint select committee. Because the Bengal and Bihar members of the committee were deeply divided on the issue, the final decision on the bill depended upon the votes of the opposition parties.

[28] J. Bondurant (ed.), *Regionalism Versus Provincialism: A Study in Problems of Indian National Unity* (Berkeley: University of California Press, 1958), pp. 79-80.
[29] *Ibid.*, p. 82.

The government leadership, therefore, quickly called a meeting of the Executive Committee of the Congress Party in Parliament to iron out the differences.

Although the Working Committee had met on August 5, three days before the meeting of the Executive Committee of the Congress Party in Parliament, the Bengal-Bihar issue was not officially discussed. The Working Committee meeting did, however, give the Chief Ministers of Bengal and Bihar a chance to hold private talks with the big three: Nehru, Pant, and Azad. Chief Minister S. K. Sinha, in private discussion with Azad, observed that he did not favor the rejection of the Bengal–Bihar Transfer of Territories Bill because it had come from the center, but there were nevertheless strong feelings in Bihar against any transfer of territory. B. C. Roy, meeting privately with Pant, said that he was already facing strong opposition to the concession of some 600 square miles and could hardly be expected to make any further concessions.[30]

Later, at the meeting of the Executive Committee of the Congress Party in Parliament, Congressmen from Bengal emphasized the importance of a corridor to unite all of Bengal and ease the burden of administration. Bihar Congressmen emphasized the difficulties Bihar would experience if the territory were transferred. Nehru intervened in support of Bengal. He asked the committee to show special consideration for Bengal's northern territorial claims. Northern Bengal, he noted, had a common frontier with Pakistan and a mixed population, as well as many internal problems. It was perfectly understandable, therefore, for Bengal to seek a piece of territory which would help her check any separatist tendencies. He saw no reason for the Muslims involved in the transfer to feel disturbed, because there were already twenty-five Muslims in the West Bengal Legislative Assembly. Moreover, since West Bengal was faced with many more difficulties than any other province, the other states

[30] Congress Party in Parliament, Unpublished Minutes of the Executive Committee, Aug. 8, 1956.

should unite in trying to help. Nehru felt that the assurances that Dhebar had given Bengal after her agreement to give up the claim to an additional 600 miles of Bihar territory had to be honored. The strip of land in dispute, he felt, should definitely go to Bengal to complete the link with the north.[31]

The Bengal–Bihar Transfer of Territories Bill, as eventually passed, provided for the corridor to the north and the transfer of the Purulia sub-district, excluding Chas and Chandil thanas, and the Patamda area of Barabhum thana. The transfers took place with little incident.[32] Except for the abortive Bihar-Bengal merger proposals, the issues in dispute between Bengal and Bihar were never submitted to the full Working Committee. The problem was handled privately between the Chief Ministers and the leaders of the central government.

The decision-making style of the Working Committee seems to have changed little since independence. The committee arrives at decisions through a process of consensus, and votes are seldom taken even to this day. Members consider themselves collectively responsible for Working Committee decisions, and, except when the leadership is divided, members have not attempted to challenge the committee's decisions openly before the A.I.C.C. or the Annual Sessions.

The persistence of this tendency to use the Working Committee as an arena for informal discussions and debate, combined with the tendency to respect the integrity and privacy of exchanges within the Working Committee and among Working Committee members, has made the Working Committee, composed as it has been since 1951 of Congressmen drawn predominantly from the parliamentary wing at the center and in the states, an excellent means of achieving center-state coordination as well as party-government cooperation. Thus, Working Committee meetings have come to provide an opportunity not only for conducting formal business relating

[31] *Ibid.*
[32] Bondurant, *Regionalism Versus Provincialism*, p. 102.

to central and state interests but also for informal consultation among senior Congress leaders who feel the need to discuss issues of concern to their states privately. So conducted, Working Committee meetings provide an important feedback mechanism by means of which national leaders can assess the reactions of state leaders toward existing or proposed national policy.

Although the style of Working Committee operations has remained relatively constant over the years, the performance of its major functions has undergone considerable change in the past two decades. The Working Committee is still the chief policy-maker for the Congress, but it has come to consider only a limited range of broad, long-term policy issues dealing primarily with such subjects as language, economic policy, planning, communal problems, and social policy. The fact that planning and language fall under state jurisdiction has led the Working Committee to become deeply involved in the problem of center-state coordination in order to facilitate the establishment of all-India policies. In addition, it has become increasingly clear that the Working Committee cannot ignore organizational affairs. Consequently, the initiative for reconstruction of the party machine derives very largely from the Working Committee. Finally, although the details of party-government coordination within the state and the selection of candidates are handled by two subcommittees—the Parliamentary Board and the Central Election Committee, respectively—it is the Working Committee which establishes policy guidelines in these areas. The proportion of time devoted to each of these major functions and the means of carrying out the responsibilities of each of these functions have undergone modification, sometimes of the evolutionary sort, sometimes revolutionary, in the years since the Working Committee made the first great transition from its role as cabinet of the movement to its role as executive of the mass organization of a dominant political party.

vii

THE DECISION-MAKING FUNCTION:
THE COORDINATION OF PARTY
AND GOVERNMENT

Although the importance of the Working Committee as a
center of decision-making in post-independence India has
fluctuated according to the degree of the committee's autonomy from the parliamentary wing, there has been a steady
trend toward a diminution of its power with the emergence
of new centers of power and decision-making corresponding
to the creation and development of the new role of the
Congress as government. The relationship between the
Working Committee and the government has passed through
three phases: a period of conflict which marked the years of
transition from 1947 to 1951; a period of parliamentary
dominance which characterized the years of centralization and
convergence from 1951 to 1963; and a period of relative
equilibrium which accompanied the years of divergence from
1963 to 1967. The role of the Working Committee in each of
these phases of development emerges clearly from an examination of the process of decision-making involved in the
shaping of major national economic, social, and language
policies. The case studies which follow demonstrate the methods of demand aggregation, consensus building, and party-
government coordination evolved by the Congress over the
past two decades.

During the freedom struggle the Working Committee had
been the unrivaled center of Congress decision-making. For
years Congressmen had looked to the Working Committee
for guidance and initiative, and, despite the emergence of the
new function of the party as government, rank-and-file Con-

gressmen expected the traditional role of the Working Committee to remain intact. They envisioned a Congress government as the handmaiden of the victorious nationalist movement whose function would be to carry out the dictates of the party organization and its Working Committee. For this reason, during the period of transition there was widespread organizational sympathy and support for Congress Presidents like Kripalani and Tandon who challenged the authority of the Prime Minister. However, the major figures in the Congress, especially Nehru and Patel, did not share this view. They saw in the new role of the party as government a separate and distinct function with its own freedom of action and lines of responsibility. The result of these conflicting expectations was a period of friction within the Congress which lasted from 1947 to 1951.

Even before Nehru assumed the prime ministership, he had in mind a model of party-government relations in which the role of the party executive in decision-making was limited. The cabinet system of government, he argued, imposed certain responsibilities on a Prime Minister and certain restrictions on the party executive. Under the cabinet system, as Nehru conceived it, the Prime Minister had a special role to play in coordinating and directing the activities of the government. Since the government would of necessity be faced with many confidential issues which could not be discussed within the party executive, the government had to be free to shape its policies and to act independently within the larger ambit of general policy laid down by the party. "Normally," Nehru insisted, "a party executive lays down the broadest lines of policy and leaves it to the government to work out."[1]

The task of adjusting the Working Committee to a role generally conforming to that envisioned by Nehru was complicated not only by the conflicting images and expectations of other Congressmen but also by the fact that the newly formed

[1] Unpublished Prasad Papers, Letter J. Nehru to J. B. Kripalani, May 2, 1947.

Cabinet, acting in accordance with its responsibilities as the Government of India, found it necessary at times to reinterpret or reject specifically articulated party policies. Since the differences between the parliamentary and organizational wings of the party were often of both a procedural and a substantive nature, the clashes which resulted were difficult to resolve. Good examples of the type of conflict which occurred during this early period can be found in the struggles which took place over the issues of vanaspati, language, and the Congress Economic Programme Committee Report.

A clear case of a conflict resulting from the government's outright rejection of party demands occurred in a dispute over legislation to enforce the coloring of vanaspati, a relatively inexpensive hydrogenated vegetable cooking fat used by unscrupulous merchants to adulterate the far more costly ghee, or clarified butter, which forms a very important element of the orthodox Hindu diet.

The vanaspati issue was of great importance to orthodox Hindus. Growing concern about the adulteration of ghee led representatives of the Go Seva Sangh to request that the Working Committee use its influence to discourage the use of vanaspati as an adulterant of pure ghee. The Working Committee decided that the importation of machinery for the manufacture of vanaspati should be prohibited and that a coloring agent should be added to vanaspati in order to prevent its use as an adulterant.[2] Yet, although the committee had taken an unmistakable stand on the issue in the presence of the Food Minister, who was attending as a special invitee, the decisions were not implemented.

Shortly after Tandon's election to the Congress presidency in 1950, renewed pressures from orthodox Hindus drew his attention to the fact that the decisions which the Working Committee had reached concerning vanaspati some eighteen months before had indeed not been implemented. This time, since there was still no suitable non-toxic coloring compound available, it was requested that hydrogenation be

[2] *Congress Bulletin*, No. 4, June-July 1949, pp. 8-9.

stopped altogether and that the use of non-ghee cooking fats be limited to the form of refined oil. Again the Working Committee was almost unanimous in its decision that hydrogenation should cease. Since the Prime Minister was not present, Tandon was authorized to communicate the Working Committee's second decision on vanaspati to the government.[3] Again the decision was not implemented.

Two months later the offensive against vanaspati had shifted to another front. At the Ahmedabad meeting of the A.I.C.C., an unofficial resolution offered by one of the members demanded that "this session of the A.I.C.C. request the Central Government to put a ban on the manufacture and circulation of vanaspati or hydrogenated vegetable oil." Azad, wishing to avert the threatened conflict between the A.I.C.C. and the government, asked the mover to withdraw the resolution, on the ground that the government was studying the matter. Instead, in defiance, an amendment was offered to force the government to implement the resolution "within a fortnight." However, Tandon, also wishing to avoid an open confrontation in spite of his disagreement with the Prime Minister, ruled that the amendment was out of order, since the "A.I.C.C. could not commit anything on behalf of the Government." Seth Govind Das, one of Tandon's close supporters, suggested that, since the Working Committee had already made its stand abundantly clear, there was little point in taking further action. Despite all these efforts to sidestep the vanaspati resolution, it was approved by a vote of 111 to 56.[4] Yet, although the A.I.C.C. and the Working Committee were essentially united on the vanaspati issue, the party was unable to prevail. Some years later, while discussing the subject of party-government relations, Nehru cited the implications of the vanaspati issue: "I remember a decision of the All-India Congress Committee some years ago about putting a ban on vegetable ghee. I told them that I could not do it. If the A.I.C.C. lays down a certain policy,

[3] *Congress Bulletin*, No. 1, Jan.-Feb. 1951, pp. 7-9.
[4] *Ibid.*, pp. 33-35.

either we will have to follow it, or, if we cannot do so, we will have to go and place our difficulties before the organization. The A.I.C.C. gives us a basic approach. Within that, the Government has a large measure of freedom."[5] Earlier, upon resigning from the Congress presidency, Tandon had also pointed to the resolution on vanaspati as an example of the government's failure to obey the resolutions of the A.I.C.C.[6]

The vanaspati issue had aroused strong feeling in certain segments of the Congress, but there was no traditional Congress commitment to any particular policy in regard to vanaspati. By contrast, there was a very specific commitment to the creation of linguistic states. After independence, rank-and-file Congressmen exerted continuous pressure, directly or through the Working Committee, for the fulfillment of this long-standing commitment, but the government refused to comply.

As early as 1920 the Congress, under Gandhi, had given full recognition to the principle of drawing the map of an independent India along linguistic lines.[7] But when the time came to act, the disruptive effects of partition and the integration of the princely states had left the Congress divided between those who feared that the creation of linguistic states would weaken the country[8] and those who foresaw a cultural renaissance based on the flourishing of the regional languages.[9] When the government-appointed Linguistic Provinces Commission headed by S. K. Dar, a retired jurist, reported late in December 1948 that the reorganization of states along linguistic lines was not at that time in the larger interest of the country, rank-and-file reaction within the Congress was such that a "requisition influentially signed" was presented to the Congress President at the Jaipur Session of

[5] *Congress Bulletin*, No. 6, Aug. 1954, pp. 290-291.
[6] *The Hindu* (Madras), Sept. 25, 1951.
[7] Sir P. Griffiths, *Modern India* (New York: Frederick A. Praeger, 1962), p. 111.
[8] Unpublished Prasad Papers, Letters Shankarrao Deo to R. Prasad, Aug. 14, 1948.
[9] *Ibid.*

the Congress "urging" the immediate redistribution of Indian provinces.[10]

In response, the Working Committee charged a three-man committee consisting of J. Nehru, V. Patel, and Congress President P. Sitaramayya with re-examining the linguistic provinces problem in light of the Dar Commission Report and the requirements of post-independence India.[11] The committee, observing that Congress policy on linguistic states had been framed when the party had not been responsible for "the practical application of this principle," concurred with the Dar Commission in recommending that the creation of linguistic states be postponed.[12] The committee did concede that new provinces might be formed if they represented "well defined areas" and did not involve "any conflict or serious dislocation vis-à-vis another province." However, the committee recognized Maharashtra and Andhra as the only two provinces which might meet these criteria.[13] With the release of the J.V.P. Report, public agitation subsided.[14]

Twice thereafter the Working Committee decided to create separate linguistic states in the South, and twice the lack of mutual agreement prevented implementation. On October 5, 1949, after hearing delegations from various southern states, the Working Committee passed a resolution laying down procedures for the creation of the provinces of Karnatak, Maharashtra, and Andhra. The resolution requested the Congress governments of the states involved to meet with the parties to the dispute and to report the results of these consultations to the Working Committee.[15] The required agreement appeared to be forthcoming only in the

[10] Sitaramayya, "Autobiography," p. 16.

[11] *Report of the Linguistic Provinces Committee* (New Delhi: A.I.C.C., 1949), p. 1. Hereafter referred to as the J.V.P. Report.

[12] *Ibid.*, p. 9.

[13] *Ibid.*, pp. 12-13.

[14] R. Retzlaff, "The Constituent Assembly of India and the Problem of Indian Unity" (unpublished Ph.D. dissertation, Cornell University, 1960), p. 477.

[15] *Congress Bulletin*, No. 6, Sept.-Oct. 1949, p. 12.

case of Andhra. Therefore, the Working Committee resolved on November 17 that the Government of India be requested to form a separate Andhra province;[16] but on January 24, 1950, the Government of India issued a communiqué stating that continued disagreement over the status of Madras city, financial arrangements, and boundaries made the formation of a state of Andhra impossible for the time being.[17]

On the eve of the First General Elections, at the height of the Nehru-Tandon dispute, the Working Committee in the absence of the Prime Minister passed the second resolution requesting the immediate creation of linguistic states in the South. This resolution, drawn up by Karnatak P.C.C. President S. Nijalingappa, a strong advocate of linguistic states, stated that "the Working Committee feel that there is general agreement on this subject among the concerned parties in South India in view of the fact that the Pradesh Committees of Tamil Nad, Kerala, Karnatak, Andhra and Maharashtra have already expressed themselves in favor of such provisions."[18] The government responded by invoking the principle of "large and broad agreement."[19] In this way, Nehru indicated that the government, unable to share the Working Committee's view of the degree of consensus existing among advocates of linguistic states, would not follow the Working Committee's direction.

The issue of linguistic states remained stalemated until after the 1951-1952 elections. The Congress Party was still committed to its traditional policy advocating linguistic states, while the government continued to invoke the principle that "the creation of linguistic provinces for administrative and governmental purposes is . . . a matter which has to be dealt with by the government and the Constituent Assembly. . . . It would make the task of the Government and the Constituent Assembly easy if the people concerned

[16] *Congress Bulletin*, No. 7, Nov.-Dec. 1949, p. 3.
[17] *Report of the General Secretaries, 1949-1950*, p. 51.
[18] *Congress Bulletin*, No. 4, July-Aug. 1951, p. 135.
[19] *The Hindu* (Madras), Aug. 23, 1951.

come to the Government with an agreed solution regarding their boundaries."[20] Even with the increased pressures, under Congress President Tandon, for the immediate creation of linguistic states, the party could not force the government to change its position. No consensus arose from the contending claimants. The government, for various reasons, refused to take the initiative or use its prestige in working out an agreement that, it was claimed, might otherwise have been forthcoming.

If, at times, the new Congress government felt compelled to resist party pressures to enact undesirable or unnecessary legislation, there were also times when the government felt it advisable to define its position as somewhat different from that set forth in party pronouncements. Perhaps the most vivid illustration of this process is provided by Nehru's attempt to dissociate the government from the party's strongly socialist Economic Programme Committee Report, a report which he himself had helped to prepare. This incident clearly demonstrates the kind of freedom Nehru felt the government needed in performing its decision-making role. The role of the party was to lay down broad, long-term goals which the government would then be free to translate into politically feasible policies.

On January 25, 1948, the Congress Economic Programme Committee submitted to the Working Committee a report, later endorsed by the A.I.C.C., which recommended nationalization of public utilities, defense production, and other key industries; abolition of the managing agency system; and a maximum profit of 5 per cent on venture capital.[21] A short time later, on February 17, on the floor of the Dominion Parliament, a Congress back-bencher moved a resolution calling for the government to adopt immediately a socialist policy "based on the principle of nationalization

[20] Unpublished Prasad Papers, Letter R. Prasad to S. Nijalingappa, May 1949.

[21] *Report of the Economic Programme Committee* (New Delhi: A.I.C.C., 1948).

of key industries and cooperative and collective farming and socialization of the material resources of the country." This resolution accorded perfectly with the Economic Programme Committee Report. But, instead of supporting the resolution, Nehru rejected it, declaring that the government had not yet worked out *its* economic policy.[22]

When the official government position was enunciated in the form of the Industrial Policy Resolution of 1948, it was a far cry from the recommendations of the Economic Programme Committee Report, for it reflected a compromise with existing economic realities. In general, the Industrial Policy Resolution provided for a mixed economy. Public ownership was confined to three industries: munitions, atomic energy, and railways. In six other fields the government reserved for itself the exclusive right to start new ventures: coal, iron and steel, aircraft manufacture, shipbuilding, telephone and telegraph materials, and minerals. Nationalization was to be postponed for a period of at least ten years, and the government guaranteed that in the interim existing concerns in these industries would remain free from government control.[23]

The striking differences between the Economic Programme Committee Report and the Industrial Policy Resolution produced a sharp reaction in the party. Shankarrao Deo, the staunchly Gandhian General Secretary of the Congress, had the secretariat prepare a report documenting item by item the divergences between the two[24]—all of which added up, in Deo's mind, to one more example of the government's cavalier treatment of the party. Throughout this period, in fact, Deo had prepared blistering attacks on the government's economic policies on the grounds that they did not embody

[22] *Indian Nation* (Patna), Feb. 19, 1948.

[23] *Hindustan Times* (New Delhi), April 8, 1948.

[24] Unpublished Prasad Papers, "Note on Congress Economic Programme Committee Report and the Industrial Policy of the Government," prepared by the Secretariat of the Economic and Political Research Department of the A.I.C.C.

the economic ideals for which the Congress had always stood. These criticisms he submitted to the Working Committee.[25] He also published them in the *A.I.C.C. Economic Review*. Deo had a fully worked out model for party-government relations in which the government appeared as merely an executive arm of the party. According to this conception, once party policy had been formulated,

> that part of the organization which is in charge of the Government should leave no stone unturned to implement the policy. . . . If, due to insurmountable difficulties, modifications or change in the policy become necessary, then it must come back to the mother organization for its consent. This alone can keep the prestige of the organization and promote confidence and faith of the people in it. Unfortunately things have been done in a different way . . . The Statement of Policy as embodied in the Economic Programme Committee's Report has been whittled down beyond recognition by unilateral declarations of the Ministers. . . .[26]

Nehru's disavowal of the Congress Economic Programme Committee Report and his adoption of a more moderate stand had been due to several factors. For one thing, at a time when India was faced with a serious lag in production stemming from the loss of business confidence in the government, the Congress Economic Programme Committee Report had created even greater uncertainty. It was attacked by the business community as being contrary to the guarantees they had received from the government at the Industrial Conference in December 1947.[27] The anxiety of the business community was vividly expressed to Congress President Prasad by a North

[25] Unpublished Prasad Papers; an example of Deo's criticism of the government's economic policy can be found in Note No. 7, dated July 16, 1949, prepared for the Working Committee.

[26] Unpublished Prasad Papers Shankarrao Deo, "Note on the Congress Organisation," prepared for the Working Committee, Jan. 15, 1950.

[27] *A.I.C.C. Economic Review* (Dec. 1, 1949), p. 6.

Indian industrialist who wrote to ask what purpose was served by "unsettling the minds of industrialists time and again by throwing such bombshells amongst them whenever they begin to show signs of settling down to serious work in the interest of national development."[28] Another factor favoring a modified stand on economic policy was pressure from Sardar Patel, who, not sharing Nehru's socialist orientations, was more sympathetic to the arguments of the business community.[29] Finally, Deo himself clearly recognized that Nehru did not feel that the government was bound to obey the dictates of the party. "After the adoption of the Economic Programme Committee's Report by the A.I.C.C.," Deo declared that Nehru had observed on February 17, 1948: "The A.I.C.C. was not an executive body. It would lay down the general policy naturally leaving it to the house to time it as it thought expedient to give certain priorities and go ahead with it at a pace which may be considered right and proper."[30]

The lack of coordination between party and government exhibited in the conflict over vanaspati, language, and the Economic Programme Committee Report came to an end following the Nehru-Tandon confrontation. At this time several factors converged to bring the coordinating potential of the Working Committee into sharp focus. Nehru's emergence as the undisputed leader of the Congress brought to a close the turbulent period of transition. Independence was a reality, the chaos of partition had been overcome, and the Congress was ready to embark on a major development program.

The party-government conflicts of early years had impressed upon Nehru's mind the necessity of preventing any further internecine rivalry within the party. The mass organization, he realized, had to be given a sense of participation in the decision-making process under the leadership and guid-

[28] Unpublished Prasad Papers, Letter to R. Prasad, Feb. 13, 1948.
[29] M. Brecher, *Nehru: A Political Biography* (London: Oxford University Press, 1959), pp. 509-510.
[30] Unpublished Prasad Papers, Shankarrao Deo, "Note on the Congress Organisation," Jan. 15, 1950.

ance of those who carried the burdens of implementing the party program. For these reasons, Nehru began to reshape the Working Committee. As Congress President, he was in a position to select his own Working Committee, to prescribe the agenda, and to guide the debate. As a result, the Working Committee became dominated by parliamentary leaders, and the Working Committee agenda came to include a large proportion of the broad policy issues facing the government.

Within the framework of these official resolutions, which for the most part the Prime Minister drew up himself, the Working Committee and the A.I.C.C. were able to discuss major policy issues. Since major modification of these resolutions was ruled out, the possibility of divergence between party and government policy was unlikely. Nevertheless, since Nehru was not insensitive to the criticisms of the party, party opinion was taken into consideration by formulating subsequent resolutions so as to incorporate a more workable consensus. While unable to dominate or dictate policy, the party could in this way play an important role in "broadly effecting that policy or pushing it in this direction or that."[31]

This pattern of party-government coordination persisted throughout the period of centralization and convergence and is perhaps best illustrated by the way in which the broad strategy for Indian economic planning was evolved over a period of several years. The pattern included extensive interaction involving the Cabinet, the Working Committee, the A.I.C.C., and the Parliament. In the end, potential conflict was averted by a workable consensus incorporating the views of the traditionalists and the modernists, the organizational wing and the parliamentary wing.

The First Five Year Plan, which placed major emphasis on agriculture, had succeeded in increasing food production. However, studies undertaken in the middle of 1953, halfway through the Plan period, indicated growing unemployment.[32]

[31] J. Nehru, "General Elections and the Congress," *A.I.C.C. Economic Review*, IX (May 1, 1957), 3-6.

[32] Planning Commission, *Second Five Year Plan* (New Delhi: Government of India, 1956), p. 110.

Party-Government Coordination

The government and the Planning Commission realized that this problem could be met only by stepping up the pace of development through more rapid industrialization.[33] This decision to accelerate the developmental process with emphasis on industrial expansion gave rise within the Congress to a great debate between the traditionalists and the modernists over the strategy for the planned economic development of India.

The modernists, represented by the more highly urbanized, socialist-oriented Congressmen, wanted new investment in industrial expansion concentrated in heavy industry within the public sector. The traditionalists, represented by the Gandhians, feared concentration of resources in heavy industry and Western patterns of industrialization. They advocated, instead, the strengthening of the cooperative, decentralized village and cottage industry sector of the economy. They considered their approach to Indian economic development to be more individualistic, humanitarian, and natural than socialism, which they saw as a mechanistic import from the West. The Gandhians called their approach "sarvodaya."

The divergence between the majority of the Congress and the Gandhian element of the party went back several years. The Tandon-Kripalani battle had led many Gandhians to secede from the party, and the leaders of the Congress were anxious to prevent any further defections, not so much because of the numerical strength of the Gandhians as because of a long-standing emotional commitment to Gandhianism and the desire to retain the concept of constructive work as a Congress organizational principle. Yet the formation of the Bhoodan Movement of Vinoba Bhave in 1951 acted like a magnet whose force was strong enough to weaken the party loyalty of even the most staunchly pro-Congress constructive workers. Disturbed by these breaches within the party, Nehru, as leader of both party and government, strove to create a broad consensus within the party by rallying it around the task of economic development. At the Hyderabad Session of

[33] Brecher, *Nehru*, p. 526.

the Congress in 1953, for instance, two resolutions were passed to demonstrate the party's unswerving commitment to Gandhian principles. The first resolution appealed to Congress governments in the states "to do their best for the success of the Bhoodan Movement."[34] The second resolution ratified the final draft of the First Plan and welcomed "the emphasis laid on the expansion and strengthening of village and small-scale industries, and the building up of the community on cooperative lines."[35] In fact, however, the First Plan's commitment to the decentralized sector of the economy was extremely small, and the Gandhians had reason for uneasiness.

The Gandhians attributed the growth of unemployment midway through the First Plan to the government's neglect of village and cottage industries. To alleviate it they demanded greater governmental support for cottage industry, especially by means of a demarcation of spheres of production which had been promised in the First Plan.[36] The First Plan had clearly stated that, whenever a large-scale industry competed with a cottage industry, a non-competitive common production program was to be evolved. Under a common production program spheres of production could be designated, expansion of large-scale industrial capacity could be prohibited, and a cess could be imposed on the products of large-scale industry.[37] Despite these commitments in the Plan, the government had seen fit to implement only the third item: the laying of a cess of three pies per yard on millmade cloth. This fell far short of the Gandhian demands that all basic consumer goods be produced in decentralized village and cottage cooperatives protected from the competition of large-scale industry. Specifically, the Gandhians wanted certain types of cloth reserved for the handloom and khadi sectors of the economy,

[34] Indian National Congress, *Report of the General Secretaries, 1953-1954* (New Delhi: A.I.C.C., 1954), pp. 153-154.

[35] *Ibid.*, p. 78.

[36] Congress Party in Parliament, Unpublished Minutes of the General Body, Aug. 10-13, 1953.

[37] Planning Commission, *First Five Year Plan* (New Delhi: Government of India, 1952), p. 318.

production of edible oils reserved for the village ghani industry, discouragement of existing hullers of rice in favor of handpounded rice, reservation of paper manufacturing to the handmade paper industry, and the manufacture of leather sandals completely reserved for the cottage industries sector. By modeling the Indian economic system on decentralized, widely dispersed village and cottage industries, the Gandhians felt they could raise the standard of living in rural areas, reduce unemployment and underemployment, and preserve a way of life which they felt was threatened by the growth of Western-style socialism based on large-scale industry.[38]

The pros and cons of the Gandhian position were perhaps best summarized by U. N. Dhebar, a former Congress President and a strong supporter of Gandhian economic ideals. Dhebar warned against creating a self-defeating "religious atmosphere" because the case for village and cottage industries could easily be detached from "sentimentalism" and defended on rational economic grounds. Thus, the most effective arguments to offer in support of the establishment and encouragement of village and cottage industries were: the need to employ a large dispersed population, the fact that a huge labor force could not be absorbed in capital-intensive schemes, the expectation that increasing demands for consumer goods like food and cloth could be met in decentralized sectors while also providing extra employment, the fact that heavy industry would absorb the bulk of capital investment and leave little for developing consumer goods industries, the need for supplemental income in overcrowded land situations, and the desire to provide for a balanced economy. Dhebar believed that the arguments in favor of village and cottage industries outweighed, even on economic grounds, the arguments in opposition. The most frequently heard arguments against village and cottage industries as cited by Dhebar were: small-scale industries put technology in cold storage, caused inflation and reduced purchasing power, had extremely high production costs and lacked markets, were difficult to accept

[38] *The Hindu* (Madras), April 25, 1955.

because of the problem of reconciling low income with increased production, produced a need for parallel development of capital goods and consumer goods industries to absorb production of heavy industry, wasted resources, and lacked the organizational framework to carry out their development.[39]

The government did not accept the Gandhian analysis of the causes of unemployment. Finance Minister C. D. Deshmukh told the Congress Parliamentary Party that unemployment could be attributed to several causes: the government's labor policies, the elimination of price controls, and the influx of new people into the labor market. Nehru added that changes in the Indian social structure, the breaking down of the joint family, and the rapidly expanding population were further causes for higher unemployment figures.[40] Reassuring his colleagues that the government was committed to the policy of creating full employment, Nehru emphasized that this goal had to be accomplished through the production of more wealth rather than through the provision of doles to the unemployed.[41]

Nevertheless, convinced that the solution to India's economic problems lay in village and cottage industries, the Gandhians continued to press their cause within the Working Committee. The first step was to persuade the committee to approve a proposal to survey the extent to which state governments had carried out the recommendations on village and cottage industries contained in the First Plan.[42] Shriman Narayan, a General Secretary of the Congress who was deeply committed to Gandhian ideals, enthusiastically undertook the task of collecting data. He addressed a circular letter to all Congress Chief Ministers, inquiring particularly into the extent to which the Plan's recommendations concerning the reservation of spheres of production had been im-

[39] *Congress Bulletin*, No. 6, Aug.-Sept. 1955, pp. 487-492.

[40] Congress Party in Parliament, Unpublished Minutes of the General Body, Aug. 10-13, 1953.

[41] *Ibid.*

[42] *Congress Bulletin*, No. 4, May 1954, pp. 183-186.

plemented. The Chief Ministers were requested to supply the requisite data within a month.[43] Meanwhile, Narayan held a press conference at which he enthusiastically proclaimed that the Congress would, at a session of the A.I.C.C. shortly to be convened at Ajmer, "chalk out a definite programme regarding the economic policy of the Congress, particularly relating to land reforms and the development of large-scale, small-scale and village and cottage industry."[44]

Subsequent Working Committee meetings proved that Shriman Narayan had overestimated the extent of Congress consensus on the issue of village and cottage industry. Meeting informally prior to the Ajmer session, the Working Committee was sharply divided on the issue; deadlock, not decision, was the result. One group strongly supported the Gandhian desire to prevent "unhealthy competition" by the assignment of spheres of production. A second group stressed the need for the development and expansion of modern large-scale industry.[45] Later, when the full Working Committee met, Narayan's expectations received a further blow. Dr. B. C. Roy, Chief Minister of West Bengal, a man contemptuous of central interference in the affairs of his state and far from sympathetic to Gandhian economics, raised several objections to the events of the weeks that had just passed. He protested the harassment from "numerous circulars" issued by the A.I.C.C. He also complained that he had been reading a good deal in the press about an informal Working Committee meeting; yet he had never been officially informed of the subjects discussed. Nor had any mention of the matter appeared in the official minutes of the Working Committee. In an attempt to lead toward consensus, Nehru reassured Roy that the circulars had been well-intentioned and harmless efforts at soliciting suggestions and that no decisions had been made at the meeting from which he had been absent.

[43] Circular letter Shriman Narayan to Chief Ministers of the States, May 25, 1953, *ibid.*, pp. 203-205.
[44] *The Hindu* (Madras), July 15, 1954.
[45] *The Statesman* (New Delhi), July 20, 1954; *The Hindu* (Madras), July 21, 1954.

Finally, after having poured oil on troubled waters, Nehru broke the deadlock by introducing three resolutions on economic policy. These resolutions, which had been drawn up independently by Nehru, were promptly ratified. Minor changes were suggested in only one of them.[46]

The Ajmer resolutions indicate that Nehru was attempting to steer a middle course between the advocates of large-scale and small-scale industry. While attaching great importance to the growth of large-scale industry, the resolutions called for the encouragement of cottage and small-scale industry as an essential part of the economy. However, even the decentralized sector was to be based on improved techniques, and spheres of production were to be provided on a selective basis and only where possible. Perhaps the most important part of the Ajmer resolutions, from the standpoint of party-government relations, was a reference to inquiries already instituted by the government into the role of cottage and small-scale industries in the Second Plan. The Working Committee took "special notice" of these inquiries and hoped that the government would give early consideration to the reports once they were received. Not only had the Ajmer resolutions been drafted by the Prime Minister, but the implication was that the government was planning to base its ultimate decisions on its own studies of feasibility.[47]

The sympathetic hearing given to supporters of village and cottage industries by the government and the compromise approach ratified by the Working Committee served for a time to calm the fears of the Gandhians about the future of village and cottage industries in a rapidly industrializing society. However, the adoption of the socialist pattern of society brought back their old doubts concerning the extent of the government's commitment.

Under the First Five Year Plan, a pragmatic and non-

[46] *Congress Bulletin*, No. 5, June-July 1954, pp. 227-230.

[47] For a copy of the Ajmer resolutions, see *Resolutions on Economic Policy and Programme, 1924-1954* (New Delhi: A.I.C.C., 1954), pp. 87-93.

doctrinaire approach to planning which had called for a mixed economy while leaving the ultimate shape of the Indian economy largely undetermined, agriculture had received the major emphasis and industrial policy had fallen roughly within the outlines of the Industrial Policy Resolution of 1948. With the government's decision, halfway through the First Plan, to accelerate the growth of the economy through more rapid industrialization, the issue of industrial policy was reactivated.

The first indication of a major shift in industrial policy came in the fall of 1954, when Nehru told the National Development Council that the pattern of development toward which he was aiming was a "socialistic picture of society." While the public debated the implications of Nehru's remarks, the Indian Cabinet reviewed the Industrial Policy Resolution of 1948 and decided that it "had to be interpreted in terms of the socialistic objective."[48] In late December, after two days of debate, the Lok Sabha passed a resolution which made the "socialist pattern" the official policy of the government and a guide to the Planning Commission in drawing up the Second Plan.[49]

After the objective of the socialist pattern of society had been endorsed by the N.D.C., the Cabinet, the Congress Party in Parliament, and the Lok Sabha, it was ratified by the Congress Working Committee and the A.I.C.C. The Congress session held at Avadi, Madras, in January 1955 passed a resolution which stated that "in order to realize the object of the Congress Constitution and to further the objectives stated in the Preamble and Directive Principles of State Policy in the Constitution of India, planning should take place with a view to the establishment of a socialistic pattern of society, where the principal means of production are under social ownership or control, production is progressively

[48] Congress Party in Parliament, Unpublished Minutes of the General Body, Dec. 2, 1954.
[49] *The Hindu* (Madras), Dec. 23, 1954.

speeded up and there is equitable distribution of the national wealth."[50]

Prime Minister Nehru later insisted that credit for the Avadi resolution should really be given to U. N. Dhebar, the new Congress President.[51] Technically, Nehru's statement was correct. Dhebar was elected Congress President late in 1954. At that time the socialist pattern concept was being endorsed by various official government bodies. In light of these actions and Nehru's speeches before the N.D.C. and Parliament, Dhebar felt that the issue should be set forth with no less clarity within the party. He therefore prompted Nehru to draw up a resolution embodying the principle already declared by the government so that there would be no doubt about the party's position on the issue. He considered the previous Congress objective of a "cooperative commonwealth" too vague and general. The socialist pattern would define the party's goals more clearly. Thus, formally, Dhebar was responsible for the adoption of the Avadi resolution.[52]

Yet it is quite clear that, as far as industrial policy was concerned, the dominant role was played by the government and not by the party. This had been true of the Industrial Policy Resolution of 1948; it had been true of the enunciation of the socialist pattern of society in 1954; and it would also be true of the Industrial Policy Resolution of 1956. On April 30, 1956, a few weeks before the submission of the Second Plan, the government presented to the Parliament an industrial policy resolution to modify the one in effect since 1948. The new Industrial Policy Resolution expanded the scope of the public sector. The number of industries reserved for the public sector rose from six to seventeen. Included in this category were all basic and strategic industries, public utilities, and industries requiring large investment. Specifically, heavy industry such as iron and steel, machine tools, and

[50] *Resolutions on Economic Policy and Programme, 1955-1956* (New Delhi: A.I.C.C., 1956), p. 1.

[51] Brecher, *Nehru*, p. 529.

[52] This account was given to the author in New Delhi in 1960 by leading Congressmen.

heavy electricals as well as mining fell under the jurisdiction of the public sector. The concurrent list of twelve industries where private sector industry was expected to supplement the dominant public sector enterprises included the production of machine tools, essential drugs, aluminum, basic chemicals, and sea and road transport. All other industries were generally to be left to the private sector. In addition, the resolution guaranteed existing facilities from nationalization, provided for expansion of existing facilities under certain circumstances, and permitted public-private cooperation in developing some of the reserved sectors.[53]

The Congress commitment to socialism was welcomed throughout most of the country. However, it created a split among the Gandhians. The more orthodox warned that the Congress commitment to socialism was a radical departure which might cause further defections among Congress Gandhians.[54] To arguments like this Shriman Narayan replied:

Is not Gandhianism, socialism of a type? In the contents of the economic policy resolution, it has been made clear what socialism is. That means full employment, more production and economic and social justice for all. We have laid emphasis on small-scale and cottage industries in order to provide fuller employment. According to our ideal, the State will be encouraged on a co-operative basis. Therefore, the contents of the Economic Policy Resolution are in no way opposed or inconsistent with the Gandhian conception. On the other hand, we are moving close to the same ideal. Gandhiji's socialism was of the Sarvodaya type and that is what we are aiming at. Ours is not of the Western type.[55]

However they expressed themselves, the Gandhians were still

[53] Planning Commission, Government of India, *The New India: Progress Through Democracy* (New York: The Macmillan Co., 1958), pp. 387-396.
[54] *Tribune* (Ambala), Jan. 17, 1955.
[55] *The Indian Express* (New Delhi), Jan. 19, 1955.

concerned about the implications of socialism. They tended to mistrust those who conceded a place to village and cottage industries out of non-idealistic motives. And yet it was economics rather than sentiment which was to give village and cottage industries a place in the Second Plan. The breakthrough came in two stages.

First, the differences between the advocates of cottage industries and the supporters of large-scale industry were miraculously (or so it seemed at the time) reconciled by an economic model drawn up by Professor P. C. Mahalanobis, chairman of the Indian Statistical Institute and adviser to the Planning Commission. On March 17, 1955, the Planning Commission released the Mahalanobis "plan frame," which proposed the creation of a large basic industries sector as the foundation for further economic development and a decentralized cottage industry sector to alleviate the problem of unemployment and provide a satisfactory flow of consumer goods. Many economists have argued that this blending of approaches was achieved on less than solid economic grounds. Dr. W. Malenbaum, for example, has noted: "Where basic decisions were not merely assumptions (as for heavy industry), they were derived from formulas in which the parameters overpriced labour and underpriced capital. The answers thus assured an allocation pattern which tended to understate the relative importance of the labour-intensive. . . . activities and exaggerated the investment flow to the capital-intensive . . . sectors. The major adjustments made between the plan-frame and the plan itself served to enhance this bias. . . ."[56]

Despite such theoretical shortcomings, the Mahalanobis blend of heavy industry and decentralized industry was a politician's dream. It was welcomed by all groups within the Congress. The National Development Council approved it in the first week of May 1955. The Working Committee, meeting at Berhampur, Orissa, only a few days later, officially endorsed the Mahalanobis strategy. Although some orthodox

[56] W. Malenbaum, *Prospects for Indian Development* (London: George Allen & Unwin, Ltd., 1962), p. 91.

Gandhians were alarmed by a passage in the Working Committee's resolution calling for greater mechanization of cottage industries, the majority were elated. For the first time, it seemed, village and cottage industries had been given an important place in Congress economic policy. It was fully expected that they would be given an equally important position in the Second Plan.

But their position was not really assured until it was decided that village and cottage industries would not only alleviate unemployment but could also play a significant role in helping to control inflation. This conclusion, which had been reached by the Indian Finance Ministry in a study of the financial implications of the Second Plan, was summarized in a note presented to the Working Committee in December 1955. Finance Minister C. D. Deshmukh, explaining the note, declared that village and cottage industry would play a key role in absorbing unemployment and checking the inflation that was bound to result from the Plan's deficit financing. The Second Plan would require austerity and economic discipline to increase savings, he warned, and greater agricultural production was needed to increase national income. The success of the Plan, he concluded, could be greatly enhanced if the Congress organization took special steps to generate popular enthusiasm for the Plan, helped organize small-scale village and cottage industry, and joined in community development and national extension service activities.[57] After Deshmukh had concluded his presentation, the Working Committee ratified the basic approach of the Second Five Year Plan.[58]

In the end, a synthesis of socialism and sarvodaya was evolved. Industrialization was to proceed on two planes: a heavy industrial sector based largely on public ownership and a decentralized sector based on village and cottage industries. The government's formula, incorporated in the Second Five Year Plan, ratified by the party, and approved in

[57] *Congress Bulletin*, No. 9, Dec. 1955, p. 696.
[58] *Ibid.*

179

final form by the National Development Council in the summer of 1956, succeeded in placating both traditionalists and modernists. Although the Plan's emphasis was clearly on the development of large-scale heavy industry, the decentralized sector was given sufficient encouragement to provide a workable consensus on the objectives of planning as exemplified in the Second Plan.

Three issues had had to be resolved before any concrete program could be drawn up. In each case the role of the government was decisive. The commitment to a socialist pattern of society was endorsed first by the National Development Council, then by the Parliament, and only after that did it become part of the party's program. The Industrial Policy Resolution of April 1956, which defined the relation between public and private sector under the socialist pattern, originated with the government and evidently was never considered by the Working Committee. The decision on the role of village and cottage industries was discussed in party and government circles from mid-1953 on, but despite party pressures it did not really receive full endorsement until the acceptance of the Mahalanobis plan frame. Only after an investigation by the Planning Commission and the Finance Ministry did any firm commitment to village and cottage industries become government policy. The party's ambivalence in the resolution of this issue and the importance of the government's leadership was perhaps best summarized by Congress President Dhebar. "Some of us are not clear. And we argue whether the social revolution should precede the economic revolution or the latter the former. Similarly, we are not clear about the methodology and the technique of the new struggle. . . . And because we are not clear we turn to the Government and ultimately to Panditji."[59]

Dhebar revealed in more specific detail the role of the party and the government in the policy process as it had related to the formulation of the Second Plan when he told the A.I.C.C. that

[59] *Congress Bulletin*, Nos. 10-11, Oct.-Nov. 1956, p. 465.

. . . the Plan Frame and the question of resources were discussed by the Standing Committee of the National Development Council on which are represented some of the
Chief Ministers who also are in their political capacity
our leaders. They have given their general approval to
the same. The matter may have been considered by the
Cabinet of the Central Government. The preparation of
a Plan Frame and consideration of the resources position
requires a very detailed study of the nation's economy
and the trends of economic development in the world.
Our leaders in the Government are in a better position
to study these questions. This I do not say with a view
to set a limit upon the discussion. But I have no doubt
that you will agree with me that we shall have to take
these into consideration before making suggestions.[60]

Thus, Dhebar in effect informed the A.I.C.C. that the Chief
Ministers and the National Development Council would be
playing the dominant roles in decision-making for the Second Plan. The chief actor was certainly not to be the party.

The pattern of party-government coordination developed
during the period of centralization and convergence continued
in slightly modified form during Shastri's brief tenure as Prime
Minister and in the early months of Mrs. Gandhi's term. From
May 1964 to May 1966 there was effective interaction between party and government, and, if anything, the Working
Committee played a slightly more important role than before.
The shift of emphasis to the Working Committee during
the period of divergence is best illustrated by the decision-
making process which led to the creation of a Punjabi Suba.
Although their demands had been rejected by the States Reorganization Report in 1955, the Sikhs had continued to agitate
for a unilingual Punjabi-speaking state. As in the case of the
bifurcation of Bombay and all other strong linguistic demands,
the center was eventually forced to give in. The particular
factors responsible for the reversal of the earlier decision on

[60] *Congress Bulletin*, No. 6, Aug.-Sept. 1955, p. 479.

Punjab involved changes in the Sikh demands, changes in the Congress leadership, and changes in the state of the nation.

A split within the militant Akali Dal was perhaps the most important development in the Sikh community. The schism promoted greater militancy in demands for Punjabi Suba while shifting the basis of those demands. Tara Singh's openly communal demand for a Sikh state had been thoroughly unacceptable to the central leadership. But the purely linguistic demand put forth by his rival, Sant Fateh Singh, was a demand that could be given a fair hearing without violation to the secular state principle. As the *Hindustan Times* said: "It is a tribute to the patriotism and political courage of Sant Fateh Singh that he wrenched the demand firmly out of its communal integument and presented it as nothing more or less than a claim for parity of status for Punjabi with the other major languages of the country which had been given territorial base. In this form, the demand was clearly one which all Punjabi-speaking communities in the state could support."[61]

Meanwhile, India was facing two major external threats as a result of the Chinese invasion of 1962 and the Indo-Pakistan war of 1965. Since Punjab is strategically situated for the defense of northern India and Kashmir, the Indian government could not run the risk of having military operations disrupted by political turmoil. As Nehru had explained to Chief Minister Sachar in 1949, Punjab's special position as a frontier province forced the central government to take a particular interest in its stability.[62] Agitation for Punjabi Suba had been suspended for the duration of the Chinese invasion, but Prime Minister Shastri was able to halt a later crisis only when the hostilities between India and Pakistan had already begun.[63] Earlier, in the summer of 1965, Shastri had refused the Punjabi Suba demand. By fall, however, as soon as the Indo-

[61] March 11, 1966.

[62] Unpublished Prasad Papers, Letter J. Nehru to B. Sachar, June 23, 1949.

[63] *The Statesman* (New Delhi), Sept. 7, 1965.

Pakistan cease-fire had been signed, the Cabinet announced the appointment of a three-man sub-committee to examine the Punjabi Suba demand afresh.[64]

Under Nehru it is less likely that such a reversal would have been possible, for Nehru had been able to see the Sikh demands only in terms of communalism. Shastri was less adamantly committed to the prevailing policy, and under pressure of the Indo-Pakistan clash he felt compelled to take a fresh look at the Punjabi Suba issue. During his short term as Prime Minister the Punjab problem was considered by the Cabinet sub-committee, by a special Parliamentary committee, and by the Congress Working Committee.[65] Shastri was followed by Mrs. Gandhi, who, as Congress President in 1959, had supported the bifurcation of Bombay. More responsive to linguistic demands than her father had been, Mrs. Gandhi pushed for a quick decision on the Punjabi Suba case.

By late February discussion was taking place at three levels. In an attempt to provide central leadership and prevent Punjab Congressmen from working at cross purposes, a Working Committee sub-committee consisting of Kamaraj, Home Minister Nanda, and U. N. Dhebar was given the job of ascertaining the views of state Congressmen. The Cabinet sub-committee, consisting of Nanda, Chavan, Jagjivan Ram, and Sanjiva Reddy, discussed the administrative, financial, and economic aspects of the Punjabi Suba proposals. Finally, a committee of Members of Parliament set about gathering information about public sentiment. By early March, under the threat of renewed agitation in the Punjab, a final decision was in the making. On March 9, the Cabinet sub-committee met with the Working Committee sub-committee, each having previously met separately with various groups from the Punjab.[66] The next day the Working Committee considered the sub-committee reports for just three hours before passing a resolution requesting the government to create a unilingual

[64] *The Hindu Weekly Review* (Madras), Oct. 5, 1965.
[65] *The Statesman* (New Delhi), Dec. 27, 1965.
[66] *The Statesman* (New Delhi), March 9, 1966.

Punjabi-speaking state. Since Morarji Desai and Darbara Singh had opposed the resolution, the Working Committee resorted to a formal vote for the first time in many years, yet the majority clearly believed that what had been conceded to other languages could not be denied to Punjabi. The principal architects of the decision, according to reports, were Kamaraj and Mrs. Gandhi.[67]

The close cooperation between the Working Committee and the government during the early years of the period of divergence broke down in the summer of 1966 over the issue of devaluation of the rupee. Despite the fact that the government had ruled out devaluation several times in the early months of 1966, on June 5 it was suddenly announced by the government that the rupee would in fact be devalued. Neither the Congress President nor the Working Committee had been consulted. The result was a rift between party and government which reflected no less a major factional split within the central leadership. At the Working Committee meeting in early July following the devaluation decision, the government presented Working Committee members with an elaborate official note justifying the action taken. However, this note was accompanied by an equally elaborate note prepared by former Finance Minister Morarji Desai who criticized the government's action.[68] The committee decided to postpone consideration of the issue until members had had a chance to study both notes. In the interim it became clear that the Working Committee's discussion would follow group lines. Atulya Ghosh, a member of the Working Committee and a supporter of Mrs. Gandhi, publicly justified the government's decision to act independently of the party on this matter by insisting that the devaluation decision was not a new economic policy so much as a consequence of the old economic policy and as such did not require consultation with the Congress President or the Working Committee.[69] At the

[67] *The Statesman* (New Delhi), March 10, 1966.
[68] *Hindustan Times* (New Delhi), July 6, 1966.
[69] *Hindustan Times* (New Delhi), July 14, 1966.

subsequent Working Committee meeting, however, those members who were not in the Cabinet and who had not participated in the decision did not view the government's action in this light. Morarji Desai, T. T. Krishnamachari, V. K. Krishna Menon, Dr. Ram Subhag Singh, and Biju Patnaik bitterly attacked the government for its action. By contrast, the Chief Ministers who had been the major supporters of Mrs. Gandhi in her election took a much softer line, accepting devaluation as an established fact requiring only suggestions for follow-up action.[70]

The struggle over devaluation brought to the surface certain fundamental changes which were taking place within the Congress. As the *Hindustan Times* observed, the devaluation controversy was not about policy. It was about attitudes, and it involved "a clash between generations, between the need for modernization and an obsolescent leadership which instinctively sees in change a challenge to its survival." In conducting this holding action "the old leadership knows it cannot press it too far but it hopes that it has pressed it far enough for the Prime Minister to be tamed."[71] And so she was, for later, when the government came under further attack stemming from the failure of the monsoon, the seeming breakdown of law and order, and government indecisiveness, Mrs. Gandhi told a press conference that "on important things we consult important members of the Congress Working Committee."[72]

The relationship between the Working Committee and the national government has thus undergone a process of evolution which has placed the Working Committee in a different role during each phase. During the period of transition, demands released by the end of colonial rule received expression through the Working Committee which was dominated briefly by state organizational leaders and by Congress Presidents intent upon asserting the independence of the organizational

[70] *Hindustan Times* (New Delhi), July 20, 1966.
[71] *Hindustan Times* (New Delhi), July 21, 1966.
[72] *The Hindu Weekly Review* (Madras), Jan. 16, 1967.

wing and together demanding implementation by the new Congress government of long-established Congress policy on social, economic, and language issues. This pressure from the party led to friction between the Working Committee and the government stemming from the rejection by the Congress leaders in the government of party demands as inconsistent with broader considerations of national unity, economic stability, and social welfare.

With Nehru's election to the Congress presidency, conflict between the Working Committee and the government came to a halt. The Working Committee became the focal point for coordinating party-government relations and for helping to aggregate the conflicting demands and interests of which the party was composed. The usefulness as well as the limitations of this new role were illustrated in the strategy for the planned development of India. The process of aggregation was slow. It involved a continuous interaction of party and government and repeated attempts to reconcile the conflicting views of the traditionalists and modernists within the Congress. And the final consensus, however it might satisfy political considerations, led as often as not to an uneconomic allocation of resources.

The decision-making role of the Working Committee underwent further transformation in the period of divergence as the cohesiveness of the central leadership gave way to a new pattern of factionalism which was reflected in the struggles for succession and which, the immediate succession crisis overcome, created renewed problems of party-government coordination. Party-government interaction at the center became what it had been at the state level for years—a camouflage for group conflict. Meanwhile, a major problem facing the Congress was how to transfer leadership to a new generation. The new leadership of the government, with a greater sense of urgency and a schedule of policy priorities differing from that of the old guard of the Nehru era, sought to counteract independently the stagnation that had overtaken the Indian economy. Resenting such a break with the consensus approach of the past and committed to previously established policies of the government, a group within the Working Committee attempted to check the government's policy initiatives. The reverberations of the resulting conflict were muffled only by the development of an internal crisis in the country and the coming of the 1967 elections. But it was only muffled, not stilled. Conflict was expected to renew itself in the form of a struggle over the prime ministership.

And so, after twenty years of rule, the Congress found itself faced with a fundamental dilemma. The consensus pattern of decision-making evolved during the period of centralization and the early years of the period of divergence had preserved unity, provided for party-government coordination, and permitted elaborate consultation with all sections and levels of the party. Yet this process of aggregation had become so "successful" that a checkmate system of decision-making was the result. There came a time when the government found itself saddled with a series of policies which had clearly brought the Indian economy, strained by two wars and natural disasters, to a point of utter stagnation but to which so many senior Congress leaders in the Working Committee were committed that the government found it difficult to put together a consensus for change. Under such circumstances the only responsible alternative open to the new leadership of the government was to begin taking policy initiative on its own. It broke with the old system of tight economic controls, opened up the fertilizer industry to foreign private capital, and devalued the rupee. Although the old guard managed to succeed in restraining a government which to them seemed to be running wild, it was clear to nearly all observers that India in the late 1960's was desperately in need of new ideas and new policies. Perhaps even more it needed new leaders capable of generating new ideas and implementing new policies. Yet the Congress at this critical juncture was deadlocked between an older generation deeply committed to the policies of the past and a new generation not yet powerful enough to carry out policies on its own. Both leadership groups looked to the election for vindication.

THE DECISION-MAKING FUNCTION:
THE ESTABLISHMENT OF
ALL-INDIA POLICY

The Working Committee has played an important role in coordinating center-state relations and formulating all-India policy. The Working Committee's role in setting all-India policy was not merely a logical development of pre-independence Congress tendencies. It stemmed mainly from the fact that the Congress became the majority party at the center and with two or three exceptions controlled all the states for the first two decades after independence. Since all Congress Chief Ministers attended Working Committee meetings either as members or as special invitees, the Working Committee emerged in these years as an important arena for informal discussions of all-India policy, discussions which served more or less officially as guidelines to the states. Thus, because of the overwhelming power of the Congress, an understanding of the functioning of Indian federalism requires an examination of the internal processes of the dominant party.

The Congress had grown up as a centralized political organization, and its central leadership had always felt that there were many areas which required some degree of national uniformity, although it was customary to permit the provincial leadership to structure details to meet widely differing local conditions. Thus, after independence the Congress considered it legitimate and the government considered it convenient for the Working Committee as the chief decision-making body for the party to attempt to establish national policy which could be used as a model by the states. Moreover, since the Working Committee was also the chief executive of the party, Congress discipline could be invoked when necessary in an attempt to persuade the state Congress ministries to take action generally in accord with the all-India policy agreed upon by the central government and the Chief Ministers in the Working Committee. Party discipline could also be invoked to control insurgence by the members of the mass organization. Although the Working Committee's policy-coordinating role has not solved all the difficulties of center-state relations, the handling of such pivotal decisions as those involved in developing land and language policies leaves little doubt that coordination would have been even more difficult if it had not been for the Working Committee.

As a coordinator of center-state relations, the Working Committee came to handle both planning and non-planning issues. Its role in these areas has varied considerably over the past two decades, but the pattern of development followed roughly the same three stages which characterized the relationship between the Prime Minister and the Congress President and which shaped the evolution of the Working Committee's relation to the central government. During the early years following independence the Working Committee was not only a convenient but in fact the sole arena in which center and state leaders could discuss policy objectives. In the years of transition from 1946 to 1951 very little coordination was attempted except for some efforts addressed to zamindari abolition and the national language question. With the beginning of the period of centralization and convergence, however, the Working Committee became a very significant center for coordination. It was during this period that the pattern for handling planning issues diverged from the accustomed pattern which still sufficed for non-planning issues.

The creation of the Planning Commission in 1951 and the attempt to carry out centralized planning within a federal system brought into sharp focus the problems of coordination between the center and the states. In drawing up the First Five Year Plan, Nehru relied extensively on the Working Committee to develop all-India policies for those subjects under the constitutional jurisdiction of the states, such as land reform. However, the experience gained by this process of consultation, the conviction that the Working Committee as a purely party organ could not give official sanction to a national plan, and the realization that it could be useful only so long as the Congress controlled the governments in all the states forced the government to develop more formal machinery for coordination. Since "in the field of policy the central and state governments have to act in close cooperation with one another," the central government found it necessary in the summer of 1952 to establish its own official decision-maker for planning, the National Development Council. It was expected that cooperation in land problems, food problems, provisions for the financing of agriculture, a common production program for small- and large-scale industry, selection of irrigation and power schemes, and conservation of mineral resources[1] would "be greatly facilitated as a result of" the National Development Council's existence. Thus a new official body came into being with the sole objective of coordinating center-state relations in planning. The National Development Council eventually came to play the dominant decision-making role in planning at the government level. But the Working Committee has continued to play a part in articulating broad policy and in prodding the state Congress ministries to action. In this way, the Working Committee came to supplement the newly created machinery in performing a role it had once monopolized.

The role of the Working Committee in establishing broad all-India economic policy emerges clearly from an examination of the development and implementation of Congress land policy, particularly the policies involving zamindari abolition and the imposition of ceilings on landholding. In the case of zamindari abolition there existed, despite poor coordination, a strong Congress consensus which facilitated action. However, although a coordination process was much more

[1] Planning Commission, *First Five Year Plan* (New Delhi: Government of India, 1952), p. 5.

extensively developed by the time the Working Committee was called upon to handle the land ceiling issue, the implementation of such a policy was less readily achieved since there was almost no basis for agreement between the modernized intellectual leadership at the center which favored it and the emerging leadership in the states which opposed a policy so damaging to its staunchest supporters.

Immediately upon resuming office in 1946, the Congress ministries in the states had begun introducing bills to abolish the zamindari system and to remove all intermediaries from the land—a long-standing objective of Congress land policy. The Working Committee encouraged the state governments to proceed expeditiously with the legislation and delegated authority to Congress President Rajendra Prasad to oversee the legislation.[2]

Under Prasad's leadership a meeting of state revenue ministers was called shortly after independence to discuss the most pressing land policy problems. Although the goal of the conference was to evolve a "reasonable amount of uniformity" in the approach to zamindari abolition, the consensus of the meeting was that conditions in the states varied so markedly that each state would have to be free to handle the problem in the way most congenial to local conditions. However, the group did agree that it would be desirable to work out a uniform program for the post-abolition stage. It was decided, therefore, to request the Congress President to appoint a special committee to study the matter and make recommendations.[3] The report of this committee, later known as the *Report of the Congress Agrarian Reforms Committee*, was published in July 1949. Although it remained an influential document, it was never officially endorsed by the party.

Having agreed to permit each state to develop its own approach to the elimination of intermediaries, Prasad care-

[2] *Congress Bulletin*, No. 4, July 1947, pp. 1-2.
[3] H. D. Malaviya, *Land Reforms in India* (New Delhi: A.I.C.C., 1955), p. 82.

fully followed the pace of zamindari abolition bills through the various stages in the state assemblies. Having always taken a very keen interest in the problem of zamindari abolition, Prasad encouraged reform even in the face of opposition from other members of the Working Committee. For instance, when Maulana Azad tried to slow down the pace of legislation in Bihar, Prasad encouraged his colleagues to proceed.[4] Another time, when objections were raised by powerful domestic interests, Prasad made inquiries but refused to intervene. Thus, when the issue of temple zamindari was raised by a member of the Birla family, who feared a loss of revenue if temples were forced to relinquish their zamindari rights, Prasad agreed to take the matter up with the state Chief Ministers.[5] After receiving their replies, he gave Birla three reasons for his inability to intervene in favor of the temples. First, the bills had already progressed too far to be changed. Second, charities would not be abolished, but zamindari would have to go. And, finally, Prasad warned that many people resented the relatively high living standard enjoyed by some of the priests.[6]

As the pace of zamindari abolition quickened, Prasad was increasingly subject to complaints from interested groups objecting to specific provisions of bills in different states and demanding the convening of an all-India conference to ensure a nationally coordinated policy. While admitting that he, too, was concerned about the lack of coordination, Prasad felt that zamindari abolition had reached a stage at which a national conference was no longer feasible.[7] He did, however, decide to place the major issues raised by petitioners before the Working Committee.[8] At a special session held on April

[4] Unpublished Prasad Papers, Letter Shankarrao Deo to R. Prasad, March 29, 1948.

[5] Unpublished Prasad Papers, Letter J. K. Birla to R. Prasad, translation from the Hindi original, dated about July 20, 1948.

[6] Unpublished Prasad Papers, Letter R. Prasad to J. K. Birla, Aug. 14, 1948.

[7] Unpublished Prasad Papers, Letter R. Prasad to Sir Ahmed Syed Khan, March 21, 1948.

[8] *Congress Bulletin*, No. 1, July 1948, p. 2.

30, 1948, and devoted to the zamindari abolition problem, the committee heard a deputation of zamindars from Bihar concerning their demands for equitable compensation.[9] The zamindars were told that Congress policy could not be changed. As for the details of specific legislation, the states had full authority to act. "We have found by experience," Prasad told one of the zamindars, "that it is very difficult for us from the centre to interfere."[10] Even so, the Working Committee did make some specific suggestions for modification of a zamindari abolition bill to the Bihar ministry. These suggestions were probably related to an issue raised by the Tata Enterprises of Bihar, which pointed out that certain provisions of the Bihar bill were contrary to the government's Industrial Policy Resolution of April 6, 1948.[11]

Although zamindari abolition was proceeding at a different pace in each state, the center tried to see that state policies were not at variance with the policies of the central government. In the case of zamindari "legislation and its implementation," said K. V. Rao, the Congress General Secretary, "the principles maintained in the manifesto as worked out by the party concerned, the instructions of the Central Parliamentary Board, and the directives of the Central Cabinet if any, should not materially differ."[12]

Following the Working Committee's meeting on April 30, Prasad refused to accept further complaints. Whenever a petition was received, he simply forwarded it to the state concerned without comment.[13] When asked, in view of the financial crisis in India, whether it would be wise to abolish

[9] *Ibid.*, p. 5.
[10] Unpublished Prasad Papers, Letter R. Prasad to Raja Sahib, May 13, 1948.
[11] Unpublished Prasad Papers, Letter Tata Iron & Steel Co. to R. Prasad, March 29, 1948; Letter Tata Iron & Steel Co. to R. Prasad, April 15, 1948.
[12] Unpublished Prasad Papers, K. V. Rao, "Note on the Functioning of the Parliamentary Board," prepared for the Parliamentary Board meeting of Feb. 16, 1949.
[13] Unpublished Prasad Papers, Letter R. Prasad to Raja of Bobbili, Aug. 23, 1948.

zamindari at such a colossal cost,[14] he replied: "The government of which Pandit Nehru is the head is in full possession of the situation in the country and the question of the abolition of zamindari is in pursuance of the previous decisions of the Congress. It is not for me to come in the way of the Government and ask them to drop a measure which has the sanction of the Congress. Any appeal therefore should be addressed to the Government and not to me."[15] In short, the Working Committee had played its role. The rest was up to the government.

Abolition of intermediaries had been one of the immediate objectives of Congress land policy. It had enjoyed rather broad support, and implementation had been slowed down only by legal battles over compensation. The Congress ministries did not require prodding before enacting such legislation. In fact, their initiative and the lack of coordinating machinery made it difficult to maintain national standards, although whatever coordination there was took place in the Working Committee. Yet, because of the differing conditions in each state and the advanced stage of the legislation, the Working Committee's role, however useful in theory, was limited in practice. In subsequent issues its role would be more extensive but not always more effective.

With the First Five Year Plan and its emphasis on increasing agricultural production, land policy was no longer merely important: it was paramount. However, as the nature of the land reforms became more complex, the degree of consensus diminished, particularly in regard to the issue of ceilings on landholdings. The lack of consensus on ceilings revealed itself largely in differences between the Congress leadership at the center and the Congress leaders in the states. The central leadership and particularly the Prime Minister were strongly committed to the imposition of ceil-

[14] Unpublished Prasad Papers, Letter Raja Durga Prasada Deva of Kurupam to R. Prasad, Sept. 6, 1948.
[15] Unpublished Prasad Papers, Letter of R. Prasad to Raja Durga Prasada Deva of Kurupam, Sept. 18, 1948.

ings. They attempted to use the Working Committee as a means of committing the Congress to the principle of ceilings by urging the Working Committee to pass a series of resolutions which could in turn be used to exhort the states to action. Even so, the Working Committee did not commit the Congress to the principle of ceilings until halfway through the First Plan period. By this time it was clear that many states were dragging their feet in implementing the Plan proposals on ceilings. Thus, in prodding the states to carry out the provisions of the Plan, the leadership was using the party machinery to carry out the policy of the central government.

The discussions of the land policy objectives contained in the First Plan took place largely in the Working Committee. During this period the government had not yet created the National Development Council, and, since the Congress ministries governed in twenty-one states, the Congress Working Committee made a convenient forum for discussion. Although the committee at the time had only fifteen officially appointed members, Congress President Nehru invited most of the central Cabinet and important Chief Ministers to attend, thus almost doubling the size of the Working Committee and transforming it into a miniature national development council. Thus, the preponderance of government members on the Working Committee was intensified by the presence of ministerial invitees with the effect that the Working Committee became an arm of the central government reaching out to influence state behavior in legislative areas inaccessible to direct central control.

At the time of the drawing up of the First Five Year Plan, the Congress Party had not officially committed itself to a policy of ceilings on landholdings. While the *Report of the Congress Agrarian Reforms Committee* had recommended a ceiling of three times the size of an economic holding,[16] the

[16] An economic holding was defined by the committee as a holding which could afford a reasonable standard of living to a cultivator while providing full employment to a family of normal size and efficient utilization of one pair of bullocks. *Report of the Congress Agrarian Reforms Committee* (New Delhi: A.I.C.C., 1951), p. 8.

report had never been endorsed officially by the party. Nevertheless, the Planning Commission in the *Draft Five Year Plan* published in July 1951 rejected the idea of ceilings on land. Among the various administrative, financial, and social reasons for this rejection, the Planning Commission singled out for special mention the problem of working out just and adequate compensation and the belief that the imposition of land ceilings would not yield a significant amount of surplus land for redistribution to the landless.[17] However, this was far from the last word on the ceilings issue.

Meanwhile, although the ceilings issue had played a role at a series of three Working Committee meetings, the difficulty of reaching a consensus prevented the passing of an official resolution until January 1953, a month after the ceilings principle had been promulgated in the First Plan. The first Working Committee meeting in this series of meetings, held in late May and early June 1952, ended in deadlock with a decision to shelve the ceilings issue for much the same reasons that had led to its rejection in the Draft First Five Year Plan.[18] Two months later, in August, the committee managed to reach a tenuous consensus in favor of ceilings. After holding a number of informal sessions[19] in addition to the usual pattern of formal sessions, the Working Committee was reported to have rejected the Planning Commission's stand on the infeasibility of ceilings on the grounds that for political reasons at the very least the principle of redistribution through the fixing of maximum holdings was desirable.[20] At this time the committee also decided to move a comprehensive resolution on land reform policy at the next session of the A.I.C.C., which was to be held at Indore.[21]

[17] S. Rudolph, *Some Aspects of Congress Land Reform Policy* (Cambridge, Mass.: Center for International Studies, Massachusetts Institute of Technology, 1957), p. 49.

[18] *The Statesman* (New Delhi), June 29, 1952; *Congress Bulletin*, No. 3, April-Sept. 1952, p. 104; *The Statesman* (New Delhi), June 30, 1952.

[19] *Times of India* (Bombay), Aug. 9, 1952.

[20] *The Hindu* (Madras), Aug. 12, 1952.

[21] *Congress Bulletin*, No. 3, April-Sept. 1952, pp. 113-115.

But only when the Congress assembled in January 1953 for the Hyderabad Session did the party officially ratify the ceilings principle in a resolution declaring that "the Congress welcomes the recommendations in the First Five Year Plan in regard to land policy."[22]

Although the Working Committee's tardiness in passing a resolution is a clear indication of the strong resistance to ceilings on the part of some state leaders[23] as subsequent attempts at implementation would more clearly reveal, the position of the central Congress leadership in favor of ceilings was just as unmistakably set forth in the final version of the First Five Year Plan. The Plan made some concessions to the states. It provided that each state was to delimit the maximum landholding within its own boundaries and that action would not be taken until the necessary data on landholdings and cultivation could be collected.[24] But the strength of the central commitment was left in no doubt when Nehru, at the Hyderabad Session, took the opportunity of his Presidential Address to stress the need for a vigorous land policy if India was to reach the objective of self-sufficiency in food. Among other things, he told the A.I.C.C. members, "we have to put a ceiling on land."[25] Shortly afterwards, the party endorsed the land reform resolution.

Endorsement, however, was only the first step. During the rest of the First Plan period the Working Committee found it necessary to pass a series of resolutions in an attempt to prod the Congress ministries in the states to implement the Plan provisions. In 1953, the Working Committee passed two resolutions on the subject.[26] The second, ratified by the A.I.C.C. at Agra, stated that "the state Governments should take immediate steps in regard to the collection of the requisite land data and the fixation of ceilings on land holdings,

[22] *Resolutions on Economic Policy and Programme, 1924-1954* (New Delhi: A.I.C.C., 1954), p. 78.
[23] *The Indian Express* (New Delhi), July 20, 1954.
[24] Planning Commission, *First Five Year Plan*, p. 189.
[25] J. Nehru, *Presidential Address, 1953*, p. 17.
[26] *Resolutions on Economic Policy and Programme, 1924-1954*, p. 79.

with a view to redistribution, as far as possible, among land-less workers."[27] Nearly a year later the Working Committee "reiterated" its plea to the states in the form of a third resolution on land policy implementation. Finally, in the early summer of 1954, the Working Committee passed a fourth resolution. This resolution, which was endorsed by the A.I.C.C. at a meeting in Ajmer, took the states to task for failing so completely to carry out the provisions of the First Plan that an accurate census of landholdings had not even been forthcoming. It was regretted that earlier requests for such information had not produced results, but hopes were expressed that the census would be expedited.[28]

Although the Second Plan reiterated the First Plan's recommendations for ceilings on land[29] and the central leadership repeatedly availed itself of all government and party channels to press the states to implement reforms, the task had still not been completed by the time of the Third Plan.[30] Even in states where ceilings legislation had been "enacted" or "promoted," it had been ineffectual. As Thomas Shea has observed, "pressure from the Working Committee or from the Prime Minister himself may force a state parliament to prepare some kind of legislation to satisfy popular demand." But the final version of the bill in such cases is usually far from vital or comprehensive. "The state party can then say with assurance to the Working Committee, 'We have produced an Act.' . . . They can add that informed opinion familiar with local conditions brought forth . . . evidence that the . . . original bill . . . would be impractical . . . and there is little valid criticism which either the Working Committee or the Planning Commission can offer."[31] Thus, as Neale has argued,

[27] *Ibid.*, p. 81.

[28] *Congress Bulletin*, No. 5, June-July 1954, pp. 221-222.

[29] Planning Commission, *Second Five Year Plan, The Framework* (New Delhi: Government of India, 1953), p. 71.

[30] Planning Commission, *Third Five Year Plan, A Draft Outline* (New Delhi: Government of India, 1960), p. 95.

[31] T. Shea, "Implementing Land Reform in India," *Far Eastern Survey*, xxv (Jan. 1956), 3.

"although in principle Congress politicians favor land reform, in fact they are often landlords, related to landlords, or members of the same caste or social groups as the landed. As a result, means of evasion are written into the tenure laws."[32] Still, the Congress remained officially if not wholeheartedly committed to the principle of ceilings, and Kamaraj, as Congress President, continued to press the issue. The goal of Congress land policy, he proclaimed, is "a land of prosperous peasant proprietors with economic holdings."[33] Now that the first struggle to embody the ceilings principle in legislation is over, the leadership must work, through persuasion, to see that the legislation is given effective force. The process of moving the states is difficult and slow but not impossible. Without central pressure, in fact, even less would have been accomplished in the way of land reform.

Attempts to coordinate center-state relations for purposes of planning gave rise to the development of several channels of communication and contact between the center and the states. However, until very recently, such elaborate communications channels did not exist for handling non-planning issues. Therefore, the Working Committee of the Congress became an important arena for developing guidelines for the states to follow in areas over which the center lacked jurisdiction. Perhaps the best illustration of the role of the Working Committee in non-planning issues appears in the case of language policy. Not only during the years of transition but during the period of centralization and convergence as well, all-India language policy was conducted through the Working Committee. With the growing devolution of authority during the period of divergence, however, the Working Committee alone was no longer a sufficiently effective center of coordination. Therefore, the government began to develop more formal channels for coordinating center-state relations,

[32] W. C. Neale, *India: The Search for Unity, Democracy and Progress* (Princeton: D. Van Nostrand, 1965), p. 73.
[33] K. Kamaraj, "The Food Crisis," *A.I.C.C. Economic Review*, XVII (Feb. 10, 1966), 38.

a development which would be inevitable should the period of Congress dominance come to an end.

In mid-1949, the A.I.C.C. office had received a series of complaints about discrimination against linguistic minorities in West Bengal, Bihar, Assam, and Orissa. Petitioners complained that children of minority groups constituted a considerable majority in a given area; yet schools teaching in the mother tongue of minority groups had been closed; state grants to education had been stopped; and teachers had been warned, suspended, or discharged. Courts had refused to accept documents in the language of the minority community; income tax offices had required merchants to submit accounts in the state majority language; and there were even complaints that electoral rolls had been ordered to be printed only in the majority language.[34]

Such administrative and educational discrimination had given rise to direct action among the Bengali minority in the Manbhum district of Bihar. A group of Bengali-speaking Congress Gandhians, who had founded a Lok Sevak Sangh to carry out constructive work, began a satyagraha to back up their demands for protection of the Bengali minority. The issue became serious enough to be considered by the Working Committee.

The Working Committee heard a representation from the Lok Sevak Sangh and appointed a special committee headed by Dr. P. C. Ghosh to study the problem.[35] The committee's report noted that the Bihar government permitted the use of the mother tongue as a medium of instruction at the primary level and up to class V of secondary school. From class V on Hindi became the medium of instruction. The com-

[34] Unpublished Prasad Papers, K. V. Rao, "Note on Teaching Facilities for Linguistic Minorities," prepared for the Working Committee meeting of April 5, 1949.

[35] The published proceedings of the Working Committee meeting of May 22 contain no reference to the decision reported here. The decision is, however, recorded in the mimeographed minutes circulated only to Working Committee members. See *Congress Bulletin*, No. 4, June-July 1949, pp. 8-11.

mittee recommended that Bengali be retained as a medium of instruction throughout secondary school until an all-India policy had been established.[36]

After receiving the Ghosh report, the Working Committee attempted to lay down national principles to guide the state Congress governments in dealing with linguistic minorities.[37] Dr. Rajendra Prasad was asked to draw up a draft resolution based on the Working Committee discussions. Prasad, as President of the Constituent Assembly, could ensure that the guidelines established for the states conformed to the thinking of the government and the Constituent Assembly.

In his draft resolution Prasad divided the bilingual problem into two categories: administration and education. For purposes of administration, the draft resolution noted, each province was responsible for naming its state language. In multilingual provinces, bilingual areas were to be demarcated and the language of the area indicated. The provincial language would be the official language for administrative purposes, but in bilingual areas all public documents for general use were to be printed in both languages. Although the state language was to be used for administrative and court purposes, any person would have the right to submit petitions in his own language. In the case of education, the Prasad resolution held that the mother tongue should be the medium of instruction at the primary level. Special class sections would be required for teaching in the mother tongue of the minority in bilingual areas provided there were a reasonable number of students enrolled. At the secondary stage the pro-

[36] Unpublished Prasad Papers, Report of Dr. P. C. Ghosh and P. Mishra, dated June 7, 1949.

[37] The Congress did not publish any minutes for the Working Committee meeting of July and August 1949. Only the final resolution was made public. The following discussion is based on the unpublished proceedings of the Working Committee which were circulated to Working Committee members only. The discussion is also based on copies of the draft resolution. Both can be found in the Prasad Papers (unpublished). The text of the resolution on bilingual areas passed by the Working Committee can be found in *Congress Bulletin*, No. 5, Aug. 1949, pp. 7-8.

vincial language was to be introduced, even if instruction continued in the minority language. Children at the secondary level were also to begin the study of the all-India language. At the university stage the medium of instruction was to be the regional language.

During the discussion of Prasad's draft resolution, the Working Committee made four changes which were incorporated in the final resolution. These changes were important from the point of view of implementation because they extended some guarantees and eliminated ambiguities in the phrasing of other provisions. The phrase "a considerable minority" was further defined as 20 per cent of the population. A possible loophole in the right to petition in the mother tongue was closed. The obligation of the states to provide instruction in the mother tongue was to be invoked for as few as fifteen students rather than thirty. Urdu was to figure as one of the languages entitled to minority rights. So amended and so strengthened, the Prasad resolution was passed.

The problems of linguistic minorities did not vanish with the passage of the Prasad resolution. Over the last fifteen years the central leadership has found it necessary to adopt resolution after resolution reiterating its earlier position. Even the passage, on the recommendation of the States Reorganization Commission, of the Seventh Amendment to the Indian Constitution, which spelled out minority language rights, did not leave the central leadership without reason to complain that "some doubts have arisen as to the method of implementation and some grievances exist about facilities offered to certain minority languages. The Working Committee, therefore, draw the attention of the Central and State Governments to this Policy and resolutions, and desire that they should be given full effect to and the directions of the Constitution carried out wherever this may not already have been done."[38] The constant reiteration of demands that the states provide the proper facilities for linguistic minorities in-

[38] Indian National Congress, *Resolutions on Language Policy, 1949-1965* (New Delhi: A.I.C.C., 1965), Working Committee Resolution, May 15, 1958, p. 12.

dicates that the Working Committee has not been wholly successful in protecting linguistic minorities. Yet the majority of states do seem to have been brought into line by those pressures from the Working Committee still being used to prod the remaining states to action.

National language policy is another area requiring center-state coordination. Here, as in land reform and other language issues, the Working Committee of the Congress has played an important role. The national language issue has always been particularly sensitive because it involves the problem of national unity and because it is so intricately bound up with educational and administrative policy. The Indian Constitution provides that each state shall specify the language of administration within its boundaries, but the center is responsible for laying down the medium of communication between the center and the states and among the several states. Since education is a state subject under the Constitution, the states may designate the medium of instruction for all education within a state, but the center is responsible for designating the language or languages in which the civil service examination may be taken. This examination is the sole means of recruitment into government service, and for the educated elite the Government of India is still the most important employer in the country. Since a candidate whose medium of instruction is other than the medium of examination is at a serious disadvantage, the national language policy has a direct impact on the personal welfare and financial prospects of the Indian educated elite. For all these reasons, the national language issue is a potentially explosive issue, and dealing with it requires the closest possible coordination between the center and the states.

Under the Indian Constitution, which took effect in 1950, Hindi was designated as the official language of the Union, but provision was made for the continued use of English for all official purposes during a fifteen-year transition period.[39]

[39] M. V. Pylee, *India's Constitution* (New York: Asia Publishing House, 1962), p. 342.

In 1963, Parliament enacted the Official Language Act to deal with the post-transition period. Under this act the central government was to continue using English as an associate language for all official purposes. At this time, no date was set for the final change-over to the use of Hindi alone, and Prime Minister Nehru personally assured the non-Hindi-speaking states that English would continue in use as long as non-Hindi-speakers felt the need for it.[40] None of these assurances could prevent anticipatory anxiety from developing in the non-Hindi-speaking states after Nehru's death, and, when in 1965 the status of English was reduced from that of an "official" to an "associate" language, violence erupted throughout the South,[41] and leaders from the non-Hindi-speaking states demanded constitutional or statutory assurances that English would remain as the alternative medium "as long as non-Hindi-speaking people want it."

When Prime Minister Shastri and Home Minister Nanda rejected these demands, the response was further violence and a revolt within the central Cabinet. C. Subramaniam and O. V. Alagesan, both from Madras, resigned from the Cabinet in protest, and at least three other Cabinet members from non-Hindi-speaking areas sympathized with their demand for statutory assurances.[42] In an attempt to pacify the non-Hindi areas, Shastri repeated Nehru's assurances on the status of English in a broadcast to the nation[43] and before a meeting of the Congress Party in Parliament.[44] But, with continued violence and unrest, pressures began to build up to force a change in this position. In Madras, Chief Minister Bhaktavatsalam promised his constituents that he would rally the Chief Ministers of the non-Hindi states to support a joint fight for "permanent statutory bilingualism."[45] Meanwhile, the Chief Minister of West Bengal pressed the center

---

[40] *Hindustan Times* (New Delhi), Sept. 5, 1959.
[41] *The Hindu Weekly Review* (Madras), Jan. 1, 1965.
[42] *New York Times*, Feb. 12, 1965.
[43] *Ibid.*
[44] *New York Times*, Feb. 14, 1965.
[45] *New York Times*, Feb. 24, 1965.

to evolve a compromise formula. Finally, on February 16, the government agreed to the demands for statutory assurances and sent a draft of the proposed amendments to the Official Language Act to the Chief Ministers of the non-Hindi-speaking states. The draft stated that English would continue to be used for all "official purposes of the Union" until the legislatures of three-fourths of the non-Hindi-speaking states resolved to discontinue it.[46] With the official announcement of these assurances to Parliament on February 17, Subramaniam and Alagesan withdrew their resignations.[47] In a meeting of the Congress Party in Parliament, Shastri laid down the decision-making pattern he expected to follow in working out the details of the government decisions. He announced that he would meet with the leaders of the opposition parties and with the Chief Ministers and that their views would be submitted first to the Congress Party in Parliament and then to the entire Parliament for approval.[48]

The Congress Working Committee and the Conference of Chief Ministers met in Delhi in late February for the purpose of evolving a language policy to calm the fears of the non-Hindi-speaking states. Independently, yet not surprisingly, considering the extent to which the two groups were composed of the same members, both the Working Committee and the Conference of Chief Ministers agreed unanimously to amend the Official Language Act to give formal effect to Nehru's 1963 assurances.[49] Also submitted to the central government was a series of recommendations for implementing these assurances.[50] Some of the recommendations fell under the jurisdiction of the central government, others under the jurisdiction of the states.

The first recommendation for implementing the language assurances stated that "in the transaction of business at the Central level English will continue to be used as an associate

[46] *The Hindu Weekly Review* (Madras), Feb. 22, 1965.
[47] *New York Times*, Feb. 18, 1965.
[48] *The Hindu Weekly Review* (Madras), Feb. 22, 1965.
[49] *The Hindu Weekly Review* (Madras), March 1, 1965.
[50] *Ibid.*

official language in the intervening period. No change will be made in these arrangements without the consent of the States." The important elements of this provision were the unspecified length of the "intervening period" and the need for state consent to changes in policy.

In the second recommendation, which was concerned with the three-language formula requiring state educational curricula to include the compulsory study of Hindi and English in addition to the mother tongue (or, in the case of Hindi-speaking states, Hindi, English, and any one of the fourteen languages in the Fourteenth Schedule of the Constitution), the Working Committee noted "with regret that the three-language formula has not so far been implemented by some of the States. The Working Committee feels it is necessary that immediate steps are taken to effectively implement the three-language formula evolved by the National Integration Conference and accepted by the country."

The third recommendation was potentially explosive, for it stated that "as soon as possible examinations for the all-India services should be held in Hindi, English and the principal regional languages and that candidates may be given the option to use any of these languages." Both at the Working Committee meeting and at the Conference of Chief Ministers, Prime Minister Shastri stressed the difficulties of implementing such a formula but agreed that the central government would study the matter before stating a position. The final recommendation called on the central government to consider the feasibility of establishing quotas for each state in the services.[51]

The Cabinet appointed a sub-committee to study these recommendations and to prepare a final report. In late May the completed report was approved by the Cabinet. On June 1, at a special meeting of the Working Committee to which all Chief Ministers were invited, the Working Committee was informed that the Cabinet had decided to defer the issue of establishing quotas in the services but that it had accepted

[51] *Ibid.*

all the other recommendations. A few Working Committee members objected to piecemeal approval of the package of recommendations. The government refused to accept this position,[52] but the Chief Ministers in the Working Committee did insist on several major points which were incorporated in the resolution drafted by Home Minister Nanda, C. Subramaniam, and U. N. Dhebar.[53] The Chief Ministers from the non-Hindi-speaking states insisted that the purposes for which English must of necessity be used in addition to Hindi be specified in the forthcoming bill itself and that only minor items be left to the government to announce by framing rules under the general authority of the act. The Working Committee also insisted that the three-language formula be introduced in all the states on a compulsory basis and that the examinations for the all-India services be conducted in English, Hindi, and the regional languages. Kamaraj stressed that English would remain the sole medium of examination until both the regional languages and Hindi could be used. The time of the change was to be left strictly to the government, but the principle seemed safely established.[54]

Explaining the Working Committee's decision in an article in the *A.I.C.C. Economic Review*, U. N. Dhebar argued that the position was not new but in fact incorporated the substance of two earlier Congress resolutions. Perhaps more important, Dhebar insisted that the three-language formula would have two important effects. It would permit administration to be conducted in a language the people could understand, and it would ensure that future generations would learn at least two languages apart from their regional language. His most telling statements were evoked by the decision on all-India examinations. He emphasized that the decision had been fought largely by vested interests in the bureaucracy to whom "anything that promises to make the Government

---

[52] *The Hindu Weekly Review* (Madras), May 31, 1965.
[53] *Congress Bulletin*, Nos. 4, 5 and 6, April-June 1965, pp. 144-147.
[54] *The Hindu Weekly Review* (Madras), June 7, 1965.

of the country more broad-based and representative of the masses, anything that makes for widening of the area of policy-making is an anathema."[55] The change would, in Dhebar's words, "tap those sources which today are absolutely neglected."[56] In short, just as the mass franchise had opened up political recruitment to new social and economic groups, so the shift in the medium of examinations would open up the bureaucracy to those groups otherwise unable to gain access.

The government eventually decided that the Working Committee's decision on the compulsory three-language formula and the medium of examination should be incorporated into a special government resolution on language policy to accompany the bill giving statutory basis to Nehru's assurances about the continued use of English. Yet both the resolution and the bill were delayed because the Union Public Service Commission had not finished studying the problem of changes in the medium of examination. As for the bill, it was reported that the final version would specify where English was to be used with Hindi in government and that it would include a provision that no further amendments to the bill could take effect until all states approved of the proposed change. Thus, the idea of a three-fourths or two-thirds majority was dropped in favor of giving each state an absolute veto power.[57] Since the outbreak of hostilities between India and Pakistan prevented the bill from being submitted to Parliament, it was not passed until late 1967. Under no circumstances would a language policy bill have been easy to compose or to sponsor, and only the close consultation among the Working Committee, the Council of Chief Ministers, and later the Parliament made possible the evolution of an acceptable formula for a national language policy, an issue on which center-state coordination was essential.

The growing importance of the Conference of Chief Minis-

[55] U. N. Dhebar, "The Language Issue and the Congress Working Committee's Resolution," *A.I.C.C. Economic Review*, XVII (Aug. 15, 1965), 11.

[56] *Ibid.*, p. 18.

[57] *The Hindu Weekly Review* (Madras), Aug. 16, 1965.

ters, its emergence as a pivotal body for coordinating all-India policy, is part of a tendency that has been going on for the past two decades during which informal party channels were gradually supplemented and partially supplanted by the development of official bodies designed to perform the same function. Perhaps this tendency to create official bodies was even more strongly enforced when the Congress decided that party channels were no longer sufficient to solve the recurrent outbreaks of interstate disputes over boundaries, river waters, and electric power. Thus, at the A.I.C.C. meeting in Bangalore in July 1965, the Working Committee in fact adopted a resolution which insisted that every effort should be made to settle these disputes by mutual negotiation, but recommended also that "in cases where such efforts do not succeed" the Government of India "should set up appropriate machinery for a speedy and final settlement."[58] Such a trend toward institutionalization is essential if coordination of center-state relations is to continue when the Congress loses control of some of the states, as it did in 1967.

In this way the coordination of center-state relations which took place solely in the Working Committee in the early period has been slowly supplemented or replaced by the development of more formal bodies at the official level. This pattern started with the creation of the National Development Council as a means of coordinating center-state relations in planning, continued with the growing role assigned to the conference of Chief Ministers as a means of coordinating all-India non-planning issues such as language, and was inherent in the Shastri government's suggestion that perhaps some form of official body must be constituted to handle interstate disputes over boundaries, power, and water. This suggestion was not immediately carried out, but it is inevitable that the Congress must replace its informal methods of coordinating center-state relations by more formal official channels if the problems of Indian federalism are to be solved within a union. Once such channels have been effectively de-

[58] *Congress Bulletin*, Nos. 7, 8, and 9, July-Sept. 1965, pp. 176-177.

veloped, the role of the Working Committee in establishing all-India policies will suffer further erosion whether or not the Congress loses power in a substantial number of states. But, whatever the future holds, the fact remains that over the past two decades the Working Committee has played a very significant role in the coordination of center-state relations and in the establishment of all-India policy.

THE WORKING COMMITTEE
AS CHIEF EXECUTIVE OF
THE PARTY

One of the most important of the traditional functions of the Working Committee has been its role as chief executive of the Congress mass organization. In the course of the struggle for independence, the Working Committee gradually became the supreme directorate of the movement. In 1934 the Working Committee's authority over the Congress movement was formally spelled out in the party constitution. This authority has been sustained and strengthened in the post-independence period, so that today the Working Committee has the executive authority to implement all decisions of the A.I.C.C.; to superintend, direct, and control all subordinate Congress committees; to invoke sanctions for breaches of party discipline; and to take all action in the interest of the Congress that it sees fit.[1] Functioning within this extremely broad grant of authority, the Working Committee has come to be known as the Congress High Command.

Since independence the Working Committee has been forced to commit a major portion of its time to running the party machine. With the development of serious intra-party conflict based on group factionalism, the Working Committee has used its broad authority over the mass organization to maintain party unity and to prevent factions in the states from annihilating each other and the party organization. In bringing about these objectives, the Working Committee has made judicious use of its authority by laying down

[1] M. V. R. Rao, *Development of the Congress Constitution* (New Delhi: A.I.C.C., 1958), p. 115.

broad policy for the organization, by establishing mediating machinery, and by intervening directly in the affairs of subordinate Congress committees to direct their reorganization. Although it might be expected that the Working Committee's intervention would be resented by state Congress leaders as interference in their internal affairs, central intervention in fact developed in response to direct requests from the organization for greater central guidance. Thus, the Working Committee came to play a major role as the final arbiter of disputes within the party organization just as the Parliamentary Board emerged with a similar role in the area of party-government coordination in the states. This role of mediation and arbitration, which developed from the necessity to maintain party unity, seems to be an indispensable element of Indian politics, for, as Brass has observed, "in the traditional order, the only procedure for conflict resolution which is acceptable to faction leaders is the mediation of impartial arbitrators."[2]

Party factionalism has performed both an integrative and a disintegrative function.[3] The principal disintegrative function has been manifested when intra-party conflict has become so intense that the party has failed to perceive external threats, with the result that Congress candidates are defeated at the polls. It was intra-party factionalism which caused the defeat of the Congress candidates in three important by-elections in 1963[4] and led to the implementation of the Kamaraj Plan as a means of revitalizing the party. The major integrative function, on the other hand, has been to recruit new groups into the Congress, thereby broadening the base of participation. As Elliott has shown in the case of Andhra, "the factions have been anxious to recruit leaders from lower castes, not only as symbols of intercaste appeal but also as

[2] P. Brass, *Factional Politics in an Indian State: The Congress Party in Uttar Pradesh* (Berkeley: University of California Press, 1965), p. 239.

[3] *Ibid.*, pp. 238-242.

[4] Kothari, "Three Bye-Elections."

insurance against later caste solidarity."[5] Over the years, in performance of the party maintenance function, the Working Committee has tried consistently to reduce the disintegrative effects by adopting procedures and policies to control internal factional conflict. These policies have focused on three major areas: membership qualifications, membership scrutiny, and party electoral machinery.

Although intra-party factionalism has had a major positive impact on Congress Party recruitment by broadening the base of participation, it has also given rise to the problem of bogus membership as competing factions have attempted to inflate the membership rolls in order to ensure their own control of the party machinery. As one Congressman who dealt with this problem for many years has observed, "the moment it was recognized that the number of members on the roll would determine the chances of success for intending candidates, attempts were . . . made to inflate the number so that the election results might to a considerable extent be influenced by its weight." In short, "bogus enlistment was resorted to."[6] Although the Congress had been forced to develop means of controlling bogus membership even before the transfer of power, the problem developed in acute form on the eve of independence. Because of the mass arrests and disruption which followed the 1942 Quit India Movement, the Congress organization was suffering from a deep-seated malaise from which it took years to recover. Clearly, the Congress organization had to rebuild itself, yet the goals of the organization were no longer plain; its members had developed conflicting views on the role of the organization, and the leadership was deeply involved in the final negotiations with the British for the transfer of power, the framing of a new Constitution for the Indian Republic, and the problems of meeting the crisis of partition. As a result, the organization, its sense of identity

[5] C. M. Elliott, "Caste and Faction in Andhra Pradesh," unpublished paper prepared for Association of Asian Studies meeting, New York, April 1966, p. 14.
[6] P. R. Chakraverti, "Malady—Organisational or Attitudinal," *A.I.C.C. Economic Review*, XII (June 1, 1960), 17.

lost, was permitted to drift. For a movement on the verge of capturing and organizing power, such drift could only have deleterious consequences.

Unlike most nationalist movements of Africa and Asia, the Congress had developed into a mass movement. Although composed at first of urban intellectuals and upper-class Indians, the impact of Gandhi had given the Congress a mass base. The basic element in the construction of this mass movement was the four anna membership. These primary members, as the base of the Congress organization, elected one delegate to the Annual Congress Session for each 50,000 people in the province.[7] Although the four anna membership had been modified from time to time by the addition of such other requirements as the introduction of khadi wearing, non-membership in communal organizations, and the labor franchise of substituting the spinning of 2,000 rounds of yarn per month, the four anna membership remained the core of the Congress organization.[8] During the Gandhian era Congress membership is claimed to have reached four to five million, and many more became associated with the movement during particular civil disobedience campaigns.[9]

Following the civil disobedience campaign of 1930-1933, however, the Congress was exhausted, and membership dropped to about a half million. In an attempt to rehabilitate the mass base of the organization, Nehru in 1936 fought for association with the trade unions and peasant leagues, but the old guard, fearing that such association would strengthen the left wing in the Congress, established instead the Mass Contacts Committee as a means of expanding membership within the existing party framework.[10] The efforts of the Mass Contacts Committee combined with the effects of the election of the Congress Ministries in 1937 pushed

[7] Rao, *Development of the Congress Constitution*, pp. 36-37.

[8] *Ibid.*, p. 51.

[9] S. K. Patil, *The Indian National Congress: A Case for its Reorganisation* (Aundh: Aundh Publishing Trust, 1945), pp. 44-45.

[10] M. Brecher, *Nehru: A Political Biography* (London: Oxford University Press, 1959), pp. 219-220.

Congress membership close to the four and one-half million mark. The Congress had certainly broadened its base. But the results were not entirely satisfactory.

The Congress organization was simply not prepared to handle such a massive influx. Party officials complained that the Congress machinery was "proving every day its utter inadequacy" for such a large membership. Party elections were becoming more elaborate than governmental elections, yet they had to be run on a voluntary basis. Moreover, since the Congress had come to wield "some power and patronage" and since there was "no possible danger in associating and identifying one's self with the organisation," new groups were attempting to capture control. Even the Pradesh office workers were accused of becoming part of the machine to favor one group over another.[11] As a result, declared the *Report of the General Secretary for 1938 to 1939,* "there have been complaints by individuals and parties that those in power and in control of the office machinery refused many times to supply books to their personal or political opponents and that in some cases where books were too freely distributed, unreal and bogus persons were enlisted as members to add to the strength of a party or a faction. Cases also have been reported of instances where persons to whom books were given, enrolled members and collected subscriptions but did not remit the money and even failed to send up the names to the District Congress Committee."[12] Taking note of these abuses, the Congress at Tripuri in March 1939 authorized the A.I.C.C. to take all necessary constitutional steps toward halting them. The result was the establishment of provincial and district election tribunals which were given the power to rule on election disputes and challenges to the legitimacy of membership rolls.[13] Almost as soon as the Congress had tasted power, factionalism arose, and the development of machinery

[11] Indian National Congress, *Report of the General Secretary, 1937-1938* (Allahabad: A.I.C.C., 1938), pp. 37-39.
[12] *Report of the General Secretary, March 1938-Feb. 1939* (Allahabad: A.I.C.C., 1939) p. 38.
[13] Rao, *Development of the Congress Constitution*, p. 66.

for resolving organizational conflict had begun. It was an accurate prophecy of what would happen after independence when the Congress was in full control of the central government and most of the states.

After the members of the Working Committee had been released from jail in June 1945, the Congress attempted to set its house in order in preparation for the transfer of power. However, the party and its leadership found themselves overwhelmed by the rapid movement of events. Three years passed before the party machine could be overhauled and a new party constitution enacted. During this period three committees were appointed to study the problem of reconstructing the Congress for the post-independence era. In each case, time and events forced postponement and re-study. By the time the third constitution sub-committee was appointed at the Delhi meeting of the A.I.C.C. in November 1947 and instructed to report by January 1948, its members had to take into account the recommendations of the committee appointed by the Bombay A.I.C.C. in 1945 and the committee appointed as a result of the 1946 Meerut Session.[14]

Several major problems confronted the Congress in the process of reconstruction. The most important of these problems was the determining of qualifications for membership in general and for organizational elections in particular, and the role of the central party organization vis-à-vis the states.

While the four anna membership had served as the basis of Congress membership since 1920, many Congressmen saw in it the cause of numerous malpractices in the party. Yet, although the sub-committee unanimously agreed on the abolition of the four anna membership, there seemed to be no entirely satisfactory substitute. The most attractive alternative seemed to be some form of adult franchise based solely on subscription to the Congress creed, but the complete elim-

---

[14] *Congress Bulletin*, No. 1, Jan. 1947, p. 36; Indian National Congress, *Report of the General Secretaries, 1946-1948* (New Delhi: A.I.C.C., 1948), p. 40.

ination of fees would place severe financial stresses on the local Congress organizations for which membership fees had represented the sole source of income for day-to-day activities.[15] For this reason the Bombay sub-committee in 1945 had recommended that all Congress members elected to committees pay a fee of one rupee,[16] a recommendation which had been rejected by the Meerut sub-committee on the grounds that it would yield little revenue and have an adverse effect on organizational work.[17] Recognizing all these difficulties, the Delhi constitution sub-committee recommended a new two-tier membership structure which nevertheless maintained the membership fee. The A.I.C.C. office continued to prefer a free adult franchise to the potentially corrupting influence of any paid membership system.[18]

The next problem which the Delhi committee faced in 1947 was the problem of establishing criteria for membership. At first, the committee considered fixing a specific number of hours which members would be expected to devote to the party's constructive, parliamentary, or organizational work. This criterion was rejected as too difficult to administer. Finally, it was decided to prescribe three specific but somewhat loose requirements for membership. A Congressman was to be a habitual wearer of khadi for at least two years; he was to subscribe to the basic policies of the Congress; and he was not to be a member of any other political party. The last requirement was a crucial step in Congress development, for it meant that the Congress would no longer function as a loose umbrella organization in which different parties could operate openly. This provision, whose effect was to

[15] Unpublished Prasad Papers, "Report of the Delhi Constitution Sub-Committee of 1947."

[16] Unpublished Prasad Papers, "Report of the Bombay Constitution Sub-Committee of 1945."

[17] Unpublished Prasad Papers, "Report of the Meerut Constitution Sub-Committee of 1946."

[18] Unpublished Prasad Papers, "Report of the Delhi Constitution Sub-Committee of 1947."

transform the Congress from a movement into a political party, received strong opposition from the Congress socialists on the committee, but they were outvoted.[19]

A third problem faced by the committee was the need to develop a means of ensuring fair and impartial elections. The Congress had recruited five and one-half million four anna members prior to the 1945-1946 organizational elections. Despite the existence since 1939 of district and state election tribunals to avert and correct abuses, the party's electoral machinery broke down under the strain of internal conflict. At all levels of the party, groups developed for the purpose of gaining control of the organization. Intra-party rivalry was accentuated by the new feeling of exclusivity directed by Congressmen of longer standing against newer members who had not "sacrificed" for the cause.[20] Ideological differences also became a source of friction within the party.[21] As a result, complaints of irregularities flooded the Congress office in such quantities that the center felt the need to intervene more directly in state party affairs. "In these elections," J. B. Kripalani observed, "the A.I.C.C. office had confined its interference to the minimum and left maximum autonomy to the provinces." He warned that the A.I.C.C. could not remain indifferent to the "abuse" of autonomy evident in several provinces.[22]

Although the Delhi committee recommended continuing the system of district and provincial election tribunals and adding to them a central election tribunal to hear appeals, the A.I.C.C. office questioned the utility of the existing machinery and therefore opposed its expansion.[23] The A.I.C.C. office had received numerous complaints to the effect that district and provincial tribunals devoted insufficient time to complaints, functioned in a partisan manner, lacked enough

---

[19] *Ibid.*

[20] *Congress Bulletin*, No. 7, Oct. 15, 1946, pp. 12-13.

[21] *Report of the General Secretaries, 1946-1948*, p. 45.

[22] *Congress Bulletin*, No. 5, Aug. 3, 1946, pp. 12-13.

[23] Unpublished Prasad Papers, "Report of the Delhi Constitution Sub-Committee of 1947."

impartial arbitrators, and in many districts simply did not exist at all. Under such circumstances the appointment of a central tribunal would add complexity to an already too cumbersome machinery. Thus, the A.I.C.C. office recommended that the provincial executive retain the responsibility for hearing complaints.[24]

Finally, the Delhi committee considered a problem raised by the A.I.C.C. office in regard to its role in relation to subordinate committees. The issue was raised in a special note prepared by the A.I.C.C. office. The note itself presents an excellent summary of the state of the Congress organization and the problems it faced:

> It has been the tradition of the AICC office to give maximum autonomy to provinces. No complaint that is received from any province is inquired into and settled except after the fullest prior consultation with the PCC. Party politics in many provinces however oblige the office to intervene in provincial affairs more than it would like to. From our recent tours we get the definite impression that a great many Congressmen want more active interference in the affairs of the provinces and continued inspiration from the President, Congress Secretaries and the Working Committee. If it is desired that the Congress organization should function effectively and undertake a number of constructive and other activities it would be necessary for the Working Committee and its individual members to function more continuously and more effectively. What form this effective functioning should take is for the Committee to determine.[25]

It is clear that the impulse to central intervention in provincial affairs came not from the center but from the states themselves, a fact which was to give the Working Committee substantial authority over the Congress organization.

The draft of the Delhi constitution sub-committee proposals was presented to the Working Committee in late January

[24] *Ibid.*   [25] *Ibid.*

1948. Since Gandhi was not satisfied with the proposals, it was decided that the constitution sub-committee should discuss them with him. After a brief meeting it was agreed that Gandhi would prepare a note setting forth his views. On the afternoon of January 30, Congress General Secretary Jugal Kishore received the draft from Gandhi. A few hours later Gandhi was assassinated.[26] Although Gandhi's proposals for the Congress organization were not to the liking of many Congress leaders, there was a tendency after his death to view them as his last will and testament. They were not easy to set aside.

Gandhi's draft proposals were indeed radical in design. They called for the end of the Congress as a political organization and for its conversion into a Lok Sevak Sangh or social service organization.[27] But Gandhi's old lieutenants, believing that the Congress was the only unifying force in India, felt they could not accept such an approach in anything like its entirety. Instead, they decided to adapt selectively some of its features, which they added to the proposals already drawn up by the Congress constitution sub-committee. These proposals so modified were adopted by the A.I.C.C. at Bombay in April 1948 and ratified by the Jaipur Session.

The new constitution created a three-tier membership of primary, qualified, and effective members. The primary member was to be at least twenty-one years old. He was to pay no fee on joining, but he could take direct part in elections only at the lowest organizational level—that is, for the village Congress panchayat. All other organizational elections were to be indirect. In order to become a qualified member, it was necessary to have been a primary member for two consecutive years and to pay a fee of one rupee. Effective members were to be qualified members of at least one year's standing who had devoted time to Congress work. Once the primary members had elected members to the primary Congress panchayat, the members of the panchayat and all ef-

---

[26] *Report of the General Secretaries, 1946-1948*, p. 42.
[27] Rao, *Development of the Congress Constitution*, pp. 237-238.

fective members were to be entitled to elect delegates based on the proportion of one delegate for each 100,000 people in the area. Credentials committees established at district and state levels were to examine applications for effective and qualified membership. Tribunals were also established at state and district levels to decide election disputes.[28]

The complex membership pattern of the new constitution was an attempt to combine the idea of the Congress as a political organization with Gandhi's idea of the Congress as a Lok Sevak Sangh. As Deo observed:

> The new Congress is . . . a compromise. The goal of *Sarvodaya*, a cooperative commonwealth, is retained as well as the means, namely, constructive work, but day-to-day political and parliamentary activities also form part of the Congress programme, instead of being excluded as advocated by Gandhiji. This was quite necessary at the present critical juncture if chaos and collapse in the country were to be avoided. . . . If the new creed is the apex of the present Congress constitutional structure, the qualified and effective members constitute its solid base. . . . The qualifications laid down for an effective member in the new Congress Constitution are practically the same as those which are prescribed by Gandhiji for the worker of the proposed *Lok Sevak Sangh*. Except for the election of the Congress Panchayat for which qualified membership is sufficient, for all higher Congress committees or bodies, effective membership is essential.[29]

Thus, effective members were to be the great constructive workers of India. Yet Deo was later to admit that the scheme had failed. Congressmen were no longer interested in constructive activity, he sadly observed. They were interested only in the capture of power.[30]

---

[28] *Ibid.*, The Jaipur Constitution, p. 72.
[29] Shankerrao Deo, *The New Congress* (New Delhi: A.I.C.C., 1949), pp. 24-25.
[30] *Congress Bulletin*, No. 2, March-April 1950, p. 52.

The Working Committee

The Congress began enrolling members under the new constitution on May 1, 1949. Enrollment was to end on August 31, but because of appeals from local Congress committees the deadline was extended several times. When enrollment was finally concluded in December, the results were staggering. The party had enrolled 30 million primary members and several hundred thousand qualified and effective members. In the enthusiasm of the moment most qualified members were expected to become effective members. However, K. V. Rao told the Working Committee: "From all reports, it is also seen that this enlistment is being done on a competitive scale by different and differing Congress groups in a number of provinces." The four anna membership had been abolished because of charges that rich people had used it as a means to support undesirable candidates. Yet, with the growth of strong personal differences among Congressmen and in an attempt to capture control of the Congress machinery for the forthcoming general elections, the new provisions had been abused on a massive scale. In fact, in one village Congress, enrollment exceeded the total population of the village. K. V. Rao doubted that even 10 per cent of the qualified and effective members really met the qualifications. The credentials committees were the only constitutional check against such bogus enrollment. "But," observed Rao, "experience has shown that these committees have become the instruments of the groups in power in certain provinces. The same is the case with certain Election Tribunals." The Congress electoral machinery had broken down again. The final official primary membership enrollment for the year was recorded as 17 million.[31] The extent of the breakdown was described by Congress President Pattabhi Sitaramayya in this way:

> It is saddening to reflect how in certain parts of the country pride and prejudice or passion and perversity have been let loose, working the general election of Pan-

[31] Unpublished Prasad Papers, K. V. Rao, "A Note on the Congress Organisation," Jan. 1950. Also see Table XIV-1, p. 343.

chayats, the *pars assini* of the new constitution. It is really impossible for any outsider, however eminent, impartial, and farseeing, to unravel the tangled web of factious fights and discords and distinguish the genuine from the fictitious amongst membership rolls, applicants to elective seats, proposers and seconders of nominators, where the originals have been replaced by counterfeits and then condemned as such. It requires weeks of labor and tons of energy to tell the genuine from the spurious and establish the triumph of truth and morality. Whole districts are sometimes involved in such palpable frauds.[32]

The role of factionalism in the competitive enrollment of members and the steps available to the Working Committee for correcting them are well illustrated by the case of Andhra, where Dr. Pattabhi Sitaramayya, T. Prakasam, and N. G. Ranga were in competition for control of the state Congress. Prakasam, who had been ousted from the chief ministership of Madras, attempted to recoup his losses by challenging his Andhra rivals in the party organization. In the organizational elections of June 1948, he joined forces with Ranga to defeat N. Sanjiva Reddy, the candidate supported by Sitaramayya, for the post of President of the Andhra P.C.C. The real showdown for Prakasam, however, occurred on the eve of the organizational elections of 1950. Whoever won control of the organization at this time would control the distribution of tickets. Therefore, the two groups competed in attempting to enroll as many people into the Congress as possible.

The only kind way to describe the enrollment process which resulted in the enlistment of 900,000 new members[33] would be to say that the workers were somewhat carried away by the urgency of the situation. In the Ranga strongholds of Guntur and West Godavari districts, 300,000 and 150,000 qualified members, or approximately 10 per cent of the population,

[32] *The Hindu* (Madras), June 25, 1950.
[33] *Report of the General Secretaries, 1949-1950*, p. 95.

were enrolled,[34] and in certain villages enrollment exceeded the adult population or, in a few cases, the total population of the village.[35] As a result, election proceedings were suspended in several areas pending an A.I.C.C. investigation.[36] Some Congressmen, dismayed by such proceedings, appealed to the state court system to settle complaints, but the Working Committee moved quickly to condemn this procedure.

Stunned by the situation in Andhra, the A.I.C.C. sent S. K. Patil to conduct a study. He was given power to take charge of the Andhra P.C.C. office—funds, records, and all—and he was to retain control until further action could be taken.[37] Patil, reporting back on September 3, 1950, informed the Working Committee that agreement between the two groups was almost impossible. He felt that elections could not be held simply by sending in outsiders to supervise. In fact, nothing could be done impartially, because all the returning officers belonged to one or another of the conflicting groups. Therefore, he felt that the issue could be settled only if the group leaders sat down together and agreed to conduct a fair election. Patil was given the authority to retain control over the P.C.C. until such elections could be held.[38] In the meantime, the Andhra P.C.C. funds were sent to the A.I.C.C. for safekeeping.

The Andhra example demonstrates the Working Committee's dilemma. While it could suspend the existing Congress machinery, it still had to work with the Congressmen who had abused it. Whatever machinery it devised, it had to rely on the integrity of party members to operate it responsibly. Nevertheless, the search for reliable machinery went on.

Because it was impossible to subject to scrutiny the vast enrollment of effective members under the Jaipur Congress constitution, the Working Committee decided to disenfranchise them by having delegates to higher committees elected

[34] Unpublished Prasad Papers, K. V. Rao, "A Note on the Congress Organisation," Jan. 1950.

[35] *Report of the General Secretaries, 1949-1950*, p. 78.

[36] *Ibid.*, p. 80.

[37] *Ibid.*, pp. 80-81.

[38] *Congress Bulletin*, No. 6, Sept.-Oct. 1950, p. 212.

solely by the primary Congress Panchayats.[39] This decision, which amounted to a censure of the party organization, was opposed at the Delhi A.I.C.C. in February 1950 by Purshottamdas Tandon and his supporters, who were on the verge of capturing control of the party organization in the states based on the new membership enrollment.[40] The debate in the A.I.C.C. was so vigorously prosecuted that, when the leadership invoked a closure vote, it passed by only ten votes. (The A.I.C.C. had always been much less willing to accept Working Committee recommendations on organizational issues than on policy issues.) In the end, the Working Committee agreed to suspend rather than to abolish the constitutional electoral provision in question. The matter was to be taken up at the next session of the Congress, and, indeed, at the Nasik Session the Congress authorized the A.I.C.C. to make the necessary changes in the party constitution.[41] The Working Committee was also requested to review the matter with specific reference to the reintroduction of paid membership, the appointment of a central election tribunal and credentials committee, the vesting of the Working Committee with adequate emergency powers, and the establishment of machinery for selecting candidates for the legislature. In short, the Congress organizational machinery was in for another overhaul.

Reform hinged on the membership question. The Working Committee recommended combining the two-tier membership scheme which had been proposed by the Delhi Congress constitution sub-committee with the one rupee membership fee proposed by the Bombay Congress constitution sub-committee, and once again there arose a major dispute over the paid membership idea. The Working Committee itself was reported to have voted to adopt the one rupee fee by the minimal margin of one vote.[42] Nehru had insisted on the one rupee fee, but many of the state P.C.C. leaders preferred a

[39] *Congress Bulletin*, No. 2, March-April 1950, p. 42.
[40] *Ibid.*, pp. 50-51.
[41] *Ibid.*, p. 53.
[42] *The Hindu* (Madras), Jan. 30, 1951.

return to the old four anna membership. Finally, a compromise resolution calling for an eight anna fee was offered. Each of the three proposals was put to a vote. The four anna fee lost by a vote of 60 to 117. The eight anna fee lost by a narrow margin of 78 to 91 on the first vote and by 87 to 106 on the second. Thus, with some difficulty, the Working Committee proposal for a one rupee membership fee was accepted. By contrast, the A.I.C.C. approved without much debate the Working Committee's recommendation for the establishment of a central credentials committee and a central election tribunal.[43] Finally, the A.I.C.C. amended the Congress constitution with an emergency provision providing that, "to meet an emergent situation, the Working Committee shall have the power to take such action in the interest of the Congress as it may deem fit: provided, however, that if any action is taken, which is beyond the powers of the Working Committee as defined in this Constitution, it shall be submitted as early as possible to the A.I.C.C. for ratification."[44] This clause gave the Working Committee the most sweeping authority it had enjoyed in its thirty-year history.

Yet, in spite of all this activity and discussion, the Congress had not really set its house in order by the First General Elections. Since the organization had not been prepared for independence and since when independence came it came so quickly, organizational reform became intermixed with the problems of new goal orientation, party-government relations, ideological struggles, and the loss of anti-British cementing force. At the same time, the leadership was too deeply involved in running the affairs of the country to plan out the future of the Congress, which was forced to limp along on crutches improvised to suit rapidly changing circumstances. During the First General Elections, however, the importance of party organization was impressed very forcefully upon the Congress.

[43] *Ibid.*
[44] Rao, *Development of the Congress Constitution*, 1950 Congress Constitution, Art. XVII(i), p. 115.

As Chief Executive Of The Party

Since the First General Elections, the Working Committee has used an amazing ingenuity in attempting to cope with organizational problems caused by factional struggles for control of the party machine. In this process, the committee has continued to focus on three major areas. First, it has manipulated the requirements for membership. Second, it has attempted to establish institutionalized checks to guard against fraudulent membership enrollment. Third, it has tried to evolve procedural safeguards for fair organizational elections. Throughout, the Working Committee has tried with some success to encourage the states to settle disputes internally while simultaneously reassuring minority factions that it would hear appeals in all cases of outright abuse and that it would continue to play a mediating role in order to maintain party unity and prevent groups from annihilating one another. In creating new machinery, however, the Working Committee has frequently been frustrated by the dilemma of devising reliable procedural safeguards without making the machinery so cumbersome as to become inoperable.

Following the 1952 General Elections, the Congress restored the four anna membership and has maintained it ever since. The Congress today has two types of members—primary and active. Most changes over the past decade and a half have dealt with the voting rights of primary members and the requirements for active membership. The voting rights of primary members have fluctuated according to whether direct or indirect elections have been prescribed. In the direct system of elections the primary members elect representatives to all higher committees. In the indirect system they elect only the lowest committee. Both approaches have been used to discourage competitive enrollment of bogus primary members. Yet both have also been more or less susceptible to corruption. The most recent system, adopted at Bombay in 1964, has represented a return to the indirect elections of the 1949 pattern according to which primary members may vote only in the election of the Block Congress Committees. All P.C.C. delegates are then elected by the active members in the block at the usual rate of one delegate per 100,000 population. Under such circumstances, it seems highly likely that there will be a sharp increase in the number of active members.[45]

Over the years the requirements for active membership have fluctuated a great deal. Sometimes the requirement has called for little more than the payment of a one rupee membership fee. Other times alternatives have been made possible, so that active membership might be obtained by collecting ten rupees for the party or by enrolling a certain number of primary members. Most curious of all, under the influence of U. N. Dhebar, the famous Gandhian yarn franchise calling for twenty-five gundhas of self-spun yarn of at least sixteen counts was reactivated in an attempt to attract the type of membership considered desirable.[46] But none of these membership requirements has had the desired effect. As one can see by examining the primary and active membership figures, membership tends to increase sharply when an organizational election is in the offing, and especially when the organizational election precedes a general election.[47] Since the Congress organization plays an important role in candidate selection, competing groups seek to dominate the party organization and control the distribution of tickets. Even the Congress practice of broadening its base by co-opting elements, such as scheduled tribes and castes, women, youth, and labor, has been used by majority groups to strengthen their position in party elections. Competitive enrollment has survived all attempts at reform.

The Working Committee has not been much more successful in establishing foolproof procedures for verifying party electoral rolls. Deadlines have been fixed for the close of membership enrollment and for the preparation of final membership lists. Various devices, including the three-level center, state, and district credentials committees as well as provincial

---

[45] P. R. Chakraverti, "Amended Congress Constitution—The Malady Persists," *A.I.C.C. Economic Review*, xvi (July 10, 1964), 9.
[46] Chakraverti, "Malady—Organisational or Attitudinal," pp. 13-19.
[47] See Ch. XIV, Table XIV-1.

returning officers and scrutiny committees, have been established to ensure against fraudulent enrollment. In each case the effort has failed. The credentials committees and scrutiny committees have become dominated by various conflicting groups because the Working Committee has had difficulty in finding enough impartial arbitrators or brokers to perform the function at the state level. As both Brass and Weiner have pointed out,[48] this function is critical for the maintenance of the party structure, but the number of Congressmen available for the function is actually declining.[49] One Congressman who has worked in the Congress office for some time has suggested that the arbitration function should be performed by Congressmen selected by the Working Committee from outside the state in which they must operate. "Congressmen must be made to feel," he warned, "that the scrutiny, verification and all forms of enquiries into complaints are left with persons . . . known for their integrity and selflessness and also strong enough to withstand all advances from the vested interests. This will only be possible when the Returning Officers are specially elected by the Congress Working Committee and deputed to function in the Pradeshes other than their own."[50] Because of such difficulties and in order to simplify the cumbersome machinery, the Working Committee finally abolished all these separate and specialized agencies. Therefore, since 1957, under the urging of Congress President U. N. Dhebar, the scrutiny function has been centered in the hands of the executive committees of the P.C.C. and the D.C.C. At the same time, the selection process for P.C.C. and D.C.C. executives was changed from nomination by the President to election by the committee members. Yet even this reform has had little effect. A majority group can elect an entire executive committee as easily as its president

[48] M. Weiner, "Traditional Role Performance and the Development of Modern Political Parties: The Indian Case," *Journal of Politics*, XXVI (Nov. 1964), 839-840; Brass, *Factional Politics in an Indian State*, p. 239.

[49] *Ibid.*

[50] Chakraverti, "Malady—Organisational or Attitudinal," p. 18.

alone.[51] In a factional fight between the Gupta and Sampurnanand groups in Uttar Pradesh, for example, disputes over membership forced the postponement of organizational elections for a year until A.I.C.C. observers dispatched to scrutinize the electoral rolls had weeded out a bogus enrollment of some 200,000 members.[52]

Finally, the Working Committee has attempted to create a workable election machinery and to ensure orderly and fair organizational elections. The election machinery evolved through the same phases as the attempts to scrutinize membership. At first, the Working Committee created election tribunals at the center, state, and district levels to decide disputes relating to the election of office bearers. When this machinery proved to be too cumbersome, provision was made for a Pradesh Returning Officer to be elected by at least three-fourths of the P.C.C. members. Anyone performing this function was not to be eligible to run for any other office during his term of service or for six months after leaving the post. It was assumed that anyone elected by a three-fourths majority would be considered to enjoy widespread support. However, this system, too, was subject to abuse owing to the use of influence and patronage, for "the prospects of finding a place in the Ministry, or any Commission appointed by the State Government, or any other high office which mostly rested on the recommendation of the State Government, or in the minimum a seat in the Legislature makes the person concerned amenable to the dictates of the leader of the Congress Legislative Party, and it becomes well-nigh impossible to stand against those powerful influences. Persons with exceptional record of integrity and selflessness have withstood it, but it has been so rare."[53] Thus, though major abuses have been brought under some control, purely procedural changes have not put an end to the problems of party factionalism. As one observer noted, it was "abundantly

[51] *Ibid.*, p. 17.

[52] *Times of India* (Bombay), Oct. 2, 1960.

[53] Chakraverti, "Malady—Organisational or Attitudinal," p. 17.

clear" that the organizational machinery functioned satisfactorily in the states which were not riven by factional rivalry. But where such disputes existed, dissident groups had "reasonable" cause for complaint.[54]

Since the time of Dhebar's presidency, the Congress has attempted to simplify its organizational machinery and to strengthen the party structure by giving the major responsibility for scrutiny of enrollment and supervision of organizational elections to the P.C.C. President and the P.C.C. executive. Over the years it has become evident, however, that even the most elaborate and cumbersome machinery of credentials committees, scrutiny committees, and election tribunals is no protection against abuses arising from factionalism. Yet neither is centralization the answer, for, since the Working Committee is theoretically responsible for supervising 20 Pradesh Congress Committees, 437 District Congress Committees, and over 5,000 Block Committees, "it becomes impossible to do justice"[55] without some decentralization.

The Working Committee has labored continually over the last two decades to establish an effective system for reconciliation of group conflict. One manifestation has been the repeated revision of the party's constitution. But document tinkering notwithstanding, the experience of the past twenty years suggests that any reasonable procedural machinery works well in states where factionalism is at a minimum. In faction-torn states, conversely, no machinery has yet been created which is immune to abuse by the dominant group as a means of suppressing its opponents. Thus, the absence of effective institutionalized forms of conflict resolution at the state level and below has necessitated frequent intervention and constant guidance on the part of the Working Committee. The major function of Working Committee arbitration and mediation has been to prevent minority groups within state Congress parties from suffering annihilation or from feeling so thoroughly isolated that they break away from the party,

[54] *Ibid.*   [55] *Ibid.*

thereby reducing party support. So long as minority factions felt they could turn to the Working Committee for protection, they were willing to continue to function within the Congress in the hope that one day they might in turn constitute the majority group. In this way, the Working Committee came to play a key role in maintaining party solidarity and Congress dominance, though it may also have prevented the states from learning the consequences of internecine rivalry while the Congress dominance overall was still sufficiently strong to permit mistakes to be rectified without too much difficulty.

In any case, the Working Committee's arbitration and mediation role could be effectively performed only so long as the central leadership itself remained united. Let the central leadership once become so divided that it is unable to intervene decisively and one of the most important stabilizing forces in the Congress will have been removed. Since it is just such a pattern which has characterized the years of divergence, party solidarity and dominance have been seriously undermined.

THE PARLIAMENTARY BOARD:
THE COORDINATION OF PARTY-
GOVERNMENT RELATIONS
IN THE STATES

The Parliamentary Board, a sub-committee of the Working Committee, plays much the same role in coordinating party-government relations at the state level that the Working Committee plays in maintaining over-all organizational unity. Although party-government coordination was successfully maintained at the center for over fifteen years, stability was by no means universally achieved at the state level. Yet the very stability of the relationship at the center permitted the Prime Minister and the central leadership to influence the resolution of conflicts in the states. This conflict between the parliamentary and organizational wings, which became the normal pattern of operation in the Congress at the state level, has been attributed to three causes: traditional, procedural, and factional. Although all three played a role, there is little doubt that party factionalism has been the supreme cause of conflict. It is for this reason that an external source of mediation is so essential to the health of the Congress at the state level. Conflict resolution by means of the Parliamentary Board is one of the most important functions of the Working Committee.

The origins of the Parliamentary Board go back to the 1937-1939 Congress ministries. In March 1937 the Congress Working Committee appointed a parliamentary sub-committee to supervise and coordinate the work of the Congress ministries. The Board in this early phase consisted of three members of the Congress inner circle—Sardar Vallabhbhai Patel, Rajendra Prasad, and Maulana Azad—and it ceased to function when the Congress ministries resigned. Following the 1945-1946 elections the Board was revived. It consisted once again of Patel, Prasad, and Azad, but, because of their preoccupation with all-India events, it was shortly expanded to include the Congress President and one of the General Secretaries of the party. In 1948 the size of the Parliamentary Board was expanded to six, and it became a permanent and official part of the Congress machine under the Jaipur constitution of 1948. The constitution provided that "the Working Committee shall set up a Parliamentary Board consisting of the President and five other members with the Congress President as its Chairman for the purpose of regulating and co-ordinating parliamentary activities of the Congress legislative parties and shall frame rules in that behalf."[1] For the next decade the dominant members of the Parliamentary Board were the major figures in the central Cabinet, important Chief Ministers, and the Congress Presidents. They were, specifically, Nehru, Maulana Azad, Pant, Morarji Desai, Jagjivan Ram, Kamaraj, Mrs. Gandhi, U. N. Dhebar, Lal Bahadur Shastri, S. K. Patil, and Y. B. Chavan. In 1963, as part of the reforms envisioned by the Kamaraj Plan, the Parliamentary Board was expanded from six to eight members.

In the process of becoming the supreme arbiter of the Congress in the post-independence period, the Parliamentary Board passed through several stages of development. The first stage, from 1946 to 1949, was a period of limited action during which the Board was unable to provide much leadership because of the pressure of all-India events. The second phase, from 1949 to 1952, was an activist phase during which the Board developed many of its procedures. It also learned the extent and limits of its authority. The third phase, following the 1952 general elections and extending well into the period of divergence, was one of orderly

[1] M. V. R. Rao, *The Development of the Congress Constitution* (New Delhi: A.I.C.C., 1958), p. 87.

functioning according to established procedures for the arbitration and mediation of intra-party disputes. Throughout, however, the Parliamentary Board's role has been complicated by the existence of traditional attitudes and modes of behavior which have increased the potentiality for conflict between the parliamentary and organizational wings and have created an environment indifferent, if not always hostile, to conciliation.

Factionalism might not have come to manifest itself as conflict between the parliamentary and organizational wings of the Congress if the party had not been traditionally divided regarding strategy and tactics between those who emphasized parliamentary means and those who emphasized non-parliamentary means. Throughout the Gandhian era Congressmen differed over the meaning of non-cooperation. During the great civil disobedience campaigns of the twenties and thirties, differences were submerged, but between campaigns open conflict developed. According to the Gandhians, non-cooperation included boycotting legislatures, while the suspension of civil disobedience meant concentration on the Gandhian constructive work program in the villages. But village work held little appeal for the moderates, who insisted on working in the parliamentary field during lulls in civil disobedience. Although Gandhi disapproved of participation in the legislatures, he recognized that "we have in the Congress a body of men who believe in council entry and who will do nothing else if they cannot have their programme. Their ambition must be satisfied."[2]

Once Gandhi had conceded a role to the Swarajists, that is, those who insisted on working in the parliamentary sphere, other leading Congressmen demanded that the Swarajists function, not as a separate party affiliated with the Congress as in the twenties, but as a part of the Congress organization and therefore guided by its policies and discipline.[3] Thus, it

[2] C. Shukla (ed.), *Reminiscences of Gandhiji* (Bombay: Vora & Co., 1951), pp. 206-207.
[3] B. Pattabhi Sitaramayya, *The History of the Indian National Congress* (Bombay: Padma Publications, 1946-1947), I, 571.

was decided to exercise tight control over those who constituted the parliamentary wing of the movement. The Congress, like many mass parties of the twentieth century, considered the Congressmen in Parliament as simply an arm of the movement subordinate to the dictates of the mother organization.[4] This attitude was to have repercussions after independence.

After the election of the Congress ministries in the states in 1937, the Congress needed a means of supervising and coordinating the work of the new parliamentary wing of the party, and the Parliamentary Board was created. Since most of the important Congress leaders did not participate in the new ministries at this time, preferring to devote full time to the movement, the supervisory task was assigned to just three of the most important members of the Working Committee: Sardar Patel, Rajendra Prasad, and Maulana Azad. At first, the Board handled problems as a whole. However, as the burdens of supervision increased, it was decided to place each man in charge of a specific group of provinces.

During this pre-independence phase the Parliamentary Board attempted to ensure that the ministries conformed to policies consistent with the goals of the movement. Although there was no interference in the day-to-day work of the ministries, the Board was able to bring about the appointment of two Chief Ministers—one in Central Provinces, the other in Bombay[5]—and to influence the composition of the ministries. The Board was also responsible for issuing the final order for the cabinets to resign in 1939. Because of such actions several British writers of the time charged the Parliamentary Board and the Working Committee with dictatorship and totalitarianism.[6] More recent observers have noted that the

[4] M. Duverger, *Political Parties: Their Organization and Activities in the Modern State* (London: Methuen & Co., 1955), p. xxxvi.

[5] N. D. Parikh, *Sardar Vallabhbhai Patel* (Ahmedabad: Navajivan Publishing House, 1953), pp. 230-273.

[6] Sir Reginald Coupland, *The Indian Problem: Report on the Constitutional Problem in India* (London: Oxford University Press, 1944), Part II, Ch. 12; Sir G. E. Schuster and G. Wint, *India and Democracy* (Toronto: Macmillan Co., 1941), p. 170.

Congress as an independence movement could not be expected to behave like the Tory Party in Great Britain.[7]

With independence it was clear that the central leadership of the Congress had no intention of following the 1937-1939 pattern of party-government relations. The major leaders of the Congress became the leaders of the new government and refused to consider themselves bound by the dictates of the party's mass organization. However, since rank-and-file behavior did not undergo a similar transformation, both ministries and government administration suffered a barrage of attacks from the organization. It was clear that the development of a satisfactory relationship between party and government would require time and a change in behavior patterns for the rank-and-file Congressman.

The chief function of the Congress in pre-independence days had been to agitate against authority. The psychology instilled by this role could not be reversed overnight. But the need for such a change could have been anticipated, for as early as 1937 the party had been advised that "our general attitude to these [Congress] ministries cannot be agitational in the old sense of the word; we cannot agitate against ourselves." Instead, party members were encouraged to present criticism in the spirit of friendly cooperation.[8] Later, on the eve of independence, the rank and file were warned that ministries might occasionally have to take action for reasons which could not be made public immediately. Therefore, party members were told to respond, not with premature and open criticism, but by approaching the ministers through the party organization. Persistent problems on any issue were to be referred to the Working Committee.[9]

But the plea for judicious conduct was ignored. The new governments were openly criticized by the organization. At all levels of administration party members attempted to in-

[7] W. H. Morris-Jones, *Parliament in India* (Philadelphia: University of Pennsylvania Press, 1957), p. 67.

[8] *Congress Bulletin*, No. 7, Dec. 1937, p. 28.

[9] Circular 10a, *Congress Bulletin*, No. 3, March 1947, pp. 8-9.

terfere with and influence decisions, ordering civil servants about as if they were party servants. The A.I.C.C. office was flooded with complaints about Congressmen meddling in state administrative affairs. During this period Congressmen were charged with such irregularities as giving "instructions to the Police and other officers in regard to . . . incidents necessitating police investigation or regarding action to be taken in view of *apprehended* incidents. . . . In some cases Congressmen have taken advantage of their position and have gone to the length of interesting themselves in behalf of parties to disputes and helping them by suggesting the arrest or release of persons, and have not hesitated even to write to Magistrates about cases pending before them." Congressmen were also charged with corruption which took the form of "taking up the cases of private parties for securing for them permits for import and export of various kinds of controlled goods, securing licenses and supplies of various kinds of goods and also obtaining licenses for running public motor transport and in so many other ways helping individuals to secure benefit from the Government. Sometimes Congressmen are themselves partners with others in such business deals."[10]

In West Bengal and Bihar, bribery and corruption were so freely talked about that it was said "not only by the general public but even by Congressmen that Congress Committees have become places for issuing or insuring permits and licenses for control of commodities, contracts, supplies, and motor routes to Congressmen and their relatives." According to the Congress General Secretary Shankarrao Deo, Congressmen justified the sale of privileges as a way of helping those who had suffered in the fight for independence. Many could see nothing objectionable in such behavior. In fact, both Congressmen and administrators were beginning to view it as the norm. Some administrators, as a result, had come to issue permits and licenses only to those who had received

[10] Unpublished Prasad Papers, Circular to all Presidents of the PCCs, dated Aug. 6, 1948, marked "not for publication."

certification from the president of the local Congress committee.[11]

Congress President Rajendra Prasad responded first by rebuking Congressmen for such irregular, illegal, and corrupt behavior.[12] He then presented to the Working Committee a note which became the basis of the Standards of Public Conduct resolution passed by the Jaipur Session of the Congress in December 1948. Before the resolution became Congress policy, however, the latent friction between the organizational and parliamentary wings came out into the open.

As originally drawn up, the Standards of Public Conduct resolution was clearly aimed at the organization.[13] But, when the time came for it to be ratified by the A.I.C.C., there was an attempt to turn it into a condemnation of the government. Mahesh Dutta Misra, one of the delegates, introduced an amendment exhorting "all Congressmen, members of the central and provincial legislatures, and more specially members of the cabinets" to "set an example and maintain a high standard of conduct." The amendment was clearly an expression of hostility toward the parliamentary wing, and Deo, who had moved the resolution on behalf of the Working Committee, declared it unacceptable. Nevertheless, the amendment was approved by a vote of 107 to 52.[14]

During these proceedings Nehru and Patel were absent. The next day Nehru told his Congress colleagues, "I was shocked when I learnt about the resolution last evening." He felt it was a "retaliatory resolution" reflecting on the Cabinet and amounting to a vote of censure against his government. He then threatened to resign if it were not withdrawn. At this point a special meeting of the A.I.C.C. was convened, and upon the demands of Nehru and Patel the committee voted 116 to 75 to reconsider the issue. A substi-

[11] Unpublished Prasad Papers, Shankarrao Deo, Madras Enquiry Report, 1949.

[12] Unpublished Prasad Papers, Circular to Presidents of the PCCs, Aug. 6, 1948.

[13] *Congress Bulletin*, No. 1, Jan. 1949, pp. 28-31.

[14] *Hindustan Times* (New Delhi), Dec. 19, 1948.

tute amendment was approved. Specific mention of "the members of the legislature and specially ministers" had been deleted, so that the new amendment read simply that "all Congressmen must set an example . . . and maintain a high standard of conduct."[15] The incident over the resolution on Standards of Public Conduct demonstrates the depth of anti-ministerial feeling among organizational Congressmen. It also provides one more example of the supremacy of the parliamentary wing of the Congress. Nehru, insisting that the resolution as originally approved by the A.I.C.C. was tantamount to a vote of no-confidence in his government, forced the A.I.C.C. to recant.

Although the central leadership refused to tolerate interference in day-to-day administration and most of the more extreme abuses were eventually eliminated, the basic issue remained. The amorphous relation between the organizational and the parliamentary wings continued to generate friction and controversy. Although many had thought that Nehru's defeat of Tandon would set the conflict to rest, the cure held good only at the central level. Ever since, conflict between the organizational and parliamentary wings has been endemic to Congress politics at the state level, and frequently it has been fatal. Consequently, it has given rise periodically to a debate now long familiar at higher Congress levels regarding the organizational and theoretical implications of such persistent antagonism. The most intensive examination of the problem, however, probably took place at the Poona Session of the A.I.C.C. in 1960.

A special note on the reorganization of the Congress had been prepared for the Poona A.I.C.C. by K. Hanumanthaiya, former Chief Minister of Mysore. Hanumanthaiya analyzed the Congress malady as a kind of schizophrenia. Although the Congress, once a movement, had evolved into a political party, he argued, its constitution had failed to reflect the change, and the idea that the organization was greater than the government tended to persist among the rank and

---

[15] *Hindustan Times* (New Delhi), Dec. 20, 1948.

file. Although India had adopted the constitutional conventions and practices of the United States and the United Kingdom, it had failed to adjust the party system in the same way. Dual leadership had led to political instability with the result that "the history of the Congress in the last decade is strewn with wreckages of ministries."[16] The source and development of this schizoid Congress Hanumanthaiya traced as follows:

Before the attainment of freedom, the parliamentary wing existed in the Congress. But it existed to play a minor role of making use of legislatures to carry on the fight for freedom in the enemy's camp. The parliamentary wing was so subordinate that many of the top leaders of the Congress remained out of it. The organisational leader was the undoubted and undisputed head of the Congress. The President of the Congress was even called "Rashtrapathi." After the attainment of freedom and assumption of office by the Congress, the top personnel from and the power and prestige of the organisational wing flowed inevitably to the parliamentary wing. The character of the Congress was changing from that of a movement into that of a political party. The conflict between the Prime Minister and the President became evident. In the States, the conflict between the Chief Ministers and the Presidents of the PCCs became widespread and intense. In the centre and in some States the dominating personalities of the leaders of the parliamentary wing so asserted [sic] as to make the organisational head adopt a policy of cooperation and smooth working. But this has been a personal remedy and not a constitutional remedy. What, in fact, has happened in some places and for the time being has now to be incorporated in the constitution of the Congress.[17]

Therefore, Hanumanthaiya proposed, as he had several

[16] K. Hanumanthaiya, *Report on the Congress Constitution* (New Delhi: A.I.C.C., 1960), p. 26.
[17] *Ibid.*, pp. 27-28.

years before, that the Congress abolish dual leadership of party and government by merging the two in the person of the leader of the parliamentary wing.

Hanumanthaiya's analysis and conclusion were corroborated by Humayun Kabir, Minister of Scientific Research and Cultural Affairs. In a parliamentary democracy, Kabir argued, the center of political gravity swings from the party organization to the Parliament just as public attention swings from organization to policy implementation. Yet the continued existence within the Congress of parallel party and government organizations was not only inconsistent with external conditions but conducive to the promotion of a kind of rivalry, which was prevented at the center only by the overlapping membership of the Cabinet and the Working Committee and by the pre-eminence of the Prime Minister. Kabir felt that this pattern should become the all-India pattern, for

> since we have accepted the parliamentary form of democracy and introduced the free and secret vote, it is very unlikely that members of the legislature in the Centre or the States will agree to a permanently subordinate position. They will be elected by thousands, if not lakhs [hundreds of thousands] of votes in secret ballot and will thus claim to be truer representatives of the people than members of any party executive. The logic of the situation therefore seems to indicate that the parliamentary wing will increase in strength and the party organisation will serve as an instrument for helping the parliamentary wing by bringing its message to the masses of the people. That this is already taking place is seen from the anxiety of party members to find a place in the legislature and if possible the cabinets in the centre and the States.[18]

J. Rameshwar Rao, introducing a report prepared by a committee of the Congress Party in Parliament, of which

[18] *Hindustan Times* (New Delhi), May 29, 1960.

he was a member, also warned that the relationship issue had to be settled. Organizational work was losing its charm. For reasons of economics as well as prestige there was a rush toward the doors of the legislatures, he declared, and even P.C.C. Presidents had been relegated to a status inferior to that of a Deputy Minister. But, if Rao's diagnosis tended to resemble Kabir's and Hanumanthaiya's, his solution was quite different:

> If it is felt that the organisation in existing form or in a modified one is more important than the Legislative Party, let all efforts be made to enhance the prestige of the organisation and its office bearers. . . . If ministerial interference in organisational affairs at different levels is to continue, there appears to be little need for a separate organisation. The Legislative Party could as well manage the affairs of the organisation and the office of Chief Minister and the P.C.C. Chief could be merged into one.[19]

The representatives of the organizational wing also had an opportunity to speak out on the occasion of the Poona A.I.C.C. Confirming the observations of Hanumanthaiya and Kabir, they deplored the fact that the Congress organization had been reduced to the task of organizing and winning elections and demanded a stronger role for the party. "In my view," said one Congressman, "the organisational wing . . . should be supreme, the Congress President should be supreme and in the states the P.C.C. President should be supreme."[20]

Taken as a whole, the debate at the Poona A.I.C.C. revealed that the Congress was divided on Hanumanthaiya's proposal to abolish dual leadership of party and government. Nehru opposed any merging of party and government offices, arguing that talk of two wings in the Congress was "meaningless." On the other hand, Sanjiva Reddy, the Con-

[19] *Report of the Committee of the Congress Party in Parliament*, pp. 2-3.
[20] *Hindustan Times* (New Delhi), June 5, 1960.

gress President at the time, told the A.I.C.C. that he personally would prefer to see the two wings of organization and government merged because of the confusion inherent in dual leadership. Dhebar, expressing the consensus of the Working Committee as a body, admitted that "a measure of confusion" and "misunderstandings" had arisen as a result of dual leadership. "But," he said, "this does not call for the abolition of the system itself but for taking remedial measures to remove the confusion."[21] Dhebar also pointed out that the organizational wing was needed as a separate entity for the purpose of keeping contact with the masses. It could act as a link between the people and the leaders of the government.

After all these reports and speeches representing the whole spectrum of opinion on party-government relations, the outcome of the Poona Session was no more than a reassertion of a position which had been maintained by the leadership ever since independence. According to this position, both organizational and parliamentary wings had separate functions to perform and should be permitted to perform these functions without outside interference. It was the duty of the Congress, therefore, to evolve coordinating procedures by which the organizational and parliamentary wings might work in harmony.

The Parliamentary Board was to provide this guidance by developing a coordinating process. It was also to arbitrate and mediate disputes as they arose. Yet the traditional differences between the parliamentary and organizational wings were to be intensified and, in fact, converted into something altogether new by the development of party factionalism. As a result, the Board found itself, in state after state, mediating between opposing factions—one in power in the ministry, the other poised in the organization as a means of seizing the ministry—rather than coordinating, as expected, two separate but equal Congress functions.

[21] *Ibid.*

Parliamentary Board

The attempt to deal with the problem of coordinating the organizational and parliamentary wings of the Congress in the states began in 1946 with the revival of the Parliamentary Board immediately following the creation of the Congress ministries in the states. As in the 1937-1939 period, the Board consisted of Patel, Prasad, and Azad; but, as was not the case in the earlier period, the triumvirate was unable to exercise detailed supervision. All three men eventually joined the new Cabinet, all were deeply involved in the negotiations for the transfer of power, and Prasad in particular was in poor health. To make it possible for the Board to carry out its functions, it was enlarged almost immediately by the inclusion of the Congress President and one of the General Secretaries. With the adoption of the Jaipur constitution in December 1948, the Board became a permanent part of the Congress machinery. Nevertheless, until 1949, the Board continued to play a limited role.

The ineffectuality of the Parliamentary Board during this first phase can be easily demonstrated. Papers dealing with ministerial conflicts in Madras went unattended for a full year.[22] In Bengal the ministry was ousted and a new cabinet appointed, then reshuffled, without any reference to the Board.[23] The Bengal P.C.C. leaders also selected candidates for assembly seats without consulting the center.[24] By 1949, however, several factors converged to stimulate the reactivation of the Parliamentary Board.

In the first place, pressure for greater central guidance began to come from the states. Secondly, the appointment of Kala Venkata Rao, former Finance Minister of Madras, as secretary to the Board, led to the first systematic thinking about the role of the Parliamentary Board in the general Congress framework. Finally, the development of serious splits

[22] Unpublished Prasad Papers, Shankarrao Deo, Madras Enquiry Report.
[23] Unpublished Prasad Papers, Letter R. Prasad to B. C. Roy, March 10, 1948.
[24] *Ibid.*

and factional disputes in practically every state called for some massive intervention from the center to prevent complete political chaos. It was during this critical period from 1949 to 1952 that the role of the Congress Parliamentary Board as umpire and arbiter began to evolve.

Pressure for more active intervention by the Parliamentary Board came largely from the organizational wing. Organizational leaders complained that no proper consultative machinery existed in the states and that the center was not functioning effectively in providing guidance. A series of related grievances had come to light at a meeting of the Presidents and Secretaries of the P.C.C.s at Allahabad in the early months of 1947. An A.I.C.C. note issued after the adjournment of the meeting had described the lack of harmony between the parliamentary and organizational wings at the state level:

> All those who spoke pointed out that there was no proper consultative machinery in existence in provinces between the PCC's and Congress ministries leading to much misunderstanding which [it] was necessary to avoid in the interest of harmonious work. Congressmen and Congress Committees could not render effective cooperation if the PCC or its representatives were not taken into consultation on vital matters. It was also pointed out that as in 1938 and 1939 the Congress Parliamentary Board was not effectively functioning. It was necessary that this Board should function more vigorously and give thought to problems arising out of the parliamentary activities of the Congress.[25]

The consensus was that, without intervention from the center, friction would continue to the detriment of the welfare of the party as a whole. But the leadership's preoccupation with other issues prevented action from being taken for some two years.

[25] Unpublished Prasad Papers, "Office Note on Conference of Presidents and Secretaries of the PCCs," Allahabad, Feb. 22-24, 1947.

Parliamentary Board

The first systematic thinking about the role of the Parliamentary Board was set down in two notes prepared by Kala Venkata Rao. The first of these notes envisioned an extremely comprehensive policy-making and coordinating role for the Parliamentary Board.[26] The proposals in this note were rejected. The second note confined itself to the problems of party-government coordination. For the first time, within this note, a suggestion was made to adopt a formal consultative procedure as a means of providing for smoother relations between the parliamentary and organizational wings of the Congress within each state.

As early as 1946, hoping to facilitate party-government relations in the states, the Parliamentary Board had laid down certain general guidelines. These guidelines, based largely on the 1937-1939 experience, suggested that a distinction had to be drawn between administrative and policy matters. Thus, the ministries had an obligation to coordinate policy, but the organization had an obligation not to interfere in administration. Policy disputes could be referred to the Parliamentary Board, administrative abuses were to be brought to the government's attention through organizational channels, and in no case were grievances to be aired publicly.[27] However, since no procedures for consultation had been prescribed, the implementation of these suggestions was uncertain.

As a corrective, Rao's note recommended that state ministers meet annually prior to the opening of the legislative session to discuss major legislation and government policy with the President and Secretary of the P.C.C. This conference was to be supplemented by a monthly meeting between representatives of the P.C.C. and the ministry to compare notes on the implementation of these programs and policies.[28] After considering Rao's note, the Working Committee instructed

[26] Unpublished Prasad Papers, K. V. Rao, "Note on Parliamentary Organisation," dated Feb. 15, 1949.

[27] *Congress Bulletin*, No. 6, Sept. 1946, p. 17.

[28] Unpublished Prasad Papers, K. V. Rao, "Note No. 13, Relationship between the Congress Government and PCC," dated Apr. 5, 1949.

the Congress President to issue a directive endorsing the proposal for yearly and monthly meetings and suggesting, in addition, that the legislative party and the P.C.C. within each state exchange ex officio members.[29] Even today this approach is considered to be one of the best means of party-government coordination.[30]

Perhaps the most urgent reason for the reactivation of the Parliamentary Board was the development of widespread factionalism based on personal rivalry, particularistic loyalties, and regionalism. A series of open challenges to Congress ministries resulted in the fall of the Congress governments of Madras, the Punjab, West Bengal, and Travancore-Cochin, despite Congress majorities in the legislative parties. Such conflict could not be tolerated. Yet the dilemma facing the Parliamentary Board was how to achieve political stability within a one-party system without stifling the debate and criticism necessary for maintaining responsibility. As Rajendra Prasad wrote in 1948: "The difficulty at the present moment is that there is no opposition party worth the name in most of the Provincial Legislatures and some opposition party is necessary for a parliamentary government of the type we have."[31] Yet by 1949 the Congress was generating its own opposition so vigorously that its own ministries could not remain securely in power. The pattern, fairly uniform wherever it occurred, involved a struggle for power between rival groups controlling the organizational and parliamentary wings for control of the state government.

It was almost a matter of course for a group which had lost power or one which was in a minority in the ministry to attempt to strengthen its position by capturing control of the party organization. Control of the organization, however, was not an end in itself. It was a means of capturing control of the ministry, for, when a dissident group controlled the party organization, it had two advantages. In the first place,

[29] *Congress Bulletin*, No. 4, June-July 1949, p. 41.
[30] *Congress Bulletin*, Nos. 7-9, July-Oct. 1962, p. 144.
[31] Unpublished Prasad Papers, Letter R. Prasad to Shankarrao Deo, March 31, 1948.

the party organization was an excellent platform from which the group could gain leverage against the majority group and attack the ministry. With this leverage it might be able to win over enough supporters in the Congress legislative party to take over the ministry. Failing this, a second alternative was available. Control of the party organization meant dominance over the party election machinery, which could be used to ensure the selection of legislative candidates from the party group. This in turn guaranteed that the group would eventually emerge as the dominant parliamentary group after the elections.

As a result of this intra-party maneuvering, it was necessary for any group desiring to remain in power to secure control of both party and government. Only when the ministerial group controlled both organizational and legislative wings could it feel safe. Where the leader of such a group was able to hold his group together and prevent it from splintering, political stability and harmonious party-government relations were achieved. Where a dominant leadership had not emerged, the consequence was continued party-government conflict creating what amounted to a two-party system of alternating elites within the dominant Congress Party. In states badly divided on the basis of factionalism, the Parliamentary Board's major role during this period was to evolve procedures for arbitrating disputes with the end of preserving party unity, maintaining political stability in the state, and preventing hostile groups from liquidating each other.

In more specific terms, the Parliamentary Board had to develop policies which would increase the ability of a basically effective ministry to survive constant threats from intra-party opposition groups within the assembly as well as from the vantage point of the P.C.C. At the same time, however, it was necessary to prevent unreasonable domination by a truculent and insensitive ruling group. Experience in dealing with crisis after crisis eventually led the Parliamentary Board to recommend a series of remedial procedures which were embodied as Working Committee resolutions. Most of these resolutions were designed to prevent political instability by strengthening the ministries.

In the first place, the Working Committee expressed its disapproval of the formation of territorial, linguistic, or ideological groups to contest party elections. It also deplored the related abuse by which cabinet portfolios were distributed among the members of the victorious group.[32]

Second, the Working Committee forbade the P.C.C.s passing no-confidence resolutions against a ministry, for ministries were to be responsible to the legislative parties, not to the organization. If grievances existed, party members were to bring them to the attention of the Working Committee or the Parliamentary Board.[33] The purpose of this resolution was twofold—to prevent the use of the P.C.C. as a springboard to the ministry and to preserve the separation of party and government functions which alone could permit the ministries to exercise their constitutional right to act without direct interference of the party machinery in day-to-day administration. This resolution had grown out of an incident in Kerala where steps to overthrow the Pillai ministry had begun when the P.C.C. passed a vote of no-confidence in the Chief Minister and demanded that the Congress assembly party take a similar vote, thereby bringing down the Congress ministry.[34]

Third, the Working Committee dispensed with annual elections for the leader of the Congress legislative parties at the center and in the states. By making the term of the leader coterminous with the life of the assembly, the central leadership hoped to discourage disruptive annual challenges to the Chief Ministers.[35] The potential danger of annual elections had been demonstrated by the case of Madras, where the annual election was tantamount to a periodic vote of confidence in the ministry. In this process, the most onerous burden of proof had rested on the ministry rather than on the op-

[32] *Congress Bulletin*, No. 6, Sept.-Oct. 1949, p. 34.
[33] *Ibid.*, p. 1.
[34] Unpublished Prasad Papers, Letter K. A. G. Menon to Shankarrao Deo, Oct. 25, 1948.
[35] *Hindustan Times* (New Delhi), Oct. 8, 1949.

position, for opposition groups were able to concentrate during the intervals between elections on building a coalition strong enough to oust the Chief Minister. At the very least an attempt was made to discredit him by bringing out charge sheets just in time for the annual election.

Finally, in an attempt to provide effective coordination without allowing the government to overwhelm the party organization, the Working Committee decided that state ministers and parliamentary secretaries could not be office bearers in the P.C.C.s or in equivalent subordinate Congress committees. Nevertheless, in an attempt to encourage party-government coordination, the committee decided that members of the government should be permitted to belong to the executive committee of the state party organization.[36] In this way, the procedure of party-government coordination used at the center in an attempt to prevent conflict between the Working Committee and the Cabinet provided a pattern for the solution to the problem in the states as well.

In addition to setting down such broad policy for party-government coordination during the 1949-1952 period, the Parliamentary Board developed its role as umpire, learning in the process both the extent and the limits of its power, particularly in the contrasting cases of the Punjab and West Bengal. In these two partitioned provinces the Congress faced some of its most difficult problems, and the Parliamentary Board was forced to take quite strong action. The West Bengal case demonstrated that the Parliamentary Board's role can be severely circumscribed when it is dealing with a leader of recognized stature who enjoys the backing of the Congressmen in his home state and refuses to succumb to central pressure. The Punjab case demonstrated the extent to which the Parliamentary Board can intervene in a province badly divided into competing factions.

The Congress Party in postwar Bengal consisted of three groups: the Gandhians, the Jugantar, and the Hooghly. The Gandhians, led by Dr. P. C. Ghosh and Suresh Banerjee,

---

[36] *Congress Bulletin*, No. 7, Nov.-Dec. 1949, p. 4.

had never developed a strong base of support, for revolutionary Bengal had never been fully convinced of the efficacy of Gandhi's teachings. The Jugantar group, led by S. M. Ghose and Kiron Shankar Roy, was strong enough to take over the leadership of the party following the ouster of the Bose group. However, their support was concentrated largely in northern and eastern Bengal, the areas which came to form East Pakistan. Finally, there was the Hooghly group, led by P. C. Sen, which took its name from the Calcutta and Hooghly River areas in which its support was concentrated. While the Hooghly group was able to gain control of the ministry from the Gandhian group, it was forced to fight a seesawing battle for control of the party organization dominated by the Jugantar group.

This group rivalry, growing political unrest in the state, and the defeat of a Congress candidate in a south Calcutta by-election convinced Nehru that radical steps had to be taken. In a report to the Working Committee he recommended that fresh elections be held for both the P.C.C. and the legislature in West Bengal. In the six months to elapse before the election could be held under the Government of India Act of 1935, he favored the formation of an interim ministry and the reconstitution of the executive committee of the P.C.C. The Working Committee endorsed Nehru's recommendation.[37]

The Working Committee was shortly to discover, however, that the Congress in West Bengal was not as malleable as the party in other provinces. Two months after the July resolution, which had been reinforced by reiteration on August 25, the only step actually taken to implement it had been the preparation of the electoral rolls. As a result, Maulana Azad went to Calcutta. He invited the leaders of the two groups to Delhi for two days of discussion with the General Secretaries. It was suggested that each group submit a

[37] Unpublished Prasad Papers, unpublished Working Committee proceedings, July 16-19 and July 27-28, 1949. The final resolution appears in *Congress Bulletin*, No. 5, Aug. 1949, pp. 2-3.

slate of 5 candidates for office bearers of the P.C.C. and 25 candidates for the executive committee. Since the P.C.C. group claimed a strength of 212 of the 324 members of the P.C.C. and 53 of the 81 members of the P.C.C. executive, they were more than willing to submit to an election. The ministerial group, for obvious related reasons, refused to do so. The General Secretaries saw little hope of an amicable resolution of the dispute.[38]

Throughout this period the absence abroad of the Chief Minister, B. C. Roy, had prevented him from taking part in the discussions. When he returned in the first week of September, however, he made it clear that, as head of the West Bengal government, he would not permit central interference. Immediately he set about scheduling a meeting of the Congress legislative party for September 10. When Kala Venkata Rao, the Congress General Secretary, called from Delhi asking him to come to the capital as soon as possible, Roy replied that he was otherwise engaged. He had to attend a meeting of the assembly party, he said. Therefore, he could not possibly get to Delhi before September 14. K.V. Rao lost no time in discussing Roy's reply with Nehru and Prasad, who decided to send a telegram to Roy requesting his immediate presence in Delhi and suggesting that a party meeting prior to his departure was inappropriate. Only after consultation with the Parliamentary Board in Delhi would a legislative party meeting be fruitful. Roy, however, repeated that he would not be able to come until after the meeting with his legislative party and pointedly remarked that he could not see why the meeting was inappropriate. At the assembly party meeting on the 10th, Roy obtained a vote of confidence of 34 to 14. The confidence resolution also requested the Working Committee to rescind its resolution calling for reorganization of the West Bengal Congress. The next day, armed with a vote of confidence, B. C. Roy went to Delhi to meet with Nehru and the Congress President.[39]

[38] Unpublished Prasad Papers, K. V. Rao, "Note on West Bengal," prepared for the Working Committee.
[39] *Ibid.*

The Working Committee

By October the Working Committee had been forced to modify its decisions by withdrawing its demand for the formation of a caretaker government in West Bengal and by agreeing to permit the P.C.C. and its executive committee to continue as constituted until the regular Congress organizational elections were held. However, the central leadership continued to insist on the holding of interim elections for the reconstitution of the West Bengal ministry. For this purpose the Working Committee appointed a five-man committee to draw up procedures for the selection of candidates.[40]

But the interim election was never held. Under the impact of a new flood of refugees streaming in from East Pakistan, both the Chief Minister and the Governor of the state of West Bengal sent communications to the Working Committee pointing out the constitutional, financial, economic, and political difficulty of holding an election under such circumstances. After studying these notes, the Working Committee decided not to proceed with its decision to reconstitute the government of West Bengal.[41]

Instability in West Bengal came to an end following the organizational election held in the normal course of affairs in September 1950, when the Hooghly group, which had controlled the government since 1948, also emerged as the dominant group in the party organization.

In the West Bengal episode the Parliamentary Board was confronted by a provincial leader whose stature was equal to that of the most powerful member of the central government. Since the new Indian Constitution had not yet been adopted, the center could not change the state administration simply by declaring President's Rule and holding new elections. The only available means for imposing central decisions on the state was through the party organization. But party channels were not strong enough to prevail over the

[40] *Report of the General Secretaries, 1949-1950*, p. 64.
[41] *Ibid.*

Chief Minister's determination to control the affairs of West Bengal within the state itself. Later, in the Punjab, the result was to be different, for the power of the Parliamentary Board, as a body dominated by ministerial elements, had been reinforced by the provisions of the new Indian Constitution.

Post-partition instability also rocked the province of the Punjab, which with West Bengal bore the brunt of partition. Because of the Punjab's strategic position as a border province and especially because the Punjab was the gateway to Kashmir, the central leadership kept a watchful eye on Congress rivalries there.

Instability in the Punjab was the result of several complex and interrelated sets of group loyalties. Partition and the high influx of refugees had created political as well as economic problems. As in West Bengal, there was conflict between those Congressmen whose support came from the portion of the province left behind in Pakistan and those whose source of power still lay within the boundaries of the Republic of India. Superimposed on this problem was the traditional rivalry between the Punjab's two largest religious communities, the Hindus and the Sikhs. To complicate things even further, conflicts due to regional-linguistic factors and intra-community rivalries also existed. The result was such prolonged ministerial instability that President's Rule was declared and remained in effect for ten months.

In the Punjab the basic conflict took place between two Hindu leaders of the Congress, Dr. Gopi Chand Bhargava and Bhim Sen Sachar. Bhargava had been leader of the opposition in the Punjab during the period of the 1937-1939 ministries. He had served as leader of the Congress legislative party in the assembly and was elected first Chief Minister of partitioned Punjab. Bhim Sen Sachar had been Finance Minister in the Punjab cabinet in pre-partition days. Sachar and Bhargava fought a seesaw battle which saw Bhargava in power from August 1947 to January 1949, Sachar from

January 1949 to October 1949, and Bhargava from mid-October 1949 to June 1951, when the center intervened and declared President's Rule until the First General Elections.

It was continued instability in the Bhargava ministry throughout 1950 and early 1951 which eventually brought massive intervention by the Parliamentary Board. The Board was determined to bring group conflict to an end in the Punjab and embarked upon the most far-reaching attempt at intervention in the history of center-state relations in India. The Board notified Bhargava that he could remain Chief Minister in the Punjab. But he would have to call an immediate meeting of the Congress assembly party. At this meeting Congress assemblymen were to elect by proportional representation ten aspirants for ministerships. Upon receipt of the list the Parliamentary Board would choose six names in consultation with Bhargava. These men would form the Punjab cabinet.[42]

Bhargava's reaction upon learning of the Board's decision was immediate and sharp. He contended that the directive represented a vote of no-confidence in his leadership. It was, moreover, a case of blatant interference with the right of a Chief Minister to select his cabinet as he saw fit.[43] He therefore rejected the plan.[44] However, faced by a solid front in the High Command, especially Nehru, Azad, and C. Rajagopalachari, who was reported to have been the originator of the idea.[45] Bhargava finally gave in.[46] He called a special meeting of the Punjab assembly party, apologized publicly for his previous refusal to obey the Board's directive, and confessed that his behavior had been tantamount to a direct insult to the Board. When the legislative party assembled, Bhargava's group was able to elect six of its members. From the Sachar group only four were elected.[47]

[42] *The Statesman* (New Delhi), April 28, 1951.
[43] *Tribune* (Ambala), April 29, 1951.
[44] *The Statesman* (New Delhi), May 8, 1951.
[45] *The Statesman* (New Delhi), April 28, 1951.
[46] *Tribune* (Ambala), May 17, 1951.
[47] *Tribune* (Ambala), May 19, 1951.

The list of ten names was forwarded to the Parliamentary Board, which, evidently recognizing the group bias of the selections, decided to substitute its own list without consulting Bhargava. The Board's selections would have created a composite ministry with the various groups equally represented.[48]

Bhargava was stunned by the Board's action. He refused to accept the Board's advice on the grounds that it would transform his majority into a minority[49] and endanger his leadership since the groups would not remain static if they knew he could no longer distribute patronage. Instead, he decided to adopt B. C. Roy's tactic of calling a meeting of the assembly party and, by arming himself with a vote of confidence and a blank check from his group, bringing the crisis to an end.[50] However, three factors operated against him. Bhargava did not have the stature of B. C. Roy. He lacked the solid party backing the Bengal chief had enjoyed. And he was faced by a new power which the ministerial members of the Parliamentary Board could exercise under the new Indian Constitution. That was Article 356, Presidential Rule.[51] Thus, when he continued to defy the Board's directive, he was asked to resign.

The decision to end the Bhargava ministry was reached after a stormy session of the Parliamentary Board during which Nehru had threatened to resign from the Board if Bhargava was allowed to continue to defy its directives.[52] Nehru argued that only a wholesale purge of the groups in the Punjab would bring order and stability to the state. He declared that he would not tolerate any further compromise settlements among the groups. Undoubtedly the communal

[48] *The Statesman* (New Delhi), May 23, 1951.

[49] *The Statesman* (New Delhi), May 24, 1951.

[50] *Tribune* (Ambala), June 7, 1951.

[51] Government of India, *The Constitution of India*, as modified up to July 1, 1960 (New Delhi: Manager of Publications, 1960), pp. 192-193.

[52] *Congress Bulletin*, No. 3, May-June 1951, p. 101; *The Statesman* (New Delhi), June 13, 1951.

257

basis of group alignments in the Punjab played an important role in arousing Nehru's opposition.

Bhargava was now faced with a clear directive that he resign immediately. After hesitating four days, he agreed, but added that, as leader of a majority in the assembly, he was prepared to form a new government.[53] The Parliamentary Board, however, had decided that no attempt was to be made to form a new Congress ministry, and shortly thereafter, upon the advice of the Prime Minister, the President of India invoked President's Rule for the first time. Thus, after twenty months of instability, the third post-independence Congress ministry in the Punjab came to an end.

The role of the Parliamentary Board in the Punjab marked the high point of the Board's interference in the affairs of the provincial ministries. The drastic action was taken because of the critical situation in the Punjab created by partition, the communal nature of the conflict, and most important of all, because of the strategic position of the state both as a border province and as the main access route to Kashmir. Thus, the second phase ended with the emergence of the Parliamentary Board as an important force in the Congress organization.

The third phase of Parliamentary Board development began sometime after the First General Elections. During this phase the Board attempted to define more specifically the roles of the party and the government; it elaborated and refined its recommendations concerning procedures for party-government coordination; and it continued to develop its umpire function.

The earlier decision of the Congress to maintain a separation of party and government functions was complicated by Nehru's decision to become Congress President, for many Chief Ministers wished to emulate Nehru's example. Nehru resisted these pressures on the grounds that it was inadvisable to concentrate too much power in the hands of one man.

[53] *Tribune* (Ambala), June 17, 1951.

He also insisted that his actions at the center were to be viewed as a temporary response to a specific crisis.

At the Hyderabad Session in January 1953, when Nehru agreed to accept a second term as Congress President, the Congress passed a resolution preventing state leaders from following Nehru's example. No ministers were to hold an office such as P.C.C. President, Vice President, or Secretary, although they might be members of the executive committee of a P.C.C. Nehru justified this position by pointing out that "the work of the Chief Minister was indeed a very hard one and the merger of the two important positions would weaken both the offices. The President of the P.C.C. was not necessarily the only person that counted in the organization."[54] By means of the Hyderabad resolution, Nehru wished to create a formula in the states similar to that which was beginning to work successfully at the center: consultation between the Chief Minister and the P.C.C. President and discussion at the P.C.C. executive committee level.[55] Beyond such coordination of broad policy as these arrangements might provide, however, each wing of the party was to function autonomously. If the organizational and parliamentary wings could not reach agreement, they would simply have to carry on within their own spheres and accept the differences growing out of disparate roles. In cases of especially serious disagreement, the Working Committee and the Parliamentary Board were to serve as cementing or mediating forces.[56] And if the dispute between the parliamentary and organizational wings arose from factional alignments, the Parliamentary Board would act as an umpire to help reconcile the cliques.

The decision to retain the separation of the parliamentary and the organizational wings led to extensive efforts to develop coordinating procedures. Suggestions were solicited from the P.C.C.s, from Congress ministries, and from Con-

[54] *Congress Bulletin*, No. 6, Aug. 1954, pp. 293-294.
[55] *Congress Bulletin*, No. 3, March 1953, pp. 95, 79-80.
[56] *Congress Bulletin*, No. 6, Aug. 1954, pp. 293-294.

gress Chief Ministers.[57] Special committees were convened in 1955,[58] 1957,[59] and 1963[60] to study the problem and to make recommendations. The most consistently reached position was, perhaps, the conviction that coordinating procedures should consist of conventions developed over a period of time rather than of elaborately specific regulations. In general, however, the following suggestions were agreed upon as basic to proper coordination.

First, it was suggested that Chief Ministers arrange meetings between ministers and P.C.C. office bearers, who were also to be invited to legislative party meetings. Second, Chief Ministers and P.C.C. Presidents were to meet as frequently as necessary; the ministries were to meet with the P.C.C. executive at least once every quarter; and P.C.C. Presidents and Chief Ministers were to be considered ex officio members of the legislative party executive and the P.C.C., respectively. Third, ministers were advised to meet with local Congress organizations to discuss their problems whenever they were on a tour of the state. Finally, it was suggested that all legislative bills be sent to the P.C.C. for comments after being published, while the party was warned particularly not to interfere in the day-to-day administration of the government, especially in matters of transfers of officials, appointments, promotions, and dismissals. As for judicial proceedings, such matters were not even to be discussed privately. At all times Congressmen were advised not to criticize the government publicly. They were to work through the organization for redress of grievances; and all problems that could not be resolved locally were to be referred to the Parliamentary Board. Finally, it was felt that the party and the government should act as an integrated whole in a spirit of cooperation.[61]

[57] *Hindustan Times* (New Delhi), Nov. 7, 1952.

[58] Indian National Congress, *Report of the General Secretaries, 1955-1956* (New Delhi: A.I.C.C., 1956), pp. 68-70.

[59] *Congress Bulletin*, Nos. 7-8, July-Aug. 1957, pp. 281-291.

[60] Indian National Congress, *Report of the General Secretary, Jan. 1964–Dec. 1964* (New Delhi: A.I.C.C., 1965), pp. 42-43.

[61] *Report of the General Secretaries, 1955-1956*, pp. 68-70.

When party-government conflict continued despite the reiteration of these procedures to ensure coordination, the Congress leadership acknowledged that it could no longer be attributed to lack of coordinating principles and clear-cut directives but rather to a failure on the part of state leaders to utilize existing procedures.[62]

The most dramatic departure in the central leadership's attempts to establish party-government coordinating procedures at the state level came with the implementation of the Kamaraj Plan in 1963, when it was decided to constitute state coordination committees in which representatives of the Parliamentary Board would participate directly. These committees were to consist of the P.C.C. President and two representatives of the organizational wing; the Chief Minister and any two ministers; and a representative of the central Parliamentary Board. The Parliamentary Board laid down procedures for these meetings which called for the convening of the meeting by the P.C.C. President in consultation with the Chief Minister, preparation of the agenda based on similar consultations, and secrecy of proceedings except for official press notes released after the meeting.[63] The whole scheme was to be closely tied to the expansion of the Parliamentary Board and the resignation of senior Congressmen from ministerial posts to devote full time to party organizational work. Yet even this scheme does not seem to have prevented party-government conflict, for factional rivalry persists in several states; and even the General Secretaries admitted "that a great deal of enthusiasm is not evinced by the states for convening the meeting of the coordination committees."[64]

The Parliamentary Board's umpire function, as it developed in the third phase, may best be seen in the procedures by which the leaders of the Congress legislative parties

[62] *Congress Bulletin*, Nos. 7-10, July-Oct. 1962, pp. 144-145.

[63] *Report of the General Secretary, 1964*, pp. 42-43.

[64] Indian National Congress, *Report of the General Secretary, Jan. 1965–Feb. 1966* (New Delhi: A.I.C.C., 1966), p. 59.

were elected and in the process of cabinet formation in the states following the 1962 General Elections. Depending on the degree of factionalism in the state, one of three broad patterns was evident. In states where party unity prevailed, the legislative party was free to elect its own leader and the leader to select his own cabinet. In this way the election of Y. B. Chavan in Maharashtra, K. Kamaraj in Madras, and B. C. Roy in West Bengal was a formality. Not only was central intervention in cabinet formation non-existent, but in these states it would also have been resented and resisted.[65]

By contrast, in states where the party was divided into factions and groups, the Parliamentary Board set down the general policy for the election of the Chief Minister. The objective in each case was to achieve party unity and government stability. The Parliamentary Board then acted as an umpire in solving any disputes. The degree of central intervention in faction-torn states was related to the degree of factionalism.

In states where one faction was clearly dominant, the Parliamentary Board attempted to prevent a contest, obtained the unanimous selection of a leader, and then ensured that the minority groups were given some representation in the cabinet. Thus, the Parliamentary Board used its prestige to secure the unanimous election of Sanjiva Reddy in Andhra and Pratap Singh Kairon in Punjab. It was then made clear to each Congress legislative party that the "desire" of the center was for the election, respectively, of Sanjiva Reddy and Kairon. Such unanimous elections as a result of central intervention placed restrictions on the chief minister in cabinet formation. Although Pratap Singh Kairon, who knew that he had a clear majority in the legislative party, "wanted the Party to be free to elect the leader" and desired for himself "unrestricted liberty to choose his colleagues," he was forced to select, in consultation with the Parliamentary Board, a "broad-based" cabinet incorporating representatives of the

[65] C. P. Bhambhri, "Pattern of Cabinet Making in Indian States," *Political Science Review*, II (1963), 72.

minority groups who had complied with Nehru's request to facilitate his unanimous election as Chief Minister.[66]

In states where the groups were more evenly divided and where the Parliamentary Board was unable to determine immediately which leader to favor with a unanimous election, the Board followed the procedure of testing the strength of the opposing groups, then seeing to the election of the leader with the greatest support. This procedure was followed in Mysore, Madhya Pradesh, and Bihar, all states where the Congress was very badly divided.

In the case of Mysore, where the party was split between P.C.C. President Nijalingappa and Chief Minister B. D. Jatti, Lal Bahadur Shastri was sent as a representative of the Parliamentary Board to achieve a compromise. Although the center would normally have insisted upon the election of Nijalingappa, whose group constituted a majority in the legislative party, Nijalingappa himself had been defeated in the election, and it was standard Congress policy that no man could be elected Chief Minister unless he could first get himself elected to the legislature. Nijalingappa was not allowed to run, but the absence of compromise still meant that a contest was in the offing between Jatti and S. R. Kanthi, a member of the Nijalingappa faction. At this point Shastri ascertained the sense of the party by an "informative poll" and appealed for the unanimous election of Kanthi, who, he said, had received the strongest support.[67]

In Madhya Pradesh the situation was even more complex. The center preferred K. N. Katju, but like Nijalingappa he had been defeated at the polls, leaving the Congress badly split between two non-candidates, the former Chief Minister and M. C. Deshlehra, the P.C.C. President. U. N. Dhebar was sent by the Parliamentary Board to Madhya Pradesh to negotiate a solution. After prolonged negotiation, "the groups agreed to elect Mr. [B.A.] Mandloi after receiving an assurance from Mr. Dhebar that the new leader would be free to choose his cabinet in consultation with the Congress

[66] *Ibid.*, pp. 70-71.   [67] *Ibid.*, p. 71.

High Command."[68] Similarly, in Bihar, the Congress was seriously divided between groups led by Chief Minister B. Jha and K. B. Sahay. Atulya Ghosh was sent as a representative of the Parliamentary Board to ascertain the strength of the two groups in the Congress legislative party. A secret ballot was held. Jha received a majority and was subsequently re-elected to the chief ministership.[69]

In all three states of Mysore, Madhya Pradesh, and Bihar, following the election of the leader, broad-based ministries were formed in order to see that the defeated factions were represented.[70] But that did not end the Parliamentary Board's work, for the Board was also responsible for keeping the factions working together in an attempt to maintain political stability. In this way, depending on the internal conditions of each state, the Parliamentary Board has played its major role as umpire, arbiter, and mediator of disputes.

The power of the Parliamentary Board has varied according to the degree of factionalism within the state just as the problem of party-government coordination has existed in fact only in those states where the Congress Party has been torn by intra-party rivalries. Where no leader has emerged with overriding stature, men of relatively equal power have competed for control of the ministry. In areas where a dominant leader has emerged, he has been able to control both party and government despite the constitutional provisions for dual leadership. Under such circumstances, the P.C.C. presidency has been occupied simply by a nonentity or trusted lieutenant nominated by the Chief Minister. In states where the Congress Party has been badly divided, as in Mysore or Madhya Pradesh, the center has been able to exercise, and *has* exercised, considerable influence. Conversely, in states with a recognized leader, such as Uttar Pradesh under Pant, Bombay under Morarji Desai, and Madras under Kamaraj Nadar, central interference has been almost nonexistent. In fact, under these circumstances, the state leaders

[68] *Ibid.*, p. 72.   [69] *Ibid.*, p. 72.   [70] *Ibid.*, p. 73.

have not only excluded central intervention in state affairs; they have also been able to make demands on the center and have been successful in doing so. This has been particularly true in the allocation of planning funds.

The Congress Party, operating as it does within a federal structure, is not the highly centralized organization many observers believe it to be. In the past decade it has seen the development of strong provincial leaders whose cooperation is essential to political stability, economic growth, and the continued existence of the party. The result has been an increasing tendency toward the development of autonomous state parties. The central leadership, however, can turn its limitations to considerable advantage by identifying emerging leaders in time to make common cause with them and by easing their confirmation in positions of power. Furthermore, the power of the Parliamentary Board has been augmented by the constitutional provision permitting the President of India, under certain circumstances, to suspend a state government and replace it by direct central rule for a period of time. The threat of central intervention expressed through the Parliamentary Board has been extremely effective. Yet the Parliamentary Board must always keep in mind that, when a Congress ministry is dissolved, a suitable replacement must be found. In the final analysis, though the center can encourage and strengthen a particular group in the state Congress, it cannot sustain indefinitely a group which lacks a strong popular base within the state.

The Congress is not the only party in India to be plagued by factionalism. But the major difference between the Congress and the opposition parties has been that the Congress leadership has learned how to manage intra-party conflict so as to prevent the complete disintegration of the Congress itself—a fate which has frequently befallen other parties in India. The management of conflict within the Congress takes the form of mediation and arbitration through persuasion and conciliation; appeals to party and national unity; the establishment of models for party-government coordination;

and, ultimately, the development of techniques for gauging the strength of competing groups so that leadership may be turned over to the majority. At the same time, minority factions are given representation in state ministries, for the objective of the Parliamentary Board's mediating approach is to achieve stability and unity without so isolating or destroying the power of factions representing significant electoral support that they break away from the Congress to strengthen the anti-Congress coalitions in the states. The overall objectives of the national party can be most effectively accomplished if Congress governments continue to control the states.

The role played by the Parliamentary Board since its creation has to a very large extent been dependent upon the existence of a united central leadership and on the presence within the national leadership of recognized arbitrators capable of getting divergent groups to work together. With the crumbling of this unity the effectiveness of the Parliamentary Board in dealing with state parties was seriously jeopardized. The states have been forced to act, if not autonomously, then with unprecedented independence of the center.

THE WORKING COMMITTEE AND THE
SELECTION OF CANDIDATES:
THE CENTRAL ELECTION COMMITTEE

The Working Committee's function as final authority in the selection of candidates for the state and national legislatures is performed by the Central Election Committee, a sub-committee of the Working Committee. The Central Election Committee consists of the members of the Parliamentary Board in addition to five members elected by the A.I.C.C. The Prime Minister is an ex-officio member of the Central Election Committee. The creation of this separate machinery for selecting candidates and conducting elections was brought about in 1948 with the adoption of the first post-independence Congress constitution. Prior to that time, candidates for both the 1937 and the 1946 elections had been selected by ad hoc committees established, according to varying criteria, especially for the purpose. Thus, in 1937, the Election Board consisted of twenty-five members, but in 1946 a seven-member body was created. The C.E.C. provides a critical point of linkage between party and government, for candidate selection remains one of the most important functions which the party performs. Moreover, the selection process tends to bring to the surface the divergent interests of which the Congress is composed since those selected are given access to power through control of Congress legislative parties. Thus, the competition for party tickets has tended to be the supreme test of the party's capacity for conflict resolution.

The C.E.C. has passed through two stages of development, which correspond to the period of centralization and convergence and the period of divergence. The contrast between these two periods in regard to the functioning of the C.E.C. reflects more than anything else the changes that have occurred within the Congress over the past two decades. During the first phase covering the elections of 1951, 1957, and 1962, when the C.E.C. played a decisive role in the process of candidate selection, centralization of the final distribution of tickets was considered decisive and was regarded by many Congressmen as "unavoidable" to the extent that "the organization at the lower levels was weak, loose and riven by group politics."[1] During the period of divergence, however, despite the fact that the subordinate levels of the organization continued to be seriously divided, there was no effective central control because of the extension of group and personal rivalries within the C.E.C. itself. The resulting breakdown of central control over conflict resolution led to major defections from the Congress in 1967.

The members of the Central Election Committee drawn from the Parliamentary Board, as might be expected, have been the senior Congress leaders who enjoy considerable stature in the party. However, the same has also been true of the elected members, for it has been customary for A.I.C.C. members to elect as a matter of course an official list of candidates informally "suggested" by the party leadership. Even so, contests have developed. Perhaps the bitterest fight over the election of Central Election Committee members occurred at the time of the Nehru-Tandon struggle in 1951. The selection of elected members in 1957 and 1962 proved to be fairly routine, but, with the death of both Nehru and Shastri, conflict over selection broke out once again.[2]

In order to guide the state Congress parties in selecting candidates, the C.E.C. has set down a series of formal criteria to be taken into consideration at the time of selection, as well as procedures to be followed in the preparation of state recommendations to the C.E.C. The formal criteria for selec-

[1] Sadiq Ali, *The General Elections 1957: A Survey* (New Delhi: A.I.C.C., 1959), p. 14.
[2] *The Hindu Weekly Review* (Madras), May 30, 1966.

tion have been worked out over the years so that, by the 1967 General Elections, the C.E.C. prescribed eight qualifications "to be taken into account generally" in the selection of individual candidates by the provincial election committees. These formal criteria called for each Pradesh Election Committee (P.E.C.) to determine: (1) whether the candidate is an elected member of the party; (2) if a sitting member, whether he has submitted a statement of his assets and liabilities; (3) his record of political, social, and economic work; (4) his agreement with the basic policies of the Congress, particularly those relating to communal harmony, prohibition, untouchability, co-operatives, social reform, and social and economic justice; (5) his experience in legislative and local bodies; (6) his contribution to constructive work and development; (7), if a sitting member, his contact with the constituency, his record in the legislature, and his past performance in paying his contributions to the party; and, finally, (8) his observance of discipline. The provincial election committees were also urged to ensure adequate representation to women and minorities.[3]

Not even such an elaboration of detail could ensure a uniform selection process, for it must be remembered that what are perhaps the most important criteria for selection are never formally proclaimed by Congress leaders. These factors, which quite naturally dominate the selection process, are usually articulated only by implication in the consideration of the candidate's "ability to win." In fact, however, it is under this rubric that the really dominant factors in individual candidate selection at both state and national levels become apparent, for, in considering a candidate's ability to win an election, it is necessary to take into account caste, community, minority, regional, and traditional loyalties. All political parties are forced to make equivalent calculations, and it is obvious that in a society of the sort found in India such considerations must inevitably play a role. Although the Congress leadership never makes them explicit, preferring to

[3] *Congress Bulletin*, Nos. 7-8, July-Aug. 1966, p. 254.

speak publicly in more general terms, observers regularly analyze the nomination and election process in communal and caste terms.

Caste factors have consistently played a role in Congress selection. In Mysore it was reported, for example, that the lists prepared by the state Congress office for scrutiny by the provincial election committee included the caste of each candidate.[4] Chavan's selection of Maharashtra candidates was heavily influenced by caste considerations.[5] In Rajasthan it was quite clear that Shastri, who played the dominant role in selecting the list of candidates in 1957, had attempted to reduce the opposition of the Rajput ex-rulers in the state by accommodating their interests in the process of selection.[6] The degree of his success can be seen from the fact that the leader of the Rajasthan Kshatriya Mahasabha, the Rajput Caste Association, urged Rajputs to vote for the Congress on the grounds that abolition of jagirdari did not prove Congress enmity toward Rajputs whose interest, in fact, only the Congress could serve.[7] A disgruntled Congressman in the Punjab charged that the official provincial election committee list of candidates had underrepresented the Jat community, and argued that he was not the only "sinner" to raise the caste issue, for "bigger sinners would be found . . . in the official camp who have informally (but no less zealously) pleaded for their candidate not only in the name of community but of narrow 'biradri' and 'gotras.' . . . In fact such factors are constantly kept in view at every stage while finalizing the choice of nominees."[8]

The Central Election Committee considers the religious community of election candidates not merely from the idealistic point of view of minority representation but also in the light of their chances of success. In Kerala, for example, in preparation for the 1962 elections, the Central

[4] *Link*, Nov. 26, 1961, p. 19.
[5] *Times of India* (Bombay), Feb. 14, 1962.
[6] *Hindustan Times* (New Delhi), Feb. 20, 1957.
[7] *Hindustan Times* (New Delhi), Feb. 21, 1957.
[8] *Hindustan Times* (New Delhi), Nov. 29, 1961.

Election Committee reversed a provincial election committee decision in order to accommodate Catholic interests. In Kottayam, a predominantly Catholic area, the provincial election committee's nomination of Mr. M. O. Mathai, a former personal assistant to the Prime Minister, caused the local Congress to rise in revolt against the imposition of an "outsider."[9] Therefore, when the Kerala list reached the Central Election Committee, the committee substituted C. J. Kappan, a Kottayam Catholic leader, to placate Catholic demands. In explaining the change officially, a spokesman said that a "better" candidate had been available than the one originally recommended.[10] The Central Election Committee also attempted to accommodate Sikh interests in the Punjab by means of the Akali merger of 1957. The accommodation of Muslim interests by representation commensurate with their population has always been a Congress goal, but it has less often been accomplished.

The Congress is also forced to consider the impact of traditional loyalties in elections involving former princes. In Madhya Pradesh, for example, a state containing some seventy-six former princely states, Chief Minister Mishra met the challenge of Congress dissidents and the defection of the Rajmata Vijaya Raje Scindia of Gwalior by negotiating for the support of the Maharaja of Rewa.[11] In Rajasthan, Chief Minister Sukhadia, faced with the defection of the pro-Jat group, tried to strengthen his position by asking the Maharaja of Jaipur, husband of the Rajasthan leader of the Swatantra Party, to resign as Indian Ambassador to Spain and seek election on the Congress ticket.[12] The extent of the central leadership's sensitivity to the challenge presented by the former princes can also be seen in the case of the Punjab, where the announcement that the Maharaja of Patiala would seek election to the Punjab assembly as an

[9] *Hindustan Times* (New Delhi), Nov. 11, 1961.
[10] *Hindustan Times* (New Delhi), Nov. 24, 1961.
[11] *Times of India* (Bombay), Jan. 4, 1967.
[12] *Times of India* (Bombay), Jan. 6, 1967.

independent led some senior Congress members to argue for his being offered the Congress ticket. Others suggested the tactic of allowing the Congress ticket to remain empty in order to forestall the Maharaja from campaigning against the party on a state-wide basis as well as in his own constituency.[13]

Thus, while the Congress leaders officially and publicly articulate many formal criteria for selecting candidates, the dominant calculations are based on the ability to win, which involves selecting candidates in accordance with the social composition of each constituency. While these calculations are most carefully weighed by the provincial election committees and Chief Ministers in the case of the more localized state assembly constituencies, it is no less clear that they play an important role at the C.E.C. level in selecting Members of Parliament and members of the legislative assemblies.

The applications filed by prospective candidates provide interesting insights into the values officially stressed by Congress politicians. The themes of service and sacrifice get particular emphasis. A candidate in Assam, for example, characterized himself as follows: "I am a selfless worker of the Council of Nationalist Muslims. I was brutally oppressed on the Direct Action Day of the Muslim League in 1946 at Noasark Muszid, Sylhet. Four times my life was endangered with serious plots against me."[14] Another applicant declared that he had "continuously served as a humble soldier in connection with the freedom movement."[15] It is interesting to note that selfless sacrifice for the greater good of the nationalist cause or the Indian people is also a frequent theme in the autobiographical sketches of Congress legislators appearing in the *Who's Who* volumes published by various state governments.

Over the years selection procedures have not evolved so much as fluctuated with successive attempts to find an ef-

[13] *Times of India* (Bombay), Jan. 3, 1967.
[14] S. V. Kogekar and R. L. Park, *Report on the Indian General Elections, 1951-1952* (Bombay: Popular Book Depot, 1956), p. 4.
[15] *Ibid.*

fective formula for screening candidates below the national level. The major problem has usually been determining the degree to which decentralization was feasible at a certain point of party development, a problem which has normally been translated into the practical question of whether to place major responsibility for selection at the state level, the district level, or below the district level. In 1952 major emphasis in selection was placed on the role of the district committee; in 1957 an attempt was made to strike a balance between the district and state levels, and provision was also made for an elaborate system of checks by A.I.C.C. observers; in 1962 a highly decentralized system gave the Mandal Congress Committees a significant role while at the same time simplifying the selection machinery and placing stress on the regular party organization.[16] In 1967 demands from state leaders led to a decision to concentrate the selection process at the state level again. Candidates were directed to apply for tickets directly to the provincial election committee, and, although it was mandatory for state leaders to consult with district leaders, consultation below that level was left to the discretion of state officials.

Yet, regardless of which level of party organization was designated as primarily responsible for candidate selection, the fact remains that the Congress has regularly received some 20,000 to 25,000 applications for the roughly 4,000 legislative tickets available. Although each candidate in turn is backed by one faction or a coalition of competing factions, it is normal for the dominant faction in a state or locality to ensure that its own supporters emerge victorious from the selection process. For this reason, procedural mechanisms for conflict resolution have never been successfully internalized with the result "that each conflict, unless resolved unanimously, tends to be channelled upward necessi-

---

[16] For an excellent series of five articles on candidate selection in 1957 and 1962, see: R. Roy, "Selection of Congress Candidates," *Economic and Political Weekly*, I (Dec. 31, 1966), 833-840; II (Jan. 7, 14 and Feb. 11, 18, 1967), 17-23, 61-76, 371-376, 407-416.

tating . . . the intervention of the top command."[17] Internal conflict in this way tends to deprive local Congress units of whatever autonomy they might otherwise have, making it possible for a strong and united C.E.C. to play a dominant role in fact as well as in theory.

Whatever the procedural details elaborated for a specific election, once the provincial election committee has scrutinized all candidates, its recommendations are forwarded to the Central Election Committee for approval. These recommendations take several forms. In some cases the provincial committee may express consensus, as when it was declared that a certain candidate "is a good Congress-worker, and a man of integrity. He has extensive personal influence in the constituency and his chances of success are sure. In the opinion of the DCC no one except him will be able to defeat the rival Socialist candidate." In many cases, however, the recommendations sent forward indicate sharp differences of opinion among the state Congress leaders. In one such case, the provincial election committee wrote that the candidate in question was "an influential Nepali leader" and an I.N.T.U.C. organizer, but that "a section of Congressmen doubt his integrity." Of another it was said that "he is a sitting MLA. He himself belongs to the labour class. . . . Although the DCC did not recommend him the PCC considers it advisable to put him for the constituency in the interests of labour."[18] These examples show the extent to which the provincial election committees may use their authority to override groups at the district, mandal, and village level. In the same way, the Central Election Committee may modify or disregard the recommendations of the provincial election committees.

Although each selection process devised by the Congress has laid great stress on elaborate machinery and carefully specified stages through which recommendations proceed

[17] *Ibid.* (Jan. 14, 1967), p. 71.
[18] Kogekar and Park, *Report on the Indian General Elections, 1951-52*, p. 4.

from the Congress committee at the lowest level to the district committee, to the provincial committee, and, finally, to the Central Election Committee for final approval, in practice candidate selection has tended to be performed by small ad hoc committees in which the Chief Minister of the state plays a central role. These ad hoc committees are designed to accommodate conflicting group interests through a complex process of bargaining. Even at the Central Election Committee level there tends to emerge a small group who bear the responsibility for making ultimate decisions in the most difficult cases. In the process of selecting candidates for the 1962 general elections, for example, several three-man committees were formed to deal with candidate selection in faction-torn states.[19] Invariably, however, Lal Bahadur Shastri and Mrs. Gandhi were the Central Election Committee members most frequently called upon to make the difficult decisions. Mrs. Gandhi's reputation as an impartial and efficient arbitrator played an important role in her subsequent election to the prime ministership of India. One of the striking features of the selection process for 1967, another consequence of the divisions among the central leadership, was the failure of the necessary, widely trusted arbitrators to emerge. As a result, selection disputes had to be settled by bargaining and horse trading on an unprecedented scale.

The precise role of the Central Election Committee and the point at which it must intervene in the selection process depends, therefore, upon conditions at the center as well as upon the level of intra-party conflict within each state. During the period of centralization and convergence in states where the leadership was unchallenged, the Central Election Committee did not come into play until the state list had been completed. Approval of the slate in such cases was *pro forma*, for in essence the state party functioned autonomously. In states where a dominant group existed in the face of a weaker but still significant minority opposition, the Cen-

---

[19] *Hindustan Times* (New Delhi), Nov. 29, 1961.

tral Election Committee occasionally played a role in the early phases of drawing up the state list, but generally it confined its activity to the final selection process by ensuring that the minority group was given some representation. Finally, in states where the Congress was badly split by factions, the Central Election Committee sometimes found it necessary to participate throughout the selection process in order to see that a fruitful accommodation was reached. Yet frequently accommodation also signified agreement on weak compromise candidates whose acceptability to competing factions was not necessarily an indication of their strength in the constituency.[20]

The Central Election Committee's role was variously limited in states where the Congress was united or where there existed an unmistakably dominant group. Thus, in 1962, the lists of candidates submitted by B. C. Roy and Atulya Ghosh of West Bengal, by Chavan of Maharashtra, and by Kamaraj of Madras were accepted with little difficulty, although some minor changes were made. The Maharashtra list was altered slightly to conform to the central leadership's demands for greater minority representation.[21] The West Bengal list was adjusted to make room for Humayun Kabir, a Muslim central minister whose name had been dropped by the provincial election committee. Otherwise, the lists from such united states were accepted as submitted,[22] a forerunner of things to come.

In those states where the center was satisfied that the leader of the dominant group was capable of providing stable leadership, the state list was scrutinized and adjusted to ensure that the Chief Minister would have a solid majority in the assembly after the elections and that significant minority groups had some representation. Such was the case in Andhra and Mysore in 1957. In Mysore, for example, the

---

[20] M. Weiner and R. Kothari, *Indian Voting Behavior* (Calcutta: Firma K. L. Mukhopadhyay, 1965), p. 7.

[21] *Hindustan Times* (New Delhi), Dec. 1, 1961.

[22] *Hindustan Times* (New Delhi), Nov. 23, 1961.

Central Election Committee saw to the accommodation of the Hanumanthaiya group, but the majority of seats were left in the hands of the Nijalingappa group.[23]

The Central Election Committee's role was more complex and more extensive in badly divided states where the factions themselves were unable to reach any kind of settlement. In such states irreconcilable rivalries may arise from various sources. In some states, in the Punjab and Orissa in 1957, for example, the Central Election Committee's main task was to accommodate the conflicting interests of new groups that had entered the Congress. In other states, such as Uttar Pradesh, Bihar, and Madhya Pradesh, the Central Election Committee was faced with the problem of reconciling internally generated Congress factionalism. If the Central Election Committee's role in states characterized by Congress unity shows the limits of its authority during the period of centralization and convergence, its role in faction-torn states shows the scope and the importance of its authority.

The Central Election Committee's role in integrating new groups into the Congress was clearly illustrated by the case of the Punjab in 1957. Prior to the 1957 General Elections, the Congress in Punjab had succeeded in co-opting practically all the opposition parties, including the Akalis, the Gandhi Janata, the Praja Socialist Party, and even some Communists.[24] Although the incorporation of these groups guaranteed Congress control of the Punjab, it created a major problem for the party in the distribution of tickets. The eradication of inter-party conflict had served simply to intensify the level of intra-party conflict. Publicly, the Punjab Congress leadership announced that the new Congressmen would be treated as individual party members and that there would be no bargaining with groups for the allocation of seats, but it was quite clear that such bargaining was the order of the day. There were two major criteria in the distribution of tickets: the individual candidate's chances of success in a

---

[23] *Hindustan Times* (New Delhi), Feb. 1, 1957.
[24] *Hindustan Times* (New Delhi), Dec. 12, 1956.

particular constituency and the ability of Chief Minister Kairon to form a government based on a secure majority in the Congress legislative party after the election. However, the problem of balancing conflicting claims between the old and the new Congressmen proved exceedingly difficult. The hardest bargaining was carried on with the Akali leader Tara Singh, who demanded forty-nine assembly seats and seven Lok Sabha seats for his supporters—a demand based on his claim that the Akalis had polled 75 per cent of the Sikh vote in the last Gurdwara elections. Instead, the provincial election committee offered the Akalis only twenty-four seats or 40 per cent of the Sikh majority districts in the Punjab.[25] Tara Singh pressed his demands in meetings with Nehru, U. N. Dhebar, Pant, and Maulana Azad,[26] but other Punjab Congressmen, calling his demands preposterous, petitioned the central leadership not to give in to them.[27]

The Central Election Committee had a difficult time balancing the conflicting interests in the Punjab. After several long meetings it was announced that the list would be drawn up by ignoring group claims and by taking individual merit alone into consideration.[28] This announcement was precipitated by the Akali strategy of releasing their list at the last minute in order to prevent lengthy scrutiny. When the Central Election Committee finally released its list of official candidates, it was easy enough to discover, in spite of public declarations to the contrary, the kind of maneuvering that had been taking place. The Central Election Committee list gave the Kairon group 55 per cent of the nominations in order to ensure its control of the legislature. The Akalis were given only twenty-six seats instead of the forty-nine they had demanded. Moreover, even those Akalis receiving tickets were not the first choice of the Akali leadership, a tactic designed to win the loyalty of those actually selected. When these de-

[25] *Hindustan Times* (New Delhi), Jan. 20, 1957.
[26] *Hindustan Times* (New Delhi), Jan. 12, 1957.
[27] *Hindustan Times* (New Delhi), Jan. 12, 1957.
[28] *Hindustan Times* (New Delhi), Jan. 22, 1957.

cisions on Akali representation were reached, the Akali observers, furious, stormed out of the Central Election Committee meeting, declaring that the selections had been designed to divide the Sikh coalition which it had taken Tara
Singh some seven years to build.[29] The reaction elsewhere
in the Punjab, however, was that the Central Election Committee had been exceedingly fair in adjusting the rival claims
and interests in the state. The new Congress members had
been accommodated, the claims of older Congress groups had
not been ignored, and rival groups had been given balanced
representation.[30] Thus, in an attempt to ensure greater political stability in the Punjab, the Congress leadership broadened the base of the party by co-opting opposition parties,
then sought to balance off the resulting conflict of interests by
the use of the party machinery in granting tickets for the
1957 General Elections.

Factionalism in Bihar was one of the most persistent problems facing the Central Election Committee. In 1957, when
Morarji Desai was sent to Bihar to supervise the selection of
candidates, there were 4,000 applicants for the 318 assembly seats and the 55 Lok Sabha seats. Upon arrival in Patna,
Desai was presented with an agreed list of candidates drawn
up jointly by the competing factions. After reviewing the list,
he is reported to have interviewed all 4,000 applicants. This
gave him some idea of the state of Congress politics in Bihar.
Then, using as an excuse the Working Committee's broad
guidelines for the selection of candidates—the replacement
of a third of the sitting members, the allocation of at least 15
per cent of the tickets to women, and the proportional representation of Muslims—he proceeded to revise the entire list.
In the process he dropped 40 per cent of the sitting members
of the state assembly, including some party stalwarts against
whom there was documentary proof of corruption. Morarji's
list was further revised by the Central Election Committee.[31]

[29] *Hindustan Times* (New Delhi), Jan. 24, 1957.
[30] *Hindustan Times* (New Delhi), Jan. 25, 1957.
[31] *Hindustan Times* (New Delhi), Dec. 26, 1956.

It is significant that these major changes in the distribution of tickets produced only a short-lived revolt in several districts of Bihar.[32]

By 1962 the problem of factionalism in Bihar had grown worse. A three-man sub-committee of the Bihar provincial election committee consisting of the Chief Minister Binodanand Jha, the dissident leader K. B. Sahay, and the P.C.C. President A. Q. Ansari had attempted to draw up an agreed list of candidates for the 1962 General Elections. But they were so divided that they could agree on candidates only for 11 of the 53 Lok Sabha constituencies and 63 of the 318 assembly constituencies. It was reported at that time that

> for the remaining there are more than two and sometimes as many as six suggestions for each seat. Group rivalries in Bihar have been so furious that the Congress President at one time expressed "disgust" at the procedure adopted by the Pradesh Congress. Congress directives have not been flouted more recklessly anywhere as in this state, where a large number of candidates including eight State Committee members, have changed their old constituencies. . . . The two main groups . . . are not the only problem, there are groups within groups, and the position is complicated by frequent changes of loyalties by aspirants for the ticket.[33]

The Central Election Committee's reaction to the Bihar situation was said to be one of amazement and anger.[34] A special sub-committee consisting of Swaran Singh, Shastri, and Mrs. Gandhi was appointed to work with Chief Minister Jha in drawing up an acceptable and balanced list of candidates. In the final list, as customary, the ministerial group was given a majority,[35] but the rival groups were also given a fair share of the tickets for the 1962 General Elections.

[32] *Hindustan Times* (New Delhi), Jan. 10, 1957.
[33] *Link*, Nov. 19, 1961, p. 10.
[34] *Hindustan Times* (New Delhi), Nov. 8, 1961.
[35] *Hindustan Times* (New Delhi), Dec. 11, 1961.

In Madhya Pradesh the provincial election committee was unable to draw up a list because of the sharp cleavage which existed between the ministerial group led by K. N. Katju and the non-ministerial group led by P.C.C. President Moolchand Deshlehra. This split was reflected in the provincial election committee where the ministerial group controlled six seats and the Deshlehra group controlled five. Because of this close division Katju and Deshlehra were authorized by the provincial election committee to bargain for their respective groups; but, still, settlement could not be reached. Finally, Lal Bahadur Shastri was requested by both groups to arbitrate the state list of Congress candidates. Both groups agreed to abide by his decision.[36] In the end, the ministerial group was given a majority, but the factional splits were so deeply rooted that many Congressmen went down to defeat in the elections, among them the Chief Minister himself. As a result of this kind of internecine group rivalry, Congress strength in the Madhya Pradesh assembly fell from 232 in 1957 to 142 in 1962, thus ending the near monopoly of power enjoyed by the Congress in Madhya Pradesh.[37] When the election was over, the ineffectual Madhya Pradesh Congress Committee was suspended by the Working Committee, and an ad hoc executive committee was formed in an attempt by the center to restore order to the party in Madhya Pradesh.[38]

The situation in Uttar Pradesh was only slightly less damaging. Although the Uttar Pradesh provincial election committee was badly divided between the Gupta and Tripathi groups, a list was prepared for submission to the Central Election Committee in which candidates for 70 per cent of the seats had been selected unanimously.[39] This appearance of unanimity, however, was deceptive, for it had been produced only under continued pressure from the center. Nehru

[36] *Hindustan Times* (New Delhi), Nov. 9, 1961.
[37] Indian National Congress, *Report of the General Secretary, Jan. 1964–Dec. 1964* (New Delhi: A.I.C.C., 1965), p. 21.
[38] *Ibid.*
[39] *Hindustan Times* (New Delhi), Nov. 12, 1961.

had warned that, if provincial election committee members voted for candidates according to group loyalties, he would have each and every case closely examined by the Central Election Committee. Nehru's threat persuaded the majority group that it could not get away with being too heavy-handed and the minority group that any stalling or obstructionism would be considered disloyal or at least unwelcome.[40] Thus, the two groups had agreed to grant tickets to all important Congress supporters in each district. In the remaining constituencies, competing candidates were "bracketed" together on the list, and the final decision was left to the Central Election Committee.[41]

The Central Election Committee may try to encourage the development of stable leadership in a divided state, but, even during the period of centralization and convergence, it could not ignore the wishes of the leaders involved. Nor could it always prevent changes from taking place. Both of these limitations are illustrated by the case of Rajasthan in 1957 and the case of Gujarat in 1962.

In the 1957 General Elections in Rajasthan, the Central Election Committee attempted to strengthen the position of the old majority group led by J. N. Vyas. Although it gave Sukhadia a majority, the Central Election Committee excluded several of Sukhadia's ministers and chief lieutenants. Sukhadia attempted to strengthen his position in the state by rebelling against the Central Election Committee. He threatened to resign from the chief ministership and to refuse to stand for office unless his ministers were restored to the list of candidates, for he considered the Central Election Committee's action a vote of no-confidence in his leadership.[42] After a hurried discussion with Nehru, Shastri, and Azad, it was agreed that adjustments should be made

[40] *Hindustan Times* (New Delhi), Nov. 16, 1961.

[41] Paul Brass, *Factional Politics in an Indian State: The Congress Party in Uttar Pradesh* (Berkeley: University of California Press, 1965), p. 79.

[42] *Hindustan Times* (New Delhi), Jan. 25, 1957, Jan. 28, 1957.

in the disposition of eight seats.[43] The Central Election Committee, under pressure from a powerful emerging state leader, was forced to reverse its previous stand.

Another interesting case occurred in Gujarat during the 1962 General Elections. When Gujarat became a separate state after the bifurcation of Bombay, a senior member of the old Bombay cabinet, Jivraj Mehta, became Chief Minister of the new unilingual state. Morarji Desai, then a senior member of the central Cabinet, tried to consolidate his support in his home state by installing in power a group loyal to him. As a means of purging the old leadership, Morarji and his Pradesh Congress Committee supporters argued for the application to the Gujarat Congress of a suggestion made by President Sanjiva Reddy in his Presidential Address at Bhavnagar in 1961, "that people who have been in power, say for a period of ten years, should voluntarily relinquish their offices and take up organisational work."[44]

The application of such a rule would have enabled the Provincial Congress Committee to replace almost the entire Mehta ministry as well as many of Mehta's other supporters in the legislature. However, Nehru and the Congress President denied the existence of such a policy.[45] Mehta himself argued that the principle was being applied arbitrarily and unilaterally to eliminate him and his cabinet. He asserted his right as Chief Minister to challenge the decisions of the Desai-controlled provincial election committee before the Central Election Committee.[46] The Central Election Committee set up a three-man sub-committee to review the provincial election committee's rejection of twenty-one applicants from the Mehta group. While denying the applicability of the ten-year rule, the Central Election Committee granted tickets to only four of the twenty-one supporters of the Chief

[43] *Hindustan Times* (New Delhi), Jan. 29, 1957.

[44] N. S. Reddy, *Presidential Address, The Indian National Congress, Sixty-sixth Session* (New Delhi: A.I.C.C., 1961), p. 9.

[45] *Hindustan Times* (New Delhi), Nov. 25, 1961.

[46] *Hindustan Times* (New Delhi), Nov. 17, 1961.

Minister. Nevertheless, Mehta considered himself vindicated.[47] Furthermore, his supporters succeeded in defeating Morarji's choice as successor to the chief ministership at the polls. In the end, however, the Desai forces were triumphant. Mehta was finally ousted from power at the time of the implementation of the Kamaraj Plan. Thus, the Central Election Committee was unable or unwilling to bolster the strength of a Chief Minister whose power was waning.

After the candidates had been selected, the Congress attempted to prevent those denied a ticket from sabotaging the election of their successful competitors. In fact, the very process of selection was designed to keep revolts at a minimum. Stress was placed on the fairness of the procedures and on the fact that ample scope had been given for airing grievances before the list of candidates was finalized. However, once the list was complete, all Congressmen were expected to support it. As a deterrent to open revolt by dissatisfied Congressmen, it was customary to issue public warnings that those engaging in open defiance of party discipline by running as independents would never again be considered as Congress candidates.[48] The first critical test of the degree of potential revolt came with the deadline for filing nominations. At this time the A.I.C.C. made a check on the number of Congressmen who had filed to run as independents or on some other party ticket. These Congressmen were expelled[49] unless they recanted before the deadline for withdrawals.

Until the 1967 elections, however, open revolt was not the major difficulty. The real problem in seeing official candidates successfully through the elections was the possibility of an attempt on the part of disappointed nomination-seekers to practice sabotage without overtly violating party discipline.[50] In an effort to detect and deter such clandestine activities, the Congress developed a system of sending observers

[47] *Hindustan Times* (New Delhi), Dec. 23, 1961.
[48] *Hindustan Times* (New Delhi), Feb. 1, 1957.
[49] *Hindustan Times* (New Delhi), Feb. 1, 1957.
[50] *Hindustan Times* (New Delhi), Feb. 10, 1957.

to investigate reports which seemed to warrant inquiry. It is at this point that the social factors in the selection of candidates come into play. The causes of such excursions in sabotage, and the Central Election Committee's attempt to prevent them by taking into consideration the social realities of the constituencies, can be seen in the case of Jhunjhunu district in Rajasthan. In this predominantly Jat area, local Congress Jats charged that the "High Command"—that is, the Central Election Committee—had "victimized" the Jats when the tickets were distributed. The charge was easily shown to be false, for, whereas three Rajputs and two Jats had been given tickets in the previous election, the new list contained four Jats and only one Rajput. The real issue, therefore, could be traced to the fact that the dominant Jat leader in the district, who had been denied a ticket, was secretly supporting an independent for whom he hoped to gain disaffected Congress Jat votes.[51]

The shrewdness of the central leadership in uniting opposing factions behind the official candidates can be seen in the case of the candidacy of Ram Ratan Gupta in the 1962 General Elections in Uttar Pradesh. Ram Ratan Gupta, an important faction leader in Kanpur and an ally of C. B. Gupta, was given a Congress ticket for Gonda parliamentary constituency after years of unsuccessful efforts to attain it. Ironically, in order to attain his long-cherished goal of becoming a Member of Parliament, "Ram Ratan had to fight in a constituency where previously he had worked with the opposition. Moreover, he had to fight in a constituency where all but one of his 'base' assembly candidates owed allegiance to an opposite factional group in the state Congress." Expecting a difficult fight in the Gonda constituency, where no local Congressman had sufficient influence or resources to compete against powerful opposition candidates, the Congress had chosen a candidate with means. In the end, Ram Ratan's financial resources proved decisive. Despite the fact

[51] *Hindustan Times* (New Delhi), Feb. 17, 1957.

that the assembly candidates were members of the rival faction, Ram Ratan's desire to become a Member of Parliament persuaded him to work out a truce by promising to finance the campaigns of the assembly candidates. The result was a total Congress victory.[52]

Thus, during the period of centralization and convergence, the elaborate formal selection procedures established by the Congress were supplemented by the creation, on an ad hoc basis, of a series of small committees whose function was to bargain over the distribution of tickets. In this bargaining process the Chief Ministers played a crucial role. But the selection of candidates for constituencies in which bargaining had failed to resolve party differences tended to fall into the hands of those central leaders who were considered the most important and impartial of all possible arbitrators. One of Shastri's strengths was his performance of this role in all three elections prior to his death. G. B. Pant and Nehru were also important arbitrators. And so was Mrs. Gandhi in the 1962 general elections. In effect, these supreme arbitrators of the Congress were the most powerful of the Congress leaders. Their ability to perform this function effectively was one of their sources of power.

Effective as it was, the pattern of candidate selection during the period of centralization and convergence was sharply modified during the period of divergence, and the resulting contrast reveals a significant shift in the locus of power within the party. The selection process during this period was characterized by a continuing split within the central leadership of the Congress, a struggle over the selection of candidates for the National Parliament, a marked decline in the role of the national party in the process of selection, a corresponding increase in the power of state leaders, and the first massive defections of dissident Congressmen since 1951.

The divisions within the national leadership of the Congress had their origins in the struggle over succession to the

---

[52] Brass, *Factional Politics in an Indian State,* pp. 79-85.

prime ministership, vacated first by Nehru and later by his successor Shastri. As in 1951, these divisions generated an open contest over the selection of the five elected members of the Central Election Committee.

Maneuvering for the election of C.E.C. members had begun while the A.I.C.C. delegates were still assembling for the May meeting in Bombay. The strategy adopted by the various groups was determined by A.I.C.C. voting procedures. Under the single transferable vote system it was essential for each group to calculate carefully the number of its supporters. The dissident group led by Morarji Desai controlled enough votes in the A.I.C.C. to guarantee that one member of the group would be elected to the C.E.C. The official group, composed of Congress President Kamaraj, the Prime Minister, Mrs. Gandhi, and the Syndicate—S. K. Patil, Sanjiva Reddy, and Atulya Ghosh—controlled enough votes to guarantee their group three of the five C.E.C. seats. The fifth seat, remaining thus in doubt, converted the election into an open contest.

As his group's first choice Morarji quickly settled on C. B. Gupta, former Chief Minister of Uttar Pradesh. The official group, however, found itself divided. Kamaraj wanted Sanjiva Reddy, D. P. Mishra, and Mohanlal Sukhadia to contest as candidates for the official group's three assured seats. Mrs. Gandhi agreed to Reddy and Mishra, but she preferred Nijalingappa, G. L. Nanda, or D. Sanjivayya for the third seat. When no agreement could be reached on the third candidate, she insisted on the selection of G. M. Sadiq, Chief Minister of Jammu and Kashmir.[53] With the official candidates of both groups determined, focus shifted to the open contest for the fifth seat. The two major groups were known to have an unofficial entry to pick up the lower preference surplus votes of their supporters. K. Hanumanthaiya represented the Morarji group and D. Sanjivayya the official group. At this point, however, other factors came into play. The small but vocal left wing of the Congress decided to

[53] *Hindustan Times* (New Delhi), May 27, 1966.

support the candidacy of K. D. Malaviya and S. N. Mishra; and the urging of some members of the Working Committee led Dr. Ram Subhag Singh, a popular parliamentary figure and member of the Working Committee, to enter the contest. All other candidates were persuaded to withdraw.[54]

As was expected, the official candidates of both groups had little trouble collecting the minimum of 89 votes needed for election. To the surprise of many, however, C. B. Gupta was one of the three candidates elected on the first round. He received 91 votes to Sanjiva Reddy's 118 and D. P. Mishra's 95. The official group's dissatisfaction with the peremptory selection of Sadiq was evident from his failure to be elected until the second round.

Still more indicative of the diverse forces at work within the Congress was the contest which developed between Dr. Ram Subhag Singh and K. D. Malaviya for the fifth seat. Only by the third ballot was Ram Subhag able to pull out ahead and win.[55] His major support came from the Syndicate. But in order to win he also needed the second preference votes of Morarji and his followers.[56] Malaviya's strength was attributed to rumors that he enjoyed the unofficial support of Kamaraj.[57] That there was some substance to these rumors is suggested by reports that Malaviya received his votes from the anti-Gupta faction in Uttar Pradesh and from the second preference votes of Madras.[58] This split within the national leadership, reflected in the open contest over the C.E.C. and intensified by the anticipation that Morarji Desai, the leader of the dissident faction, would renew his bid for the prime ministership following the General Elections, was manifest at every stage of the selection process.

As the selection process for the Fourth General Elections

[54] *The Hindu Weekly Review* (Madras), May 30, 1966.
[55] *Ibid.; Hindustan Times* (New Delhi), May 24, 1966.
[56] *Hindustan Times* (New Delhi), May 24, 1966.
[57] *The Hindu Weekly Review* (Madras), June 6, 1966.
[58] *Hindustan Times* (New Delhi), May 24, 1966.

went its course, it revealed the unmistakably shrinking influence of the central leadership in the nomination process. This reduced role was evident not only, as in the period of centralization and convergence, in the states with a strong united leadership or in the states under the control of a dominant group but also in states badly torn by factionalism. In such cases the active authoritative intervention of earlier years gave way to a policy of sanctioning the continuance of the status quo. Y. B. Chavan summarized the limited role of the C.E.C. quite adequately when he observed: "I found that the provincial election committees had the real say. Where the P.E.C. nominations were unanimous, the C.E.C. made slight changes, if at all. When they came up with divided lists, in most cases we let the status quo (sitting members) remain."[59]

For example, in states where the party was controlled by a dominant faction, such as Gujarat, Madhya Pradesh, Madras, Maharashtra, Mysore, Orissa, Rajasthan, and West Bengal, the list of candidates was drawn up by the Chief Minister with few appeals to the C.E.C., which approved the list with little or no change. In faction-ridden states such as Andhra, Bihar, Assam, and Uttar Pradesh, there was a tendency for faction leaders to apportion the seats through a process of bargaining under the mediation of a member of the C.E.C. Only when no agreement could be reached did the C.E.C. play a significant role, and even then its decisions were restricted to names already appearing on the conflicting lists.

Even the central leadership's long-standing role as arbitrator and mediator was substantially reduced. There were no instances of active intervention as in the past. Although Mrs. Gandhi and Kamaraj, especially the latter, emerged as the final arbiters, the number of unresolved disputes requiring their help was fewer than ever before. Instead, there had been developed a new procedure which came to be

[59] *Times of India* (Bombay), Jan. 9, 1967.

called the Andhra formula because it had been originally formulated to help reconcile conflicting groups in this important South Indian state.

The Andhra rift seems to have originated in attempts by Sanjiva Reddy and D. Sanjivayya, both former Chief Ministers of Andhra and members of the Indian Cabinet, to strengthen their hold over their political base. The Reddy-Sanjivayya group intended to ensure that their followers formed the majority group in the state legislature so that, after the election, either Reddy, Sanjivayya, or one of their followers could be elected Chief Minister.[60] As the deadline for nominations approached, the Andhra Congress found itself split from top to bottom.[61] Although the incumbent Chief Minister controlled six of the eleven P.E.C. seats, the dissidents had strong support at the center, for Sanjiva Reddy was a member of the C.E.C. Nevertheless, the official list submitted by the P.E.C. excluded most of the sitting members unsympathetic to the Chief Minister. Dissatisfied with such meagre representation, the dissidents withdrew from the P.E.C. and drew up a separate list. Both lists were submitted to the C.E.C.[62]

At this point, Kamaraj tried to heal the breach in the Andhra Congress by proposing a compromise formula calling for the retention of all sitting members against whom there were no serious complaints.[63] But only after the C.E.C. had established a sub-committee consisting of Patil, Chavan, and Morarji did the rival groups manage to hammer out their differences.[64] Finally, with the aid of the sub-committee, a list was devised which gave the Chief Minister a large enough majority to ensure his re-election and which also gave the dissidents a substantial representation.[65]

The brilliance of the compromise can be seen in the fact

---

[60] *The Economic and Political Weekly*, I (Sept. 24, 1966), 231-233.
[61] *Times of India* (Bombay), Nov. 1, 1966.
[62] *Times of India* (Bombay), Nov. 9, 1966.
[63] *Times of India* (Bombay), Dec. 2, 1966.
[64] *Times of India* (Bombay), Dec. 5, 1966.
[65] *The Statesman* (Calcutta), Dec. 18, 1966.

that, although the ministerial group was given a majority, tantalizing possibilities were created for the dissidents. Because the C.E.C. had assigned some of the Chief Minister's seats to constituencies in areas where the Congress was traditionally weak, the official group would have to work hard in order to maintain its majority, while the dissidents had a stake in winning as many seats as they could. The C.E.C. formula raised hopes among the dissidents to such an extent that Subba Reddy, a follower of Sanjiva Reddy, was found making a statement that he would contest for the chief ministership after the election. Aware that the ministerial group had an edge over the dissident group in terms of the number of candidates selected, he was confident that the dissidents would win more seats in the election with the result that he would be in a position to be elected Chief Minister.[66] More broadly, as a result of the C.E.C.'s decision, it was reported that Congress prospects in the state of Andhra had improved considerably.[67] And Kamaraj, having intervened skillfully without annihilating either of the groups, retained his position of power and influence in the South.

The Andhra solution proved so effective that it became the model for solving disputes in the remaining problem states of Assam, Bihar, and Uttar Pradesh. It was officially adopted by the C.E.C. as part of a three-point formula proposed by C. B. Gupta. First, the C.E.C. would give preference to sitting members unless serious charges had been raised against them. Second, the C.E.C. would be the sole judge in determining if a *prima facie* case of misconduct existed. Third, no person would be given a ticket who had violated party discipline by voting for non-Congress candidates for monetary or other considerations.[68] After this formula was put into practice, problem states suffered the least turnover of candidates,[69] for the status quo was maintained as the

[66] *Times of India* (Bombay), Jan. 3, 1967.
[67] *Times of India* (Bombay), Dec. 23, 1966.
[68] *The Statesman* (Calcutta), Dec. 24, 1966.
[69] *Hindustan Times* (New Delhi), Dec. 25, 1966.

only solution to the problem. Because the competing groups were able to bargain for seats and maintain their power in the state party, the problem states witnessed fewer, and less organized, defections than those states with a strong leadership or dominant group.

In states controlled by a dominant group the pattern also was different than in the past. By contrast with previous elections, dissident minority groups were not only given very few seats on the original lists as drawn up by the Chief Minister: they also failed to receive any support when the lists were submitted to the C.E.C. In the case of the Punjab, for example, the counter list prepared by the dissidents was simply ignored by the C.E.C. As a result, Darbara Singh, one of the dissident leaders, was reported to have told Kamaraj that, in view of the shabby treatment accorded his followers, he would surrender his own ticket.[70] The reasons behind such ungenerous behavior were fairly evident. Faced by the increased likelihood of serious competition from the opposition parties through united fronts, most Chief Ministers wanted to ensure their control of the state by selecting where possible only loyal candidates, thereby minimizing the potential strength of dissident factions within the legislative party. Such calculations were not unrelated to the Prime Minister's concern to strengthen her hand in the almost inevitable contest for the prime ministership following the elections. It was reported that the Prime Minister had agreed to guarantee the Chief Ministers a majority in the legislatures in return for the right to select Members of Parliament. As a result, there were many disputes in the C.E.C. over parliamentary tickets.

The refusal to accommodate dissidents' demands for changes in the Chief Ministers' lists of candidates led to a series of major defections from the Congress in almost every state, the first such massive defection since 1951. During the Nehru era minority factions had been reluctant to leave the party largely because of the accommodating attitude of the

[70] *Times of India* (Bombay), Jan. 4, 1967.

central leadership. There was also the prestige of the Congress under Nehru's leadership to reckon with. In 1967, however, isolated from power by the Chief Minister and his dominant majority, able to expect little support from the central leadership, the minority factions in most states began to split off. As a *Times of India* editorial observed: "Minority factions which are so well entrenched that they can depend on receiving a fair share not only of tickets but of the spoils of office, as in U. P. and Bihar, have no compulsive reason to quit. They know that the dominant groups cannot entirely ignore their claims and live in the hope of some day making a bid for power and coming out on top."[71] The situation was far different for the weak and poorly organized factions. Theirs was a constant struggle just for survival.

Although in India such defections are popularly viewed in terms of frustrated personal ambition, the problem goes much deeper. It is, indeed, very largely true that the Congress, as a broad aggregating party, contains interests constantly seeking expression through group networks. Thus, as the *Times of India* noted, "quite often rival interests of castes, communities or districts are involved in what appear on a superficial view to be mere clashes of personalities" but which as in Kerala and West Bengal are very much deeper.[72] In Kerala a few years ago a large group of Christians broke from the Congress to establish the Kerala Congress. In Bengal the issue was one of the relative power of districts within the state.[73]

And there were many other related incidents. In Rajasthan the dissidents consisted of the pro-Jat Arya group with a strong local base in Bikaner. In Gujarat the demise of the influence of Saurashtra played a role, while in Madhya Pradesh the dissidents were found among the leaders from the old Madhya Bharat. Thus, the most significant defections occurred, not in those states where the groups within the Congress were relatively equal in power, but in states where

[71] *Times of India* (Bombay), Dec. 27, 1966.
[72] *Times of India* (Bombay), Dec. 8, 1966.
[73] *Ibid.*

they were a distinct and impotent minority. Even when the Chief Ministers had given them representation, it was seldom what they had expected. Isolation drove them to revolt from the Congress and to run as a separate party. Their chances could hardly be worse.

The shift in the locus of power revealed in the selection of candidates for the 1967 election was accompanied by a new development involving open disputes among conflicting groups within the C.E.C. over the selection of Members of Parliament. The expectation of a contest over the prime ministership directly after the elections gave both state and national leaders a totally new perspective and an acute interest in the selection of nominees to Parliament. In the past the Lok Sabha had been used by many Chief Ministers as a dumping ground for dissident leaders from the states. However, during the contest between Mrs. Gandhi and Morarji Desai over the prime ministership, they learned that their influence among the state parliamentary delegations could be extremely important, but that, so long as many Members of Parliament were exiled dissidents, the Chief Minister's influence within his state delegation would be seriously limited. Yet, just as the Chief Ministers became more deeply concerned about their nominees to the Lok Sabha, the Prime Minister and the national leadership had also developed a substantial stake in the selection of parliamentary candidates. As a result of this intensified interest in parliamentary candidates, many of the disagreements within the C.E.C. focused on the nomination of members of the Lok Sabha.

There was little doubt that the split within the national leadership was reflected in the nomination process during which national leadership groups attempted to assert their authority in the selection of parliamentary candidates. The controversy over the nomination of V. K. Krishna Menon was perhaps the most prominent, but certainly not the only, such instance. In the Menon case, the Bombay P.E.C. under the influence of S. K. Patil had decided to refuse V. K.

Krishna Menon a ticket for his constituency in Bombay. When the Bombay list reached the C.E.C., it led to a serious dispute among the major groups within the national leadership. Although personally unenthusiastic about Menon's candidacy, Mrs. Gandhi felt compelled to meet Patil's open challenge by supporting him. Kamaraj, who strongly favored Menon's candidacy, had even supported one of Menon's followers for election to the C.E.C. The opposition consisted of a coalition including Morarji Desai, C. B. Gupta, the members of the Syndicate, and Dr. Ram Subhag Singh.[74]

Open confrontation was unusual in C.E.C. history. Traditionally, the C.E.C. had operated through consensus. Votes were seldom taken. Therefore, hoping to extricate itself from the difficulties created by Menon's candidacy, the C.E.C. decided to delay public announcement of its decision to back the P.E.C. until Menon's response to several offers of alternative tickets could be ascertained. When he adamantly refused to contest a seat in another constituency, the C.E.C. announced its decision to drop him.[75] Thus, in the face of the coalition which had succeeded in electing Ram Subhag Singh to the C.E.C., the Prime Minister and the Congress President found themselves unable to impose their will in the C.E.C. Mrs. Gandhi attributed Menon's defeat to his supporters' failure to speak up for him in the committee.[76] Atulya Ghosh, on the other hand, argued that Menon was not granted a seat in accordance with a long-standing Congress convention that the C.E.C. does not upset a unanimous recommendation by a P.E.C.[77]

The decision to maintain the status quo in faction-torn states practically guaranteed the re-nomination of sitting members. But the parliamentary delegates from those states with a stable dominant leadership experienced a high turnover which led to disputes over specific seats as leaders of

[74] *Times of India* (Bombay), Nov. 25, 1966.
[75] *Times of India* (Bombay), Dec. 3, 1966.
[76] *Hindustan Times* (New Delhi), Dec. 15, 1966.
[77] *Hindustan Times* (New Delhi), Dec. 16, 1966.

the major groups at the center fought to protect their supporters. Thus, for example, when the Kerala list was considered, Morarji and Gupta made an unsuccessful attempt to include Ravindra Varma on the ground that his good parliamentary performance entitled him to renomination. The bid failed.[78] Mrs. Gandhi attempted a similar but more successful intervention to secure seats for several of her ministers.[79] Kamaraj was also involved in maneuvering for parliamentary tickets in his repeated attempts to hold a seat open for T. T. Krishnamachari.[80] Finally, in Andhra[81] and Orissa[82] the C.E.C. insisted on the selection of certain sitting members who had been denied tickets at the state level.

Although it is difficult to document the degree to which the Prime Minister and the Chief Ministers negotiated the selection of Members of Parliament, it would seem that enough evidence is available to show that the possible contest over the prime ministership and the differences among groups at the center had an important impact on candidate selection, and that, in light of the dominant role played by the Chief Ministers in the selection of candidates, many of the conflicts over parliamentary seats within the C.E.C. were actually attempts by national leaders to protect loyal sitting members.

The recruitment process for the Fourth General Elections, then, revealed a great deal about existing Congress leadership, the locus of power in the party, and the factors influencing candidate selection. For one thing, it revealed that the national leadership of the Congress continued to be seriously split and that one of the most important results of this split in the national leadership was the attempt on the part of state leaders to consolidate their position at home and in Parliament, which in turn brought about massive defec-

[78] *The Statesman* (Calcutta), Dec. 22, 1966.
[79] *Times of India* (Bombay), Jan. 4, 1967.
[80] *Times of India* (Bombay), Jan. 5, 1967.
[81] *Times of India* (Bombay), Dec. 17, 1966.
[82] *Times of India* (Bombay), Dec. 18, 1966.

tions among dissident state groups. In this and other ways, the recruitment process of 1967 seemed reminiscent of 1951. At that time, the party was split between Nehru and Tandon; there was also a massive enrollment of largely bogus members and a proliferation of major defections. However, whereas the conflict in 1951 acquired an ideological flavor, owing largely to the tacit encouragement of Nehru, the split in 1967 produced no such pattern, although Menon's candidacy could have sparked this reaction had his supporters been more broadly based and had the Prime Minister made common cause with them.

The defections from the Congress have had both a disintegrative and an integrative impact on the Congress. To the extent that each group had some social base, the withdrawal of the dissidents certainly weakened the Congress in some areas. Yet, though defections forced the Congress to face the election with more external competition, there was a corresponding reduction of intra-party competition and of the danger of internal sabotage. In fact, the greatest threat to the Congress came, not from the dissidents as such, but from the ability of the opposition parties to form a united front against the Congress.

Perhaps most important and most irreversible of all, the events leading up to the 1967 elections demonstrated not only the split in the national leadership but also a major shift in the locus of power from the center to the states. The two are closely related. The open split in the Congress made it impossible for the weakened national leadership to intervene in the selection process in any decisive way. Thus, though strong Chief Ministers have always played an important role in candidate selection, they enjoyed in 1967 a much stronger voice than ever before. Perhaps even worse from the point of view of the national leadership, the center had to content itself with the rather passive expedient of preserving the status quo in faction-torn states where it previously was able to dictate a favorable solution.

The selection of candidates is the one function performed

by the Congress organization which makes control of the party a jealously coveted prize once every five years. As a result, a study of the nominating process can be expected to reveal a great deal about the Congress Party. As E. E. Schattschneider has observed: "The nominating process is obviously one of the points at which parties can be studied most advantageously for no other reason than that the nomination is one of the most innately characteristic pieces of business transacted by the party. . . . By observing the party process at this point one may hope to discover the locus of power within the party, for he who has the power to make the nomination owns the party."[83]

During the period of centralization and convergence the role of the C.E.C. in the final distribution of tickets in a party torn by severe intra-party factionalism was critical. Since all factional groups in the Congress had only one ultimate aim—the control of the ministry and the patronage and power appertaining thereto—the selection process became the focal point of group conflict. Yet competing groups, unable to settle these disputes locally, were forced to look to, and thus even in victory remain beholden to, the C.E.C. as the final arbitrator.

The period of divergence, however, was characterized by a split in the central leadership which contributed to the devolution of power to the states and the increasing federalization of the Congress. State leaders as usual attempted to strengthen their position at home by reducing the role of dissident groups within the party and, what was not so usual in earlier days, often succeeded all too well in doing so, for the central leadership, weakened by internal divisions, was unable to intervene decisively. The result was the development of the first massive wave of defections from the Congress since 1951. These defections, in combination with the formation by opposition parties of united fronts on an unprecedented scale, threatened in 1967 to bring an end to Congress dominance.

[83] E. E. Schattschneider, *Party Government* (New York: Rinehart & Co., Inc., 1942), p. 100.

THE CHANGING ROLE OF THE WORKING COMMITTEE

The role of the Working Committee in independent India evolved through three phases each of which reflected political developments within the country and changes in the party. During each of these phases the major functions of the Working Committee underwent considerable change as the internal structure of the party was pragmatically adjusted and adapted in an attempt to achieve the maintenance of party solidarity and the continuance of Congress dominance in India. The period of transition from 1946 to 1951 was a period of conflict and disorder during which the party structure of the pre-independence period found itself unable to cope with the myriad of problems arising from the early years of transforming the Congress movement into a governing political party. The period of centralization and convergence from 1951 to 1963 witnessed the emergence of a process of accommodation, coordination, and conflict resolution under the guidance of the central leadership of the party. The period of divergence from 1963 to 1967 has reflected the devolution of authority and the growing autonomy of the state Congress parties and has raised major problems of solidarity, coordination, and cooperation to such an extent as to pose a threat to the unity of the party.

During the period of transition from 1946 to 1951 the leadership of the Congress was so preoccupied by the problems of partition, the integration of princely states, the framing of a new Indian Constitution and by the other difficulties accompanying the transfer of power that matters pertaining to the inner structure of the party were permitted to drift.

The Working Committee

As a result, the first four years of the post-independence period were marked by conflict and disorder throughout the party. Friction was manifest between the Congress Presidents and the Prime Minister; a struggle developed over control of the Working Committee; the mass organization attempted to impose policies on the government; center-state relations lacked effective coordination. There was open interference by Congress members at all levels of administration. In several states Congress ministers were overthrown despite large Congress legislative majorities as factionalism under the cover of party-government conflict raged out of control. The party was divided on policy, goals, and tactics. Yet, throughout this period organizational problems went unattended, and time after time the much needed reconstruction of the party was postponed.

For a brief moment in 1946 the autonomy of the party seemed to have been guaranteed by Nehru's decision to resign as Congress President in order to become leader of the new Interim Government. Instead, there ensued a very critical debate over the composition of the Working Committee. The mass organization attempted to prevent the newly constituted parliamentary leadership from continuing to sit on the party executive. When initial efforts to block dual leadership of party and government failed, the party adopted a constitutional amendment restricting the parliamentary wing's representation on the Working Committee to one-third of the total committee membership. This prohibition placed the Congress President and the P.C.C. Presidents in a majority on the Working Committee for a brief and ineffectual period of time. It was not a coincidence that this condition prevailed in the stormy periods during which Kripalani and Tandon presided. Even at its most harmonious, this transitional phase was threatened by a quiet antagonism between party and government at the national level. At this time many Congressmen still believed that the traditionally dominant position of the Working Committee would remain unchanged. They envisioned the new government as the handmaiden of the triumphant nationalist movement. Expecting the new government to implement uncritically the long-standing policies of the Congress, the party reacted with hostility when the government felt it necessary to reject, rewrite, or ignore the policies adopted by the mass organization.

Meanwhile, independence had released a series of deeply rooted social forces long submerged during the struggle against the British raj. The communal, caste, linguistic, and ideological interests which had been united under the Congress umbrella were suddenly given individual expression through the Congress organization. Thus, the orthodox Hindus in the Congress, the government's policy of secularism notwithstanding, expected the new government to satisfy their repeated demands for the banning of vanaspati and the outlawing of cow slaughter. The advocates of linguistic states expected the new Congress government to implement immediately the long-standing Congress pledge to create unilingual states. Socialist intellectuals within the party expected the new government to embark immediately upon a socialist economic policy while the Gandhians, for whom constructive work and Gandhian economics had become a philosophy of life, expected the government to begin the reconstruction of Indian society along Gandhian lines. But, however their demands differed or even conflicted in substance, all interests converged in expecting that a Congress government would carry out the dictates of the party mass organization as expressed through its decision-making organs.

The leadership of the government, meanwhile, perceived these divided councils and particularistic demands as threats to the unity and stability of the country. Thus, despite differences in philosophy and outlook, the men of the national leadership sought to compromise their ideological differences and to resist party pressures for the implementation of such demands. The result, as we have noted, could only be a period of conflict between party and government.

In the case of vanaspati, organized interests operating

301

through the Working Committee of the Congress sought to place a ban on its manufacture. When the government ignored the Working Committee's decision to do so, the Congress President was authorized by the Working Committee to inform the government of the party's policy on the issue and to request immediate action. Again the government took no action. As a result, the issue was raised in the A.I.C.C., and attempts were made to instruct the Congress government to implement the party's directives within a fortnight. Despite these pressures the government refused to yield, insisting that the party did not have the authority to commit the government to such a specific policy. The party could lay down broad objectives, but the timing and implementation were to be left to the government's determination.

The linguistic states demand proved to be an even more delicate issue for the government, for it involved demands for implementation of a long-standing and clearly articulated Congress policy. The government's position on linguistic states was clearly spelled out for the first time in the Dar Commission Report, which insisted that the creation of linguistic states be postponed indefinitely and that only minor adjustments be considered immediately. This recommendation was given party sanction with the adoption of the J.V.P. Report, which asserted that the principle of linguistic states had to be reconsidered in the light of changed circumstances. Throughout the debate on the linguistic states issue the party insisted that a boundary consensus existed, but repeatedly in attempting to work out the details of implementation the government found that such agreement did not in fact exist. As a result, a specific Working Committee directive to create the state of Andhra was shelved, and eventually, despite repeated Working Committee pressure, the resolution of the issue of linguistic states was postponed.

The case of economic policy, during the transition period, was somewhat different, for the government was forced to move much more cautiously, in fact, than the Prime Minister was willing to admit. Thus, though Nehru had helped to prepare the Congress Economic Programme Committee Report with its strong socialist and Gandhian objectives, the impossibility of implementing such a program at that time forced him to repudiate it. Nehru's relations with Patel, domestic economic difficulties, and the concern over maintaining confidence within the business community compelled the Prime Minister to develop a much more moderate economic program for India. This compromise policy was embodied in the Industrial Policy Resolution of 1948.

Thus, during the transition period from 1946 to 1951, demands long submerged during the struggle against the British raj quickly surfaced and received expression through the Congress organization. The new Congress government was expected to implement policies clearly articulated by the party. Instead, many of the policies laid down by the party were rejected outright by the Congress government on the ground that these policies conflicted with the broader responsibility of the government to consider the larger interests of the country.

If the relationship between the Working Committee and the national government was marked by conflict during the transitional period, the relationship between the Working Committee and the state governments was totally ineffective even where it was not non-existent. The Congress ministries in the states, with little guidance from the national party, except for the advice of individual leaders, had undertaken almost immediately after the 1946 election to implement the long-standing Congress commitment to abolish the zamindari system. Since the zamindars as a group had divorced themselves rather early from the nationalist movement in order to support the British raj, the state Congress ministries encountered little opposition within the party in passing legislation to abolish the zamindari system. Zamindars could only seek to head off the passage of such legislation by appeals for intervention addressed to the Congress President and Working Committee. Although state legislation was adjusted slightly to ensure coordination with national policy, the

Congress President made it clear that land reform was the sole responsibility of the new Congress governments. The central party would not intervene on behalf of the zamindars. Zamindari abolition represented one of the few issues in which there was an attempt to coordinate national and state policy through the Working Committee. Yet, even here, coordination could only be minimal because of the diversity of conditions in each state, the rapid progress which the legislation had made through the state legislatures, and the determination of state leaders to implement the policy as soon as possible.

The Working Committee's role as chief executive of the party during the transitional period was weakened by the absence of central initiative and guidance. The national leadership had become overwhelmed by the rapid movement of events and the problems of the transfer of power. The party machine, first debilitated by the mass arrests of the Quit India Movement and then flooded by an influx of new members, was in desperate need of reorganization but was permitted to flounder as organizational reform was postponed from year to year. The writing of a new party constitution which began in 1945 was not completed until 1948. Moreover, the new constitution, which attempted to combine the functions of a conventional political party with those of a Lok Sevak Sangh, or Gandhian social service organization, proved to be unworkable. The party machinery collapsed under the massive enrollment of new members by factions competing at the state level to gain control of the party organization and its election machinery in time for the First General Elections. The Working Committee's valiant last-minute attempt to set the party's house in order was unable to prevent major defections from the party. Perhaps more disheartening was the Working Committee's discovery in the case of Andhra, for example, that central intervention could only go so far in taking over a state Congress organization. In the end, the national party had to work with the groups which were functioning within the state. It was confined to mediating their disputes in an effort to restore a workable harmony within the state party.

One of the most significant developments in the role of the Working Committee in the transitional period was the revival in 1946 of the Parliamentary Board and its formal incorporation into the Congress machine in the 1948 party constitution. Although the Parliamentary Board was ineffectual during the first few years of its revival, it began by 1949 to emerge as a decisive force within the Congress. This rapid development of the Parliamentary Board's effectiveness led to the strengthening of the Congress ministries in the states, the beginning of a coordination procedure, and, most important of all, the emergence of a formalized process of conflict resolution between the state parties and the state governments which was to aid significantly in the maintenance of cohesion, unity, and dominance of the Congress for the next decade.

The establishment of a formal procedure for candidate selection was another major contribution of the period of transition. Until the establishment of the Central Election Committee, candidates had been selected by ad hoc committees specifically created to perform this function. The 1948 party constitution, however, made the C.E.C. a permanent part of the Congress. Since it could determine the composition of the Congress ministry by selectively distributing party tickets, candidate selection itself became the major point of linkage between party and government. Moreover, the very composition of the C.E.C. provided important connections between the Working Committee's coordinating function performed by the Parliamentary Board and the selection of candidates, since the members of the Parliamentary Board held a majority of the seats on the C.E.C.

The period of transition from 1946 to 1951 can thus be characterized as a period of disorder and uncertainty as well as conflict in the midst of which the party nevertheless succeeded in adapting itself to the task of governing. The major contributions of this period to Congress development were the emergence of the supremacy of the Prime Minister, the decision to permit overlapping membership between party and government, the development of the role of the Parliamentary Board, and the establishment of a formal process of candidate selection within the party. The major failure was the leadership's inability to effectively reorganize and rehabilitate the party organization. The party was permitted to drift, and the problems of the party did not receive the attention they warranted until much too late in the succeeding period of convergence.

The election of Nehru as Congress President in 1951 marked the beginning of the period of convergence. Party-government conflict at the national level was brought to a halt as Nehru merged the office of Congress President and Prime Minister and established the parliamentary wing's dominance over the Working Committee. The emergence of the state Chief Ministers as a powerful force in the country and within the Congress Party Working Committee enhanced the capability of the Working Committee as a means of coordinating center-state relations. While the party machine did not receive much attention until the late 1950s, the mediating, arbitrating, and conciliating role of the Working Committee became highly developed and effective in keeping an increasingly diverse party working together.

As Congress President, Nehru reshaped the Working Committee to meet the needs of coordination, economic development, and change. With the removal of all restrictions on the membership of leaders of the parliamentary wing in the Working Committee, most of the P.C.C. Presidents were replaced by the most powerful Chief Ministers. Those P.C.C. Presidents who received seats on the Working Committee tended to come from states so badly divided by factional conflict that there was no clearly recognized leader. Consequently, their tenure was short, and their status could not compare with that of the established state leaders who dominated the party in their home state. The presence of major central Cabinet members in addition to the Prime Minister and the Chief Ministers ensured that the hard core of the Working Committee would consist of the leaders of the parliamentary wing at the center and in the states. The very composition of the Working Committee in this way determined to a large extent the functions which the committee was able to perform effectively.

In time, as a body composed largely of members of the parliamentary wing, the Working Committee came to play an important role in providing policy leadership to the party organization, in coordinating party-government relations, and in accommodating the conflicting demands of Congress leaders representing the broadening base of the party. The Working Committee became a sounding board by which the Prime Minister could test the acceptability of new policies as well as an important feedback mechanism by which to assess the reactions of party and state leaders. All major government policies were thoroughly discussed as policy resolutions in the Working Committee before submission to the A.I.C.C. for debate and ratification. In fact, a regular pattern developed in which the Prime Minister would draw up major policy resolutions, adjust them to the demands of state leaders in the Working Committee, and then in the course of A.I.C.C. debate assess party attitudes toward them. In the A.I.C.C., members would discuss the content of an official Working Committee resolution, criticize specific shortcomings of the resolution and of the government policy it endorsed, and move amendments which, having served as a basis for debate, would be withdrawn to permit unanimous passage of the resolution. Although amendment was rare, many of the criticisms expressed in this manner were not ignored, nor were they futile. Judging the temper of the party, the Prime Minister would attempt to adjust subsequent resolutions to achieve the widest possible consensus. Altogether, these Working Committee resolutions served not only to articulate the broad objectives of the government but also to educate and influence the opinions of the leaders of the mass organization and the attitudes of the country as a whole.

This process of accommodation and consensus building was clearly illustrated by the decisions involving the development of the basic strategy for planned economic growth. Partly because there were at least two basic issues involved, it took several years for this strategy to evolve into a workable formula. The first problem was the necessity to ensure coordination of party and government. The second involved the difficulty of reconciling basic philosophical differences between the traditionalists and modernists in the Congress. The central government and the Planning Commission were dominated largely by westernized, highly urbanized intellectuals, who were devoted to the modernization of India through industrialization based on the development of heavy industry in the public sector. To Gandhian Congressmen, however, such policies were unacceptable as completely foreign to Indian tradition; and because the government seemed consistently to place insufficient emphasis on rural development, economic decentralization, and social service, the Gandhians had become increasingly alienated from the Congress, a process which was of considerable concern to Nehru.

Just as the Congress movement had united a multitude of divergent groups behind the goal of political independence, Nehru's goal as leader of party and government was to unite as many groups as possible behind a new consensus of Indian economic development. This goal required that the Congress Party be an open, all-inclusive organization united behind a series of consistent but broadly based principles. The adoption by the government of the Mahalanobis Plan Frame, which finally offered an acceptable compromise between the aspirations of the traditionalists and the modernists, between the claims of socialism and sarvodaya, was an important example of the consensus-building approach. Yet the history of the Mahalanobis compromise suggests also the inadequacies of the consensus approach. The formula as it turned out did not prove to be feasible, for the unsuccessful results of the rural industrial program were not commensurate with the expenditure incurred.[1] This defect might have been detected had not the compromise seemed for a while to be so politically perfect. Thus, attention to consensus can be a source of strength and stability but can also lead to unwise and uneconomic policies.

During the period of centralization and convergence the Working Committee also came to play an important role in establishing all-India policy for the guidance of state Congress ministries. In the case of planning issues, the government had turned to the Congress Working Committee as the major coordinating instrument for developing the basic policy objectives of the First Plan—especially on those issues such as land policy which were under the direct jurisdiction of the states. However, experience proved that, if coordination took place only in the Working Committee, there was a danger that the Plan would be viewed simply as a party plan rather than as a national plan. Moreover, it was clear that the Working Committee could not give official sanction to the Plan. This realization led the government very early in the planning process to establish an official body, the National Development Council, to carry out the major policy-making function of coordinating center-state planning policies. The Working Committee, however, was still being used as a means of supplementing such official coordination at the party level and, perhaps more important, as a method whereby the national leadership could prod the states to act. Thus, during this phase when the Congress controlled the national government and most of the state governments, the Working Committee remained an important meeting ground where the more intellectual, urban-oriented leaders of the party could attempt to persuade the new leaders of the more rural, pragmatic, and interest-based sectors of the Congress to conform to the broad objectives of the Plan.

[1] George Rosen, *Democracy and Economic Change in India* (Berkeley: University of California Press, 1966), p. 175.

The Working Committee

At the non-planning level, the Working Committee provided the single means of establishing and coordinating all-India policies on subjects not under the jurisdiction of the central government, such as language. Again, Working Committee resolutions were designed to exhort rank-and-file Congressmen as well as state leaders to consider the national implications of their actions and to inhibit advancement of narrow parochial attitudes. Although the national leadership could not compel acquiescence in planning or non-planning issues, its persuasive power was not inconsiderable. As the devolution of political power grew stronger toward the end of the period of centralization and convergence, the Congress leaders found that the old informal methods of coordination were no longer sufficient. It became essential to create official bodies to handle non-planning issues just as the National Development Council had been created to handle planning issues. The result was an increase in the frequency of meetings of the Conference of Chief Ministers, which, though it had no constitutional duties, became a very important body.

It was during the period of centralization and convergence that the arbitrating, mediating, and conciliating roles of the Working Committee became most highly developed. If the Congress was to be the all-inclusive force for economic development that Nehru envisioned, it was essential that the Congress broaden its base of recruitment to include all social strata. With this accomplished, or nearly so, the role of the central leadership was, by persuasion, encouragement, cajolery, accommodation, reconciliation or whatever, to get these diverse elements to work together, invoking discipline only rarely and in the absence of all other alternatives. The central leadership exerted all its power to prevent majority groups in the states from crushing or ignoring dissidents, particularistic interests, or other minority groups. The leadership tried to accomplish its integrative role by establishing formal procedures to ensure security and also acted as a final court of appeal and umpire when the procedural safeguards were abused. The party failed, however, to institutionalize the integrative function. Dominant groups consistently adapted the intricacies of each formal procedure to suit their own ends. As a result, the party became heavily dependent on the integrity, intelligence, and ingenuity of the national leadership to settle disputes which could not be settled locally. Several dangers were inherent in this system. If ever the central leadership ceased to be united or to produce effective individual arbitrators, the integrity and thus the dominance of the party would be severely threatened. The Congress would come to depend more and more on the resources and ability of each state leader to hold the party together within his state. Such developments would lead to increased federalization.

During the period of centralization and convergence, in short, major emphasis was placed upon maintaining the open, broad-based character of the Congress in support of a program of planned economic development of the country. Nehru's dual role of Prime Minister and Congress President, his ability to dominate later Congress Presidents, his development of an effective system of consultation between parliamentary and organizational wings at the center, enabled him to function as supreme arbitrator of party and government affairs. It also enabled the central government to play an important role in shaping all-India policy by using the Working Committee to pressure, prod, and persuade the states to enact legislation considered important to national unity and growth. The Working Committee's role as arbitrator, conciliator, and mediator for the party machine in the event of factional strife within the state parties, and its role in the selection of candidates for the state and national legislatures became highly developed and helped to keep the open, broad-based party operating successfully. Yet perhaps the greatest failure during this period was the continued neglect of the party machine as such. Attempts to build a party organization at the district level and below were not begun until the presidency of U. N. Dhebar and were not implemented until after the 1957 elections, and by 1959 there were renewed demands for a thorough restructuring of the Congress. However, the leadership failed in its attempts to institutionalize effective organizational procedures and to limit the intensity of factionalism within the party as the period of centralization and convergence began to give way to a period of divergence.

With the period of divergence from 1963 to 1967 there developed a new equilibrium between party and government and between the center and the states. The resurgence of the party had begun as early as 1959 when demands for widespread changes in the party organization culminated in the acceptance of the principle of an elective element in the Working Committee. The tempo of change increased with the introduction of the Kamaraj Plan, which had been framed as a means to restore dignity to the organization by rekindling the old Congress ideal of renunciation of power and thus by providing for a return of talent to the party organization. While the original goals of the Kamaraj Plan were frustrated, interest in the Congress presidency was renewed when the most likely candidates for successor to Nehru expressed interest in becoming Congress President. At this point, at a critical point of transition, the election of the first leader of stature to the Congress presidency since 1948 placed the party in a position of strength such as it had not enjoyed for over a decade. The status of the organization was further enhanced by the significant role played by the Congress President and the Working Committee in the first succession. These developments, each tending to diminish the centralized power of the 1951 to 1963 period, breathed new life into the deliberations of the A.I.C.C. and the Annual Sessions. After a long dormancy each body seemed to be springing to life with a spirit of questioning and criticism which gave rise to freer debate, more open criticism, and more vigorous efforts to amend official resolutions.

At the same time, the devolution of power to the states

which had been under way for almost a decade created a new equilibrium in center-state relations until by the late fifties the emergence of powerful state leaders and the rising power of new social groups began to be reflected at the national level. When Congress President U. N. Dhebar resigned, expressing criticism of bossism in the Congress and of the intractability of state leaders, he was publicly recognizing the culmination of a process which had been much accelerated during his term by the reorganization of states in 1956. In a sense, Nehru had encouraged the emergence of the Chief Ministers by strengthening their position vis-à-vis the party organization through the Parliamentary Board, and, in 1952 following the First General Elections, he had supplanted most of the P.C.C. leaders on the Working Committee by the most important Chief Ministers. However, in the years following, while the state leaders continued to increase their power by building political support on a strong social base at home, the central leadership was weakening. First, Nehru's dominance was shaken by the Chinese invasion and by his deteriorating health. Then the struggle for succession split the central leadership in such a way that the competing leadership groups felt compelled to reach out to the states for support. When the Chief Ministers played the decisive role in the second succession, this trend toward the devolution of power had reached its apogee.

The changes in the relationship between party and government and between the center and the states produced corresponding changes in decision-making. The long-standing pyramidal structure of Congress decision-making fell into a polycentric system in which power was distributed among several institutional groups: the Working Committee, the Chief Ministers, the Cabinet, and the Congress Party in Parliament. Thus, Shastri's consensus approach was not only a matter of personal style but also a reflection of the political reality of the time. Moreover, consultation with Chief Ministers became so essential to the decision-making process that it could no longer be adequately performed in the Working Committee alone. The frequency with which the Conference of Chief Ministers met to handle all-India policy in non-planning areas such as language and food was a good indication of the growing importance of state party leaders and of the consequent institutionalization of non-party channels of communication among Congressmen.

Yet the checkmate system which emerged during Shastri's prime ministership created grave difficulties for the Congress and the country. As George Rosen has observed, the difficulties that India faced after 1961 were only partly due to natural causes. "Equally, they arose from the crisis within the Congress party, a crisis of ideas and leadership. . . . The leadership, for reasons of age and health, no longer proved capable of generating new ideas to serve as a basis for policy. The Prime Minister no longer led the party, he held it together. At the same time a conflict arose between the old ideas and the interests of powerful new groups within the party."[2] It was this pattern from which Mrs. Gandhi tried to break out.

Upon first assuming the prime ministership, Mrs. Gandhi moved as cautiously as Shastri had, but by the middle of 1966 she was asserting her independence from the Congress President and the Working Committee and attempting to move in new directions of policy and leadership. While following the consensus approach on the Punjabi Suba issue, Mrs. Gandhi reached the decision to devalue the rupee by depending for advice, not on her senior colleagues in the Working Committee, but on a new group of young policy-oriented members of her Cabinet. The result was a rift between the Prime Minister and the Congress President which was exacerbated by a split between the Cabinet and important non-Cabinet members of the Working Committee. Deterioration of law and order, the failure of the monsoon, and the forthcoming elections all conspired to force Mrs.

[2] *Ibid.*, p. 278.

Gandhi back to the pattern of close consultation on important issues.

Perhaps more important than the impact on decision-making of these shifts in power from the center to the states and of the split in the central leadership was their critical impact on conflict resolution. This became most evident in the selection of candidates for the 1967 General Elections. The recruitment process revealed that the national leadership of the Congress continued to be split and that one of the most important results of this split was the attempt by state leaders to consolidate their position at home and among their state parliamentary delegations. This attempt at consolidation by state leaders brought about massive defections among dissident state groups who, feeling isolated from power within the party because of the inability of the central leadership to intervene to protect them, withdrew from the Congress. Underlying these defections was the basic Congress dilemma: "To dominate, Congress must accommodate; yet accommodation encourages incoherence which destroys the capacity to dominate."[3]

The Congress entered the 1967 General Elections without Nehru at the helm, the government shaky, the national leadership seriously divided, smarting from massive defections of dissident groups and facing an unprecedented series of united fronts forged by the spectrum of opposition parties. The results of that election were a shock to both party and country, for it appeared that the period of Congress dominance had come to an end. For the first time the Congress was forced to consider itself seriously in the role of opposition as well as majority party. A new phase in the evolution of the Congress was imminent.

With each of these stages the function of the Working Committee underwent modification which enabled it to func-

[3] W. H. Morris-Jones, "Dominance and Dissent," *Government and Opposition*, 1 (July-Sept. 1966), 460; see also "The Indian Congress Party: A Dilemma of Dominance," *Modern Asian Studies*, 1 (April 1967), 109-132.

tion effectively despite changes in the country and the party. During its period of dominance the Working Committee passed through a phase of conflict and transition from 1947 to 1951, a phase of convergence and centralization from 1951 to 1963, and a phase of divergence from 1963 to 1967, each marked by certain characteristic patterns of decision-making and conflict resolution. Playing a no less significant role in the maintenance of Congress dominance during the first two decades of independence, however, were corresponding shifts in the nature of Congress recruitment and leadership.

PART III

THE LEADERSHIP OF THE
CONGRESS PARTY

xiii

THE ORIGIN AND PRE-INDEPENDENCE
DEVELOPMENT OF THE CONGRESS ELITE

The capacity of the Congress organization to adapt its structure and functioning to changing circumstances would have
been insufficient to sustain the Congress in power after independence if the Congress had not also evinced the ability
to recruit leaders and members from an ever-broadening
social base. Certainly the Congress would not have been
able to maintain support throughout its long history if it
had not been able to harness the social changes let loose by
the forces of modernization, industrialization, and democratization which have swept over India in the past century.
One of the most important results of the Western impact on
India was the creation of a new elite which was eventually
to arouse India to the sense of national identity that
would bring an end to British rule. Yet because of the protracted nature of the nationalist struggle in India, the new
elite was itself subject to modification and adaptation over
the years as new and more diverse social elements were politically activated and recruited into the movement. The
stability of post-independence India, in fact, has to a large
extent been an outgrowth of the Congress Party's ability
to incorporate new elements and to develop organizational
means for enabling these diverse social elements to work
together, if not always harmoniously.

The evolution of the Congress elite can be divided into
four periods, each of which produced a slightly different
type of leader drawn from a different complex of social strata.
There was the period of the moderates from 1885 to 1900,
the period of the extremists from 1900 to 1920, the Gan-

319

dhian era from 1920 to 1946, and the post-independence period from 1946 to the present. Yet in no case did a new wave of Congressmen completely inundate the old. Instead, the tendency was for the new elite to coexist with the old, giving rise to the mosaic which is the Congress Party today. Thus, though the Congress began with a fairly homogeneous upper-caste, upper middle-class, urban, modernized elite, it was slowly Indianized by a process of drawing upon an ever more traditional social base. As a result, it would be difficult to characterize the Congress leadership today in terms of a purely modern or a purely traditional elite. It would be more accurate to visualize the social composition of the Congress membership and elite as a continuum in which the modernized elements blend by various transitional stages into more traditional elements as one moves down the leadership pyramid from national to state to village levels.[1]

The nature of the modernized Indian elite from which the Congress elite was first to be drawn was largely determined by the earliest British contacts. The first Indians to become somewhat westernized were the servants and agents of the East India Company and the Indian merchants who served them. It was these two groups and their descendants who were the first recipients and patrons of English education. These were the Indians who first broke through the rigidities of the caste order and began the creation of a social pattern outside the traditional social structure.[2]

The key to the further development of the Indian elite was the need for the Company to staff the administrative, legal, and educational system which had arisen as its responsibilities for governing India increased. Although some Indians had received a Western education in the early years of the Company's rule, largely through private schools and missionary groups, it was not until 1835 that the direction of what was to become the massive Indian educational

[1] W. H. Morris-Jones, *The Government and Politics of India* (London: Hutchinson University Library, 1964), pp. 67-71.

[2] B. B. Misra, *The Indian Middle Class* (London: Oxford University Press, 1961), p. 343.

system was settled. At that time, Macaulay's famous memo, closing a long debate between the orientalists and the Anglicists in favor of the latter, called for the creation of a new "class," which was to be "Indian in blood and colour, but English in taste, in opinions, in morals and intellect."[3] Therefore, in the words of Bentinck's Order in Council, "all the funds appropriated for the purpose of education would be best employed on English education alone."[4] This educational policy made modern education available, not to the masses, but to the Hindu elite and especially to the Brahmins.[5]

From 1835 on, the new elite grew slowly but steadily with the expansion of educational facilities. By 1854, some two decades later, a conservative estimate placed the number of English institutions at 180 with some 30,000 students in attendance. By 1857, with the establishment of major universities in Calcutta, Bombay, and Madras,[6] the English educational system in India had assumed its basic form, and education as a whole became more widely available. It was estimated that by 1860-1861 there were 368 government and mission schools with an enrollment of 43,232 students.[7] As career opportunities and the market value of English education increased, the resistance on the part of the more orthodox upper-caste Hindus broke down, and the system continued to grow in response to quickening demand.[8]

By 1885, fifty years after the famous educational decision

[3] *Ibid.*, p. 11.

[4] B. McCully, *English Education and the Origins of Indian Nationalism* (New York: Columbia University Press, 1940), pp. 69-70.

[5] R. Bendix, "Public Authority in a Developing Political Community: The Case of India," *Archives of European Sociology*, 4 (1963), 50; S. Tangri, "Intellectuals and Society in Nineteenth Century India," *Comparative Studies in Society and History*, 3 (July 1961), 383.

[6] McCully, *English Education and the Origins of Indian Nationalism*, p. 144.

[7] *Ibid.*, p. 129.

[8] It is important to note that Muslims did not share this enthusiasm for English education. The result was that the Muslim community fell far behind the Hindus in developing modern skills and leadership.

and nearly three decades after the establishment of the earliest universities, estimates placed the size of the English-educated elite at about 55,000.[9] This new elite was over-whelmingly Hindu.[10] Drawn from a very narrow social base, it represented upper-caste, middle and low income urban groups rather than the old native aristocracy.[11] In 1891, eleven groups of castes totalling just under 14 per cent of the population provided more than half of the literate com-munity.[12] Most of this new elite was either government serv-ants or members of the new modern professions of law, medicine, education, or civil engineering. Of the professions, law attracted the most talented men.[13]

Having created a new elite, the British found themselves facing the demands of this group for a greater share in the administration of India. These demands took organizational form in 1885 with the creation of the Indian National Con-gress. That this organization reflected the dominance of the new English-educated elite can be seen by the representa-tion at the first Congress meeting in Bombay. The seventy-two delegates, who came from all the Indian provinces, were predominantly Hindu, and their occupations showed a "re-markable correlation with those pursued by the educated elite of India."[14]

Although politically and socially reformist in orientation, this new Congress elite was not anti-British.[15] Their attitudes were clearly reflected in the resolution, passed at that first meeting in Bombay in 1885, which called for a Royal Com-mission to investigate the working of the Indian administra-

[9] McCully, *English Education and the Origins of Indian Nation-alism*, p. 177.

[10] *Ibid.*, p. 184.   [11] *Ibid.*, pp. 185, 187.

[12] K. Davis, *The Population of India and Pakistan* (Princeton: Princeton University Press, 1951), p. 156.

[13] McCully, *English Education and the Origins of Indian Nation-alism*, p. 191.

[14] *Ibid.*, pp. 384-385.

[15] R. I. Crane, "The Leadership of the Congress Party," in R. Park and I. Tinker (eds.), *Leadership and Political Institutions in India* (Madras: Oxford University Press, 1960), p. 171.

tion with a view to freer access to the Indian Civil Service examinations. It also demanded the introduction of an elective element in the Indian Councils. Even at this stage, the Congress opposed British imperial policy as it affected India, and called for a reduction in military expenditures and an end to the annexation of Upper Burma.[16] But none of these demands could be called revolutionary. The loyalty of the members of the new Congress was displayed in their outspoken acknowledgement of the benefits of British rule. In the course of discussions at Bombay, for instance, one delegate declared: "Gentlemen, had it not been for English education and Western civilization, persons inhabiting different parts of this vast country, . . . would not have this day met together in this Hall to interchange thoughts, give expression to their common grievances and aspirations, and discuss in a most constitutional manner the means for redressing those grievances and fulfilling those aspirations." Another delegate found it within himself to say: "Without discanting at length upon the benefits of that [British] rule, I can summarize them in one remarkable fact, namely, that for the first time in the history of the Indian population there is to be beheld the phenomenon of national unity among them, of a sense of national existence, and of common solicitude for the well-being and honour of their common country."[17] And yet, though the Congress delegates to the founding meeting in Bombay have been called moderates and may be described as wholly loyal to British India, there was in their references to a new-found national unity a significant proto-revolutionary flavor. On sentiments such as this a separatist movement can rise and flourish, as it did in India.

An examination of the religious, caste, and social composition of Congress delegates from 1892 to 1909 indicates that the Congress elite remained constant throughout the first two decades of the organization's existence. During

[16] M. V. Ramana Rao, *A Short History of the Indian National Congress* (Delhi: S. Chand & Co., 1959), p. 8.

[17] McCully, *English Education and the Origins of Indian Nationalism* p. 386.

these years there were 13,837 delegates to the annual meetings. Hindus accounted for 12,383 of the total, an overwhelming majority. Only 912 delegates were Muslim, but there were 210 Parsis and 177 Christians. Of the Hindus, almost half were Brahmin.[18] In terms of occupation, 9,119 delegates were drawn from the professions. The only other groups represented among them were the landed gentry, which accounted for 2,629 delegates, and the commercial classes, which sent 2,091 delegates. Among the professions the lawyers predominated with 5,442 delegates. Journalists, doctors, and teachers each accounted for about 400 delegates.[19] In short, the delegates to the early Congress sessions were clearly a homogeneous group drawn from the new English-educated elite which was predominantly Hindu, upper caste, and professional. In this sense the early Congress was almost totally divorced from the bulk of the Indian population in terms of outlook, education, occupation, social origin, and goals.

Yet, even while the English-educated elite was emerging to provide a new type of leadership in India, developments were taking place which were to have a profound impact on the composition of the Indian elite and on the leadership of the Congress for the next several decades. In the years immediately following 1835, the major educational impetus had been confined to the universities. However, English education began to expand more rapidly during the 1870's. Expansion was particularly marked at the secondary level, and by the early 1880's there were already in existence some 486 secondary institutions with an enrollment of some 60,000 students.[20] As a result, the 1881 census showed a ratio of 1 to 3,300 for Indians in secondary schools compared to a ratio of 1 to 22,055 in colleges and profes-

[18] Dr. P. C. Ghosh, *The Development of the Indian National Congress, 1892-1909* (Calcutta: Firma K. L. Mukhopadhyay, 1960), p. 23.

[19] *Ibid.*, p. 24.

[20] McCully, *English Education and the Origins of Indian Nationalism*, pp. 165-166.

324

sional institutions.[21] Clearly, not all those who completed secondary school would find a place in college. The emerging elite, though more numerous, was to be less highly educated as a group, both in duration and content of their education,[22] than the first products of English education had been.

Therefore, although a larger group in this period came into contact with the West and with Western ideas, it did so less intensely and with a totally different effect than in the earlier generation. The attraction of English education, as before, was largely economic, but the economic slots destined to be filled by many of the new generation were of a vastly different nature. Rapid population increases due to the restoration of peace by the British and the growing fragmentation of landholdings led members of many of the priestly and literary castes to seek enough English education to fill the expanding lower ranks of government and business offices. They became clerks. When they, in their turn, became politically active, they were called by Lord Dufferin the "Babu politicians."[23]

The second generation of Indians, with regard to the nationalist movement, were more responsive to a new kind of nationalism based on Hindu revivalism than to the liberal nationalism espoused by the earlier generation of moderates, from whom they differed so markedly in social origins, education, and degree of contact with the West. The new nationalists were drawn from the lower-income groups who found it difficult to obtain employment in the modern sector of the society. As a result, they developed grievances based on personal, economic, and social frustrations, for which they tended to blame the British. Moreover, deriving as they did from sectors of society which by uninterrupted tradition were carriers of orthodox Hinduism and having

[21] *Ibid.*
[22] Tangri, "Intellectuals and Society in Nineteenth Century India," p. 372.
[23] Misra, *The Indian Middle Class*, p. 348.

tasted Western values only in the diluted dosage of secondary school, they tended to be attracted to a different type of leadership and to a degree of militancy repugnant to the earlier generation.[24] They responded positively to the militant and revivalist leadership provided by Bal Gangadhar Tilak with its emphasis on traditional values, its mass participation techniques of boycott and hartal, and its militant demands for swadeshi.[25] Moreover, with the partition of Bengal in 1905, the new militancy was at an opportune moment given an emotionally charged issue against which these new techniques could be employed.

The emergence of this new leadership resulted in a head-on clash with the older moderate leadership of the Congress which for some time left sharp cleavages within the nationalist movement between the moderate and militant wings.[26] Only by 1907-1908 did the newer leadership succeed in incorporating some of its slogans as official Congress goals.[27] Yet the success of this more militant Hindu revivalist leadership in broadening the base of the Congress to include hitherto untouched Hindu social and economic groups tended also to embitter Hindu-Muslim relations and to undermine thereby the development of the more broad-based Indian nationalism which had been envisioned by other older Congress leaders.

Meanwhile, the process of change in the fabric of Indian life which had already precipitated two phases of leadership began to accelerate in the early part of the twentieth century. The most important influences on the future development of the Indian elite were the increase in economic activity, especially as a result of World War I, the further growth of urbanization, and the expansion of literacy in English and the vernaculars.

[24] Crane, "The Leadership of the Congress Party," p. 176; Tangri, p. 272.

[25] Crane, p. 176.

[26] Bendix, "Public Authority in a Developing Community: The Case of India," pp. 56-58.

[27] Crane, p. 171.

Origin And Pre-Independence Development

Perhaps the most important of these factors, especially in the degree to which it introduced a largely new element in the composition of the Indian elite, was the growth of Indian industry. Increased industrial progress, particularly during and after World War I, in turn stimulated the development of a managerial and technological elite and led to a considerable increase in industrial employment.[28] As a result, the growth of the Indian elite, which had previously been derived from changes in the educational, judicial, and administrative sectors, began to be derived from expansion in trade and industry as well. No less important, the growing Indianization of business provided a major source of funds for nationalist activity.[29]

Increased economic activity also gave impetus to the trend toward urbanization. The urban population rose from an estimated 6 per cent in 1835 to 10 per cent in 1901 and 11.2 per cent in 1921. The growing diversity of this new urban population provided a broad base for recruitment into the nationalist movement. It also provided the leadership which later would attempt to organize the great mass of the Indian population still living in the rural areas and still untouched by the vast changes of the past century. Although literacy in English had spread from the coastal enclaves to the interior, it was still concentrated in urban areas.[30]

The expansion of education during this phase took place most dramatically at the university and secondary levels. English education, though still the privilege of a minority, became more widely dispersed, and literacy in the vernaculars began to seep down to entirely new social strata, helping to broaden still further the base of recruitment for the elite of the nationalist movement. By 1921 the literacy rate in India was 8.2 per cent of the population over ten years of age and as high as 14.2 per cent among males.[31] Yet, while the educational system had expanded, it was still top-heavy at the

[28] Misra, *The Indian Middle Class*, p. 396.
[29] *Ibid.*, pp. 249-250.
[30] Davis, *The Population of India and Pakistan*, p. 159.
[31] *Ibid.*, p. 151.

university and secondary levels. Primary education, conducted for the most part in the vernacular languages of
India, expanded less rapidly.[32] The slow growth of primary
education in proportion to higher education has been attributed to several factors. The most important was the fact
that the upper and middle classes in the urban areas had the
money to develop educational facilities for their children,
while people in the rural areas did not. Since British policy
placed major emphasis at the time on private as opposed to
public education, the expansion of rural education could not
possibly proceed as rapidly as in the urban areas.[33] Whereas,
in 1901, 8.5 per cent of the literates were literate in English, by 1921 the figure was 12.1 per cent and a decade later
14.9 per cent; by 1931 the census listed 3.5 million Indians
as able to read and write in English.[34] While this figure is impressive, it nevertheless constituted an extremely small elite
of 1.2 per cent of the population. By 1921 total college enrollment had reached 59,595, or a five-fold increase over
1886; total school enrollment stood at 8.32 million.[35]

Moreover, during the years after 1920 with the stirring
of greater material consciousness, the caste distribution of
literacy began to expand so as to broaden the base of political recruitment. This change was significant because there
had been a fairly rigid correlation between social position
and degree of literacy. At one time observers had feared
that distribution of literacy would become frozen in this pattern because of discrimination on the part of the high-caste
members who controlled education. As the Census Report
of 1901 put it:

> The officers of the Education Department, with whom
> the decision practically rests as to the localities where
> new schools are to be opened and what grants-in-aid

[32] S. Harrison, *India: The Most Dangerous Decades* (Princeton:
Princeton University Press, 1960), p. 58.

[33] Misra, *The Indian Middle Class*, p. 284.

[34] Davis, *The Population of India and Pakistan*, p. 159.

[35] McCully, *English Education and the Origins of Indian Nationalism*, p. 304.

should be given belong almost exclusively to the small privileged group of high castes. In Bengal, for example, excluding 44 Europeans and Eurasians, . . . there are 137 officers of the Education Department, of whom no less than 111 are Brahmins, Baidyas and Kayasths, only 9 are Muhammadans, 5 are Native Christians and 12 belong to other castes. The lower grades of the community are entirely unrepresented.[36]

It was also feared that the educational system might serve in this way "to enforce and even widen the existing cleavages between the Classes [castes] in the community."[37] In spite of these forebodings, by the 1930's literacy among lower castes began to show a more rapid increase so that by 1940 caste mobility had also increased. Intermediary castes were pushing into modernized sectors of the economy, and some lower castes were even moving into the occupational preserves previously monopolized by Brahmins and Vaisyas.[38] It was these nationalists, drawn from the lower castes and educated in the vernacular, who were to become politically active for the first time in response to Gandhi's leadership.

While the new Indian elite continued to grow in size and diversity, the Congress elite remained basically middle class and urban. Yet at a critical turning point, just after World War I, Indian nationalism was to receive a new thrust with the emergence of a leader who possessed the capacity not only to galvanize the old Congress elite divided into moderates and extremists but also to mobilize the newly emerging groups in such a way as to transform the Indian National Congress into a mass movement.

Gandhi, then, emerged as a leader of the Congress at a major turning point. The forces of economic change, urbanization, and education, in addition to the death of Tilak, placed him in a critical position from which he was able to appeal to all segments of the movement. As a Western-edu-

[36] Davis, *The Population of India and Pakistan*, p. 156.
[37] *Ibid.*   [38] *Ibid.*

cated lawyer, he had the credentials to attract the more modernized element in India, while his use of traditional symbols enabled him to attract the more traditional groups and to link the largely middle-class, urban elite with the masses of the countryside. Through the use of satyagraha Gandhi was able to broaden the base of the Congress by recruiting new elements into the movement. This gave the Congress the impetus to develop organizational methods of reconciling conflicts among such diverse elements; the benefits of the resulting conflict-resolution techniques would be particularly apparent after independence. For a very brief period, largely because of the peculiar circumstances of the Khilafat Movement, even the Muslim elite were brought into the Congress. However, the marriage was brief, and after 1923 the Muslims went their own way.

Gandhi had begun to attract adherents as early as 1917 during his Champaran campaign to alleviate peasant oppression on the indigo plantations in Bihar. This early activity attracted Rajendra Prasad, a young Bihar lawyer, and Acharya J. B. Kripalani. Several other early converts were Vallabhbhai Patel, Jawaharlal Nehru, and C. Rajagopalachari, all of whom like Gandhi were lawyers. Gandhi's response to the oppressive Rowlatt Bills and the Amritsar tragedy also attracted idealistic, highly educated, upper-caste Indians. However, it was not until after the Congress had officially adopted the policy of non-cooperation in 1920 that Gandhi's appeal began to attract larger and more diverse elements.

The first civil disobedience campaign called for a boycott of the 1920 elections conducted under the Indian Councils Act, a boycott of government schools, and a boycott of the law courts. Although this campaign lasted fourteen months, the response was limited. Few students left their studies to participate in the movement. Yet some lawyers, of whom the most famous were C. R. Das and Motilal Nehru, did respond by giving up their practices.[39] Many lesser figures

[39] M. Brecher, *Nehru: A Political Biography* (London: Oxford University Press, 1959), p. 73.

Origin And Pre-Independence Development

were also inspired to give up the practice of law and join
the movement before an outbreak of violence in a remote
area of Uttar Pradesh prompted Gandhi to call the first civil
disobedience campaign to a halt. It had lasted only a little
more than a year, but it had had a significant impact. Jail-
going had become respectable even for the newly recruited
middle- and upper-class professional men.[40] Moreover, as a
report of the Viceroy indicated, the movement had begun
to have a measurable impact on the lower classes and, to
a somewhat lesser extent, on village India: "The lower classes
in the towns have been seriously affected by the non-cooperation movement . . . and although [its] influence . . .
has been much smaller in the rural tracts generally, in certain
areas the peasantry have been affected, particularly in parts
of Assam Valley, United Provinces, Bihar and Orissa and
Bengal."[41]

The changes that occurred in the Congress as a result
of Gandhi's early impact can be seen in the changing composition of the A.I.C.C. from 1919 to 1923. There was a
sharp shift from the larger cities and provincial capitals to
the district towns. In 1919, 59 per cent of the A.I.C.C.
delegates came from the larger cities while only 41 per cent
came from the district towns. By 1923 the balance was reversed: only 35 per cent came from the cities and 65 per cent
from the towns. It was also at this stage that women began
entering the Congress. However, the Congress retained its
high-caste orientation, for Brahmins constituted 40 per cent
of the membership in 1919 and 34 per cent in 1923. Occupationally, the professionals, especially the lawyers, continued to play a dominant role.[42]

The second great civil disobedience campaign, the salt
satyagraha, began on March 12, 1930, when Gandhi and
seventy-eight disciples began a march from Ahmedabad to
the sea. When Gandhi was arrested, demonstrations broke

[40] *Ibid.*, p. 81.   [41] *Ibid.*, p. 78.
[42] G. Krishna, "The Development of the Indian National Congress
as a Mass Organization, 1918-1923," *The Journal of Asian Studies*,
xxv (May 1966), 422-424.

331

out in every major city in India. The British responded with mass arrests. It was estimated that by the end of 1930 arrests totaled somewhere between 60,000 and 90,000.[43] By this time the movement had gained wider attention, and new groups were recruited to the cause, particularly the small landholding rural gentry. It was from this group that the key leaders of the Indian states would be drawn some thirty years later. The decade from 1932 to 1942, more than any other period in Congress history, was responsible for broadening the base of the movement by making possible the recruitment of non-urban elements and lower, non-Brahmin, castes.

Some indication of what happened to the Congress movement under Gandhi can be seen in the development of Congress leadership in Maharashtra and Madras. In Maharashtra the Congress was dominated by Brahmins for the first thirty or forty years of its history. In spite of his mass appeal, even B. G. Tilak, the great Maharashtrian leader of the Congress, supported the theory of Brahmin superiority. Thus, in its early years, the Congress in Maharashtra did not appeal to non-Brahmins. Because of their alienation from the Congress in both Maharashtra and Madras, where a similar situation obtained, non-Brahmins were willing to operate the new institutions created by the British constitutional reform program. They entered the legislative councils in 1920-1921 and in fact helped the British to suppress the non-cooperation movement which was favored by the Brahmin-dominated Congress organization.[44]

This early non-Brahmin hostility to the Congress diminished slowly beginning in 1928. In Madras, until then, the non-Brahmins had been preoccupied with regional struggles, and the non-cooperation movement of 1920-1921 was, therefore, largely unsuccessful in these areas. By the late twenties, as regional objectives were accomplished and

[43] Brecher, *Nehru*, p. 153.
[44] M. Patterson, "A Preliminary Study of the Brahmin Versus Non-Brahmin Conflict in Maharashtra" (unpublished M.A. thesis, University of Pennsylvania, 1952), p. 109.

national politics became more compelling, the Tamil areas had become involved in the nationalist struggle. By the thirties they were joining the Congress.[45] In Maharashtra the non-Brahmins began joining the Congress as the Brahmins became increasingly identified with the Hindu Mahasabha. The result was a decline in the image of Congress exclusivity and a gradual transformation of the composition of the Congress movement. However, it was not until about 1934 or 1935 that significant sectors of non-Brahmins entered the Congress in Maharashtra.[46] At this time the leadership of the Maharashtra Congress movement was in the hands of Brahmins like Shankarrao Deo, B. G. Kher, and N. V. Gadgil.

By independence, the non-Brahmins in the Maharashtra Congress were in sight of abolishing Brahmin leadership. In the First General Elections the Congress was forced to select many non-Brahmins as candidates, though not in proportion to the population since Congress prestige was sufficient to serve as an endorsement for almost any candidate. In the ensuing Bombay cabinet all the Maharashtra ministers were non-Brahmins.[47] By the 1960's all D.C.C. presidents and secretaries and about 75 per cent of the candidates in the 1962 elections were non-Brahmins.[48] In 1966 non-Brahmins constituted about two-thirds of the Maharashtra cabinet. In the North the process was somewhat slower. But the total effect of Congress activity throughout India in the thirties and forties was to broaden the base of the membership by attracting lower castes into the movement. These recruits have now become the elite in South and West India. In North India the struggle for leadership status, still under way, is one of the major causes of instability.

[45] E. Irschick, "The Brahmin-Non-Brahmin Struggle for Power in Madras" (unpublished paper prepared for the Association for Asian Studies Conference, San Francisco, 1965), pp. 8-9.

[46] Patterson, *A Preliminary Study of the Brahmin Versus Non-Brahmin Conflict in Maharashtra*, pp. 116-117.

[47] *Ibid.*, p. 127.

[48] *Link*, Feb. 18, 1962, pp. 14-15.

Congress Party Leadership

In summing up Gandhi's impact on Congress recruitment, a British historian wrote that Gandhi "quickened patriotic sentiment in the hearts of the middle classes and, above all, he took Indian nationalism to the masses. What had been almost totally an affair of the educated few, became the concern of every Indian, rich or poor, learned or ignorant, lawyer, shopkeeper or agriculturist."[49] More recently, a prominent Indian observer concluded that Gandhi not only widened the party's appeal to include the masses but also made the middle class more Indian in outlook.[50] All in all, the new leadership of the Congress represented the more traditional forces in society. "From the Gandhian upheaval new classes of leaders had emerged, the majority comprising small-town lawyers, doctors, and social workers with a leavening of urban intellectuals, politically conscious peasants and workers, students and, not least important, a vast array of women."[51] No longer was the Congress leadership drawn only from the upper-caste professionals of the coastal provinces of Bengal, Madras, and Bombay. They came as well from Uttar Pradesh, Bihar, Andhra, the Central Provinces, and Gujarat—the interior areas which had been less subject to Western influences.

A cross section of the Congress in recent years reflects the patterns of leadership recruitment during the Gandhian era in much the same way as the rings of a tree reflect the patterns of its growth. When analyzed by age groups ten years apart, the membership of the Second Lok Sabha, for instance, illustrates clearly the process by which representatives of different groups were recruited in response to changing conditions in the successive decades of the twentieth century.[52]

[49] P. Griffiths, *Modern India* (New York: Frederick A. Praeger, 1962), p. 73.

[50] Frank Moraes, *India Today* (New York: The Macmillan Co., 1960), pp. 67, 75.

[51] *Ibid.*, p. 76.

[52] The data on the Congress members of the Second Lok Sabha were collected by the author in cooperation with Dr. Surindar Suri, former Director of the Diwan Chand Information Center.

The membership of the A.I.C.C. in 1956 and of the Third Lok Sabha confirms these patterns of recruitment,[53] but in the detailed discussion that follows the evidence will be drawn from the far more extensive data relating to the membership of the Second Lok Sabha.

Whatever the index by which successive generations of Congressmen are compared—source of income or occupation, social origin, landholding, education or caste—the pattern is the same: from decade to decade there was a gradual broadening of the recruitment base for the Congress elite. The trend was from urban to rural, from high caste through the middle castes to the lower castes, from the modernized professions to the more traditional pursuits. In general, the impulse to join the Congress came at some time between age twenty and age thirty. Therefore, those joining the Congress during any one decade tended to belong roughly to the same age group. Thus, the impact of the Gandhian era is revealed by the configuration of four Congress generations: the early Gandhians born between 1891 and 1900, the generation of the first civil disobedience campaign born between 1901 and 1910, the generation of the second civil disobedience campaign born between 1911 and 1920, and the generation of the Quit India Movement born between 1921 and 1930.

Table XIII-1 on occupation indicates clearly that successive decades of the Gandhian era attracted leaders from different social strata. The early Gandhian period attracted the most devoted followers, men who were drawn into the movement and remained from that time on as full-time Gandhian workers. By contrast, those identifying themselves as public workers, who joined the Congress during the Quit India Movement, tended to be young leaders of the newly politicized lower castes devoted to the improvement of their own caste rather than to general village uplift. Professional men were strongly attracted to the Congress in the early Gandhian period and even more strongly during

[53] These studies were carried out by the author. See Chapters XIV and XV below.

TABLE XIII-1

OCCUPATION OF CONGRESS MEMBERS OF THE
SECOND PARLIAMENT, 1957-1962, BY AGE GROUPS*

Occupation	1891-1900		1901-1910		1911-1920		1921-1930	
	No.	%	No.	%	No.	%	No.	%
Public work	17	44.7	14	20.3	16	24.6	11	28.9
All professional	13	34.2	27	39.1	17	26.1	9	23.7
Law only	6	15.8	23	33.3	14	21.5	7	18.4
Agriculture	4	10.5	18	26.1	22	33.9	10	26.3
Business	2	5.3	5	7.2	6	9.2	7	18.4
Other	2	5.3	5	7.2	4	6.2	1	2.6
Unknown	0	—	0	—	0	—	1	—
Total	38	100.0	69	99.9	65	100.0	39	99.9

* In Tables XIII-1 to XIII-6 only those born between 1891 and 1930 were included. Not included were five whose ages were unknown, two born after 1930, and six born before 1891. The percentages do not always add up to 100 because of rounding.

The data on the Congress members of the Second Parliament were based on interviews with 224 of the 375 members of the Congress Party in Parliament in 1960. Since only non-ministers were included in the study, the sample is composed of about 70 per cent of Congress back-benchers. All tables are based on the standard frequency distribution program of the Computer Center of Pennsylvania State University.

the period of the first civil disobedience campaign when Gandhi issued his call to the educated classes to boycott the British raj. The first heavy influx of non-urban Congress members came in the thirties when the rural gentry began to join in large numbers. Although some businessmen have always belonged to the Congress, their numbers increased impressively as independence drew near. Perhaps most important of all, the table on occupation reveals that the base of Congress recruitment was most limited during the early Gandhian era and that by the time of the Quit India Movement the Congress was recruiting its future elite from nearly all sections of society.

These observations are substantiated by the data on social origins in Table XIII-2, on landholdings in Table XIII-3,

TABLE XIII-2

FATHER'S OCCUPATION OF CONGRESS MEMBERS OF THE
SECOND PARLIAMENT, BY AGE GROUPS

Occupation	1891-1900		1901-1910		1911-1920		1921-1930	
	No.	%	No.	%	No.	%	No.	%
Agriculture	15	39.5	29	42.6	30	46.9	16	42.1
Professional	4	10.5	13	19.1	3	4.7	6	15.8
Public work	0	0.0	1	1.5	1	1.6	1	2.6
Government service	11	28.9	12	17.6	10	15.6	4	10.5
Business	4	10.5	10	14.7	14	21.9	8	21.0
Raja or zamindar	4	10.5	3	4.4	6	9.4	3	7.9
Unknown	0	—	1	—	1	—	1	—
Total	38	99.9	69	99.9	65	100.1	39	99.9

TABLE XIII-3

LANDHOLDINGS OF CONGRESS MEMBERS OF THE
SECOND PARLIAMENT, BY AGE GROUPS

Landholdings	1891-1900		1901-1910		1911-1920		1921-1930	
	No.	%	No.	%	No.	%	No.	%
Under 20 acres	10	26.3	20	29.0	17	26.2	10	26.3
21-100 acres	10	26.3	19	27.5	21	32.3	5	13.2
Over 100 acres	2	5.3	7	10.1	5	7.7	6	15.8
Size unknown	1	2.6	5	7.3	3	4.6	3	7.9
None	12	31.6	18	26.1	17	26.2	14	36.8
Other	3	7.9	0	0	2	3.1	0	0
Unknown	0	—	0	—	0	—	1	—
Total	38	100.0	69	100.0	65	100.0	39	100.0

and on major source of income in Table XIII-4. While all
generations of Congressmen have some rural roots, the percentage of the elite drawn from agricultural families rose
steadily from generation to generation until it reached a high
of 47 per cent in the decade of the thirties. By contrast,
Congress leaders from families in government service
joined the Congress in largest numbers during the early
Gandhian phase, then declined steadily over the next three

TABLE XIII-4

Main Source of Income of Congress Members of the
Second Parliament, by Age Groups

Main Source of Income	1891-1900		1901-1910		1911-1920		1921-1930	
	No.	%	No.	%	No.	%	No.	%
Parliament	13	34.2	17	25.0	10	15.6	11	28.9
Agriculture	13	34.2	30	44.1	34	53.1	18	47.4
Business	3	7.9	6	8.8	7	10.9	6	15.8
Professional	4	10.5	13	19.1	10	15.6	2	5.3
Other	5	13.2	2	2.9	3	4.7	1	2.6
Unknown	0	—	1	—	1	—	1	—
Total	38	100.0	69	99.9	65	99.9	39	100.0

decades. Congressmen from professional families joined mainly in the twenties and again at the time of the 1942 Quit India Movement.

Land ownership, as represented in Table XIII-3, is another indicator of social origin. The largest number of Congressmen with no connection with the land belonged to the early Gandhian generation and the Quit India period. Those Congressmen most intimately connected with the land tended to join during the twenties and thirties. Yet there is an interesting variation between the recruits of these two periods. Whereas the Congressmen of the twenties were predominantly small landowners owning less than 20 acres —a typical landholding among the professional families from which urban Congress recruits of this generation were largely drawn—the Congressmen of the thirties were drawn from the middle-level peasantry owning between 21 and 100 acres and depending upon agriculture as a major source of income, as Table XIII-4 suggests. The Lok Sabha members drawn from the early Gandhian public workers and many of those coming from families of civil servants tend to depend on their parliamentary salary for income. The generation of the twenties, as might be expected, draws upon agricultural income, parliamentary salaries, and professional fees.

The educational distribution of the Congress members of the Second Lok Sabha, as shown in Table XIII-5, con-

TABLE XIII-5

EDUCATION OF CONGRESS MEMBERS OF THE
SECOND PARLIAMENT, BY AGE GROUPS

Education	1891-1900		1901-1910		1911-1920		1921-1930	
	No.	%	No.	%	No.	%	No.	%
Matriculation	6	17.6	11	17.7	15	24.2	7	18.4
Some college	2	5.9	4	6.5	5	8.1	6	15.8
B.A.	6	17.7	6	9.7	12	19.4	13	34.2
M.A.	6	17.7	4	6.5	3	4.8	3	7.9
Prof. degree	13	38.2	34	54.8	26	41.9	9	23.7
Other	1	2.9	3	4.8	1	1.6	0	0
Unknown	4	—	7	—	3	—	1	—
Total	38	100.0	69	100.0	65	100.0	39	100.0

firms earlier observations. The heavy influx of professionals in the first civil disobedience campaign is clearly demonstrated by the fact that the highest percentage of Congressmen holding professional degrees falls in this period. The generation which stands out most sharply in the educational category is the generation of the thirties, which was caught up in the Gandhian boycott of schools and was drawn predominantly from the rural areas. Therefore, it shows the lowest educational attainment. The highest educational attainment, on the other hand, was reached by the early Gandhians.

The composition of the Congress elite by castes, as demonstrated in Table XIII-6, reveals a steady shift from higher to middle to lower caste groups with each generation. Interestingly, those who insisted when interviewed that they did not believe in caste and to whom caste had lost its meaning were most numerous among the highly idealistic and reformist early Gandhians. Their numbers declined

TABLE XIII-6

CASTE OF CONGRESS MEMBERS OF THE
SECOND PARLIAMENT, BY AGE GROUPS

Caste	1891-1900		1901-1910		1911-1920		1921-1930	
	No.	%	No.	%	No.	%	No.	%
Kayastha	3	8.3	1	1.5	1	1.6	1	2.9
Brahmin	4	11.1	23	35.4	7	11.3	2	5.7
Kshatriya	8	22.2	6	9.2	8	12.9	2	5.7
Vaisya	7	19.4	8	12.3	5	8.1	2	5.7
Harijan	2	5.6	6	9.2	15	24.2	13	37.1
Tribal	1	2.8	5	7.7	6	9.7	5	14.3
Non-Hindu	3	8.3	4	6.2	4	6.5	4	11.4
Sudra	2	5.6	6	9.2	11	17.7	3	8.6
Anti-caste	6	16.7	6	9.2	5	8.1	3	8.6
Unknown	2	—	4	—	3	—	4	—
Total	38	100.0	69	99.9	65	100.0	39	100.0

sharply as political activity became a means by which caste status might be improved. Many of the early rebels against caste had been Brahmins, which helps to account for the low percentage of those declaring themselves as Brahmins in the early Gandhian generation. With the influx of great numbers of highly educated professionals during the first civil disobedience campaign, Brahmin leadership reached its height, then declined. The decade of the thirties saw the entrance of future Harijan and Sudra leaders. Particularly numerous among the recruits of this period were those from Sudra castes ranking as dominant agricultural castes in various parts of India (e.g. Reddis in Andhra, Lingayats and Vakkaligas in Mysore, Marathas in Maharashtra). The sharpest increases in the generation of the forties were shown by Harijans and Tribals. In general, the trend has been for the higher castes to decline in percentage of membership and for the lower castes to increase in strength. Because of the reservation of Harijan and Tribal seats in the Lok Sabha, the percentage from these groups ranks higher than the percentage for the Sudra castes, who are dominant at the state level and whose full strength will eventually be reflected in Parliament.

Thus, all socio-economic indices demonstrate that, with each major civil disobedience movement of the Gandhian era, the Congress attracted a broader and broader segment of the Indian population, so that by the time of independence it was no longer the strictly middle-class, urban movement it had been before 1920. It had acquired a mass base. Gandhi's ability to accomplish this feat was based partly on his charismatic leadership and partly on the fact that Indian society itself had undergone major changes under the impact of urbanization, education, and economic change. By reorganizing the Congress along linguistic lines, Gandhi was able to harness the hitherto untouched political potential of growing literacy in the vernacular, which eventually led to the decline of the high-caste monopoly of Congress leadership.

Although the new heterogeneity of the Congress created greater problems from the point of view of aggregating diverse and sometimes conflicting interests, there is little doubt that the broader social base of the Congress gave the post-independence leadership elite greater strength and stability than it would otherwise have had. Unlike many nationalist movements of Asia and Africa, the Congress emerged into power as a broadly based organization reflecting more than the middle-class, professional, urban interests of a highly Westernized elite. It boasted a leadership which extended into the countryside, which was Indian in outlook, and which therefore was in contact with the masses. Nor did the dynamic of evolution within the Congress elite cease with independence and the close of the Gandhian era. It has continued to respond to changes within the society brought about by the introduction of the mass franchise, the continued modernization of Indian society, and the political awakening of previously neglected segments of the population.

THE COMPOSITION OF THE
MASS ORGANIZATION

Since independence the composition of the Congress mass organization has undergone a major transformation. Under the impact of universal adult suffrage the rural leadership recruited into the Congress during the thirties and forties is beginning to move into positions of power in the Congress elite, while the base of the Congress continues the process of transformation in which competing Congress elites seek to mobilize mass support in the struggle for control of the Congress ministries. The nature and effect of these changes in the composition of the Congress mass membership can be understood most clearly by analyzing the membership patterns of each level of the party separately. Although there is still a lack of data, enough information is available to provide at least a profile of total Congress membership and to suggest the nature of Congress recruitment and its relationship to the society in which it functions.

The base of the Congress consists of two types of members: primary members and active members (Table XIV-1). The development of intense factional struggles within the Congress since independence has led to wide fluctuations in both types of membership as competing factions have worked to recruit supporters in their efforts to win control of local, district, and state Congress committees. The result has been an extensive circulation of elites at the base of the Congress instead of the stagnation which might have developed from a monopoly of power by those groups which had participated in the pre-independence nationalist movement.

The most intense factional rivalry occurred in the years

Composition Of The Mass Organization

TABLE XIV-1

PRIMARY AND ACTIVE MEMBERSHIP
OF THE CONGRESS, 1949-1967

Year	Primary	Active
1949-50[a]	17,000,000	400,000
1952[b]	8,804,516	298,877
1953[c]	6,290,290	82,776
1954	3,160,063	40,689
1955	7,582,473	73,171
1956[d]	4,848,884	73,320
1957	4,509,614	68,015
1958	10,087,190	133,964
1959	2,664,023	57,770
1960	4,681,736	88,279
1961	9,458,005	138,518
1962	4,291,459	44,168
1963	2,646,113	66,730
1964	5,308,440	72,920
1965	17,349,043	332,081
1966-67[c]	11,041,847	208,954

[a] Indian National Congress, *Report of the General Secretaries, January 1949–September 1950* (New Delhi: A.I.C.C., 1950), p. 95.

[b] Indian National Congress, *Report of the General Secretaries, October 1951–January 1953* (New Delhi: A.I.C.C., 1953), p. 79.

[c] Membership figures for 1953-1955 and 1966-1967 were given to the author by the A.I.C.C. Secretariat.

[d] Data for 1956 to 1965 taken from Indian National Congress, *Report of the General Secretary, 1965–1966* (New Delhi: A.I.C.C., 1966), pp. 98-99.

preceding the First General Elections when primary Congress membership rose from 5.5 million in 1945-1946 to 17 million in 1949-1950. Following the elections, as might be expected, primary membership declined to 8.8 million, and remained below this figure for the next few years. Then, preceding the organizational elections of 1958, it climbed back up to 10 million, reflecting the efforts of those Congress factions which had been excluded from the ministries formed in 1957 to gain a strong foothold in the organization. Primary membership then declined considerably and did not revive until preparations were begun for the 1962 General Elections. By 1964 the primary membership was

343

back up to 5.3 million, and in 1965, in anticipation of the Fourth General Elections, it once again reached the phenomenal figure of 17.3 million. Surprisingly, despite the severe electoral reverses in the 1967 General Elections, primary membership declined only to 11 million, a figure well above the average for the past fifteen years. It is likely that this figure reflects the expectation that interim elections will be held in many states so soon that no Congress group, hoping to control the state organization, can afford not to sustain its efforts to maintain peak strength. Because these primary membership figures rise and fall in accordance with the opportunities of competing factions to gain advantage by seeing that the electoral rolls are as full as possible, even to the extent of padding the rolls with bogus members, the primary membership does not accurately reflect the true level of firm Congress support.

A more accurate measure of the extent of Congress identification can perhaps be found in the active membership, which provides the base from which all elected party officials are selected. Active membership has also fluctuated a good deal over the years but not to the same degree as primary membership. While much of the fluctuation is attributable to factional struggles, some has also been caused by the practice of varying the criteria for active membership from time to time in an attempt to minimize the effects of bogus enrollment. Even so, there is a direct relationship between the number of primary members and the number of active members. When primary membership is high, active membership is also high. Thus, the phenomenal enrollment of 17 million primary members in 1949-1950 was matched by an equally impressive enrollment of 400,000 active members. Shortly after, active membership dropped to a little less than 300,000. For the next decade, much as in the case of the primary membership, it fluctuated from year to year. A low of 40,000 was reached in 1954 when very stringent qualifications for active membership were adopted, but the number of active members rose to 138,000 in 1961 prior to the 1962 general elections and reached a high of 332,000 prior to the 1967 general elections. The average during the post-independence period was about 80,000—a much more reliable index of Congress strength than that provided by the primary membership figures.

To obtain some idea of the composition of the active membership base of the Congress, a survey of active members in three states was conducted in cooperation with local Congress offices.[1] In the resulting sample of 13,461 active members for whom complete information was available, 8,594 (64 per cent) were drawn from the state of West Bengal, 3,189 (42 per cent) from Maharashtra, and 1,678 (12 per cent) from Gujarat. Material from these three states gives a fairly accurate profile of active Congress membership, since it takes into account two of India's largest cities, Bombay and Calcutta, as well as the smaller cities of Ahmedabad (1.2 million) and Poona (737,426). Altogether, the urban sector accounts for 6,251 (46.6 per cent) active members in the sample. The rural portion of the sample includes thirteen predominantly rural districts of Maharashtra, fourteen in West Bengal, and the non-urban portions of Ahmedabad and Baroda districts in Gujarat. The thirteen Maharashtra districts contain twelve cities with a population in excess of 100,000, and the fourteen West Bengal districts contain eight cities of a similar size; but, since this is a typical pattern in rural districts of India, the presence of these cities in otherwise rural districts does not make the data unrepresentative of rural India as a whole. In all, the largely rural districts account for 7,210 (53.4 per cent) of the active members in the sample. The analysis of these 13,461 active members of the Congress takes into consideration several demographic variables including occupation, age, religion, caste, and linguistic group.

Since occupation is one of the most important indices of

---

[1] Complete data were available for only 13,461 active members in the three states surveyed. However, age data were available for a slightly larger number, and this higher figure is used in Tables XIV-4 and XIV-5.

Congress Party Leadership

social class, it can reasonably be expected that the distribution of occupations among the active membership of the Congress will shed a great deal of light on the nature of the Congress base. As seen in Table XIV-2, the active mem-

TABLE XIV-2

OCCUPATION OF ACTIVE MEMBERS AND URBAN-RURAL
DISTRIBUTION, 1958[a]

	Urban		Rural		Total	
Occupation	No.	%	No.	%	No.	%
Agriculture	869	13.9[b]	2,919	40.5	3,788	28.1
Service	1,946	31.1	1,376	19.1	3,322	24.7
Business	1,899	30.4	1,096	15.2	2,995	22.2
All professional	1,079	17.3	1,400	19.4	2,479	18.5
Education	692	11.1	890	12.3	1,582	11.8
Other professional	387	6.2	510	7.1	897	6.7
Public work	305	4.9	232	3.2	537	4.0
Student	63	1.0	53	0.7	116	0.9
Other[c]	90	1.3	134	1.8	224	1.6
Total	6,251	99.9	7,210	99.9	13,461	100.0
Urban–rural distribution	6,251	46.6	7,210	53.4	13,461	100.0

[a] The data on active members of the Congress, based on a study of the total active membership in the states of West Bengal, Maharashtra, and the Baroda and Ahmedabad districts of Gujarat, were compiled in 1960 from party records with the aid of party officials. The information is based on the 1958 party enrollment lists.

[b] Most of these agriculturalists are found in the district of 24 Parganas which surrounds Calcutta.

[c] Housewife, labor leader, laborer, etc.

bers exhibit a considerable diversity of occupations and thus confirm the generalizations which have frequently been made about the broad-based nature of the party. The largest single occupational group among the active members in the sample were agriculturalists, followed by service workers, businessmen, and professional men, in that order. Public workers and students, while represented, were present in much smaller numbers. The urban working classes and agricultural laborers were almost non-existent in the sample, and the latter in particular are unorganized and unrepresented.

The fact that the occupational distribution varies significantly from region to region (see Table XIV-3) demon-

TABLE XIV-3

OCCUPATION OF ACTIVE MEMBERSHIP
BY STATE, 1958

Occupation	West Bengal		Maharashtra		Gujarat		Total	
	No.	%	No.	%	No.	%	No.	%
Agriculture	2,559	29.8	677	21.2	552	32.9	3,788	28.1
Service	2,059	24.0	743	23.3	520	31.0	3,322	24.7
Business	1,330	15.5	1,237	38.8	428	25.5	2,995	22.2
All professional	2,267	26.4	143	4.5	69	4.1	2,479	18.5
Education	1,564	18.2	10	0.3	8	0.4	1,582	11.8
Other professional	703	8.2	133	4.2	61	3.6	897	6.7
Public work	188	2.2	282	8.8	67	4.0	537	4.0
Student	91	1.1	13	0.4	12	0.7	116	0.9
Other	100	1.2	94	2.9	30	1.8	224	1.6
Total	8,594	100.2	3,189	99.9	1,678	100.0	13,461	100.0

strates the difficulty of generalizing from a single province to the all-India level. Perhaps the greatest variation occurs in the professional category. In the sample as a whole the professions accounted for 18.5 per cent of the active members. However, it would seem that this rather high percentage is due to the peculiar situation in West Bengal, where 92 per cent of all the professionals in the sample were to be found. Thus, whereas 26.4 per cent of the active members in the West Bengal group were professionals, only 4.5 per cent of the Maharashtrians and 4.1 per cent of the Gujaratis were professionals. In Brass's study of the Congress in Kanpur in Uttar Pradesh, professionals accounted for 7 per cent of the active membership.[2] Thus, it would seem that Bengal

[2] Paul Brass, *Factional Politics in an Indian State: The Congress Party in Uttar Pradesh* (Berkeley: University of California Press, 1965), p. 183.

is an exception to the general pattern as seen in the three other states for which figures are available. This deviation may be attributed partly to the extremely high literacy rate and widely dispersed middle class in Bengal, which was the first area in India to experience the Western impact and to benefit from Western education.

But perhaps the major reason for the unusually large number of professionals in the West Bengal group was the extremely high proportion of active members who classified themselves as educators. Some 12 per cent were educators and only 7 per cent belonged to all the other professional occupations. However, almost all the educators (that is, 1,564 out of 1,582) came from Bengal. As a result, the educators constituted 18 per cent of the West Bengal active membership while the other professions contributed only 8 per cent, a figure somewhat closer to that in other states. This high proportion of educators may indicate the success of the Bengal Congress machine headed by Atulya Ghosh in using education as a source of party patronage. As Brass has observed in Uttar Pradesh:

> The private schools are run by managing committees of men of influence. When a grant is given to a district school, the members of the committees, the teachers, and the parents of the students are benefited. The Education Minister also has scholarships to distribute and under certain circumstances, may grant admissions to schools. Thus, if the Education Minister wants to appoint a teacher to a private school, he is not likely to encounter opposition. The managing committees themselves are often run by politicians or political aspirants. Local Congressmen associate themselves with district schools to acquire support for themselves in the community, while the members of the managing committees and often the teachers have a built-in political organization among their colleagues and students if they care to run for an Assembly seat.[3]

[3] *Ibid.*, pp. 213-214.

In general, it is probably safe to say that professionals constitute about 4 to 8 per cent of the active membership of the Congress. This rather small percentage of professionals in the mass base of the Congress—a percentage which is certainly closer to their representation in the total population[4]—is in sharp contrast to their predominance in the elite of both party and government.

The remaining non-agricultural occupations pursued by the active members in the sample showed a consistent pattern with relatively minor fluctuations from state to state. The businessmen ranged from a high of 39 per cent in Maharashtra to 25.5 per cent in Gujarat and 15.5 per cent in Bengal. Service workers or white-collar workers ranged from 31 per cent in Gujarat to 24 per cent in both Maharashtra and West Bengal. The Kanpur study reveals a similar pattern with businessmen constituting 41 per cent of the active membership and service workers 35 per cent.[5] By contrast with the professionals, both businessmen and service workers are markedly underrepresented at all leadership levels of the Congress.

The public workers are perhaps one of the most interesting categories of Congress active members. They are to be found in both urban and rural areas. Although the public workers derive from the volunteer tradition of the Gandhian constructive worker, many of the activities in which they are now engaged receive considerable government support, and many of the workers themselves are "often on salary, in governmental or quasi-governmental bodies. . . . Today the term constructive worker refers to the party worker engaged in ordering those who are particularly needy, whether or not the activity is wholly non-governmental."[6] The propor-

---

[4] For an analysis of the size of the professional middle class, see George Rosen, *Democracy and Economic Change in India* (Berkeley: University of California Press, 1966), pp. 296-297.

[5] Brass, *Factional Politics in an Indian State*, p. 183.

[6] Myron Weiner, "Traditional Role Performance and the Development of Modern Political Parties: The Indian Case," *Journal of Politics*, xxvi (November 1964), 837.

tion of constructive workers among active members averaged 4 per cent for the sample as a whole. The smallest percentage (2 per cent) was to be found in the Bengal group and the largest (9 per cent) in Maharashtra. Constructive workers accounted for 4 per cent of the active members in the Gujarat sample and for 3 per cent of those in Kanpur.[7] As in the case of the professionals, the small percentage of public workers to be found among the active members at the base of the Congress hierarchy contrasts sharply with the relatively large proportion of Congressmen among the leadership elite who identify themselves as public workers.

In rural areas the active membership of the Congress is dominated by the agriculturalists drawn from the non-Brahmin middle peasantry. Taking the present sample as a whole, 40.5 per cent of the active members in predominantly rural areas were agriculturalists. However, because of the peculiar influence of the West Bengal segment of the sample, it is doubtful whether this percentage is representative of the true strength of the agriculturalists at the base of the Congress in rural areas. In Bengal only 33 per cent of the rural Congressmen were agriculturalists, while in the rural districts of Maharashtra and Gujarat some 60 per cent of the active members identified themselves as agriculturalists. That the figures for Maharashtra and Gujarat are probably a more accurate reflection of the strength of the agriculturalist element in the Congress is confirmed by a study of the Belgaum district of Mysore where they made up 64.2 per cent of the total in 1959.[8]

Not only is the percentage of agriculturalists within the Congress in the rural areas high: it is growing. In Belgaum district, for example, the proportion of agriculturalists increased from 56.6 per cent in 1952 to 64.2 per cent in 1959.[9] Moreover, as several observers have noticed, the nature of the Congress elite is changing. Rural Congress lead-

---

[7] Brass, *Factional Politics in an Indian State*, p. 183.

[8] Weiner, "Traditional Role Performance and the Development of Modern Political Parties," p. 847.

[9] *Ibid.*

ers are beginning to attempt to capture control of the Congress at the district level,[10] and the dominance of the Brahmins and other high castes is giving way under the influence of the non-Brahmin middle peasantry.[11] There appears to be a sharp contrast between the two types of rural leadership groups, the traditional village notables and the emerging middle peasantry, which increasingly are to be found vying for control of the local Congress organizations. Although Weiner has observed that it would still be "accurate to say that the most active party members . . . come from those families which in the past have wielded power,"[12] the functioning of these traditional village notables varies substantially from the style of the middle peasantry as it emerges from the stage of incipient political consciousness to political power. Thus, among the Reddis of Warangal, Elliott observes: "A traditionally wealthy landowning Reddy has built a consciously intercaste faction. . . . a middle class Reddy lawyer seeking to establish himself has gathered a consciously Reddy group. Throughout the state it is remarkable that the politicians with the strongest caste orientation are from the middle-peasant status rather than the notable status."[13] Nevertheless, factional divisions have almost always forced factional leaders to recruit support from other and lower castes.[14]

In spite of the preponderance of agriculturalists, there is a considerable diversification among the non-agricultural groups represented among the active Congress membership in rural areas.[15] These are the service employees, the busi-

[10] R. Kothari, "Three Bye-Elections," *Economic Weekly*, XVII (June 19, 1965), 988-989.

[11] W. H. Morris-Jones, *The Government and Politics of India* (London: Hutchinson University Library, 1964), pp. 67-68.

[12] Weiner, "Traditional Role Performance and the Development of Modern Political Parties," p. 847.

[13] C. M. Elliott, "Caste and Faction in Andhra Pradesh" (unpublished paper prepared for the Association of Asian Studies meeting, New York, April 1966, p. 8.

[14] *Ibid.*, p. 14.

[15] Weiner, "Traditional Role Performance and the Development of Modern Political Parties," p. 847.

nessmen, the professionals, and the public workers, whose
representation has been somewhat overstated in the sample
as a whole on account of the special character of the Bengal
Congress. Yet the total figure is somewhat more characteristic than the breakdowns, for the number of service workers
and professionals was much higher in Bengal than in Maharashtra and Gujarat while the number of businessmen was
much lower. In West Bengal 24 per cent of the active members in the predominantly rural districts were in service as
compared to 3.5 per cent in Maharashtra and 7.8 per
cent in Gujarat. The professionals accounted for 26 per cent
in Bengal, 3.6 per cent in Maharashtra, and 2.5 per cent
in Gujarat, while businessmen constituted 12 per cent in
Bengal, 17 per cent in Maharashtra, and 28 per cent in
Gujarat. In none of this data is there evidence to refute
Weiner's conclusion that the "Congress . . . recruits its active
members and its leaders from the small merchant community, the professionals and the five per cent of the landowning population with more than 30 acres of land."[16] Yet
there is some evidence that the Congress is attempting to
broaden its base by mobilizing the poorer and more backward classes which at present are poorly represented at
the Congress base. In Madras the Congress under the leadership of K. Kamaraj deliberately worked to create among
the economically backward classes a base from which to
draw a new cadre and new leaders.[17]

Although no official statements exist regarding the proportion of Congressmen who have joined the party since
independence, the data from the active membership sample seem to indicate clearly that the Congress has not been
static and that it has been able to recruit new young members. According to Table XIV-4, at least 20 per cent of the
sample of active membership in 1958 was post-independence
in origin for the very simple reason that the age of these
members would have made it impossible for them to have

[16] *Ibid.*, p. 848.
[17] *The Congress Socialist* (April 15, 1965), p. 2.

TABLE XIV-4

AGE DISTRIBUTION OF ACTIVE MEMBERSHIP, 1958

Age	No.	%
20–30	2,708	20.0
31–40	4,789	35.3
41–50	3,887	28.6
51–60	1,717	12.7
Over 60	470	3.5
Total	13,571	100.1

participated in the nationalist movement. Yet even older active members demonstrate that much Congress membership is of relatively recent origin. The generation occupying the largest segment of the sample was the group from ages 31 to 40, who were born between 1918 and 1927 and who would not have reached age 20 until the last phase of the freedom movement. Even if recruited before independence, they could not possibly have participated in anything but the Quit India Movement of 1942. The second largest group consisted of those between the ages of 41 and 50, who were born between 1908 and 1917 and would have been able to participate in the second civil disobedience campaign. Only 12.7 per cent of the sample could have played a role in the first civil disobedience campaign, and only 3.5 per cent remained from the early Gandhian phase. Thus, over one half of the Congress active members in the sample were under 40, which is hardly an indication of senility in the Congress. When Congressmen talk of the need for new leadership, what is referred to is the need to give these younger elements access to political power, which is still monopolized by older Congressmen. In order to accomplish such a transfer of power to the younger generations of Congressmen, there have been suggestions such as the ten-year rule for limiting the duration of an individual's service in the legislature and the proposal to retire a third of the legislature with every election. So far no action taken has relieved the frustration of young Congress members, which remains a real problem.

According to Table XIV-5, Maharashtra had the youngest

TABLE XIV-5

AGE DISTRIBUTION OF ACTIVE MEMBERSHIP BY STATE, 1958

Age	West Bengal		Maharashtra		Gujarat	
	No.	%	No.	%	No.	%
20–30	1,586	20.1	827	20.6	295	17.7
31–40	2,686	34.1	1,512	37.6	591	35.3
41–50	2,259	28.7	1,140	28.4	488	29.2
51–60	1,089	13.8	437	10.8	191	11.4
Over 60	260	3.3	101	2.5	109	6.5
Total	7,880	100.0	4,017	99.9	1,674	100.1

membership. This no doubt reflects the major shift that has occurred in the social base of the Maharashtra Congress since the thirties. Gujarat, on the other hand, had the oldest membership, which reflects the greater stability of the Gujarat Congress. The age levels of Maharashtra and Gujarat active members are reflected in the respective state legislatures. In Maharashtra the largest single age group in the legislative assembly in 1957 consisted of those under 40; in Gujarat the largest group fell in the 40-50 range.[18] Whereas in Gujarat 30 per cent of the members were over 50, only 23 per cent in Maharashtra were in this category. Thus, in Maharashtra, where the Congress leadership had passed into the hands of a more broadly based leadership, both the active members of the party and the members of the legislative assembly were younger than in Gujarat. If the situation in Maharashtra represents the trend of the future, as it seems to, then it probably bodes well for the ability of the Congress to recruit new young members.

[18] The studies of the Maharashtra and Gujarat Legislatures of 1957 were carried out by the author based on biographies contained in *Bombay Legislative Congress Party Directory*, 1958.

Composition Of The Mass Organization

The social pattern of the Congress as reflected in the religious, caste, and linguistic makeup of the active members varied more substantially from state to state than the indices of age and occupation. There was also a marked difference between the urban and the rural districts. In Bengal, where Muslims constitute about 19 per cent of the population, they were slightly underrepresented in the Congress and accounted for only 16 per cent of the active members. Muslim representation in rural and urban areas in West Bengal was about the same, but in Maharashtra the situation was different. Although Muslims constituted only 5.4 per cent of the active membership in the rural districts of Maharashtra, the figure increased to 8 per cent in the smaller urban areas and to 9.4 per cent in Bombay. It is possible, however, that Muslim representation in relation to Muslim population was more constant than the raw data indicate. That is, Muslims may be more numerous in the cities, where they formed a larger proportion of the active membership. Moreover, in both Calcutta and Bombay, each known as a cosmopolitan city with a widely diversified population, almost all the religious groups in India were represented among the Congress active membership: Christians, Jains, Buddhists, and Sikhs.

The distribution of active membership according to caste is very significant, for it documents many of the generalizations that have been made recently about the importance of the dominant landed caste groups in the Congress. In Maharashtra, including Bombay, 16 per cent of the Congressmen were Brahmins and 66 per cent were non-Brahmin Marathas. This accounts for the charge made in 1962 that all the District Congress Committee Presidents and Secretaries in Maharashtra were Marathas and that 75 per cent of all Congress candidates in the 1962 General Elections were also of this group.[19] The caste distribution in Maharashtra varied significantly between urban and rural areas. Whereas the ratio of Brahmins to Marathas in urban areas was 16 to 63, the

[19] *Link* (Feb. 18, 1962), pp. 14-15.

ratio in rural areas was 15 to 68. In addition to these two major social groups, the sample from Maharashtra also indicated the presence of two significant caste minorities: the Lingayats, who are present in large numbers in several Maharashtrian districts, and the Gujarati Banyas.

In Gujarat the dominance of the most numerous landed caste was also evident. The major landowning caste of Patidars constituted 65 per cent of the active members. Next came the Vaisya groups with 18 per cent and the Brahmins with 7 per cent. The lower castes in both Maharashtra and Gujarat were very poorly represented. Thus, it would seem clear that in the predominantly rural districts, as Morris-Jones has observed, "the politics of adult franchise has . . . raised the influence of the non-Brahmin middle peasants who are at once numerous and—as compared with the hardly less numerous untouchables—economically substantial. Men from these groups seem to be more prominent in Congress than before."[20]

The diversity of the Congress membership in the city of Bombay, the capital of Maharashtra and once the capital of the bilingual state also called Bombay, was clearly evident from the distribution of the sample among various linguistic communities. The largest single group were Gujaratis, who made up 31 per cent of the active membership and outnumbered the Maharashtrians who represented only 27 per cent of the active members in the city. These figures clearly demonstrate what was at stake for the Gujaratis in the bifurcation issue. Other major linguistic groups were from Uttar Pradesh (20 per cent), Madras (8 per cent), and Sindh (2 per cent). Also represented were members from Mysore, Kerala, Punjab, Bengal, and Rajasthan. Each of these groups represented less than 1 per cent of the sample. In short, the active membership of the Bombay City Congress was an extremely diverse group faithfully reflecting the cosmopolitan character of the city.

As the figures from the sample of active members in three

[20] Morris-Jones, *The Government and Politics of India*, pp. 67-68.

states indicate, the Congress has a fairly well diversified base in terms of occupation, age, and social makeup. This base varies somewhat according to state and according to whether the area is urban or rural. The greatest diversity is to be found in urban areas. In the rural areas the Congress in most states appears to be in the hands of the dominant non-Brahmin middle peasant caste, but even in these areas about 40 per cent of Congress active members are drawn from a variety of non-agricultural occupations. Yet, as different as the urban active membership is from the rural active membership, in response presumably to the difference between urban and rural constituencies, at election time the urban Congress candidates are less frequently successful than the rural candidates. As a result, the legislative representatives of the Congress tend to represent the more predominantly rural districts and tend to support programs more in the interest of rural areas than urban areas. This disproportionate representation suggests a potential source of friction within the Congress. It also suggests the possibility of a future alienation from the people of the urban areas. The politics of mass franchise has forced the Congress to extend its influence to the rural areas, but the Congress cannot afford to cut itself off from the urban constituencies.

As one passes from a study of the active membership which composes the mass base of the Congress to a survey of the various levels of the party elite in the organizational and parliamentary wings, it becomes evident not only that the decision-makers do not reflect a cross section of society but also that they do not even reflect a cross section of the party base itself. This disparity is clearly demonstrated within the Congress party organization by a juxtaposition of the composition of the mass base with the composition of the elite who serve in the A.I.C.C. and the Working Committee, the two major decision-making organs of the party organization. The difference in membership composition between those two levels of the party is evident in almost all the basic demographic variables.

Congress Party Leadership

From Table XIV-6, it would appear that the Working Committee and the A.I.C.C. both contain a preponderance of professionals and public workers. The representation of businessmen and agriculturalists seems strikingly reduced, and the service group has disappeared entirely. The natural conclusion would be that at the elite levels of the national party organization there is a massive shift to dominance by middle-class professionals, especially lawyers. This was certainly the case with the Working Committee from 1946 to 1954, although an analysis of the membership of more recent Working Committees would show some broadening of the leadership base. The A.I.C.C. figures, however, require some adjustment before they can be interpreted meaningfully.

Although 56 per cent of the A.I.C.C. members described themselves as professional men—31 per cent as lawyers and 24 per cent as educators—the number of unknowns in

TABLE XIV-6

OCCUPATION OF ALL-INDIA CONGRESS COMMITTEE AND WORKING COMMITTEE

Occupation	A.I.C.C. in 1956[a]		W.C. 1946-1954[b]		A.I.C.C. in 1956		W.C. 1946-1954	
	No.	%	No.	%	No.	%	No.	%
Agriculture	71	11.1	0	—	71	20.6	0	—
Business	42	6.6	1	1.7	42	12.2	1	2.5
All professional	192	30.0	29	48.3	192	55.8	29	72.5
Law	108	16.9	14	23.3	108	31.4	14	35.0
Education	84	13.2	7	11.7	84	24.4	7	18.0
Public work	21	3.3	7	11.7	21	6.1	7	17.5
Service	5	0.8	0	0	5	1.5	0	0
Other	13	2.0	3	5.0	13	3.8	3	7.5
Unknown	295	46.2	20	33.3	0	—	0	—
Total	639	100.0	60	100.0	344	100.0	40	100.0

[a] All data for the 1956 A.I.C.C. delegates were obtained from biographies contained in: Indian National Congress, *Delegates Directory, 1956*, New Delhi, 1956.

[b] S. Rudolph, *The Working Committee of the Indian Congress Party* (Massachusetts Institute of Technology, mimeo., 1955), Appendix II, p. 65.

358

the data is rather high—295 out of 639, or 46 per cent. From other indices such as education, it seems reasonable to conclude that only the more highly educated, modernized A.I.C.C. members supplied information on education or occupation. Thus, a substantial proportion of the 295 unknowns undoubtedly were agriculturalists. If this is so, the number of agriculturalists in the A.I.C.C. would be higher than Table XIV-6 indicates, with the result that the proportion of professionals would fall to some 30 per cent of the total A.I.C.C. membership in 1956. Another factor which, if taken into consideration, would tend to reduce the proportion of professionals is the tendency of political leaders, as Meynaud has observed, to respond with a profession no longer practiced or an occupation considered politically more respectable.[21] Evidence to support this observation is clearly present in the data on Congress Members of Parliament in the Second Lok Sabha. Of the 52 lawyers who constituted 23 per cent of the Congress back-benchers, 14, or 27 per cent, actually received their major source of income from the land. It is also interesting to note that in the *Who's Who* volumes published by some state legislative assemblies there are some Congressmen who describe themselves as "lawyer agriculturalists." Further evidence for the close relationship between the land and the professions in rural areas is provided by Weiner's study of Belgaum. He observed that the Belgaum District Congress was dominated until the thirties by Brahmins with substantial landholdings who lived in Belgaum town and practiced law.[22] Today in Belgaum, however, Weiner finds that the new district Congress leaders are largely non-Brahmin non-professionals with less wealth and education and closer connections with ordinary rural life.[23] It should be noted that district leaders play a very important role in the A.I.C.C. Thus, the membership

[21] J. Meynaud, "The Parliamentary Profession," *International Social Science Journal*, XIII (1961), 521.

[22] Weiner, "Traditional Role Performance and the Development of Modern Political Parties," p. 835.

[23] *Ibid.*

of the A.I.C.C., while not a mirror of the mass membership, certainly reflects the nature of the mass base with less distortion than does the Working Committee.

Many of the observations made about the representation of professionals are also applicable to the public workers, who at the higher levels of the party are simply full-time politicians.

While businessmen associate themselves with the Congress in rather large numbers at the active membership level, they are not represented at the leadership levels in the same proportion. This is particularly true at the highest echelons of the Congress elite. Perhaps the explanation for this pattern is that in India business is the best organized of the associational interests and that businessmen prefer to influence decision-making indirectly rather than through direct representation.[24]

While the middle peasantry have come to dominate the Congress in the rural areas and are showing up in increasing numbers at the intermediate elite levels as members of the state legislative assemblies and as back-benchers in the Lok Sabha, their numbers decline as one moves still further up the elite hierarchy in the party. Over and over again the data serve as a reminder that changes have taken place at the lower and intermediate levels which have yet to be fully reflected at the top of the pyramid in the central and state ministries. The top elite is still largely, though not exclusively, composed of the members of the privileged social strata in terms of caste, education, and social status.

Yet just as the agriculturalists have begun to fight for control of the local Congress and to demand greater representation in the legislatures, so these demands will eventually be reflected in greater representation in the upper levels of the party hierarchy. The recruiting of more agriculturalists into the leadership circles does not mean that they will come to dominate numerically. The intellectuals of the towns

[24] M. Weiner, *The Politics of Scarcity* (Chicago: University of Chicago Press, 1962), pp. 97-129.

and cities will continue to play a crucial role at the leadership levels because their skills are essential to the operation of the party. The indispensability of the intellectuals does not mean that they will exercise total control. Agriculturalists will be able to play an important role at the local level, not only because their major interests lie there but because they will have the time and the proximity needed to play the role. Agriculturalists need not be represented at the highest leadership level in order to make their demands known and to make them effective. So long as the leadership remains open and responsive to their demands, the disproportionate representation of intellectuals will persist, though not in the same proportion as in the past. Moreover, the type of intellectual in the Congress will also change as new regional language elites come into their own. There will be a continuation of the tendency of the Congress leadership to become less Western in orientation and more Indianized in outlook.

During the Nehru era the Working Committee and the A.I.C.C. consisted largely of Congressmen of long standing, many of whom had been associated with the movement ever since the early years of the Gandhian era. As shown in Table XIV-7, most of the Working Committee members had joined in the early Gandhian period and remained active over the years. During the same period the A.I.C.C. consisted predominantly of members who joined the Congress during the late twenties and early thirties. The mass membership, as we have seen, consisted to a large extent of those who joined the Congress in the late thirties and early forties. Thus, whereas 55 per cent of the membership sample was under age 40, only 31 per cent of the A.I.C.C. membership was under 40. Whereas 60 per cent of the A.I.C.C. membership belonged to the generation of the second civil disobedience campaign, only 41 per cent of the mass membership belonged to that generation. Two major reasons seem to account for this difference in age between the mass base of the Congress and the A.I.C.C. In the first place, older Con-

Congress Party Leadership

TABLE XIV-7

AGE DISTRIBUTION OF ALL-INDIA CONGRESS COMMITTEE,
ACTIVE MEMBERSHIP, AND WORKING COMMITTEE

Age	A.I.C.C. in 1956		Active Membership in 1958		W.C. in 1954*	
	No.	%	No.	%	No.	%
20–29	32	5.4	2,708	20.0	0	—
30–39	146	24.7	4,789	35.3	0	—
40–49	204	34.6	3,889	28.6	7	15.2
50–59	137	23.2	1,717	12.7	23	50.0
60–69	55	9.3	470	3.5	7	15.2
Over 70	16	2.7	0	—	3	6.5
Unknown	49	—	0	—	6	13.0
Total	639	99.9	13,571	100.1	46	99.9

* The age groupings used by the author of the Working Committee study were: 41-50, 51-60, etc. S. Rudolph, *The Working Committee of the Indian Congress Party* (Massachusetts Institute of Technology, mimeo., 1955), Appendix II, p. 63.

gressmen wish to be associated with the A.I.C.C. because of its importance during the struggle for independence. Although younger Congressmen also aspire to A.I.C.C. membership, they are not motivated by nostalgia. They seek membership in the A.I.C.C. as a means of gaining access to the central leadership so as to be able to express grievances or group concerns. However, they are often frustrated in their attempt to gain membership in the A.I.C.C. There is a tendency for Indian politicians to be reluctant to retire. Thus, older Congressmen normally attempt to retain any position of power as long as possible. Only 7.5 per cent of the A.I.C.C. members joined the Congress after independence, although at least 20 per cent of the active members of the Congress joined since independence. If room is not made in the A.I.C.C. for young members, it will hardly encourage new recruits.

An interesting feature of the A.I.C.C. data (Table XIV-8) is that it corresponds very closely to the generational profile

Composition Of The Mass Organization

TABLE XIV-8

OCCUPATION DISTRIBUTION OF MEMBERS OF THE ALL-INDIA CONGRESS
COMMITTEE, BY AGE GROUPS, 1956

upation*	Born before 1886		1887-1896		1897-1906		1907-1916		1917-1926		1927-1936	
	No.	%	No.	%	No.	%	No.	%	No.	%	No.	%
↓d	1	10.0	2	7.4	15	22.0	28	24.8	18	22.8	3	25.0
iness	1	10.0	1	3.7	10	14.7	17	15.0	8	10.1	0	—
fessional	8	80.0	23	85.2	35	51.5	56	49.6	42	53.1	7	58.3
lic work	0	—	0	—	6	8.8	6	5.3	6	7.6	1	8.3
er	0	0	1	3.7	2	3.0	6	5.3	5	6.4	1	8.3
nown	2	—	22	—	65	—	88	—	67	—	19	—
Total	12	100.0	49	100.0	133	100.0	201	100.0	146	100.0	31	99.9

The occupation distribution of the 49 A.I.C.C. delegates whose ages are unknown
ot included.

revealed by the data on the Second Lok Sabha. The early
Gandhian generation was overwhelmingly professional; the
generation of the first civil disobedience campaign predominantly professional with a significant admixture of businessmen, agriculturalists, and public workers. In both samples
the generation of the second civil disobedience campaign
stands out with a remarkable proportion of agriculturalists.
In both cases, the most recent recruits were drawn from the
broadest base, thus confirming the conclusion that there has
been a growing diversification of recruitment.

The trend toward diversification of the party elite can
be further demonstrated by comparing the occupational composition of the A.I.C.C. in the early Gandhian period with
the A.I.C.C. in 1956 (Table XIV-9). Unfortunately, because
of the high number of unknowns in some of the years for
which information is available, only the broadest trends are
visible. The most important changes that have taken place
in the A.I.C.C. between 1919-1923 and 1956 are apparent
in the distribution of members among the occupational categories of agriculturalist, professional, and public worker.

The proportion of agriculturalists rose to a high of 11 per

TABLE XIV-9

OCCUPATION DISTRIBUTION OF ALL-INDIA CONGRESS COMMITTEE, 1919-1923 AND 19..

Occupation	1919[a]		1920		1921		1922		1923		195.
	No.	%	No.	%	No.	%	No.	%	No.	%	No.
Agriculture	7	4.4	8	4.9	4	2.5	8	2.4	5	1.5	71
Business	11	6.9	12	7.4	14	8.6	19	5.6	15	4.4	42
Professional	129	80.6	128	79.0	116	71.2	125	37.0	127	37.6	192
Law	104	65.0	105	64.8	83	50.9	78	23.1	72	21.3	108
Other[b]	25	15.6	23	14.2	33	20.3	47	13.9	55	16.3	84
Public work	—	—	—	—	1	0.6	15	4.4	27	8.0	21
Other	8	5.0	9	5.6	10	6.1	23	6.8	22	6.5	18
Unknown	5	3.1	5	3.1	18	11.0	148	43.8	142	42.0	295
Total	160	100.0	162	100.0	163	100.0	338	100.0	338	100.0	639

[a] The data for 1919–1923 were taken from: Gopal Krishna, "The Development of Indian National Congress as a Mass Organization, 1918-1923," *The Journal of A Studies*, XXV (May 1966), 424.

[b] Medicine, education, journalism.

cent in the 1956 A.I.C.C. from a previous high of 5 per cent in 1920. However, on account of the large number of unknowns and the shift in the kind of agriculturalist represented, it seems certain that the actual nature of the change was greater. The agriculturalists who were early identified with the Congress belonged to the older landed elite of zamindars and other propertied interests. The agriculturalists attracted during the Gandhian era, those who have begun to move into positions of power since independence and who have become the new establishment of the countryside, were drawn from among the owner-cultivators with medium-sized holdings.

The professionals have shown a steady decline, from 81 per cent of the A.I.C.C. in the early Gandhian period to 30 per cent in the 1956 A.I.C.C. Gandhi's early impact seems to have been greatest among lawyers. By the time of the first civil disobedience movement other professionals—doctors, journalists, and educators—became attracted to the Congress. But from 1922 on, the proportion of professionals declined steadily.

Perhaps the most important element in the early years was the emergence of a new class of professional politicians who called themselves public workers and became completely identified with the Congress cause. They did not make their appearance until the first civil disobedience campaign, but thereafter their numbers increased rapidly. With independence their strength declined steadily.

Although it is interesting to trace the relative importance of the various occupational groups in the A.I.C.C. at any one time and at various times during and after the struggle for independence, the most important information that Table XIV-9 reveals is that the A.I.C.C. was the most broadly based in occupational terms in 1956 and that in 1919 its base was the narrowest. This widely dispersed support, spreading out in concentric circles from the first professional core, has been a significant contribution to the success and stability of the Congress.

The membership composition of the Working Committee and the A.I.C.C., according to religion, as shown in Table XIV-10, reveals that the elite levels of the party were al-

TABLE XIV-10

RELIGION OF WORKING COMMITTEE MEMBERS, 1946-1954,*
AND ALL-INDIA CONGRESS COMMITTEE, 1956

Religion	W.C.		A.I.C.C.	
	No.	%	No.	%
Hindu	54	90.0	582	91.5
Muslim	4	6.7	24	3.8
Sikh	2	3.3	28	4.4
Christian	0	—	22	0.3
Unknown	0	—	3	—
Total	60	100.0	639	100.0

* S. Rudolph, *The Working Committee of the Indian Congress Party* (Massachusetts Institute of Technology, mimeo., 1955), Appendix II, p. 67.

most exclusively Hindu. Muslims constituted 7 per cent of the Working Committee membership, but only 4 per cent of the A.I.C.C. (Sikhs were about equally represented in the A.I.C.C. and the Working Committee.) But, although Muslims may have greater representation at the Working Committee level than at the A.I.C.C. level, it must be noted that minority representation is one of the most important factors taken into consideration in the selection of the Working Committee. There is always at least one Muslim on the committee and sometimes more. The negligible proportion of Muslims in the A.I.C.C. clearly demonstrates that while Congress leaders have been concerned about ensuring minority representation at all levels of the party, the most success has been achieved by appointment rather than by election. The same generalizations hold true for the representation of women, who constituted only 4 per cent of the A.I.C.C. but who have traditionally held one or more seats on the Working Committee.

In educational levels the Working Committee and the A.I.C.C., as indicated in Table XIV-11, also show a significant contrast. Only two members of the Working Commit-

TABLE XIV-11

EDUCATION OF WORKING COMMITTEE MEMBERS, 1946-1954,* AND ALL-INDIA CONGRESS COMMITTEE, 1956

	W.C.		A.I.C.C.	
	No.	%	No.	%
High school	2	4.3	7	3.3
College	11	24.0	68	32.0
Post-graduate	25	54.3	138	64.8
Private	3	6.5	0	—
No record	5	10.9	0	—
Unknown	14	—	426	—
Total	60	100.0	639	100.0

* S. Rudolph, *The Working Committee of the Indian Congress Party* (Massachusetts Institute of Technology, mimeo., 1955), Appendix II, p. 66.

tee had less than a college education, about half held professional degrees, and almost a quarter were educated
abroad. The figures on education for the members of the
A.I.C.C. can only be approximated because data are available on only a third of the delegates. Of the 213 A.I.C.C.
members in 1956 who supplied educational information, 65
per cent were post-graduates and 32 per cent had some college education. However, since it is likely that the less educated
members were prone to leave out their educational background, it might be more accurate to take the number reporting in each educational category as a percentage of the
whole. In this case, only 20 per cent of the 639 delegates in the A.I.C.C. sample would be counted as holders of
professional degrees. An additional 13 per cent would have
reached matriculation. Yet even this lowest of all possible
percentages is high considered in relation to India's literacy
rate. It indicates that the A.I.C.C., while closer to the educational attainment of the society as a whole and to that of the
mass base, is well above average levels. Interestingly, however, the A.I.C.C. members are not so highly educated as the
members of the government elite.

In short, as one moves up the hierarchy from the mass-
membership to the A.I.C.C. and the Working Committee,
one finds that the Congress Party elite in the fifties was still
dominated by Congressmen drawn largely from the modern
professions and recruited during the early Gandhian period
or during the first civil disobedience campaign. The generational pattern began changing in the late fifties as a new
generation was brought into Working Committee leadership
circles, and with the death of Nehru and then of Shastri
power began to be passed to these new generations.

The younger generation, the generation which is now attempting to consolidate its position, was born during the decade between 1910 and 1920. It includes among others Prime
Minister Indira Gandhi, Sanjiva Reddy, Y. B. Chavan,
Sukhadia, C. Subramaniam, and Asoka Mehta, all of whom
are in their late forties or early fifties. This younger generation

shares power with the generation of 1900 to 1910, which was brought into the Working Committee by Nehru and which included such important Congressmen as Kamaraj, Atulya Ghosh, S. K. Patil, Nijalingappa, and Jagjivan Ram. Most formidably challenging this two-generation coalition for power is Morarji Desai, who, born in 1896, considered himself the logical successor in age to the Nehru-Prasad-Pant-B. C. Roy generation of the 1880's. It is this conflict of generations from each side of the twentieth-century milestone which has produced friction between party and government as younger Congressmen have come of age and sought to give new direction to Indian development.

Although the Congress Party today, as before independence, is composed largely of professionals, agriculturalists, businessmen, white-collar workers, and professional politicians, the mixture has changed significantly over the years. The introduction of the mass franchise has forced the party to shift attention from the urban centers to the smaller towns and larger villages with the result that middle-caste agriculturalists have displaced the older dominance of the educated upper castes, and the party has become more rural in orientation as well as composition. At the local level the Congress has been receptive to aspiring elites who have sought access to the Congress for a number of reasons, though most often because of its position of dominance, and who have been received into the Congress partly because of intra-party factionalism which has forced competing party elites to seek outside support and partly because of the traditional openness of the party organization itself.[25] The resulting changes at the base of the Congress tend to seep gradually upward into the leadership of the parliamentary wing, as we shall see in the next chapter.

If the Congress has until recently been dominated by a

[25] M. Weiner, *Congress Party Elites* (the Carnegie Seminar on Political and Administrative Development, University of Indiana, Bloomington, Indiana, 1966), pp. 17-19; see also his forthcoming book, *Party-Building in a New Nation: The Indian National Congress* (Chicago: University of Chicago Press, 1967).

highly modernized elite, the change in the Congress base is giving rise to leaders who have emerged in a different atmosphere from that which gave rise to the old nationalist leaders. The new elite are Congressmen who have succeeded in the competitive politics of their own states and who represent to an unprecedented degree the more traditional forces in the society. Yet they are not necessarily traditional themselves. Having been brought onto the national scene, they have been forced to view problems in a broader context and in terms of the modernized leadership of their predecessors. They are thus a blend of the modern and the traditional and as such are perhaps more sensitive to the demands of their supporters and to the pressures of the electorate than those who came before them.

THE COMPOSITION OF THE
PARLIAMENTARY WING

Elite theorists have argued for some time that a society's electorate does not elect representatives that reflect itself: elective leadership is drawn from the top of the social structure.[1] In India this is particularly true of the Congressmen at the highest levels of elective office. But it is also true that one finds, as one moves down the governmental hierarchy from the central legislature to the state assemblies to the village councils, that members of each successive group are drawn from social strata closer to the indigenous social order and traditional social forces.[2] Thus, by degrees, as revealed by an examination of the Congress parliamentary wing at national, state, and district levels, modern political elites give way to more traditional elites.

In his study of the impact of panchayati raj in Rajasthan,[3] Potter shows that, as one moves up the ladder from village to district level, the type of leadership undergoes substantial alteration. Thus, of the 5,689 village sarpanches for whom information was available, most of whom were Congressmen, 83 per cent were agriculturalists, 13 per cent were village businessmen, and 1.4 per cent were public workers. At the block level of leadership, however, the proportion of agriculturalist pradhans declined to 68 per cent, the businessmen increased to 17 per cent, and the public workers to 5 per cent. Still more significant, at the block level, lawyers

---

[1] D. R. Matthews, *The Social Background of Political Decision-Makers* (New York: Random House, 1954), p. 6.

[2] W. H. Morris-Jones, *The Government and Politics of India* (London: Hutchinson University Library, 1964), p. 69.

[3] D. C. Potter, *Government in Rural India* (London: G. Bell and Sons, 1964), pp. 53-54.

appeared for the first time as representatives of village interests. At the district level even greater changes took place. Of the 26 pramukhs, only 29 per cent were agriculturalists, 17 per cent were businessmen, 17 per cent were public workers, and 38 per cent—the largest group of all—were lawyers.

In a similar study of panchayati raj in Maharashtra, which revealed that 85 per cent of those elected to Zilla Parishads were agriculturalists, 6.9 per cent were lawyers, and 3.8 per cent were businessmen, Sirsikar found that "the hold the richer peasantry have on the political life of rural areas is indicated by the fact that most of the wealthier respondents were either presidents or vice-presidents of the Zilla Parishads or at least chairmen of the Panchayat Samitis."[4] Thus, even at the lowest levels of government, leadership becomes differentiated on the basis of skill and income. Those with the most resources are also those in the best position to move into positions of leadership. The possession of skills enhances the individual's capability for dealing with the world beyond the village, and income provides for flexibility, availability, and deference. Thus, one is prepared to find that leadership becomes more and more differentiated at subsequent levels of the Congress hierarchy.

At the state legislative level the elite broadens to include a greater diversity of occupations. Agriculturalists, doctors, lawyers, educators, journalists, businessmen, industrialists, and public workers all abound. Perhaps most conspicuously absent are the white-collar workers, who hold few elective posts although they form some 25 per cent of the Congress membership. The major reason for their exclusion is undoubtedly economic. Salaries are not high, and career patterns lack the flexibility enjoyed by the self-employed. Hence, white-collar workers cannot afford the insecurity of a political career. Also absent from the leadership elite are manual workers and agricultural laborers. The former, when represented, are represented by middle-class intellectuals, and the

[4] V. M. Sirsikar, "Leadership Patterns in Rural Maharashtra," *Asian Survey*, IV (July 1964), 931.

latter are largely unorganized and unrepresented. Although the base of the elite broadens considerably at the state level, there is increasing evidence of a growing ruralization of Congress legislative representatives. The result of this tendency is evident in West Bengal where, according to Weiner, "by virtually all measurements, Congress is the most rural party in West Bengal."[5]

Changes in the social characteristics of state Congress legislators have been gradual, not sudden—a more or less faithful reflection of the changes gradually taking place in the composition of the party's mass organization. Because of the openness of the Congress, alterations in the social base of the party exert a strong and rapid impact at the organizational level, but only after some time do they appear at the legislative and ministerial levels of state party leadership. This time lag between the first occurrence of change in the organization and its reflection at other levels has been due in part to legislative recruitment patterns which tend to narrow the recruitment base, thus tempering the effects of rapid change arising from the absorption of new social groups into the Congress.

Because many factors may intervene during the selection process to narrow the legislative recruitment base,[6] the selection of candidates becomes a critical point in the election process. The results of legislative recruitment in the Congress are no exception to this observation. A study of candidate selection for the state assembly in Bihar in 1961, for instance, shows that the 2,050 applicants varied considerably in age, education, and occupation from the 318 candidates selected from among them. Thus, in terms of age, older men tended to win out over younger applicants. Whereas 46.7 per cent of the applicants were under 40, only 35.2 per cent of those selected were in the younger age group. Looking at it the other way, some 51.4 per cent of the applicants

[5] M. Weiner, *Political Change in South Asia* (Calcutta: Firma K. L. Mukhopadhyay, 1963), p. 184.

[6] J. Meynaud, "The Parliamentary Profession," *International Social Science Journal*, XIII (1961), 524.

were over 40, but 57.2 per cent of those selected were over 40.[7] In terms of education, almost two-thirds of the applicants had less than a B.A. degree, while only half of the group selected had failed to attain this level of education. To put it differently, only 23.4 per cent of the applicants had attained at least the B.A. level of education, but 28.9 per cent of the candidates had a B.A. or higher degree.[8] In terms of occupation, 52 per cent of the applicants were agriculturalists, but 46.8 per cent of the candidates were agriculturalists. Although only 28 per cent of the applicants were full-time politicians, 34.6 per cent of the candidates were full-time politicians. Professional and business representation remained about the same. Thus, 18.2 per cent of the applicants were in the professions, and 17.7 per cent of the candidates were professionals. However, lawyers constituted 8.9 per cent of the applicants but 12.6 per cent of the candidates. Businessmen accounted for 0.7 per cent of the applicants and 0.9 per cent of the candidates. In general, then, recruitment tended to favor the older candidates, those with the best education, and the full-time politicians.[9]

As a result of recruitment patterns, change at the legislative level tends to be gradual. This certain, if slow, evolution is demonstrated in the occupational distribution of members of the Uttar Pradesh assembly over a period of fifteen years.[10] Representation of the landed interests in Uttar Pradesh, as shown in Table XV-1, increased from 39 per cent in 1952 to 42 per cent in 1962. This 42 per cent figure corresponds roughly to the all-India average for agriculturalists as a percentage of Congress party membership. Yet more surprising, perhaps, is the fact that the representation of landed interests by agriculturalists increased by only 3 per cent from 1952 to 1962.

[7] R. Roy, "Selection of Congress Candidates–IV: Socio-Demographic Characteristics of Applicants," *Economic and Political Weekly*, II (Feb. 11, 1967), 372.

[8] *Ibid.*, p. 373.   [9] *Ibid.*

[10] The author wishes to thank Mr. Meyer for permission to use the above data.

Congress Party Leadership

TABLE XV-1

OCCUPATION OF CONGRESS MEMBERS OF THE UTTAR PRADESH
LEGISLATIVE ASSEMBLY, 1952-1962[a]

Occupation	1952 Assembly		1957 Assembly		1962 Assembly	
	No.	%	No.	%	No.	%
Agriculture	151	38.7	108	37.8	105	42.2
All professional	126	32.3	89	31.0	71	28.5
Education	29	7.4	31	10.8	28	11.2
Law	86	22.1	49	17.1	39	15.7
Medicine	11	2.8	9	3.1	4	1.6
Business	54	13.8	41	14.3	33	13.3
Public work	15	3.9	11	3.8	9	3.6
Labor	9	2.3	5	1.7	6	2.4
Other[b]	35	9.0	32	11.2	25	10.0
Total	390	100.0	286	99.8	249	100.0

[a] The data on Congress members of the Uttar Pradesh Legislative Assembly were collected by Ralph Meyer in India in 1962 and are part of a study of the patterns of leadership in the state of Uttar Pradesh since independence.

[b] Government service, housewife, unknown.

As might have been expected, there has been since the First General Elections a corresponding decline in the total number—if not in the variety—of professionals in the state legislatures. The decline is particularly apparent among lawyers. In Uttar Pradesh the total number of professionals decreased from 32 per cent in 1952 to 29 per cent in 1962. In the process, while the percentage of educators moved up from 7 per cent to 11 per cent, most of them were school teachers from rural districts. They represent a latent but potent political force for the future. As the Indian educational establishment continues to expand in its mission to impart literacy to the masses, the local school teachers may prove as influential a force as they have become in Ceylon.[11]

[11] W. H. Wriggins, *Ceylon: Dilemmas of a New Nation* (Princeton: Princeton University Press, 1960), pp. 362-369; also M. R. Singer,

Yet they will represent a type of leadership different from that of the older, more Westernized intellectuals, for they will be educated largely in the regional languages.

Businessmen in the Uttar Pradesh legislative assembly held their own at about 14 per cent. The same was true of public workers. The number of former government servants, previously represented in insignificant numbers, showed a perceptible increase in all areas, thus providing further evidence that Congressmen are aware of the need for skills. In an attempt to meet the demands of administering a modern state, former civil servants have been recruited into the Congress and given ministerial posts.

The occupational characteristics of the ministerial level in Uttar Pradesh for the first fifteen years of independence show a marked but diminishing contrast to that of the state Congress legislative party as a whole. Of the 65 ministers who held office from 1947 to 1962, some 30 per cent were lawyers, 28.6 per cent were agriculturalists, 14.3 per cent were public workers, 12.7 per cent were educators, and 9.5 per cent were businessmen. Thus, taking this period as a whole, among ministers, lawyers rather than agriculturalists were the largest single group. However, in more recent years, the rank order of occupations of Uttar Pradesh ministers has come to approximate more closely the composition of the Congress legislative party. The lawyers are being replaced by agriculturalists as the largest single group.

The occupational distribution of state ministers as an all-India pattern tends to follow the Uttar Pradesh pattern. Despite the decline of professional skill groups at the assembly level, the trend is only beginning to affect the ministerial elite, which, as shown in Table XV-2, continues to be dominated by lawyers. A study of the Council of Ministers in eight Indian states since 1947[12] shows that 75 per cent of the ministers have been drawn from the professional

---

The Emerging Elite: A Study of Political Leadership in Ceylon (Cambridge: Massachusetts Institute of Technology Press, 1964).

[12] This study was conducted by the author. See note in Table XV-2.

TABLE XV-2

OCCUPATION OF CONGRESS MEMBERS OF THE COUNCIL
OF MINISTERS IN EIGHT SELECTED STATES, 1946-1965*

Occupation	No.	%
Agriculture	20	9.9
Business	8	4.0
All professional	151	74.7
Law	102	50.5
Journalism	19	9.4
Education	11	5.4
Other professions	19	9.4
Public work	10	5.0
Service	13	6.4
Total	202	100.0
Unknown	200	49.8
Total	402	149.8

* The states included in this study were: Madras, Maharashtra, Orissa, Rajasthan, Andhra, Mysore, Gujarat, Madhya Pradesh. The data were collected from published biographies in the following sources: The Times of India, *Directory and Year Book including Who's Who* (volumes for 1947-1966); Parliament of India, *Who's Who 1950* (New Delhi: Manager of Government of India Publications, 1950); Trilochan Singh, ed., *Indian Parliament, 1952-1957* (New Delhi: Arunam & Sheel, n.d.); Parliament of India, *Council of States, Who's Who, 1952* (New Delhi: Council of States Secretariat, 1953); Parliament of India, *House of the People, Who's Who, 1952* (New Delhi: Parliament Secretariat 1952); S. P. Singh Sud and Ajit Singh Sud, *Indian Elections and Legislators* (Ludhiana: All-India Publications, 1953); *Lok Sabha Who's Who, Supplement* (New Delhi: Lok Sabha Secretariat, 1959); *Rajya Sabha, Who's Who, 1962* (New Delhi: Rajya Sabha Secretariat, 1962); Parliament of India, *Third Lok Sabha, Who's Who, 1962* (New Delhi: Lok Sabha Secretariat, 1962); *Directory of the Bombay Legislature, 1946-1947* (Bombay: Bombay Legislative Congress Party, n.d.); Homi J. H. Taleyarkhan, ed., *Bombay Legislative Directory, 1953* (Bombay Legislative Congress Party); *Bombay Legislative Congress Party Directory, 1958; Directory of the Madras Legislature, 1950* (Madras Legislative Congress Party); *Madras Legislative Congress Council, Who's Who, 1961*; *Madras Legislative Assembly, Third, Who's Who, 1962* (Legislative Assembly Department); *Almanac for Mysore and Who's Who, 1958*; *Mysore Legislative Assembly, Who's Who, 1959* (Bangalore: Director of Printing); *Mysore Legislative Assembly, Who's Who* (Bangalore, 1963).

categories. Two-thirds of these professionals were lawyers. Ministerial posts have also been filled by agriculturalists, businessmen, former government servants, and public workers. Thus, an analysis of the Indian ministries at the state level, as shown in Table XV-3, seems to confirm what Gutts-

TABLE XV-3

OCCUPATION OF CONGRESS MEMBERS OF THE COUNCIL OF MINISTERS IN
EIGHT SELECTED STATES, BY AGE GROUPS, 1946-1965*

| | Date of Birth | | | | | | | | | |
| | Before 1890 | | 1891-1900 | | 1901-1910 | | 1911-1920 | | 1921-1940 | |
pation	No.	%	No.	%	No.	%	No.	%	No.	%
culture	0	0	5	11.6	5	9.8	5	7.8	4	17.4
ness	1	8.3	3	7.0	2	3.9	0	0	1	4.3
professions	11	91.7	31	70.1	39	76.5	48	75.1	16	69.5
aw	8	66.7	19	42.2	29	56.9	33	51.6	10	43.5
urnalism	0	0	9	20.9	2	3.9	4	6.3	3	13.0
ducation	0	0	0	0	3	5.9	5	7.8	3	13.0
ther professions	3	25.0	3	7.0	5	9.8	6	9.4	0	0
ice	0	0	3	7.0	2	3.9	6	9.4	1	4.3
ic work	0	0	1	2.3	3	5.8	5	7.8	1	4.3
nown	1	—	4	—	8	—	10	—	2	—
Total	13	100.0	47	98.0	59	99.9	74	100.1	25	99.8

Occupations of 184 (45.8%) of the 402 members of the Council of Ministers for
m information was available in eight selected states by age groups.

man has pointed out in the case of Britain: there is a time lag between the first occurrence of changes at the legislative level and their reflection in the ministry.[13] The professionals have declined from a high of 92 per cent among ministers drawn from the pre-Gandhian generation to 69.5 per cent of those born after 1920 who entered the Congress during the forties and fifties. Not only has there been a decline in the proportion of professionals in the councils of ministers; there have been major changes in the types of professionals represented in the ministerial elite. Lawyers

[13] W. L. Guttsman, "The Changing Social Structure of the British Political Elite," *British Journal of Sociology*, II (1951), 133-134.

declined from a high of 67 per cent in the pre-Gandhian generation to 43.5 per cent in the youngest generation now represented. Moreover, many of the young lawyers, as one might suspect, have substantial connections with landed interests. Meanwhile, those in another professional category, the educators, have risen from no representation among the oldest generation to 13 per cent of the youngest. A second major trend is reflected in the fact that agriculturalists constitute 17 per cent of the youngest generation of ministers. Thus, the growing rural composition of the state legislatures is just beginning to be reflected at the ministerial level.

The Council of Ministers at the national level shows a similar pattern,[14] with one exception: the number of public workers is much higher than at the state level, a fact which vividly emphasizes the higher average age of the national elite. Otherwise, the ministers at the national level display the familiar ascendency of professionals, who in 1962 accounted for almost half of the 47 members of the Council of Ministers. The professionals were divided fairly equally among lawyers and educators. In order of numerical importance, the other occupations represented in the Council of Ministers were public workers, agriculturalists, businessmen, and former government servants.

Occupation is only one index of social stratification in India. Especially in rural areas, caste represents another important dimension. In caste terms, power in the Congress has been passing into the hands of the dominant castes in each of the states. Thus, Sirsikar shows that 71.2 per cent of those elected to the Zilla Parishads in Maharashtra were members of the Maratha caste, the caste which constitutes about 40 per cent of the total state population.[15] As noted in Chapter XIV, the Marathas accounted for 66 per cent of the active members of the Congress in Maharashtra as well as all D.C.C. Presidents and a substantial portion of M.L.A.s and members of the state cabinet.

---

[14] This study, conducted by the author, was based on the 1962 Lok Sabha's *Who's Who.*

[15] Sirsikar, "Leadership Patterns in Rural Maharashtra," p. 930.

In Bihar a similar pattern has prevailed. In the early years of Congress history in Bihar, the Kayastha caste of scribes held the dominant leadership position. Later, however, when Brahmins and Rajputs were attracted to the movement, Congress politics became a struggle for power among these castes.[16] Since land ownership has been concentrated in the hands of these three upper castes, they have continued in their position of dominance, although factional divisions among them have forced them to reach out, as have dominant groups in other states, for support from the lower castes, thus politicizing the subordinate castes and bringing them into the political system.[17]

In Rajasthan the Congress began largely as an urban movement led by the Brahmin and Mahajan castes. In recent years a major struggle for control has been taking place between this urban-based leadership and the leaders of the most important agricultural caste in Rajasthan, the Jats. Since the Jats consider themselves the most advanced of the rural groups, they see themselves as the eventual leaders of a Congress dominated by the rural interests of the state. In the meantime, until the rural peasantry become more conscious in modern political terms, the Jats have backed Sukhadia for Chief Minister as an adequate temporary leader.[18] Similar patterns have been reported for the Punjab,[19] Madras,[20] Mysore, and Andhra.[21]

Although, as Table XV-4 indicates, the national Parliament continues to reflect a greater diversity of representation

[16] George Rosen, *Democracy and Economic Change in India* (Berkeley: University of California Press, 1966), p. 62.

[17] Roy, "Selection of Congress Candidates," pp. 372-375.

[18] L. L. Shrader, "Politics in Rajasthan: A Study of the Members of the Legislative Assembly and the Development of the State's Political System" (unpublished Ph.D. dissertation, University of California, Berkeley, 1965).

[19] B. R. Nayar, *Minority Politics in the Punjab* (Princeton: Princeton University Press, 1966), pp. 149-168.

[20] A. Beteille, "Politics and Social Structure in Tamilnad," *The Economic Weekly*, xv (July 1963), 1161-1167.

[21] M. Weiner, *Congress Party Elites* (the Carnegie Seminar on Political and Administrative Development, University of Indiana, Bloomington, Ind., 1966).

TABLE XV-4

OCCUPATION OF CONGRESS MEMBERS OF PARLIAMENT, 1952-1962

Occupation	1st Lok Sabha[a] 1952		2nd Lok Sabha 1957		3rd Lok Sabha[b] 1962	
	No.	%	No.	%	No.	%
Agriculture	62	21	54	24.2	93	27.2
Business	37	11	25	11.2	26	7.6
All professional	165	47	68	30.5	144	42.3
Law	130	30	52	23.3	90	26.4
Other professional	35	17	16	7.2	54	15.9
Public work	67	20	63	28.2	59	17.3
Service	8	2	7	3.1	13	3.8
Other	0	0	6	2.7	6	1.8
Unknown	0	—	1	—	16	—
Total	339	101	224	99.9	357	100.0

[a] All data on the First Lok Sabha is taken from W. H. Morris-Jones, *Parliament in India* (Philadelphia: University of Pennsylvania Press, 1957), p. 123.

[b] All data for the Third Lok Sabha was compiled from Parliament of India, *Third Lok Sabha, Who's Who, 1962* (New Delhi: Lok Sabha Secretariat, 1962).

than is evident in the state legislatures, it appears to be undergoing a process of transformation analogous to that which has already been clearly demonstrated at the state level. Members of the professions still dominate the Lok Sabha, but their proportion has declined from 1952 to 1962. The unusually sharp drop in professionals in the Second Lok Sabha can be attributed partly to the nature of the sample, which excluded ministers, but it is also attributable to the trend in recruitment patterns as revealed in the low proportion of professionals in the Third Lok Sabha. Among professionals, as usual, the largest single group were the lawyers, who constituted 30 per cent of the First Lok Sabha, 23 per cent of the Second, and 26 per cent of the Third.

The most numerous single group in the Lok Sabha today are the agriculturalists, who have increased over the last three parliaments from 21 per cent to 27 per cent. Most of these agriculturalists were recruited into the Congress during the Gandhian era, their numbers increasing with each generation to feel the impact of Gandhi. In both the Second and the Third Lok Sabha the agriculturalists constituted only 15 per cent of the early Gandhians. They increased to 29 per cent of the generation of the first civil disobedience campaign and to 33 per cent of the generation of the second civil disobedience campaign. A more revealing indication of future trends lies in the fact that recruitment into the Third Lok Sabha, including those retained for an additional term, showed a higher proportion of agriculturalists.

The most interesting contrast between the state and the national parliamentary levels lies in the large number of Congressmen in the Lok Sabha who identify themselves as public workers. Yet even at the center their number is declining. The proportion of public workers reached a high in the Second Lok Sabha when they accounted for 28 per cent of the Congress back-benchers. By the Third Lok Sabha they declined to only 17 per cent of all Congressmen in Parliament. Yet the public worker is an emerging occupation as well as a dying one. Although many of the old Gandhian public workers, who had established records of service in their home areas before being elected to the Lok Sabha, are growing old, retiring, and dying, a new breed of public workers is in the offing. They are springing up among the low-caste Harijans and the Tribals. Often such men, who lack the educational opportunities to gain advancement in other occupations and whose landholdings are small or nonexistent, become full-time public workers devoted to the uplift of their caste or community and perhaps also to securing a place for themselves in the political life of the country.

Although the number of businessmen in the Lok Sabha has been increasing over the past years, their representation in the Congress Party in Parliament has been decreasing. They constituted only 8 per cent of the First Lok Sabha, but

13 per cent of the Second;[22] yet among Congress members the proportion of businessmen dropped from 11 per cent in the First Lok Sabha to 8 per cent in the Third. It is no secret that many businessmen tend to be attracted to opposition parties, such as the Swatantra Party.

In short, the evidence seems incontrovertible that Congress leadership, like Congress membership, draws upon a more and more diverse base with a greater and greater proportion of higher caste and highly educated professionals at each successive level of the hierarchy. It remains true in spite of the fact that the dominance of the older professional elite is declining, and the rural leadership already reflected at the state level is beginning to have an effect at both state and national cabinet levels as well as in the national Parliament. Yet this process of change has been very slow, partly because of the impact of recruitment practices.

The importance attached to certain skills can be seen not only in the persistence of the extremely high proportion of professionals holding ministerial positions at both state and national levels, but also in the recruitment of civil servants and in the tendency of certain groups in the society to see that they are represented by men thoroughly capable of dealing with the outside world.[23] At the state level this liaison role has been assigned to the lawyers of the district towns, and it is gradually becoming one of the roles of the rapidly expanding educational establishment. Thus, the Indian electorate, like most electorates, has not sought a leadership mirroring its social composition, but rather one capable of representing and protecting its interests in the councils of government. The exceptions to this pattern have been the Harijans and Tribals, who by reservation have been given special representation in both state and national legislatures. Yet, insofar as these special seats tend to be filled

[22] Surindar Suri, "Pattern of Membership," *Seminar* 66 (February 1965), 16.

[23] F. G. Bailey, *Politics and Social Change: Orissa in 1959* (Berkeley: University of California Press, 1963), pp. 58-68.

by Tribals and Harijans drawn from the more highly educated members of each community, the exceptions do not
disprove the generalization. Moreover, the reservation of
seats has not prevented Harijans and Tribals from being
underrepresented at the ministerial level.

The Congress, as the data on all levels of Congress membership and leadership indicate, is neither a landlord's party
nor a businessman's party, although it has been called both.
Instead, it represents nearly all the groups in Indian society
whose diverse and sometimes conflicting interests it has
sought to aggregate through its complex but largely effective
decision-making processes. Moreover, over the years the social base of the party has been undergoing important
changes.

Perhaps a clearer and more specific picture of the nature
of the Congress leadership and the changes which it has
been undergoing can be obtained by a careful scrutiny of at
least one level of the Congress elite. The material which
follows is based on detailed interviews with 224 of the 375
Congress members of the Second Lok Sabha.

As Meynaud has suggested, a legislator's main source of
income may be a more accurate index of his economic orientation than his professed occupation.[24] This is certainly the
case in India, where a large number of legislators and ministers declare themselves to be lawyers or public workers
in spite of the fact that their source of livelihood turns out
to be entirely different. In discussing their occupation some
25 per cent of Congress members of the Second Lok Sabha
declared themselves to be agriculturalists. However, as shown
in Table XV-5, some 43 per cent of them identified land as
their major source of income. Moreover, only 29 per cent
of these Congress legislators can be said to be so totally divorced from rural India that they owned no land at all.
Thus, some 71 per cent of the Congress Members of Parliament still had some stake in the land.

Most of the Congress members of the Second Lok Sabha

[24] Meynaud, "The Parliamentary Profession," p. 521.

TABLE XV-5

MAIN SOURCE OF INCOME OF CONGRESS MEMBERS
OF THE SECOND PARLIAMENT

Main Source of Income	No.	%
Land	95	43.4
Business	27	12.3
Professional fees	30	13.7
Parliamentary salary	54	24.7
Other	13	5.9
Unknown	4	—
Total	224	100.0

who were landowners tended to have small to medium-sized holdings. Some of the smaller landholders were obviously agriculturalists only in the sense that they shared in their family's land, which they themselves did not have responsibility for cultivating; thus, they had no direct connection with land, a status probably most applicable to the 27 per cent who owned less than twenty acres. Of the 35 per cent who owned more than 20 acres, some 15 per cent were in the 20-50 acre range and 11 per cent in the 51-100 acre range. Some 9 per cent owned more than a hundred acres. These figures lead to the conclusion that the majority of the Congress landholders in the Second Lok Sabha were drawn from the middle peasantry, which forms the base of the Congress leadership in the rural areas. This conclusion can be further substantiated by an examination of the landholdings of those who declared land as their major source of income. Among these agriculturalists, 33 per cent owned under 20 acres, 41 per cent owned between 20 and 100 acres, and 16 per cent owned more than 100 acres. Altogether, some 50 per cent of the Congress legislators most directly connected with the land were small or medium landholders, and the majority of these were in the middle peasantry.

The growing strength of this middle peasantry at the national level is reflected in the changes in recruitment from the First Lok Sabha to the Second Lok Sabha. The Congressmen newly elected to the Second Lok Sabha not only had a larger percentage of landowners than the sitting members (72 per cent as compared to 69 per cent), but their holdings were also more likely to fall in the medium range. Thus, whereas the distribution of landholders in the First Lok Sabha showed 32 per cent owning under 20 acres and 26 per cent owning more, in the Second Lok Sabha there were only 20 per cent with fewer than 20 acres and 49 per cent with more than 20 acres. Thus, it would seem that it is the middle peasantry in particular, rather than the agriculturalists as a whole, who are beginning to gain greater and greater representation at the national level. Eventually this greater representation will undoubtedly be reflected in the Indian Cabinet.

The growing number of Congress legislators from the middle peasantry notwithstanding, Table XV-6 shows that the

TABLE XV-6

CASTE OF CONGRESS MEMBERS OF THE SECOND PARLIAMENT

Caste	No.	%
Brahmin	41	19.5
Kayastha	6	2.9
Kshatriya	25	11.9
Vaisya	24	11.4
Sudra	22	10.5
Harijan	38	18.1
Tribal	17	8.1
Non-Hindu	16	7.6
Anti-caste	21	10.0
Unknown	14	—
Total	224	100.0

Congress members of the Lok Sabha were still drawn largely from the higher castes. For purposes of an all-India profile of social stratification in the Congress, we have used a slightly modified version of the traditional four varnas as the most practicable way of representing caste patterns within the Congress in generally relevant terms. Using this method of stratification, it becomes quite clear that, in spite of the reservation of seats for Harijans and Tribals and in spite of the growing number of legislators from the middle peasantry, the Brahmins are still predominant among Congress back-benchers. (Their strength would be even greater with the inclusion of the Council of Ministers, of whom 46.4 per cent were Brahmins.[25]) Of the other twice-born castes, 2.9 per cent were Kayasthas, 11.9 per cent were Kshatriyas, and 11 per cent were Vaisyas. Thus, the top three caste categories account for 46 per cent of the seats in the Congress Party in Parliament although they number only 90 million or 20 per cent of the total Indian population.[26] By contrast, the great variety of Sudra castes (e.g., Reddis in Andhra, Lingayats and Vakkilagas in Mysore, Marathas in Maharashtra) account for only 10 per cent of the Congress seats in the Lok Sabha, although they are drawn from a group which constitutes 250 million, or over half of the Indian population. As a group, the Sudra castes are the least represented of all major communities in India. However, it is this group which has governmental power in many of the states and which is slowly beginning to move into positions of authority at the center. The two major groups which in one sense fall outside the Hindu hierarchy and which in another sense form the bottom level of the Hindu social structure are relatively well represented in the Congress. This is due not only to the fact that seats are specially reserved for them but also to the fact that these two groups have given the Congress strong support. Thus, the Harijans, who constitute only 15 per cent of the population, occupy 18 per cent of the seats in the Congress parliamentary party, while the Tribals, who constitute only 7 per cent of the population, have 8 per cent of

[25] R. L. Park and I. Tinker, *Leadership and Political Institutions in India* (Madras: Oxford University Press, 1960), p. 110.
[26] H. R. Isaacs, *India's Ex-Untouchables* (New York: John Day & Co., 1964), pp. 25-27.

the Congress seats.[27] Both Tribals and Harijans are well represented in the Congress although they were the latest groups to be recruited into the Congress.

One of the interesting groups in our sample were those Congressmen who were so adamantly opposed to the idea of caste that they refused, despite continued prodding, to reveal their caste origins. This group, which insisted that caste was irrelevant and declared that they did not believe in such forms of social stratification, composed about 10 per cent of the sample. Most of this group were probably Brahmin, for they tend to be drawn from the highly Westernized early Gandhian generation, the generation which was perhaps most profoundly affected by Gandhi's leadership and teaching.

The predominance of high-caste members among the Congress Members of Parliament, as Table XV-7 indicates, is

TABLE XV-7

CASTE OF CONGRESS MEMBERS OF THE SECOND
PARLIAMENT, BY AGE GROUPS

Caste	1891-1900		1901-1910		1911-1920		1921-1930	
	No.	%	No.	%	No.	%	No.	%
Kayastha	3	8.3	1	1.5	1	1.6	1	2.9
Brahmin	4	11.1	23	35.4	7	11.3	2	5.7
Kshatriya	8	22.2	6	9.2	8	12.9	2	5.7
Vaisya	7	19.4	8	12.3	5	8.1	2	5.7
Harijan	2	5.6	6	9.2	15	24.2	13	37.1
Tribal	1	2.8	5	7.7	6	9.7	5	14.3
Non-Hindu	3	8.3	4	6.2	4	6.5	4	11.4
Sudra	2	5.6	6	9.2	11	17.7	3	8.6
Anti-caste	6	16.7	6	9.2	5	8.1	3	8.6
Unknown	2	—	4	—	3	—	4	—
Total	38	100.0	69	99.9	65	100.0	39	100.0

undergoing a process of erosion, symbolized by the fact that Lal Bahadur Shastri, a Kayastha, assumed the prime ministership after Nehru, a Brahmin. The changes in recruit-

[27] *Ibid.*

ment between the First and the Second Lok Sabha showed an increase in the recruitment of Kshatriyas, Sudras, and Tribals and a decrease in the recruitment of Vaisyas, Harijans, and caste rejectors, while Brahmin recruitment remained stable. Another indication of a change in caste composition emerges from the age distribution of Congress Members of Parliament. Brahmin Congressmen were an aging group. Some 95 per cent of them entered the Congress before independence, while 75 per cent had joined prior to 1930. Moreover, 18 per cent of the Brahmins were over 60, a full 59 per cent were between 50 and 60, and only 23 per cent of them were under 50. The same trend was evident among those who have rejected caste.

The youngest groups in the Congress Party in Parliament, on the other hand, were the Harijans and the Tribals. Some 53 per cent of the Tribals joined the party after independence, as did 29 per cent of the Harijans. Moreover, over 50 per cent of the Congress legislators in the sample between age 30 and 39 were either Harijans or Tribals, who also constituted some 34 per cent of the age group from 40 to 49. These figures clearly reflect the fact that Harijans did not really begin to become politically active until the thirties, when with the signing of the Poona Pact the Congress attempted to develop a generation of Harijan leaders. The post-independence system of reserving educational seats, legislative seats, and civil service or government jobs has assisted a great deal not only in seeing that the Harijans have been represented, but also in their development into loyal Congress supporters. The development of Tribal leadership has been a largely post-independence phenomenon reflecting the incorporation of new areas into the Indian Union. Thus, with the high castes and the lowest social groups well represented in the Congress, it can be expected that the most significant future changes in the composition of the Congress elite at the national level will come from the increasing strength of the predominantly agricultural Sudra castes.

Composition Of The Parliamentary Wing

A particularly interesting feature of Congress parliamentary leadership, as revealed in Table XV-8, is the high

TABLE XV-8

COMPARISON OF FATHER'S OCCUPATION WITH OCCUPATION OF
CONGRESS MEMBERS OF THE SECOND PARLIAMENT

Occupation	Father		Member of Parliament	
	No.	%	No.	%
Agriculture	95	43.2	54	24.2
Business	37	16.8	25	11.2
All professional	26	11.8	68	30.5
Law	12	5.4	52	23.3
Government service	40	18.2	7	3.1
Public work	3	1.4	63	28.2
Raja or zamindar	19	8.6	1	0.4
Other	0	0	5	2.2
Unknown	4	—	1	—
Total	224	100.0	224	99.8

degree of social mobility reflected in the relationship between the occupation of the father and the occupation of the legislator son. In a country where role is supposed to be ascriptive, it comes as something of a surprise to discover that there has been a higher degree of occupational mobility than in many highly developed countries. In short, Congress Members of Parliament have not followed in their fathers' footsteps. This fact has important implications in terms of the character and outlook of the Congress legislators and in terms of their relation to the traditional society. Not only is there some tendency for Congress Members of Parliament to deviate from customary norms, but the correlation between occupation of father and occupation of legislator son is extremely low. Whereas some 25 per cent of the members of the sample called themselves agriculturalists, 43 per cent of their fathers had been agriculturalists. Whereas 30 per cent of the Lok Sabha members were professionals, only 12 per cent of their fathers had been professionals, and another 18 per cent had been civil servants. Whereas 11 per cent of the Members of Parliament were businessmen, 17 per cent of their fathers had been engaged in business. Moreover, some 28 per cent of the Congress Members of Parliament in the sample were full-time politicians who had broken away completely from all other occupational categories. Even major source of income data substantiate the considerable occupational mobility of Congress Members of Parliament.

The social origins of Congress Members of Parliament is perhaps most interesting for the light it sheds on the origins of the Congress elite. According to Table XV-9, the fam-

TABLE XV-9

OCCUPATION OF THE FATHERS OF CONGRESS MEMBERS OF THE SECOND PARLIAM
BY MAIN SOURCE OF INCOME OF M.P.

Father's Occupation	*Un-known* No.	*Parlia-ment* No.	%	*Agricul-ture* No.	%	*Busi-ness* No.	%	*Profes-sional* No.	%	*Oth* No.
Professional	2	7	13.2	8	8.6	2	7.4	6	20.0	1
Business	0	7	13.2	7	7.5	16	59.3	5	16.7	2
Service	1	19	35.8	8	8.6	1	3.7	7	23.3	4
Public work	0	0	0	1	1.1	2	7.4	0	0	0
Raja or zamindar	1	2	3.8	9	9.7	3	11.1	1	3.3	3
Land	0	18	34.0	60	64.5	3	11.1	11	36.7	3
Unknown	1	1	—	2	—	0	—	0	—	0
Total	5	54	100.0	95	100.0	27	100.0	30	100.0	13

ily background of the 95 legislators who received their major source of income from the land shows that 64 per cent came from landed families, while another 10 per cent were the sons of rajas or zamindars. Thus, roughly three-fourths of the group came from landed families. The fathers of the remaining 25 per cent of the legislators who claimed land as a major source of income were either professionals, businessmen, or government servants.

Composition Of The Parliamentary Wing

The family background of those who received their major source of income from Parliament is even more revealing, especially in terms of providing data on the origins of the old nationalist elite. Only 34 per cent of this group came from landed families. Some 36 per cent were the sons of government civil servants. The rest were drawn from business and professional families. Thus, almost half of the full-time professional politicians in the Congress, those fully committed to the cause, came from the more modernized sectors of the society and renounced their privileged positions to join Gandhi in his boycott of the British raj. The extent of their divorcement from the land can be seen in the fact that 33 per cent of the families of the professional politicians owned no land and another 35 per cent owned less than twenty acres. Thus, 68 per cent of the professional politicians came from families with little or no land, while 62 per cent of them owned no land whatsoever in their own right. Among those full-time politicians still owning land, those with the smaller holdings were Harijans while those with large holdings were Brahmins.

Interestingly enough, the group whose major source of income was professional fees derived from the same background as the professional politicians. Some 23 per cent of the professionals came from civil service families, which means that about two-thirds of the forty Members of Parliament in the sample whose fathers were civil servants were either full-time politicians or professional men whose major source of income was professional fees. Of the remaining legislators in this category, some 37 per cent came from landed families, 20 per cent from professional families, and the rest from a business milieu. As in the case of the professional politicians, two-thirds of the professional group came from families with little or no land. But, unlike the professional politicians who tended to be among the earliest recruits to the nationalist movement, the professionals were well represented among all generations.

Next to the agriculturalists, the businessmen in the Congress Party in Parliament showed the highest correlation between occupation of father and occupation of son. Almost 60 per cent of the businessmen in the sample came from business families. The remainder came from professional families, landed families, or were the sons of rajas. Some 67 per cent of the businessmen owned little or no land, but the remainder had substantial landholdings. It is particularly interesting to note the shift among traditional business castes from their traditional calling. Only 38 per cent of those belonging to the various Vaisya caste groups claimed to receive their major source of income from business, while 21 per cent depended on income from land and another 21 per cent depended on parliamentary salaries.

Thus, in terms of social origins, it seems clear that Congress Members of Parliament have been drawn disproportionately from the more modernized sectors of Indian society. Yet, while also pursuing non-traditional occupations, they have frequently not followed in their fathers' footsteps. Although coming from the families of the new English educated civil service and professional families—or perhaps because of this—they did not pattern their careers after their fathers'. Having grown up in an atmosphere more conducive to self-direction and in an era of greater political consciousness, they became alienated from the British raj and responded to Gandhi's appeal to join the nationalist movement. While these leaders drawn from the more modernized sectors of society were among the earliest recruits to the Congress movement, the message gradually began to permeate to the less Westernized sectors of modern India, then spread to attract the sons of the middle peasantry of India. Supported financially by their families' landholdings, this rural generation was also able to participate full time in the Congress movement, and after independence their strong support in their home districts made them ideal candidates for office. Although, by comparison with earlier recruits, these Congressmen must be called rural and traditional, it must be remembered that they were drawn from the more modernized and educated sectors of the rural community. They tend to come from the towns rather than from the outlying villages.

In fact, as Table XV-10 shows, the Congress Lok Sabha

TABLE XV-10

POPULATION OF PLACE OF RESIDENCE OF CONGRESS MEMBERS OF THE SECOND PARLIAMENT

Population of Place of Residence	No.		%	
Village less than 500	12		5.5	
Village 500–2,000	33		15.1	
Village 2,000–10,000	24		11.0	
Total village		69		31.6
Town 10,000–50,000	56		25.6	
Town 50,000–100,000	24		11.0	
Town 100,000–250,000	24		11.0	
Total town		104		47.6
City I 250,000–500,000	12		5.5	
City II 500,000–1 million	8		3.6	
City III over 1 million	26		11.9	
Total city		46		21.0
Unknown		5		—
Total	224	224	100.2	100.2

members in the sample were drawn largely from the large towns and the small cities of India. (These areas, ranging in population from 10,000 to 250,000, will be called simply "towns" for the sake of easy identification in the following discussion.) Almost half of the Members of Parliament came from such towns as against 32 per cent who came from villages and 21 per cent who came from the larger cities. The geographic mobility of the Congressmen in the sample has been relatively restricted, yet they have enjoyed greater mobility than their fathers. Whereas 71 per cent of the Congress Members of Parliament have remained in their birthplace, 91 per cent of their fathers have stayed put. Of those legislators who did migrate away from their place of birth, the majority moved from village to town or from town to city. Occupationally, the businessmen and professionals were concentrated largely in the towns and the cities. The professional politicians were distributed equally among villages, towns, and cities. Except for the large landholders, who tended to live in towns and cities, the agriculturalists lived in the villages. The distribution of legislators according to dwelling place naturally conforms to the pattern of Congress strength in India, which tends to be concentrated in the towns of predominantly rural districts and in the villages. Thus, while a large percentage of Congress Members of Parliament can be said to come from the more modernized and Westernized sectors of society in terms of occupation and mobility, they are certainly far from divorced from the traditional society and its base in rural India.

J. Meynaud has observed that "the stability of a party always means that the average age of its parliamentary representatives will show a gradual rise."[28] This aging process has certainly been true of the Congress in spite of the fact that the party followed a conscious policy of retiring at least one-third of the members of the First Lok Sabha in distributing tickets for the Second General Elections.[29] Congress members of the Second Lok Sabha, as disclosed in Table XV-11, were clearly recruited from the older generation of Congress leaders. The proportion of Members of Parliament under 40 declined from 27 per cent in the First Lok Sabha to 19 per cent in the Second Lok Sabha and to only 12 per cent in the Third. A similar trend occurred in the 40-59 age group, which decreased from 64 per cent in the First Lok Sabha to 59 per cent in the Third. The number of Congressmen over 60, however, increased from 9 per cent in the First Lok Sabha to 20 per cent in the Second and to 28 per cent in the Third. The largest single age group in all three parliaments consisted of those between 50 and 59 years of age.

[28] Meynaud, "The Parliamentary Profession," p. 519.
[29] Sadiq Ali, *The General Elections, 1957: A Survey* (New Delhi: A.I.C.C., 1959), p. 16.

Composition Of The Parliamentary Wing

TABLE XV-11

Age	1st Lok Sabha* 1952		2nd Lok Sabha 1957		3rd Lok Sabha 1962	
	No.	%	No.	%	No.	%
20–29	13	4	2	0.9	2	0.6
30–39	75	23	39	17.8	41	11.7
40–49	99	30	65	29.7	102	29.2
50–59	111	34	69	31.5	105	30.1
60–69	30	9	38	17.4	91	26.1
Over 70	1	—	6	2.7	8	2.3
Unknown	0	—	5	—	8	—
Total	329	100	224	100.0	357	100.0

* W. H. Morris-Jones, *Parliament in India* (Philadelphia: University of Pennsylvania Press, 1957), p. 121.

There is little doubt, therefore, that the average age of Congress Members of Parliament has been increasing despite the enforced turnover under the one-third retirement policy and the attrition caused by defeat at the polls. The high-age phenomenon may also be attributable to the fact that ambitious young Congressmen during the Nehru era preferred to focus their attention at the state level where they stood a better chance of achieving positions of power outside the overriding presence of the senior nationalist leaders. Moreover, since a Member of Parliament receives a reasonably high salary for Indian conditions, many of the older Congressmen who have long been oriented toward national politics have been reluctant to retire or have felt that a parliamentary ticket was a justifiable reward for past services. Whatever its causes, the steadily increasing average age of Congressmen in positions of power has been frustrating to many younger Congressmen, who have supported periodic calls for the retirement of a third of the sitting members, for setting a maximum of ten years on office-holding, or for the retirement of senior Congressmen from government so that they may put their long experience to work in rebuilding the party.

The degree to which older Congressmen dominate at the central parliamentary level can be seen in the tendency for newly recruited members of the Lok Sabha to belong to the same generation as those they replace rather than to younger generations. In spite of the one-third retirement rule, only 21 per cent of the new members in the Second Lok Sabha were below age 40, 66 per cent were between 40 and 59, and an astonishing 36 per cent were more than 60 years old. The high average age of Members of Parliament has prevented the Lok Sabha from feeling the full impact of the changes which have been taking place at the state level. Now that a new generation has come to hold the top leadership positions in the ministry at the center, however, it is likely that some interesting changes in the composition of the membership of the Lok Sabha will be in the offing.

Perhaps the most important variable affecting the age distribution of Congress Members of Parliament is geographic. The course of development of the various state Congress parties has been extremely uneven, so that entirely new generations have come to power in some states while others have not yet undergone such renovating experiences. Geographically, the youngest Congress legislators in the sample came from southern India where the composition of the Congress has undergone a major transformation under the impact of anti-Brahmin movements. The youngest of all tended to come from Madras and Maharashtra where the emergence of a new Congress membership mixture is symbolized in the leadership of K. Kamaraj and Y. B. Chavan. Other states with a relatively young leadership are Rajasthan, Andhra, Assam, and the Punjab. The states with the highest percentage of older Congressmen tend to be those in which the Congress drew its earlier strength—Bihar, Uttar Pradesh, West Bengal, and Gujarat.

The degree to which jail-going is no longer the most significant criterion in political recruitment is another sign of the change that is gradually overtaking the Congress. In the selection of candidates for the First Lok Sabha jail-going was an extremely important factor. Subsequently, as revealed in Table XV-12, the Congress leadership discov-

TABLE XV-12

NUMBER OF YEARS SPENT IN JAIL BY CONGRESS MEMBERS
OF THE SECOND PARLIAMENT

Number of Years in Jail	No.	%
Less than one year	27	12.2
1–2 years	14	6.3
2–5 years	53	23.9
Over 5 years	23	10.4
None	105	47.3
Unknown	2	—
Total	224	100.1

ered that the skills required to build an effective legislature did not necessarily coincide with the willingness to court arrest during the independence struggle. Therefore, fewer tickets for the Second Lok Sabha were distributed to Congressmen merely for loyal participation in the nationalist movement. The greater competition characterizing the Second General Elections also encouraged the Congress to favor the man with the ability to win above all. As a result, in the Second Lok Sabha, almost half of the Congress members had never been to jail. Although 66 per cent of the sitting members who were able to win re-election to the Second Lok Sabha had been to jail, only 40 per cent of the new recruits had so distinguished themselves. Geographically, those without jail records tended to be distributed in the same areas and proportions as the younger members discussed in the previous paragraph. Some 62 per cent of the Lok Sabha members from the South had no jail experience. Of those from the non-Hindi North, 53 per cent had never been to jail. But only 38 per cent of the Members of Parliament representing the Hindi-speaking states of the North had never been jailed during the nationalist movement.

Those Congressmen surviving as legislators who also had jail records had clearly been extremely active in the nationalist movement. Only 18 per cent had been in jail for less than two years, 24 per cent had spent from two to five years in jail, and 10 per cent had been in jail more than five years. The sample did not include Congress ministers like Nehru, who spent considerable time in jail; their inclusion would clearly raise the percentage of all Congress Members of Parliament having been to jail and the duration of time spent there. The breakdown between re-elected members of the Second Lok Sabha and new recruits is especially significant. Among sitting members some 17 per cent had been in jail for less than two years, 32 per cent from two to five years, and 5 per cent for more than five years. Among the new recruits only 20 per cent had been jailed for under two years, 16 per cent from two to five years, and a mere 4 per cent for over five years. Thus, though the criterion of jail-going has decreased in importance and will decrease more as time goes on, it is still considered to reflect favorably on the level of a Congressman's activity during the independence struggle, and therefore it is not ignored when tickets are distributed.

The educational level of the Congress members of the Second Lok Sabha, as shown in Table XV-13, had fallen somewhat below that of the old Legislative Assembly, but it was still quite high in comparison with the average educational level in India. Most members of the present sample of the Congress Party in Parliament had at least some college education, while the great majority had advanced degrees or professional degrees, largely because the leadership has insisted that tickets be granted only to those with a certain degree of potential legislative skill and effectiveness. The most poorly educated members, as might be expected, were drawn from the lower castes whose access to education has been limited by many factors. Even those with advanced degrees tended to be educated wholly in India. Whereas some 80 per cent of the Lok Sabha sample had attended college for some time, only 40 to 50 per cent of the members of the Uttar Pradesh legislature had been to college.

TABLE XV-13

EDUCATION OF CONGRESS MEMBERS OF PARLIAMENT, 1952-1962

Education	1st Lok Sabha* 1952		2nd Lok Sabha 1957		3rd Lok Sabha 1962	
	No.	%	No.	%	No.	%
School	5	1	24	11.7	22	6.6
Matriculation	50	15	17	8.3	19	5.7
Undergraduate	49	15	18	8.8	60	18.0
Graduate	213	63	37	18.1	46	13.8
M.A.	0	—	18	8.8	36	10.8
Professional	0	—	86	41.9	126	37.8
None recorded	0	—	5	2.4	22	6.6
Other	18	5	0	—	2	0.6
Unknown	0	—	19	—	24	—
Total	335	99.0	224	100.0	357	99.9

* W. H. Morris-Jones, *Parliament in India* (Philadelphia: University of Pennsylvania Press, 1957), p. 121.

Among college graduates at the state level, moreover, those with professional degrees are being replaced by recruits holding simply a B.A. degree or, at the most, an M.A. degree. At the state level the trend of the future seems to point to a plateau at the matriculation level. The future educational plateau for the Lok Sabha is likely to fall at the B.A. level.

This analysis of Indian decision-makers drawn from various levels of the elite seems to indicate that, as one moves up from village to district to state to national levels, and from the secondary legislative elites to the top of the elite pyramid as represented by the central and state ministers, one finds Indian decision-makers drawn increasingly from the top of the social pyramid in terms of occupation, caste, education, and social status. Yet it is also clear that the elite has not been static. Especially at the state level there has been a considerable circulation of elites, and these changes are beginning to be felt at the national level.

New groups, especially from the middle and lower castes, are being recruited into the Congress elite. But it is important to remember that, while the lowest castes are not represented in the Congress active membership in proportion to their population, they are represented well at the secondary elite level because of the system of reserving seats for Harijans and Tribals. Now securely placed within the legislatures, they are demanding more responsibility in the cabinets. Yet at the lower levels of the Congress organization they have failed to develop an effective caste solidarity. They have allowed themselves to become divided among the factional competitors of the middle castes. Thus, as Elliott has observed: "Low caste groups still accept the legitimacy of dominant caste rule and have not been able or willing to follow their own caste leaders into politics. Thus they are divided before politics but without the advantages of traditional dominance. One might say they are most in need of caste solidarity to overcome traditional subordination, but are most prevented from realizing it."[30]

Some observers have suggested that, if the older conflicts within the Congress have involved struggles between the higher castes and the middle castes for access to the elite, there are now "some signs that in the future the main political conflict is likely to be between non-Brahmins and Harijans." Thus, as the Harijans become sufficiently aware of their political importance, they will demand even greater concessions from the government than they now enjoy. But many non-Brahmins are resentful of the privileges already conferred on the Harijans.[31]

Many critics of the Indian scene have bemoaned the decline in skill levels among legislators and ministers at both

[30] C. M. Elliott, "Caste and Faction in Andhra Pradesh" (unpublished paper prepared for the Association of Asian Studies Meeting, New York, April 1966), pp. 14-15.

[31] Beteille, "Politics and Social Structure in Tamilnad," p. 1163.

state and national levels. Thus, one reads: ". . . if one en-quires about the quality of legislation, the manner in which Bills are scrutinized in parliament and the level of debates, it has to be confessed that matters require a great deal of improvement."[32] While much of such criticism may be true, it must be remembered that the old Legislative Assembly was based on a limited franchise. Even though there has been some decline of skill levels under the universal franchise, it has not been drastic. Nor does the skill level of legislators by any means approximate that of the general population. The reasons for the continued high educational attainment of legislators are two. The leadership has enforced certain standards in the process of recruitment, and the electorate has clearly shown the desire to be represented by individuals capable of dealing effectively with the world outside the village.

It has been observed that in situations of revolutionary change the early phases of the revolution tend to be led by the alienated intellectuals but that after the revolution has achieved its objectives there is a tendency for the intel-lectuals to be replaced by party bureaucrats.[33] To a certain extent it can be argued that the Congress is undergoing such a change. As Sisir Gupta has observed, during the freedom struggle the Congress developed a mechanism for tackling complex organizational and parliamentary problems. But the specialists responsible for these developments were not the great heroes of the nationalist movement. With the transition to the post-independence period, it becomes more and more evident that men with such organizational and administrative skills are needed, and therefore a new breed of Congressmen is beginning to come into power.[34] The trend seems clearly to point to the continued development of party bosses in the states, the decline in the strength and

---

[32] K. Santhanam, "Guarantee for the Future," *Seminar*, 66 (February 1965), 23.

[33] H. D. Lasswell and D. Lerner, *World Revolutionary Elites* (Cambridge: Massachusetts Institute of Technology Press, 1965), p. 100.

[34] S. Gupta, "Competing Elites," *Seminar*, 51 (Nov. 1963), 41.

numbers of intellectuals, and the emergence of leaders closely tied to the organization and, above all, capable of maintaining a balance between the conflicting social groups of which the Congress is composed and which these new leaders represent. These new state leaders gain positions of power because of their skill in the technique of balancing group conflict generated by diverse social pressures.

Men like Kamaraj, Chavan, and Sanjiva Reddy certainly do not possess the intellectual stature of Nehru, Azad, or Rajagopalachari, but it is possible that they have a much more thorough understanding of the conflicts and changes being generated at the local level by the social pressures in India today. These new leaders have been born in the towns or in the villages of India. They come from lower castes, are slightly less well educated, and have a closer connection with the Congress membership than their predecessors had. They have mastered the technique of building majority group support and of maintaining that support in the face of continued challenges. These skills learned at the state level may become more and more important as the Congress faces increased competition at the national legislative level.

It is clear, then, that the Congress has undergone a major transformation over the years since 1885. Moreover, as Morris-Jones has recently observed, perhaps the extent of the transformation accomplished during the pre-independence Gandhian era has been somewhat exaggerated, for post-independence developments seem to indicate that the "Congress under Gandhi only went part of the way toward introducing part of the masses to certain aspects of politics."[35] But with independence and the introduction of the mass franchise, diverse groups began to move into the Congress, often beginning the process of politicization as a result of intra-party factionalism. In other cases, new groups were attracted to the Congress primarily because of its position of dominance. Largely because of the very openness of the party, these changes in the composition of the Congress were felt

---

[35] Morris-Jones, *The Government and Politics of India*, p. 30.

first at the organizational level. New groups, gathering strength and support, began by capturing control of the party organization. That accomplished, they sought expression through the parliamentary wing, which is normally dominated at this stage by a rival group. Thus, in many states, power has passed back and forth from organizational to parliamentary wings with the general elections serving as "the great conveyer belt which enables large-scale transmission between the two structures to occur."[36] In addition, although factionalism has characterized the Congress for some time, its sources have not been the same at each point in time. Shrader describes the process in Rajasthan as a three-stage phenomenon, beginning as a regional struggle, shifting to a generational conflict within the dominant urban elite, and finally evolving into a significant interest-based cleavage. The trend of this dialectic, then, has been toward a rational and modern political process. Thus, for all its divisive and negative aspects, factionalism in the Congress has served to articulate diverse interests, to broaden the base and eventually the elite of the Congress, and to extend political awareness to an even larger segment of Indian society—a development which also has its tantalizing negative and positive aspects.

If the composition and leadership of the Congress have in the past influenced policy implementation, it can be expected that their effect on policy-making in the future will be no less important. As pointed out in the chapter dealing with the role of the Working Committee in coordinating policies not under the jurisdiction of the central government, the strong agricultural base of the Congress among the middle peasantry has definitely affected land reform legislation and especially the implementation of land ceilings. Congress language policy has been significantly influenced by the emergence of regional elites who have insisted that the medium of instruction in the universities be the regional

[36] L. Shrader, "Politics in Rajasthan" (unpublished Ph.D. dissertation, University of California, Berkeley, 1965).

language and that the civil service examinations be given in the regional languages. Weiner has speculated about the implications of changes in the elite on the relative freedom with which policy-makers now operate.[37] More specifically, Rosen has argued that since independence there has been a diffusion of political and economic gains in India which has meant greater power to village, town, and state at the same time that the commitment to achieving balanced economic growth has probably slowed down the general rate of economic growth,[38] a pattern of development attributable largely to the changes that have taken place in the Congress over the past two decades. If Rosen is correct, however, "the economic ideas with which the Congress party took power that provided the basis for the successful policies and plans in the past have worn out their usefulness in all but the broadest sense."[39] Only new ideas, new leadership, and a political coalition strong enough to support both will serve to break the stagnation of the Indian economy and accelerate economic growth sufficiently to meet the rising expectations generated during the last decade. The big question is whether the Congress as presently constituted, or even as its membership and elite continue to evolve, will be able to provide the ideas, the leaders, or the consensus without which neither can be effective.

The passing of the old Westernized elite need not be viewed with alarm. The old elite, however comfortable their dominance might have made Western observers, were not the only possible modernizers of India. The newly emerging regional elites are perhaps more conscious of the needs of Indian society as a whole than were their predecessors. They also have a much more flexible, empirical, and pragmatic approach. It is not impossible, even if not inevitable, that they may provide precisely the kind of stimulus and leadership which is needed for the third decade of Indian independence.

[37] Weiner, *Political Change in South Asia*, p. 286.
[38] Rosen, *Democracy and Economic Change in India*, p. 211.
[39] *Ibid.*, p. 242.

POSTSCRIPT

THE LOSS OF HEGEMONY

The results of the 1967 General Elections produced a shock wave which was felt not only within a badly divided Congress but throughout the Indian political system. If, in fact, twenty years of one party dominance had come to an end in that electoral upheaval, both the Congress and India had reached a new turning point in post-independence development, for the Congress would have to adjust to its loss of hegemony while the Indian political system adjusted to a shift from one-party dominance to multi-partyism. At the very least, the Congress could no longer claim to be the only possible repository of public trust; it was simply the largest among many parties with demonstrable popular support.

To many in India the 1967 elections amounted to a revolt at the ballot box, for the Congress had been returned to power at the Center with a greatly reduced majority and it had failed to win an absolute majority in eight of the Indian states. A closer look at the election results, however, suggests that the great revolt was merely the continuation of a trend. As seen in Table XVI-1, the 1967 elections were an acceleration of the gradual erosion of Congress power over the past two decades. Congress strength in Lok Sabha elections declined from 364 seats and 45 per cent of the votes in 1952 to 284 seats and 40.9 per cent of the votes in 1967. At the state level, similarly, Congress support declined from a high of 2028 seats and 45.7 per cent of the votes in 1957 to 1693 seats and 40.1 per cent in 1967. Table XVI-2 indicates, as might be expected in India's single-member district plurality electoral system, that a small shift in the per cent of votes received often led to a disproportionate loss of state assembly seats. Moreover, although Congress

Postscript

TABLE XVI-1

CONGRESS POSITION IN THE GENERAL ELECTIONS, 1952-1967[a]

I. LOK SABHA

Year of General Election	Total seats	Seats won by Congress	Percentage of seats won	Votes polled by Congress	Percentage of votes polled by Congress
1952	489	364	74.40	47,665,875	45.00
1957	494	371	75.10	57,579,593	47.78
1962	494	361	73.07	51,509,084	44.72
1967	520	284	54.60	59,538,197	40.92

II. LEGISLATIVE ASSEMBLIES

Year of General Election	Total seats	Seats won by Congress	Percentage of seats won	Votes polled by Congress	Percentage of votes polled by Congress
1952[b]	3199	2183	68.20	43,445,655	42.12
1957[c]	3102	2038	65.70	55,661,165	45.65
1962[d]	3334	1957	58.37	50,374,463	43.42
1967[e]	3487	1693	48.60	56,972,083	40.07

[a] Indian National Congress, *The Fourth General Elections: a statistical analysis* (New Delhi: A.I.C.C., 1967), p. 2.

[b] Excludes the figures of the erstwhile Delhi and Himachal Assemblies.

[c] In 1957 General Election only Telangana Area of Andhra Pradesh went to the polls. Figures of 1955 mid-term elections to Andhra included.

[d] Elections were not held to Kerala and Orissa Legislative Assemblies in 1962. Figures of 1965 General Elections to Kerala and 1961 mid-term election to Orissa Legislative Assemblies included.

[e] 1962 and 1967 figures include the results of J. & K., Goa, Daman and Diu, Himachal, Manipur and Tripura Legislative Assemblies also.

Note: Elections in 3 Assembly constituencies have not yet been completed. (Assam—1; Jammu & Kashmir—2)

TABLE XVI-2

RELATIVE CONGRESS POSITION IN STATE ASSEMBLIES, 1962-1967[a]

States	% of seats won in 1962	% of seats won in 1967	Increase or decrease in % of seats	% of votes polled in 1962	% of votes polled in 1967	Increase or decrease in % of votes
Andhra	58.2	57.5	(−) 0.7	47.25	44.67	(−) 2.58
Assam	75.2	58.1	(−)17.1	48.25	43.47	(−) 4.78
Bihar	58.1	40.3	(−)17.8	41.35	32.82	(−) 8.53
Gujarat	73.3	55.4	(−)17.9	50.84	45.93	(−) 4.91
Haryana	57.4	59.3	(−) 1.9	40.41	41.40	(+) 0.99
Jammu & Kashmir	—	82.2	—	—	52.58	—
Kerala	27.1	6.8	(−)20.3	33.58[b]	35.40	(+) 1.82
Madhya Pradesh	49.3	56.4	(+) 7.1	38.54	40.66	(+) 2.12
Madras	67.4	21.4	(−)46.0	46.14	41.49	(−) 4.65
Maharashtra	81.4	75.2	(−) 6.2	51.22	47.94	(−) 3.28
Mysore	66.8	58.3	(−) 8.5	50.22	49.56	(−) 0.66
Orissa	58.6	22.1	(−)36.5	43.28[c]	30.73	(−)12.55
Punjab	57.5	46.2	(−)11.3	45.63	37.42	(−) 8.21
Rajasthan	50.0	48.4	(−) 1.6	40.02	41.44	(+) 1.42
Uttar Pradesh	57.9	46.8	(−)11.1	36.33	32.13	(−) 4.20
West Bengal	62.3	45.4	(−)16.9	47.29	40.97	(−) 6.32
Himachal	79.6	56.7	(−)22.9	51.50	42.45	(−) 9.05
Tripura	56.7	90.0	(+)33.3	43.31	57.26	(+)13.95
Manipur	51.7	55.2	(+) 3.5	28.89	32.59	(+) 3.70

[In the table above (+) indicates *increase* and (−) indicates *decrease* in percentages.]

[a] Indian National Congress, *The Fourth General Elections: a statistical analysis* (New Delhi: A.I.C.C., 1967), p. 1.

[b] Percentage of vote of Kerala given is of 1965 General Elections and of Orissa of 1961 mid-term elections.

[c] It indicates how a small change in the percentage of the total votes polled by the Congress could lead to a serious reduction in the total number of seats won by the Congress in a number of states.

losses varied considerably in extent and impact from state to state, they were particularly severe in Orissa, Bihar, Punjab, and West Bengal. Clearly, the Congress had been humbled. It had reached another turning point in its history. But it continued to be the largest and most highly organized political party in India.

Postscript

Several factors contributed to the Congress reversal in 1967. First and most important, the fact that the central leadership, divided itself, was unable to perform its traditional function of moderating and neutralizing factional splits within the party resulted in a near disintegration of the Congress organization in many states. Rival groups were actually encouraged by the example of blatant factionalism among the central leaders, and for the first time since 1951 the Congress suffered massive defection. Dissidents, isolated by dominant groups in the state party, unable to appeal to a united central leadership, felt so hopelessly in the minority that departure seemed the only alternative. As a result, disaffected Congressmen in independent Congress parties functioned in nearly all the states, and they played a decisive role in the defeat of the Congress in West Bengal and Orissa. In states where party factions were more evenly balanced and where no open break occurred, the party suffered from a more insidious factionalism that was manifest in untold instances of the sabotaging of official candidates. The effects of such internal sabotage were particularly critical in faction-torn states like Punjab, Bihar, Uttar Pradesh, and Haryana. Altogether, then, the major failure of the Congress in 1967 was internal, for the post-Nehru leadership failed to perform what had become the central leadership's most vital function —the mediation of intra-party disputes and divisions.

Widespread resentment growing out of economic stagnation, gnawing inflation, and food shortages also contributed substantially to the Congress defeats in 1967. Although the Congress had been realistic enough to expect some reverses as a result of this resentment, it was also felt that the consequences would be minimal because of the fragmentation of the opposition.[1] In 1967, however, the opposition parties were able to forge alliances on an unprecedented scale, thereby effectively concentrating the resources and the votes to be gained from the growing anti-Congressism in the electorate.

[1] *Hindustan Times* (New Delhi), March 3, 1967.

The Loss Of Hegemony

A third factor might be called the "generational revolution." The Congress simply failed to attract the votes of those to whom the independence movement was a fact of history rather than a matter of personal involvement. "It has been the experience of all the Congress candidates," declared a report of the Bihar P.C.C., "that in the same family, while the older ones vote for the Congress, the youngsters have gone against the Congress."[2] A similar force was at work when the electorate purged the party of such old stalwarts as Kamaraj, S. K. Patil, Atulya Ghosh, P. C. Sen, K. B. Sahay, Bhaktavatsalam, Kamalapati Tripathi, and G. S. Musafir.

Complacency, at all levels of the party, was a fifth major contributor to the reverses experienced by the Congress. Assuming that the party's position of dominance would continue as a matter of course, most Congress leaders overlooked such obvious signs of increasing discontent as defections from the party and dissension within. Nor did they seem more than vaguely aware of the real hardships suffered by the Indian population in the years since the previous general elections. Even within the divided central leadership there was a snug complacency that factionalism within the Working Committee could continue with impunity because of Congress dominance.

Finally, a series of regional and local factors also played an important role in sapping Congress strength. Muslim support declined in areas of communal disturbances; the anti-cow slaughter agitation hurt the Congress in parts of North India, while opposition to central government language policy took its toll in the South; state government employees dissatisfied with government wage policy revolted against the ruling party (which was, of course, the Congress); and so on. Altogether these factors were able to bring an end to Congress hegemony in India.

For almost six months after the 1967 elections the Congress Party, afflicted by defeat, dissension, and defection, seemed almost paralyzed as an organizational entity, although

[2] *Hindustan Times* (New Delhi), March 3, 1967.

there was more than enough internal activity. No sooner was the election over than there developed a struggle for control of the new government. Conflict between the Prime Minister and the Congress President was renewed, the old ideological debate over the ends of the party rekindled. Factionalism and open defection threatened the authority of the High Command, and the issue of center-state relations took on a new meaning with non-Congress governments assuming power in more than half the states. Thus, at a time when the Congress Party was more than ever in disarray, it was faced by a situation requiring more than ordinary unity and creativity.

At first, a contest for the prime ministership seemed inevitable. However, the party's severe electoral reverses had generated tremendous pressures for a consensus on the leadership issue in order to avoid a schism in the already weakened party. In the selection process Congress President Kamaraj, despite his defeat at the polls, once again emerged as an important figure, and once again the Congress presidency provided the machinery through which a settlement was achieved. The compromise formula by which Mrs. Gandhi was unanimously re-elected to the prime ministership and Morarji Desai appointed Deputy Prime Minister[3] and Minister of Finance was the product of a closely bargained consensus among the fragmented Congress leadership which, only under great stress, was able to prefer the survival of the party to the achievement of personal ends.[4]

Mrs. Gandhi's resumption of the prime ministership, however, brought renewed conflict between the Prime Minister and the Congress President. It was the pattern of the previous two successions all over again. The Congress President played a prominent role in selecting a Prime Minister who,

[3] The position of Deputy Prime Minister was first created for Sardar Vallabhbhai Patel. It lapsed after his death. It was revived in 1967 to accommodate Morarji Desai.

[4] For an excellent study of the process of selection, see M. Brecher, "Succession in India: The Routinization of Political Change," *Asian Survey*, VII (July 1967), 423-443.

once installed, set out to assert the independence and primacy of the parliamentary leadership. Not only did Mrs. Gandhi exercise her right to select her Cabinet without consulting the Congress President, but she even challenged him openly by insisting on the nomination of Dr. Zakir Husain, a Muslim, as the Congress candidate for President of the Indian Republic. While Mrs. Gandhi held that the selection of Husain would be a firm demonstration of Congress commitment to secularism, Kamaraj, who preferred the re-election of Dr. S. Radhakrishnan, considered Husain's nomination an unacceptable risk. However, in spite of Kamaraj's misgivings about the opposition's decision to support a single candidate and the possibility of North Indian Hindu Congress defections in protest against a Muslim candidate, Husain's victory confirmed Mrs. Gandhi's judgment, re-asserted her role as party leader, and, in the solidarity of the Congress response, restored confidence to the badly shaken party. It was an important stage in the rehabilitation of the Congress after its post-election paralysis.

The Prime Minister tried to continue her consolidation of power at the time of the election of a new Congress President in December 1967. Again, she had to compromise. The drama began when Mrs. Gandhi made it clear that she would not support Kamaraj for a third term. She then tested party reaction to the idea of her following in her father's footsteps by taking over the Congress presidency, thus uniting party and government leadership. The old guard was not prepared for quite so blatant a takeover, and the proposal was not heard again after Morarji made it clear that such a maneuver would result in a contest with him. Mrs. Gandhi then attempted to secure the uncontested election of her own nominee, G. L. Nanda, but this time she was thwarted by the threat of a direct contest on the part of S. K. Patil supported by the remnants of the Syndicate, Atulya Ghosh and Kamaraj. At this stage, fearing the divisive consequences of an open contest, the Working Committee requested Mrs. Gandhi and Kamaraj to find a candidate both could support. Despite several meetings, no agreement was forthcoming. Negotiations were broken off the day before nominations were due. Hours later, at a midnight meeting at the Prime Minister's house, members of the Working Committee in the absence of Kamaraj persuaded a reluctant S. Nijalingappa, Chief Minister of Mysore, to accept the nomination. Although Kamaraj disapproved of the circumstances surrounding Nijalingappa's candidacy, he readily endorsed him. With the withdrawal of all the other candidates Nijalingappa was declared unanimously elected.[5] For the second time in less than a year the pressure for consensus prevented a potentially divisive contest over the Congress leadership.

The Prime Minister thus succeeded in blocking the re-election of Kamaraj, who was unacceptable to her. But factional politics within the national leadership were such that, while it was conceded that the Prime Minister should certainly approve of the person selected for the Congress presidency, she should not be permitted to gain complete control of the party organization, and the power of the old guard was still strong enough to prevent her from effecting a complete consolidation of power. Nijalingappa's emergence as the compromise choice can be accounted for in several ways. He was a leader of sufficient stature and seniority to stand up to the Prime Minister while still being acceptable to her. His election was welcome to his one-time Syndicate colleagues, Atulya Ghosh, S. K. Patil, and Kamaraj, and was palatable to Morarji. Finally, he satisfied the desire to elect a southerner so that the replacement of Kamaraj could not be interpreted as an attempt to ignore or suppress the South. Though the Prime Minister in all likelihood could have won in a direct contest over the Congress presidency, it would probably have been a hollow victory, if not actually splitting the party, at least leaving behind enough bitterness to hamper party reconstruction.

These successive struggles for control of the Congress demonstrate that the leadership, though divided, places a high

[5] *Hindustan Times* (New Delhi), December 1, 1967.

value on the survival of the party. Factionalism at the center operates within reasonably well-defined limits. Thus, in 1966, when the party was still in a position of dominance at the center and in the states, a contest for the prime ministership seemed like an effective method for testing the support of the leading candidates. However, the very different conditions in 1967 dictated that a bargained consensus replace open conflict. The compulsions of party survival have set limits to factionalism, at least to the extent that the divided leadership seems to have evolved a system for the management of conflict among its members. At the very least, the party seems unified in the belief that a functioning High Command is essential to the continued functioning of the rest of the party organization.

If the relationship between the Prime Minister and the Congress President following the 1967 General Elections consisted of one conflict after another, party-government coordination had been no more harmonious. The 1967 election temporarily created a lame duck Working Committee, for a large number of some of the most important members had been defeated at the polls.[6] These difficulties, combined with the Prime Minister's post-election Cabinet changes, reduced the ministerial element in the Working Committee. There was a corresponding increase, of course, in the size of the non-ministerial group, which was intent upon using the Working Committee to keep a check on the re-elected Prime Minister. Thus, the group's insistence that Mrs. Gandhi take Morarji into the Cabinet as Deputy Prime Minister was motivated not only by a desire to prevent an open contest and possible split in the party but also by a determination to use Morarji as a check on Mrs. Gandhi and her "Kitchen Cabinet"—and also on Chavan.[7] Similar considerations weighed heavily in their attempt, first, to retain Kamaraj as Congress President against the wishes of the Prime Minister and, then,

[6] Among those defeated were Kamaraj, Atulya Ghosh, S. K. Patil, D. Sanjivayya, Biju Patnaik, and General Secretary T. Manaen.

[7] Brecher, "Succession in India: The Routinization of Political Change," p. 441.

to prevent the selection of a party leader considered to be the Prime Minister's nominee. Thus, the composition of the present Working Committee serves to emphasize the extent to which the nature of the Working Committee membership can impede or aid party-government coordination.

The existence of a lame duck Working Committee and the continued divisions within the central leadership have produced a serious lapse in party-government coordination. Party-government coordination at the center had come to depend on the ability of a united ministerial element in the Working Committee to provide policy initiatives and to block proposals considered impractical or contrary to the larger interests of the country. A divided ministerial leadership and a divided party leadership were bound to reduce effective coordination if the rhetoric and technique of party-government coordination should become a camouflage for group conflict—and that is exactly what happened during the week-long Working Committee meeting of May 1967.

The first meeting of the Working Committee after the elections had degenerated into a mutual recrimination session, during which the organizational leaders blamed the shortcomings of government policy for the party losses while the Prime Minister and members of the new government placed major emphasis on the disintegration and ineffectuality of the party organization. The debate ended only when Kamaraj as Congress President accepted full responsibility for the reversal. When subsequent piecemeal discussions provided no blueprint for the future, it was decided that a week-long meeting of the Working Committee should be held to discuss the major issues confronting the party. The May meeting was the result.

The Working Committee meeting in May was unique for several reasons. First, such an extended session was in itself extremely unusual. Secondly, from all indications, it seems that there was very little preparation for this meeting. None of the items on the agenda was accompanied by detailed studies designed to provide substance and guidance for discussion. Thirdly, attendance at the meeting was unusually limited. The size of the Working Committee itself had been reduced to seventeen because of its four unfilled vacancies; in addition, several important members failed to attend all of the sessions, and the number of invitees, which often in the past had exceeded the number of members proper, was this time confined to U. N. Dhebar, Swaran Singh, C. Subramaniam, C. B. Gupta, Asoka Mehta, K. D. Malaviya, and Manubhai Shah. Neither the P.C.C. Presidents nor the leaders of the legislative parties in the states attended these sessions. As a result, the two resolutions to emerge from the meeting were passed by a very small group of leaders, and, though superficial consensus was achieved, it was achieved only by throwing coherence and feasibility to the wind.

The most controversial of the resolutions passed at this Working Committee meeting was a broad policy resolution which became known as the Ten Point Program. Defeat, defection, and dissension had left the Congress leadership groping for a way to refurbish the badly tattered party image. Within the Working Committee a group led by Kamaraj, Nanda, and K. D. Malaviya[8] was convinced that the key to a Congress revival was a more radical ideological posture and action to match, which would close the frequently cited gap between policy and implementation. Moreover, a clearly articulated and zealously activated ideology would, they believed, enable Congressmen to transcend factional rivalries, so that cohesion would be restored to the party. The Ten Point Program would indeed require cohesion, for it called for social control of banks, nationalization of general insurance, abolition of princely privileges, removal of monopolies, curbing of urban landholding, and state trading in imports, exports, and food grains. Neither the Prime Minister nor the Deputy Prime Minister raised objections to any of the items in the Ten Point Program, each evidently hoping the other

[8] K. D. Malaviya was invited to attend Working Committee meetings as a spokesman for the left wing of the Congress following V. K. Krishna Menon's resignation from the Congress.

would take the responsibility for blocking the new progressive image. As a result, an elaborate program was adopted without having first been submitted to serious discussion, much less intensive study.[9]

The offhand and hands-off attitude of both government leaders was repeated at the A.I.C.C. meeting to which the Ten Point Program was submitted for ratification, with the result that the leadership lost control of the resolution to the delegates led by the small but vocal group of left-wing Members of Parliament encouraged by some members of the Working Committee. This group insisted that social control of banks be interpreted to mean nationalization and even succeeded in amending the resolution from the floor by calling for the abolition not only of princely privileges but of princely purses as well. The success of the floor revolt was a rarity in Congress post-independence history and happened largely because the divided leadership sat by silently and did nothing.[10]

With the ratification of the Ten Point Program, however, the government found itself under pressure from Kamaraj, the Working Committee, and the A.I.C.C. to bring about its immediate implementation. The implications of the Ten Point Program had given rise to speculation and debate, creating throughout the country an intense interest in exactly what the government was going to do about it. Meanwhile, however, the Cabinet was deeply divided on three major issues of the Ten Point Program—bank policy, privy purses, and general insurance policy. Particularly troublesome was the complication introduced by the popular tendency to define "social control of banks" as "nationalization," a policy that was in fact strongly advocated by many Congressmen and some members of the Cabinet. Morarji Desai, taking a stand as Deputy Prime Minister and Finance Minister, not

[9] The account presented here was obtained from interviews with leading Congressmen in New Delhi in October 1967.

[10] *Congress Bulletin*, Nos. 6-7, June-July 1967, pp. 96-105.

only refused to support such a policy but threatened to resign if it were adopted.[11]

The impending crisis was averted by means of a compromise worked out at the Jabalpur meeting of the A.I.C.C. At the customary Working Committee meeting on the eve of the session Kamaraj asked the government to explain what was being done to implement the Ten Point Program. The Prime Minister responded by enunciating the principle made familiar during her father's time: that, while the government accepted the objectives of the party, it was the government's responsibility to determine the manner and timing of the implementation of those objectives. Morarji then explained the government's position in regard to that aspect of the Ten Point Program which had aroused so much controversy. He outlined his plan for achieving social control of banks short of nationalization, adding that nationalization of general insurance, though accepted in principle, would not be implemented for some time.[12] The government's reply to Kamaraj satisfied the Working Committee, but, in order to blunt any attacks from the A.I.C.C. floor, it was decided that there would not be any resolution on the subject of the Ten Point Program submitted to the larger body. Instead, after a brief introduction by Kamaraj, Mrs. Gandhi and Morarji Desai would explain the government's position to the A.I.C.C. The tactic succeeded, and compromise, devised and supported by a united leadership, once again carried the day.

While, at the long May meeting of the Working Committee, the Ten Point Program received major attention and very nearly precipitated a crisis in party-government coordination, a second resolution dealt specifically with the issue of party-government coordination. It embodied, for the first time since independence, an official attempt to define the respective duties of government and party and to prescribe a formal mechanism for their coordination at the center, a

---

[11] *The Statesman* (New Delhi), October 26, 1967.
[12] *Hindustan Times* (New Delhi), October 28, 1967.

procedure ironically similar to that laid down unsuccessfully for use at the state level several years before. The resolution stated:

> It is the responsibility of the Congress to lay down policies of the Congress in economic, social, and other fields. These policies are broadly stated in the manifestos and are laid down in greater detail in the resolutions it passes from time to time. It is obviously the duty of the Congress Governments to carry out these policies. A suitable machinery should be set up by the Working Committee to assess and review the implementation of these policies and programmes.[13]

Liaison committees had been part of the trend, particularly strong since 1963, to institutionalize party-government coordination in the Congress. The organizational reforms adopted after the implementation of the Kamaraj Plan had called for liaison committees, though at the state level alone. After the 1967 election debacle, Kamaraj and others in the Working Committee pressed for the establishment of similar machinery for the center so that the party might maintain closer contact with the government. Many Working Committee members, reading their newspapers, found confirmation of their suspicion that the government was keeping them in the dark about issues they felt they had a right to know more about. The liaison committee prescribed by the May resolution on party-government coordination, however, had not been brought into existence by the end of 1967, and, even if it ever is formed, the chances are that it will go the way of the state liaison committees which, while constituted, seldom met.[14]

Party-government coordination must take place either at the level of the party executive or not at all. Specifically created coordination machinery has always been either unnecessary or ineffective. If the Congress party leadership is united,

[13] *Congress Bulletin*, Nos. 4-5, April-May 1967, p. 43.
[14] See Ch. X, pp. 259-261.

then special liaison committees are unnecessary. If, however, the leadership is divided, then past experience indicates that all the liaison machinery Congress ingenuity may devise will fail. The May 1967 Working Committee resolution on party-government coordination was simply an admission of continued dissension at the top of the Congress pyramid.

The Working Committee's role as coordinator of center-state relations is not so much changing as disappearing. During the first two decades of independence the Congress settled problems of center-state relations largely within the party. Differences were handled as a kind of family quarrel to be mediated by Congress elders. With the loss of Congress hegemony a whole new range of difficulties confronted the Congress government at the center, for problems once dealt with quietly as intra-party affairs henceforth required more or less public negotiation through a process of center-state bargaining. In the area of policy, moreover, the center encountered a major problem in maintaining national uniformity in the face of attempts by non-Congress governments to pursue, for various reasons, divergent goals. The center was alarmed, for example, by the tendency of non-Congress state governments to make major alterations in the hitherto fairly uniform system of community development and panchayati raj. Finally the center requested state governments to suspend making such changes until a meeting of the Conference of Chief Ministers could be convened for the purpose of evolving an all-India consensus.[15] Earlier such problems could have been disposed of by the Working Committee. As altered circumstances thus enhance the role of the Conference of Chief Ministers and call into action the National Development Council and zonal councils as well, these extra-parliamentary organs will become the primary organs of center-state coordination. If the Working Committee's role is not yet eliminated, it has certainly been substantially reduced, for its members are, in many states, drawn not from the governing party but from the opposition. Today's Working Committee

[15] *The Statesman* (New Delhi), November 11, 1967.

resolutions are an enunciation not of Indian policy, but of Congress policy.

Changes in the Working Committee's other functions have contributed to important changes in the role of the Working Committee as chief executive of the party. The factionalism which embittered party-government relations at the center and the loss of hegemony which complicated center-state relations have encouraged the devolution of power to the state parties which had begun long before the 1967 elections had taken their toll. Differences between Mrs. Gandhi and Kamaraj, for instance, created major embarrassment for the Congress when Mrs. Gandhi attempted to dissolve the West Bengal P.C.C. as a prelude to toppling the United Front government only to have her actions nullified by Kamaraj's refusal to cooperate. In other states the Working Committee was faced by demands that the party organizational elections, postponed because of the India-Pakistan war and finally scheduled for late 1967, be held off still longer. Such state parties were preoccupied with ministry-toppling, beside which intra-party affairs seemed paltry indeed. Even in states where organizational elections did take place, party electoral procedures again and again gave way under the impact of factionalism. In the state of Andhra, for instance, while the ministerial group had a majority in both the party and the government, the fact that the Pradesh Returning Officer for the organizational elections was a dissident enabled the minority to paralyze the electoral machinery and eventually to win a bargained consensus which gave them more seats in the P.C.C. than their actual strength called for.[16] In other states as well, the existing election machinery, having proved inadequate, was supplanted by a pattern of mutual bargaining between conflicting groups. The tinkering of twenty years has not yet evolved a reliable, much less foolproof, mechanism for controlling and channelling internal conflict.

This problem is accentuated by the continuing inability of the Congress to devise a viable system of membership en-

[16] *Link*, November 19, 1967, p. 14.

rollment, scrutiny, and organizational elections. Unfortunately, organizational reconstruction was ignored during the four years of Kamaraj's tenure as Congress President. At best his performance was very uneven, reaching a crescendo with each of the three successions, but each time followed by little but intermission. The inertia of the President affected the entire organization and particularly the central office. "Never before," according to one observer, had the A.I.C.C. office in Delhi "been reduced to such idleness and irrelevance."[17] Ironically, the man who came to the Congress Party leadership in the name of party reconstruction failed most conspicuously to carry out this primary task. If anything, the organization deteriorated during these years, and this deterioration was reflected in the results of the 1967 General Elections.

The role of the Congress Parliamentary Board is also in a state of flux. The changed and changing role of the Parliamentary Board was reflected in and affected by the election of state leaders, the process of cabinet formation, and the settlement of disputes which came in the wake of the 1967 elections.

After the elections the Parliamentary Board tried to set the tone for the new role of the Congress as opposition and tried to provide guidelines for Congress governments ruling by a slender majority. It was clear from the Parliamentary Board's decisions that the central leadership had decided that the best strategy for the Congress would be to give non-Congressism a chance to show what it could do—if only to hang itself. Therefore, the Board suggested that state Congress parties should be in no hurry to form a ministry where they lacked an absolute majority in the legislative assembly. Entering into coalition government was also ruled out. Next, in order to avoid the appearance of flouting the public will, Congress legislative parties were directed to select a leader only from the elected members of the assemblies, thereby ruling out the too easy return to power of defeated Chief Ministers. Finally, the Board agreed that rebel Congressmen might support the

[17] *Hindustan Times* (New Delhi), December 7, 1967.

Congress in legislative assemblies but that, support notwithstanding, they could not be readmitted to the party.[18] The strategy, in short, was to bend gracefully before the strong feelings of non-Congressism demonstrated in the elections and thus allow the diverse United Front governments to fall under the weight of their own incompatibilities. The decisions were also designed to maintain Congress solidarity by preventing defectors from being offered cabinet positions in exchange for renewed support. Aside from forbidding the resurrection of defeated Congress Chief Ministers, the Board recognized its inability to intervene decisively in state Congress affairs and gave state legislative parties an officially free hand in selecting a leader. Thus, the pattern to which the Board had reluctantly acquiesced in 1962 for states with a strong or undisputed leadership became the pattern for all states in the increasingly federalized party of 1967.

In states where the Congress had received an absolute majority as a result of the 1967 elections and in states where the party's position in the assembly had been drastically reduced, the selection of a leader for the Congress legislative party proceeded uneventfully. In the faction-torn states of Punjab, Bihar, and Uttar Pradesh, however, bitter struggles for control of the party ensued. Not even genuine external threats could generate a sense of solidarity. In Punjab, for example, a week-long delay in reaching agreement on a leader enabled the initiative to pass to the opposition, which was able to consolidate and form a United Front government despite the fact that the Punjab Congress legislative party came very close to controlling an absolute majority in the assembly.[19] Altogether, the bitter factional infighting in such states created the impression that the Congress had learned little from its election ordeal.

The diminution of the Parliamentary Board's authority and mediating influence was equally evident in the delicate task of ministry-making in Congress-controlled states. The

[18] *Hindustan Times* (New Delhi), February 28, 1967.
[19] *Hindustan Times* (New Delhi), March 8, 1967.

The Loss Of Hegemony

Parliamentary Board's technique for maintaining party dominance had been to insist on the accommodation of diverse elements within each state ministry, a pattern that had worked well under a united central Congress leadership and a position of dominance in which the road to power lay strictly through the Congress. With a divided leadership added to reduced majorities, the accommodation process was, if anything, more important. Yet it was far more difficult to achieve. Although the Parliamentary Board urged state Congress leaders to accommodate all sections of the party, state Chief Ministers one after another ignored such temperate advice in an attempt to consolidate the power of their own groups. Thus, not only had the Parliamentary Board admitted the limits of its authority by proclaiming that Chief Ministers should by and large enjoy a free hand in ministry formation, but it found that, even where it attempted to intercede with advice designed to strengthen a Chief Minister, it met with little cooperation. It was this failure to accommodate minority Congress groups which brought down the Congress governments in Haryana, Uttar Pradesh, and Madhya Pradesh, where Congressmen from under-represented socio-economic groups countered exclusion by defection.

The Congress had been returned to power in the state of Haryana, for instance, with an absolute majority, and it appeared that the leadership issue would be arranged expeditiously, when the Haryana legislative party entrusted G. L. Nanda, former Home Minister, with the task of recommending a leader.[20] Nanda's participation was expected to avert a rift between the Jat and non-Jat factions within the party, and Bhagwat Dayal Sharma, a Brahmin, was elected Chief Minister. Nanda then urged Sharma to select a small cabinet in which all sections of the party would be accommodated. But Sharma, fearing a revolt in his own group, preferred to draw his cabinet primarily from his own Brahmin-Bania supporters. Not only did he give little representation to the important Jat community, but he selected from among their

[20] *Hindustan Times* (New Delhi), March 1, 1967.

representatives the least important, to whom he then awarded minor portfolios. He could hardly have done more to alienate the Jat community. As a result, shortly after the new government took office, a group of Congress Jats and allied castes rebelled against the Chief Minister on a crucial vote. Demanding his immediate resignation, they charged that Sharma had "tried to get leaders of all the opponent groups defeated in the election and then systematically kept them out while forming the ministry."[21] The Parliamentary Board was furious over the demonstration of "tactlessness" which had precipitated the crisis. Despite a series of consultations with central leaders, neither Sharma nor the dissidents would compromise.[22] The result was the fall of the Congress ministry in Haryana and the formation of a United Front government in which the Congress dissidents were handsomely rewarded with ministerial posts. The prestige of the High Command suffered badly from this very obvious failure to quell a rebellion in the Haryana Congress party.

Shortly afterward, the Haryana debacle was repeated, with certain variations, in Uttar Pradesh. Having fallen just short of a majority when it received 198 seats in the 423-man Uttar Pradesh assembly, the Congress was able to win over enough independents to form a government under the leadership of C. B. Gupta. Mrs. Gandhi had persuaded his chief rival, Charan Singh, to permit Gupta to be elected unanimously as leader of the Congress legislative party. Yet, within eighteen days of the state government's formation, a group of Congressmen led by Charan Singh engineered a Jat-Ahir revolt against the Brahmin-Bania dominated ministry of C. B. Gupta.[23] Charan Singh, who had refused to join the Gupta ministry, became the Chief Minister of a non-Congress United Front government in Uttar Pradesh. A second Congress government had fallen as a result of the defection of important socio-economic groups.

[21] *The Statesman* (New Delhi), March 18, 1967; *Hindustan Times* (New Delhi), March 18, 1967.
[22] *Hindustan Times* (New Delhi), March 19, 1967.
[23] *Weekend Review,* December 2, 1967, p. 8.

The Loss Of Hegemony

Although the lessons of Haryana and Uttar Pradesh were lost on the Chief Minister of Madhya Pradesh, who also contrived to bring about the collapse of his Congress government, the Congress leaders in other states took note and acted accordingly. Those who had ignored Congress dissidents in cabinet formation immediately embarked on ministry expansion in order to accommodate those whose disaffection could be disastrous. This corrective action may have prevented the fall of further Congress governments, yet it could only have harmful effects on an already badly shaken Congress party discipline. Defection, once the road to obscurity, no longer means the political wilderness. It is instead an important path to power either within the Congress or in non-Congress United Fronts, and the High Command so far has been able to do little to counteract it.

The growing decentralization of the Congress has left state leaders almost completely dependent upon their own capacity to hold together the diverse groups of which the state parties are composed. The days of the *deus ex machina* are gone. The Parliamentary Board, no longer the irresistible mediator, continues to establish broad policy for the guidance of state Congress parties. Yet, even in this aspect of its role, the Board has become heavily dependent upon the wishes and needs of particular state leaders—even when faced with the practical necessity of creating stability in states where non-Congressism and Congress ineptitude destroyed Congress hegemony without creating a viable alternative.

The 1967 General Elections marked the beginning of a transformation of the Indian political system from a dominant one-party system to multi-partyism. Yet, despite the loss of Congress hegemony, which is the most acute symptom of this transformation, the Congress remains the largest, the most highly organized, and the only all-India party. It also remains the most successful of the nationalist movements of Asia and Africa, especially insofar as it has completed its own transformation from nationalist movement to political party and, on a limited scale, from dominance to opposition. Its success cannot be traced solely to the charisma of Nehru nor even to the magic tradition of the nationalist movement. It must be attributed to the ability of the Congress to adapt to the conditions of governing and to the changes which have been taking place in the Indian environment. This adaptability, which is the keynote to the development of the Congress during the past eighty years, is not likely to be abandoned in 1967 when there will be more reason than ever for seeing that the distribution of power within the party, its internal authority structure and patterns of conflict management, and the nature and sources of its leadership conform to the requirements of a new political reality.

The inevitability of a struggle over the distribution of power within the Congress grew out of its origins and its pre-independence traditions. Like most mass-based, democratic parties in the twentieth century, the Congress grew up outside the parliamentary framework and in its early history was primarily concerned with non-parliamentary activities. Thus, unlike earlier parties, such as the British Conservative Party, which developed within the parliamentary framework and created a mass organization gradually in response to the expansion of the franchise, the Congress was abruptly faced with the dilemma of determining the relationship between the mass organization and the party as government.

The Congress constitution had never formally spelled out the relationship of the party to the government, but pre-independence Congress tradition emphasized the predominance of the organizational wing. During the Gandhian era it was the politics of civil disobedience, and not parliamentary activity, that formed the mainstream of the national movement. When a parliamentary role was accepted during the 1937-1939 Congress ministries, the parliamentary wing was made subordinate to the mass organization. Most senior leaders remained outside the ministries, and a three-man directorate was created to supervise the work of those within. Thus, a strong pre-independence tradition developed in which the parliamentary wing was subordinate to the extra-parliamentary organs of the party.

The post-independence course of events has seen that tradition turned almost completely upside down. Following a brief period of conflict, the Prime Minister and the parliamentary wing came to dominate the mass organization by controlling the Congress presidency and the Working Committee. The party was granted the role of laying down the broad outlines of policy, but the government asserted its jurisdiction over the timing, content, and implementation of specific measures. Even in the formulation of that broad general policy, which was from time to time incorporated in party resolutions and election manifestos, the initiative was supplied by the parliamentary leadership, who dominated the thinking of the Working Committee. If party pressure was capable of modifying policy, largely by attempting to influence the thinking of the leadership during debates on Working Committee resolutions at the A.I.C.C., the resolutions themselves were seldom modified or rejected.

During the period of divergence the smooth functioning of the coordination processes established during the period of centralization and convergence was significantly disrupted, and the parliamentary wing's monopoly of power underwent certain changes. From this fragmentation of the centralized power developed during the Nehru era there emerged a polycentric pattern in which previously dormant institutional centers of power began to assert their role in party, government, and all-India policy-making. The authority of the Congress presidency was partially restored with the election of Kamaraj and the role he played in the two successions. By bringing about the resignation of the most important members of the central Cabinet, the Kamaraj Plan also undermined the parliamentary wing's dominant position in the Working Committee by creating an important non-ministerial group in the party executive. The role of the Congress Chief Ministers in the election of Mrs. Gandhi in 1966 dramatically demonstrated the new reciprocal relationship between center and state leaders. Even the more broadly based organs of the organizational and parliamentary wings, the A.I.C.C. and the Congress Party in Parliament, began to demand and get a greater voice in the affairs of party and government, a trend that was furthered and strengthened at times of leadership conflict or deadlock when these bodies were energized by competing elites.

Accompanying these shifts in the relative power of party and government institutions, and contributing to the difficulty in assessing them, was the development of factionalism within the leadership elite. Although a collective leadership had emerged after Nehru's death, Shastri's widespread support within the party and within the party elite clearly placed him above the rest of Nehru's lieutenants. During his less than two years as Prime Minister he was on the verge of establishing his pre-eminence as leader of both party and government. With his death, however, lack of consensus forced the leadership to resort to an open contest which resulted in the election of Mrs. Gandhi as Prime Minister. This outcome was viewed, even by Mrs. Gandhi's supporters, as an interim arrangement. Therefore, when she attempted to act as Prime Minister in her own right, rather than as vassal to her elder organizational colleagues, there was conflict. Earlier, such conflict had eventuated in the more or less willing recognition of the Prime Minister as supreme Congress leader, but this time the Prime Minister was not so secure nor so pre-eminent that conflict could be abated. Thus, factionalism between leaders of relatively equal strength took on the appearance of party-government conflict when the Congress President and the Working Committee attempted to apply checks to the Prime Minister. Both sides looked to the election for vindication.

Instead, 1967 brought an end to Congress hegemony. In the resulting shake-up of the Congress elite, no one emerged strong enough to achieve his ends unaffected by the pattern of consensus, compromise, accommodation, and bargaining which had once been encouraged as part of the Congress dedication to democratic ideals but which increasingly, especially after the Fourth General Elections, became the sole means of party (and personal) survival.

The Congress in the post-election period of 1967 has, thus, been passing through a new period of transition remarkably similar to the years immediately after independence —but with an important exception: this time competition has focused on the prime ministership, not as a usurper, but as the true seat of power, prestige, and patronage available to Congress aspirants to leadership. Although the Congress President has played an important role in the succession process, each new Prime Minister has re-asserted the supremacy of the Prime Minister as leader of party no less than government and, to this end, has contrived to prevent the leadership of the organizational wing from falling into hostile hands. Thus, Shastri insisted on the re-election of Kamaraj despite Morarji Desai's objections, and Mrs. Gandhi, despite her inability to get her own candidate elected unopposed, successfully exercised a veto over the election of a candidate unacceptable to her. So long as the Congress remains in power, the Prime Minister will enjoy a pre-eminent role.

Congressmen in both organizational and parliamentary wings look to the Prime Minister for leadership, for the Prime Minister's power, prestige, and patronage add up to an overwhelmingly commanding position. Because no Congress President can match these resources, there can be no real dual leadership at the top of the Congress pyramid. Formal provisions notwithstanding, the Prime Minister is the *de facto* leader of party and government. No elected Congress government will accept the dictation of the party President. The influence of a Congress President will depend, therefore, not only upon his own leadership capacities but also upon the degree to which he enjoys the confidence of the Prime Minister. The Congress President may play a certain resurgent role in transition periods during which a new Prime Minister is consolidating power, but, once the government gets under way, the leader of the organizational wing will again be reduced to lieutenancy.

There is another important reason why Congress Presidents may influence, but not dictate, policy. The Prime Minister of India is more than the leader of the majority party: the Prime Minister is leader of all the nation. With the loss of Congress hegemony this fact has become more, not less, important than ever before. The Prime Minister must be acceptable not only to the Congress but to the opposition parties, and especially to opposition Chief Ministers, if the government is to function smoothly and if Indian unity is to be preserved. It was this very acceptability, in 1966 no less than in 1967, which elected Mrs. Gandhi to the prime ministership.

Altogether, then, the elaborate ceremony surrounding the election of the Congress President and the attempt to preserve the myth of the Congress *rashtrapathi* have become anachronistic. During the period of one-party dominance the argument that power in the party should not be concentrated in the hands of a single person perhaps had some validity. But with the end of Congress hegemony the argument holds little force. There is no likelihood that the leadership will be able to push through a change which would permit the *de jure* appointment of a party President or Chairman by the Prime Minister. The pattern of the past will persist. When the leadership is united, there will be little difficulty in nominating a candidate, whose election will be a mere formality. When the leadership is divided, there will be either a bargained consensus or an open contest staged to test the strength of competing elites. Yet it is essential that the Congress leadership be able to transcend any such divisions. Without unity there will be government paralysis and party inaction; there will be no effective party-government coordination, and factionalism will be encouraged in the states. The ultimate danger of continued division is a checkmate system in which the only agreement attainable will be agreement on the preservation of the status quo, a consensus which will be of no service to the health of either the nation or the Congress.

The Working Committee's role is somewhat different from, and essentially more vital than, that of the Congress President. The peculiar features of Indian federalism, in which Congress federalism is embedded, necessitate close cooperation between national and state leaders, and, with the loss of Congress hegemony, this coordination must more than ever take place in the Working Committee insofar as it takes place within the Congress. The Working Committee in 1967, as before, consists of the most important members of the Indian Cabinet as well as the Chief Ministers or leaders of the Congress legislative parties in the states where the Congress is functioning in opposition.[24] Taken together, these Congressmen constitute the national leadership of the party. Almost everyone who really counts in the party is either a member of the Working Committee or an invitee. Since the Congress is a federal party in a federal system, the state leaders are bound to play an important role on the national scene as well as at home.

To dominate the Working Committee is to control the mass organization, for, although the formal structure of power recognizes the Working Committee as simply the executive arm of the Congress, charged with carrying out the program laid down by the A.I.C.C. and Annual Sessions, the informal and actual structure of power is quite the reverse. It is the Working Committee which makes policy for the mass organization. The "official resolutions" submitted for ratification to the A.I.C.C. and Annual Sessions are seldom modified or rejected. When serious challenges do occur at such meetings, they are usually a manifestation of divisions within the dominant elite, involving attempts to mobilize support by and for antagonistic points of view within the leadership. So long as it dominates the Working Committee, therefore, the

[24] It is interesting to note that, with the loss of Congress hegemony, the Chief Ministers were replaced, not by P.C.C. presidents, but by the leaders of the Congress legislative parties in the states.

parliamentary leadership is in a strategic position to control the mass organization and ensure party-government coordination. As Mrs. Gandhi remarked recently, "Who is the Working Committee? We all constitute the Working Committee. If we do not like a particular thing, we can always defeat it there. . . ."[25] Party-government coordination must take place within the Working Committee or not at all, and for this reason, despite recurrent enthusiasm for them, special liaison committees have failed to provide a solution to the problems of party-government coordination. The Working Committee resolution of May 1967 ordaining the establishment of a central coordinating committee similar to that earlier appointed (and ignored) for the states was simply a recognition that the party leadership is badly divided. The issue of party-government relations is more often than not a matter of intra-party factionalism, in which the dialogue of competition for ultimate power in the parliamentary wing disguises itself as the problem of coordinating parliamentary and organizational wings.

The Working Committee's tendency to dominate decision-making for the mass organization does not mean that the oligarchic tendencies in the Congress prevail unchecked. The Congress, like most highly centralized political parties, has developed an elaborate procedure for consulting the mass organization. Since the mid-1950's a pattern has emerged in which the A.I.C.C. meets twice a year and the Congress session once. Consultation with these decision-making organs of the mass organization is not always *pro forma*, for resolutions, once presented, must be debated and ratified. Thus, even when it is not exercised, the organization possesses the latent power to reject or modify the policy initiatives of the party executive. Even during the period of centralization and convergence, the A.I.C.C. had occasionally asserted itself, though most frequently on *dal-roti* issues of party organizational affairs. In the case of policy resolutions the party was usually more than willing to give wide latitude to the govern-

[25] *The Hindu Weekly Review* (Madras), June 5, 1967.

ment leadership and the Working Committee. Since 1963, however, the A.I.C.C. has become much more vocal on both organizational and policy issues. Delegates have challenged the "bonafides" of the Kamaraj Plan as a "deliberate action to deprive some people of power"[26] and have even pressured the government to change its policy on the renunciation of nuclear weapons. Perhaps the most forceful challenge to the leadership of the Working Committee came at the Jaipur Session of the Congress in February 1966, when the A.I.C.C. attempted to force a change in the government's policy on food zones. Only after the Prime Minister had assured the delegates that the government would re-examine its policy was a direct confrontation avoided.[27] Although no change was made in the food zone policy, it was clear that henceforth the leadership would have to be prepared to defend its actions more often and more vigorously than ever before.

The resurgence of the A.I.C.C. has even resulted in a major policy initiative, a rarity in Congress post-independence history. At the Delhi meeting of the A.I.C.C. in June 1967, the delegates succeeded in amending the Working Committee's Ten Point Program so as to direct not only the abolition of princely privileges but of princely purses as well. In initiating this action the A.I.C.C. was substantially aided by divisions within the central leadership and was in fact encouraged by some members of the High Command. The A.I.C.C.'s power to upset the applecart often depends on its availability for mobilization by competing elites rather than on its strength as a quasi-popular body. This point was clearly demonstrated at Jabalpur in October 1967, when a united Working Committee succeeded in modifying the very Ten Point Program adopted so enthusiastically by the A.I.C.C. only a few months before. In general, however, while the Prime Minister and the Working Committee will continue to carry the day, at least so long as they are united, it is clear that the views of the party will have to be given more weight

[26] *Congress Bulletin*, Nos. 7-9, July-September 1964, pp. 341-347.
[27] *Hindustan Times* (New Delhi), February 12, 1967.

and that the leadership will have to develop a meaningful dialogue between party and government if the kind of overt conflict which marked the first transition period is not to characterize the second as well.

Although debates within the A.I.C.C. can be viewed as part of the dialogue between party and government, another significant contribution to debate must be kept in mind. Just as there is a substantial overlap between party and government leaders in the Working Committee, so a large portion of the approximately 700 A.I.C.C. delegates are M.P.s, M.L.A.s, and state ministers. In A.I.C.C. debates, moreover, M.P.s have come to play a very important role. There are several reasons for this development. In the first place, because M.P.s are entitled to free first-class rail travel anywhere in India, they can turn out in sufficient force to form a disproportionate percentage of the 300 to 400 delegates who actually attend A.I.C.C. meetings. Secondly, M.P.s have begun to use the A.I.C.C. as a forum for debate and criticism of government policy. Many of them feel uneasy about criticizing ministers openly at meetings of the Congress Party in Parliament or on the floor of the Lok Sabha because of their dependence on ministers for their promotion within the party and for redressing the grievances of their influential constituents and supporters. At A.I.C.C. meetings, however, particularly when they can mobilize additional strength among other A.I.C.C. delegates, they feel less hemmed in and less isolated. An examination of the speakers at A.I.C.C. meetings would show that many of the most vocal are actually Congress Members of Parliament. Finally, a large proportion of A.I.C.C. delegates who put in an appearance are really not interested in policy issues. They come to meet with the national leadership and to discuss largely local problems. Insofar as they are interested in larger issues, they are concerned with organizational matters rather than with the formulation of substantive policy. In short, it would be a mistake to view A.I.C.C. debates in strictly party-government terms. These debates are most often a slightly more dramatic segment of the more or less continuous dialogue by which the Congress attempts to aggregate conflicting interests and bring about a workable consensus on broad objectives. For the most part, so long as the leadership is united, it has a remarkably free hand in forming policy, which is almost always ratified by the A.I.C.C. and Annual Sessions.

The authority structure of the Congress, like the distribution of power, has changed considerably over the past two decades. The formal structure of authority as it is spelled out in the Congress constitution provides for a highly centralized party. The Working Committee, Parliamentary Board, and Central Election Committee are given vast powers over the party organization, the coordination of party-government relations, and candidate selection. As chief executive of the party, the Working Committee has the power to superintend, direct, and control all subordinate Congress committees, invoke sanctions for breaches of party discipline, and take all action it sees fit to take in the interest of the Congress. The Parliamentary Board has the power to frame rules for the regulation and coordination of Congress legislative parties. The Central Election Committee has the final authority in the selection of candidates and not only may overrule the recommendations of lower committees but may nominate a candidate who has not even applied for a ticket. Thus, the formal structure of authority is highly oligarchic.

Although the center exercised much greater authority before independence than it does today, the Congress organization has never been as highly centralized in practice as its formal structure of authority would make it appear. Moreover, over the past two decades the authority of the center has undergone gradual erosion from the assertion of greater autonomy by state and local units. As a result, the Congress has been federalized into a coalition of state parties which are themselves coalitions of quasi-independent district organizations. Although there remains a complex pattern of interdependence among various strata and various groups, the party's authority structure, far from being oligarchic, is

437

in 1967 essentially balkanized. The higher levels of the party have increasingly been forced to defer to the wishes, needs, and demands of the lower strata,[28] even while the lower strata have become increasingly dependent upon the higher strata for patronage and dispute settlement.[29] The degree of interdependence has been determined by the degree of factionalism within the state, and the unity of the party has been heavily dependent upon the mediating capacity of a united central leadership. Divisions within the central leadership before and after the 1967 elections reduced the authority of the center, produced a breakdown of the established system of conflict resolution, and increased the autonomy of state leaders, who became more than ever dependent upon their own skills in holding together the factional networks within each state party. The breakdown in central mediation resulted in defections as well as a new pattern of dispute settlement based on mutual bargaining.

The changes in the authority structure of the Congress were most clearly visible in the case of candidate selection, but the pattern can also be seen in the role of the Working Committee as chief executive of the party and in the role of the Parliamentary Board. The process of candidate selection was exhibiting the pattern of autonomy and interdependence even during the period of centralization and convergence. By 1962, though able to intervene decisively in badly factionalized states, the Central Election Committee was accepting with little or no alteration a list of candidates submitted by a strong Chief Minister presiding over a dominant coalition within his state. By 1967, the pattern that applied earlier only to dominant states had become the pattern for the Congress as a whole. The almost total breakdown of the center's mediating role resulted in the passing of ultimate power over candidate selection to the Provincial Election Committee. In badly divided states a pattern of

---

[28] R. Roy, "Selection of Congress Candidates—V," *Economic and Political Weekly*, II (February 18, 1967), 409.
[29] M. Weiner, *Party Building in a New Nation,* concluding chapter.

mutual bargaining based on the maintenance of the status quo emerged. The process of federalization in the Congress party was complete.

Accompanying the shift in the locus of decision-making in candidate selection from the center to the states was the development of even greater pressure for decentralization of candidate selection within the states themselves. Lower levels of the party have demanded a decisive voice in the selection of candidates, and, as Roy has shown, the degree of their success depends on the degree of unity within the local party units.[30] The Provincial Election Committee, like the Central Election Committee of earlier times, is able to play a role largely when factionalism at the bottom forces settlement to higher levels of the party. Thus, the Congress cannot be viewed as a great pyramid in which all authority moves down from the top. During the past twenty years the politics of mass franchise, the extension of party organization into the district and below, and the creation of unilingual states have resulted in a devolution of power within the Congress to the point where the party has become essentially federalized and every level has developed substantial autonomy.

Yet some considerable degree of interdependence remains. Control of the central government and the existence of a united national leadership are still important to the general health of the party as an all-India entity. Serious divisions at the top of the Congress elite are a threat to the existence of the entire party, for such divisions encourage factionalism at all other levels of the party. An open split within the Congress elite, leading, say, to an open contest over the Congress presidency, could galvanize strictly local state factions into an all-India coalition, and the result might be such a rift in the Congress that there would be brought into being a potentially strong opposition party complete with a well-organized party network. It is interesting that the defections which took place in many states on the part of dissident Congressmen who rebelled for largely local reasons led

[30] Roy, "Selection of Congress Candidates—V," pp. 413-415.

to the setting up of a new all-India party. Yet, though such a party, the Bharatiya Kranti Dal (B.K.D.), did in fact come into existence after the 1967 elections, it failed to establish an all-India solidarity because of the desire of constituent state units to retain sufficient maneuverability at the local level to permit, if advantageous, re-merger with the larger Congress body. Had the dissident groups been homogenized into a single party as the result of a bitter struggle for control with opposing Congress elites, they would have emerged with a powerful potential for national leadership. If this time the coalition remained unstable, the same cannot necessarily be predicted of future coalitions.

A united national leadership is also important because of the party's position as ruling party at the center. Control of the central government is crucial to the state Congress parties, to those in embattled governments and those reduced to opposition, because of the peculiar nature of Indian federalism, which requires coordinated action by center and states. Moreover, the center's presence in state politics in the guise of state governors and by way of its power to declare President's Rule can have a decisive impact, not only on the politics of the state but on the internal politics of the Congress as well. President's Rule can be invoked to end the instability resulting from intra-party coalitions no less than that stemming from inter-party coalitions. Thus, by imposing President's Rule in Haryana, the center deprived a fractious Congress of the fruits of office after all its efforts to topple the previous ministry. In the final analysis, a strong mutual interdependence exists between central and state Congress units. When it controls the national government, the central leadership can invoke President's Rule, and, though President's Rule in itself cannot engineer unity within the state or within the state Congress and though it cannot be exercised arbitrarily or purely for party advantage, it can provide time for the party to consolidate and determine a strategy for recovery. With all the resources of central power, however, the Congress must depend upon its state parties to win and keep a majority in the states and at the center. Otherwise, power will pass more fully to the opposition—a situation which, should that opposition be unprepared, can only mean uncontrolled political instability or an authoritarian solution.

The changes which have taken place in the internal structure of the Congress have been accompanied by significant changes in the party membership. The end of the British raj and the introduction of the mass franchise accelerated the process of change in the composition of the Congress which had begun during the mass civil-disobedience campaigns of the pre-independence period. In order to win and hold power, the Congress sought to extend its hold over rural power elites and attract newly politicized groups into the Congress fold. The accomplishment of this aim was facilitated by the open character of Congress membership, the position of dominance enjoyed by the party, and the development of intra-party factionalism, which encouraged competing elites to reach out for support willingly provided by aspiring social groups who saw the Congress as a means through which to achieve their ends. Through this process the once atypical Congress adapted itself to the traditional social structure, thereby enabling the party to maintain its position of dominance. At the same time, the changing nature of the social structure and the internal conflict generated by elite competition created serious problems for the maintenance of party solidarity. Yet the system survived, owing to the well-exercised pattern of conflict resolution which the Congress was able to develop as a result of its long history of dealing with problems of organizational diversity.

The growing balkanization of the Congress was thus to a very large extent due to the growing heterogeneity of the party itself, which in turn derived from the emergence of new regional elites based on coalitions of caste, regional, and communal factions representative of the social conflicts of the particular states. Thus, it became increasingly difficult to talk about *the* Congress, as though it were a monolithic homogeneous entity. In fact, as the older generation of national leaders were gradually replaced, the state parties came to mirror more and more accurately the society in which they functioned, and the party's strength depended on the degree to which it could accommodate emerging social groups. The upshot has been that leadership in the Congress has been slowly passing from the hands of an upper caste, urban, upper middle-class leadership into the hands of peasant proprietors, businessmen, bazaar merchants, and politically conscious caste and community groups—from the hands of the intellectuals into the hands of the party managers. The process of change begun at the local level has slowly percolated up to the state level, so that state Congress parties have become more or less strong coalitions of caste, communal, and regional groups. Thus, in Rajasthan, for example, the Congress at the time of independence was dominated by urban, high caste leaders. When a generational split developed within the elite, Mohanlal Sukhadia succeeded in building around his own faction a broad coalition of regional and caste groups.

The result of such intra-party competition was twofold. First, at the same time that it destroyed the power of the old freedom-fighter generation, it prevented the total stagnation of the party. This aspect is reflected in Sadiq Ali's description of the state of the Maharashtra Congress in 1967:

> We all know in a general way that the Congress in Maharashtra was a strong and vital organisation. There are many young people who are MLAs and MPs in Maharashtra. Those who man the Congress organisation also largely belong to the younger generation. It is possible that some old Congressmen have received raw treatment but the infusion of a heavy dose of new blood has made the Congress organisation strong in the state of Maharashtra.[31]

The power of the Congress in Maharashtra in 1967 is al-

[31] Sadiq Ali, "The Study Tour," *AICC Economic Review*, XIX (October 15, 1967), 3-4.

most completely dependent upon the support of the Maratha community, which is the largest in the state and which succeeded quite early after independence in displacing the previously dominant Brahmin leadership in the Maharashtra state Congress.

A second result of this conflict, however, is that it can completely shatter the party, destroying its solidarity as well as its position of dominance. Thus, in Bihar, where the Congress fell apart into a complex multi-factional system characterized by a continuous process of "mutual sabotage,"[32] coalitions of factions based largely on caste have succeeded in destroying Congress hegemony itself. Especially in the North, moreover, where the process of elite change has been much slower than in the South, internal sabotage has reduced Congress strength to the point that new opportunities are open to those who are dissatisfied with their progress within the Congress. In a system of Congress dominance, aspiring social groups felt compelled to work within the dominant party as the road to power. Under the conditions of 1967, however, there was an alternative to the Congress. Thus, by failing to accommodate dissidents, the Congress was faced by a new kind of defection, which led to loss of dominance.

The key to political stability no less than Congress dominance in India has been the Congress Party's ability to attract and absorb newly politicized groups and the Congress leadership's ingenuity in constructing meaningful coalitions able to accommodate the diverse communal, social, and regional factions peculiar to each state. In most states the party system was thereby able to moderate social conflict by aggregating the diverse demands of otherwise conflicting groups. In a state like Kerala, by contrast, mutually antagonistic caste, communal, and regional groups have been concentrated in separate political parties, unable to cooperate for long under any conditions for fear that one particular

[32] *Ibid.*

group may gain disproportionately, and the result has been continuous instability. So far, fortunately, the situation in Kerala has not been duplicated elsewhere in India.

The loss of Congress hegemony has been brought about by the growing strength of parties which are largely regional in their appeal; there has emerged no all-India party capable of replacing the Congress, and the experiments with non-Congress United Fronts have turned out to be failures. Non-Congressism could not bring about needed change so long as it remained a mere negative force. The bulk of the leadership's time was spent trying to keep coalitions together—to say nothing of the energy spent in trying to improve the position of each party vis-à-vis any others in the coalition. As these anomalies became more visible, there was growing disillusionment with the stagnation and instability of opportunistic coalition building. Thus, while some see the 1967 elections as the beginning of the end of the Congress umbrella and as the first stage in an inevitable realignment of political groupings from right to left, with the ultimate pattern a so-called rational party system based on ideological bipolarization, a more likely result of the collapse of the Congress would be the total atomization of Indian politics. The bipolarization model is based on a unidimensional political perspective which does not fit Indian parties.

Any all-India party is bound to be a coalition of diverse forces. The devolution of power has made even the Congress a decentralized party, for the Congress itself has become a coalition of state parties which in turn are coalitions of quasi-autonomous district organizations. It is held together by a leadership that has a high stake in keeping the Congress intact and by some eighty years of experience in dealing with the problems of welding and holding diverse coalitions together. If the Congress, with all its experience and institutionalized patterns of behavior is unable to prevent fragmentation, if the Congress cannot channel the social forces let loose by democratization, industrialization, and modernization, then atomization—and not polarization—of Indian politics will result. In that event, the inevitable development will be stagnation and political instability. Thus, the immediate future of the Indian political system is still very much dependent upon developments within the Congress.

The Congress has received a major shock, and the test now will be how effectively it can respond. Even so, it has won a reprieve of five years, for, although it lost control of many states, it was able to retain its majority at the center. Though paralyzed at first, the Congress has shown some signs of revival. Despite its divisions the national leadership succeeded in settling the leadership issue by the unanimous election of both Prime Minister and Congress President. The smooth installation of these officers is essential to achieving coordination between party and government. The next crucial contest for control of the party will not come until 1969, when the Congress holds its organizational elections and selects a new Congress President in preparation for the 1972 General Elections. The leadership will thus have time to devote its attention to party reconstruction in the interim. There is much work to be done, but, if there is the will, there is no lack of time.

Despite the loss of Congress hegemony the Congress parties in the states remained relatively intact despite a number of defections. The 1967 organizational elections created a minimum of havoc because state party leaders managed to achieve a bargained consensus without the aid of central mediation. Moreover, the consensus on the selection of party and government leaders at the center avoided the opening of a rift, with its long anticipated potential for giving rise to two all-India coalitions of rival groups. Surprisingly, even party membership has held up. Evidently, those remaining in the party have attempted to use the new opportunities created by the 1967 election shake-up to enhance their position within the party organization in preparation for the inevitable mid-term polls that will follow in several states. There are even signs that many of the defectors are seriously weighing the possibility of returning to the Congress fold.

Postscript

In all, the 1967 General Elections have had at least five important positive results. First, a shock was administered to an increasingly complacent Congress, which has been forced to do some re-thinking about its future. The fact that the Congress maintained its majority at the center has not only given India valuable stability at a time of transition but has also given the Congress time to regroup and recoup its losses. Next, the election opened new possibilities for a number of non-Congress parties. For the first time since independence many opposition parties feel they have a genuine chance to win power. The effect has been a moderation of policy positions in those parties which see themselves as potential all-India rivals to a Congress which they see as eventually and inevitably doomed to collapse. A third positive result has been that, while non-Congressism as such has been a failure as a cementing force, opposition leaders have had a chance to experience the problems of running a government. In the case of the D.M.K. in Madras and the Swatantra-Jana Congress coalition in Orissa, such parties have shown themselves capable of effective government. Fourth, the 1967 election was a psychological boost to all those who had placed their faith in the system which came to life with Indian independence, for it renewed confidence in the effectiveness of elections and the politics of the mass franchise. A new source of power was created in 1967 when Indians demonstrated that the ballot was more than an exercise in futility. The Fourth General Election, in fact, has been characterized as a peaceful revolt through the ballot box. Finally, the 1967 elections have intensified the process of evolving permanent extra-party machinery for institutionalizing center-state relations and, in the course of doing so, have brought the bargaining process out into the open. In all these ways the existing political system has been strengthened.

However, the 1967 elections have also had several negative effects. Although faith in mass franchise has been strengthened, there is greater disillusionment with party politics. The behavior of non-Congress coalitions and of the Congress in opposition has been far from exemplary. When Chavan described Haryana instability in terms of *Gaya Ram* and *Aya Ram*, he expressed a widespread disillusionment with the buying and selling of ministerial positions. Despite the success of the D.M.K. in Madras and of the two-party coalition in Orissa, there is a strong feeling that the opposition has failed to use constructively the power given to it in February 1967. A second problem has been the disproportionate disharmony in center-state relations that has developed. Opposition coalitions, on the brink of failure, have tended to blame their difficulties on the center's determination to destroy them instead of on their own internal inadequacies. Neither of these developments is a healthy sign.

Since the 1967 General Elections have broken the near monopoly of power enjoyed by the Congress for two decades, the inevitable result will be a greater variety of political patterns and behavior. In some states the Congress will undoubtedly remain in power for some years to come. In other states it will have to govern as the largest party in a two- or three-party coalition. In still other states it will have to learn to function as opposition, unless and until the state leadership can rebuild the party and its base of support. As for the party as a whole, its most important task will be to develop a more cohesive organization with a more highly trained cadre to carry out the ideas of a new generation of Congress leaders. At the same time, it must never forget the importance of developing and maintaining a skillful articulation process by which a diverse party can be held together. It is not an impossible assignment, but it will not be easy for the Congress to do all that it must do before 1972.

APPENDICES

PRESIDENT OF THE CONGRESS

Nominated by any 10 delegates
Elected for two years by delegates

PARLIAMENTARY BOARD

Congress President and Chairman
and 7 other members selected
by Working Committee

WORKING COMMITTEE

Congress President and 20 members
7 elected by A.I.C.C.
13 appointed by President
Treasurer and General Secretary(ies)
appointed by President
from among W.C. members
All members must be members of
A.I.C.C. or elected to it within
six months after appointment

CENTRAL ELECTION COMMITTEE

Members of Parliamentary Board, Leader
of Congress Party in Parliament, and
5 members elected by A.I.C.C. The C.E.C.
is formed only during election years

ALL-INDIA CONGRESS COMMITTEE

Meets at call of Working Committee
or at request of 50 A.I.C.C. members

⅛ of P.C.C. members elected from among themselves	President and ex-Presidents of Congress, provided still active members	P.C.C. Presidents	Leader of Congress Party in Parliament	15 members elected by Congress Party in Parliament	Leaders of Congress parties in state legislatures and of legislative assemblies in union territories	*Members co-opted by W.C. from special elements not otherwise adequately represented	*Representatives of organizations and institutions in India

* co-opted and nominated members may not vote and may not contest any election.

ANNUAL CONGRESS SESSIONS

Meets annually (usually in January) and
consists of Congress President and all other
delegates (all members of Pradesh Congress
Committees are delegates)

APPENDIX II

THE STRUCTURE AND COMPOSITION OF THE FIELD ORGANIZATION OF THE CONGRESS PARTY

PRADESH CONGRESS COMMITTEES

20 Pradesh Congress Committees, 6 Territorial Pradesh Congress Committees, and Andaman District Congress Committee

Members elected by active members of block at rate of 1 member per 100,000 population	Ex-P.C.C. Presidents still active members	D.C.C. Presidents	A.I.C.C. members residing in Pradesh	MLAs elected by legislative party at rate of 5% of P.C.C. (15% max.)	*Members co-opted from special elements not adequately represented	*Representatives of organizations and institutions working in area

DISTRICT OR CITY CONGRESS COMMITTEES

There are 437 D.C.C.s of which 62 are City Congress Committees. The D.C.C. covers an area prescribed by the P.C.C.

Two members elected by active members of each block	Block C.C. Presidents (not eligible to be D.C.C. President or Secretary)	Ex-D.C.C. Presidents still active members	P.C.C. members living in or elected from district	MPs and MLAs from district if active members	Leaders of Congress parties in corporation, municipality or district board and of zilla parishad or jana-pads if active members	*Members co-opted by D.C.C. executive from special elements not adequately represented	*Representatives of organizations or institutions working in area

BLOCK/WARD CONGRESS COMMITTEES

About 5015** each with an area comprising a population of 60,000 coterminous with the Development Block. May be constituted only if there are at least 25 active members in the block.*** Membership consists of (a) members elected by the primary members at the rate of 1 for every 2000 population and (b) members of the D.C.C. who reside in or have been elected from the block.

Committees subordinate to the block are determined by the P.C.C.

MEMBERSHIP

PRIMARY

Any person over 18 years old who accepts the objectives of the Congress, pays 4 annas annually, and is not a member of any other political party, communal or other, which has a separate membership, constitution, and program.

ACTIVE

Any primary member who has served two years and who pays a one rupee annual subscription, is 21 or older, habitually wears hand-spun and hand-woven khadi, abstains from alcoholic beverages, does not observe or recognize untouchability, believes in communal unity, respects the faith of others, and undertakes to accept minimum training and to perform minimum tasks prescribed by the Working Committee (i.e., collects 12 rupees annually and enrolls 50 primary members).

---

* Co-opted and nominated members may not vote and may not contest elections.
** *Report of the General Secretary, 1964*, p. 67.
*** *Report of the General Secretary, 1965-1966*, pp. 94-95.

Constitution

of

The Indian National Congress

(AS IN FORCE FROM JUNE 25, 1967)

ALL INDIA CONGRESS COMMITTEE
7, JANTAR MANTAR ROAD
NEW DELHI-1

Article I

OBJECT

The object of the Indian National Congress is the well-being and advancement of the people of India and the establishment in India, by peaceful and constitutional means, of a Socialist State based on Parliamentary Democracy in which there is equality of opportunity and of political, economic and social rights and which aims at world peace and fellowship.

Article II

CONSTITUENTS

The Indian National Congress will include the annual and special sessions of the Congress and,

  (i) The All India Congress Committee,
 (ii) The Working Committee,
(iii) Pradesh Congress Committees,
 (iv) District/City Congress Committees,
  (v) Block Congress Committees,
 (vi) Committees subordinate to the Block Congress Committees to be determined by the Pradesh Congress Committee concerned.

Note:

(i) In this Constitution wherever the word "Pradesh" occurs, it will include "Territorial"; the word "District" will include "City" and the word "Block" will include "Town" or "Ward" as required by the context.

Appendices

(ii) Provided that in such Pradeshes, where there are no Blocks, the Working Committee will have the right to take necessary steps to delimit appropriate Committees.

Article III

TERRITORIAL DIVISIONS

(a) Pradesh Congress Committees shall ordinarily be constituted in the Pradeshes named below with the headquarters mentioned against each;

Pradesh	*Headquarters*
1. Andhra	Hyderabad
2. Assam	Gauhati
3. Bihar	Patna
4. Bombay	Bombay
5. Delhi	Delhi
6. Haryana	Chandigarh
7. Gujarat	Ahmedabad
8. Himachal	Simla
9. Jammu & Kashmir	Srinagar
10. Kerala	Trivandrum
11. Madhya Pradesh	Bhopal
12. Maharashtra	Bombay
13. Mysore	Bangalore
14. Punjab	Chandigarh
15. Rajasthan	Jaipur
16. Tamilnad	Madras
17. Tripura	Agartala
18. Utkal	Bhubaneshwar
19. Uttar Pradesh	Lucknow
20. West Bengal	Calcutta

(b) Territorial Congress Committees shall be constituted in the territories named below with the headquarters mentioned against each:

Territory	*Headquarters*
1. Chandigarh	Chandigarh
2. Goa	Panjim
3. Manipur	Imphal
4. Nagaland	Kohima
5. NEFA (North East Frontier Agency)	Bomdilla
6. Pondicherry	Pondicherry

(c) A Pradesh Congress Committee may, with the previous sanction of the Working Committee, change its headquarters.

(d) The Working Committee may, after ascertaining the wishes of the Pradesh Congress Committee or Committees concerned, constitute a new Pradesh, abolish an existing Pradesh, merge any existing Pradeshes into one or assign to a Pradesh, a district or a portion or portions of a district from any other Pradesh.

Appendices

(e) The Working Committee shall have the power to give representation in such manner as it thinks proper to areas in the Union of India as have not been included in the jurisdiction of any PCC and/or direct that such an area or part thereof be included in a neighbouring Pradesh.

Article IV

MEMBERSHIP

(a) (i) Any person of the age of 18 or over, who accepts Article I, shall, on making a written declaration in Form 'A' and on payment of an annual subscription of twenty-five paise only, become a primary member of the Congress provided that he is not a member of any other political party, communal or other, which has a separate membership, constitution and programme.

    (ii) No person shall become a primary member except in his permanent place of residence or where he carries on his work.

    (iii) The year of membership, primary and active, shall be from 1st January to 31st December.

(b) Any person, who has been a primary member for two consecutive years, may become an active member on payment of an annual subscription of Re. 1/- if he fulfills the following conditions and signs a declaration in Form (B):

    (i) He is of the age of 21 or over;

    (ii) He is a habitual wearer of hand-spun and hand-woven Khadi;

    (iii) He abstains from alcoholic drinks;

    (iv) He does not observe or recognise untouchability in any shape or form;

    (v) He believes in communal unity and has respect for the faith of others;

    (vi) He undertakes to have a minimum training and to perform a minimum task as may be prescribed by the Working Committee.

(c) Every active member shall enrol 50 primary members each year.

(d) Active membership shall be continuous so long as the annual subscription is paid according to rules made thereunder and the other conditions prescribed are fulfilled.

(e) The annual subscriptions paid by primary and active members shall be distributed in the following proportions between the various Congress Committees:

AICC	10%
PCC	25%
DCC	25%
Block CC	40%

Appendices

TERM OF CONGRESS COMMITTEES

The term of every Congress Committee and of its office-bearers, Executive Committee and members shall ordinarily be two years.

Article VI

REGISTER OF MEMBERS

(a) Permanent registers of active members shall be maintained by the PCCs and DCCs.

The Pradesh Congress Committees shall supply lists of their active members to the Office of All India Congress Committee and keep it informed of the changes made therein.

(b) The registers shall contain the full name, address, age, occupation, place of residence and date of enrolment of every member.

(c) Membership shall cease by death, resignation, removal or non-payment of annual fee.

Article VII

QUALIFICATIONS OF VOTERS AND CANDIDATES

(a) Voters:

Every primary member, whose name appears in the roll of primary members prepared in accordance with the rules framed in this behalf by the Working Committee, shall be entitled to vote in the elections to the Block Congress Committees under sub-clause (a) of Article IX of this Constitution.

(b) Candidates:

Only an active member, whose name is in the register of active members, shall be eligible for election as a member of any Congress Committee.

Article VIII

ASSOCIATE, CO-OPTED AND NOMINATED MEMBERS

No associate member shall have the right to vote or to be an office-bearer or a member of the Executive of any Congress Committee, but he shall have the right to participate in the deliberations; however, no person who is an associate member shall be debarred for that reason from seeking election or co-option to full membership of any Committee in the normal manner. The co-opted and nominated members at the AICC, PCC and lower levels shall not exercise any voting right in any organisational election nor shall they contest any election in the organisation.

Appendices

BLOCK/TOWN OR WARD CONGRESS COMMITTEES

A Block Congress Committee shall cover an area having a population of about 60,000 coterminous with a Development Block and shall consist of:

(a) Members elected by the primary members of the Congress at the rate of 1 for round about 2,000 population;

(b) Members of the DCC who reside in or have been elected from the Block.

Provided that it shall be constituted only if there are at least 25 active members in that Block.

Article X

DISTRICT CONGRESS COMMITTEES

A. A DCC shall cover an area prescribed by the PCC in its Constitution and shall consist of:

(a) Two members elected by the active members of the Block;

(b) Presidents of Block Congress Committees, provided that they shall not be eligible to become either President or Secretary of the DCC.

(c) Ex-Presidents of the DCCs who have completed one full term* and are active members;

(d) Members of the PCC who reside in or have been elected from the District;

(e) Members of the Legislature Congress Parties, both Central and State, from the district, provided that they are active members;

(f) Leaders of the Congress Parties in Municipal Corporations, Municipalities and District Boards/Zilla Parishads or Janapads in the District, provided that they are active members;

(g) Members co-opted by the Executive of the DCC from special elements not adequately represented and others in accordance with the rules prescribed by the Working Committee;

(h) Representatives of organisations or institutions working in the area in accordance with the rules prescribed by the Working Committee;

B. The PCC shall fix the number under each category in accordance with the rules prescribed by the Working Committee.

---

* Full term signifies the interval between two District Congress Committee elections or two years, whichever is less, provided that such of the ex-Presidents who have been Presidents for 365 days or more before 7-1-1964 shall continue to be ex-officio members of the DCC.

Appendices

PRADESH CONGRESS COMMITTEES

A. A Pradesh Congress Committee shall consist of:

(a) Members elected by active members of the Block at the rate of one for about a lakh of population forming a single member constituency to be coterminous with Block areas as far as possible, as delimited by the concerned PCC, the method of voting being in accordance with the rules prescribed by the Working Committee.

Provided that

(i) A delegate Constituency shall be eligible to elect a delegate in case a Block/Town Congress Committee has been duly constituted in that constituency;

(ii) From the Pradeshes of Bombay and Delhi there shall be 56 and 30 members respectively and in the following Pradeshes there shall be 25 members each;

1. Goa, Daman and Diu
2. Tripura
3. Manipur
4. Nagaland
5. NEFA
6. Pondicherry

and (iii) From the territory of Chandigarh there shall be 7 members;

(b) Ex-Presidents of the PCC who have served one full term* and are active members of the Congress;

(c) Presidents of the DCCs provided that they shall not be eligible to become either President or Secretary of the PCC;

(d) AICC members who reside in the Pradesh;

(e) Members co-opted by the PCC Executive from special elements not adequately represented and others in accordance with the rules prescribed by the Working Committee;

(f) Representatives of organisations and institutions working in the area in accordance with the rules prescribed by the Working Committee;

(g) Members elected by the Congress Legislature Party at the rate of 5% of the number of PCC or TCC members subject to a maximum of 15.

B. Every member of the PCC shall pay an annual fee of Rs. 15/- to the PCC of which Rs. 10/- shall be remitted to the AICC as delegate fee. He shall receive a certificate duly signed by one of the

---

* Full term signifies the interval between two PCC elections or 2 years, whichever is less, provided that such of the ex-Presidents who have been Presidents for 365 days before 7-1-1964 shall continue to be ex-officio members of the PCC.

Secretaries of the PCC to the effect that he is a member. No member who has not paid his fee shall be entitled to exercise any of his functions. The PCC shall forward to the AICC office a certified list of the members not later than the date fixed by the Working Committee in that behalf.

C. Every Pradesh Congress Committee shall:

(a) ordinarily function through the District Congress Committees;

(b) subject to the general supervision and control of the AICC be in charge of the affairs of the Congress Committees within its own Pradesh and to that end frame its Constitution, not inconsistent with this Constitution, which shall come into operation only with the previous sanction of the Working Committee;

(c) submit to the Working Committee an annual report of the work done by the Congress Organisation in the Pradesh including audited balance sheets;

(d) pay to the AICC the share due to it out of the members' fees (vide Article IV (e) and Clause B above) before a date to be fixed by the Working Committee.

D. The Pradesh, which has not completed the formation of the PCC on or before the date fixed by the Working Committee, may, at the discretion of the Working Committee, be disentitled to be represented at the Congress Session.

E. On the failure of any Pradesh Congress Committee to function in terms of the Constitution or in accordance with the direction of the Working Committee, the Working Committee may suspend the existing PCC and form an Ad-hoc Committee to carry on Congress work in the Pradesh.

Article XII

DELEGATES

All members of the Pradesh Congress Committees shall be delegates to the Indian National Congress.

Article XIII

ALL INDIA CONGRESS COMMITTEE

A. The All India Congress Committee shall consist of:

(a) One eighth of the number of the PCC members elected by them from amongst themselves by proportional representation according to the system of single transferable vote, provided that the number is not less than five; however one member shall be elected from Chandigarh TCC;

(b) President of the Congress;

(c) Ex-Presidents of the Congress, who have completed one full term* and are active members of the Congress.

* Full term signifies the interval between two AICC elections or two years, whichever is less, provided that such of the ex-Presidents who have been Presidents before 7-1-1964 shall continue to be ex-Officio members of the AICC.

(d) Presidents of the Pradesh Congress Committees, provided that they shall not be eligible to become either President or Secretary of the AICC;

(e) Leader of the Congress Party in Parliament;

(f) Leaders of the Congress Parties in the State Legislatures and Legislative Assemblies in Union Territories;

(g) 15 members elected by the Congress Party in Parliament according to the system of single transferable vote;

(h) Members co-opted by the Congress Working Committee from special elements not adequately represented and others in accordance with the rules prescribed by the Working Committee;

(i) Representatives of organisations and institutions working in India in accordance with the rules prescribed by the Working Committee;

B. (a) The President of the Congress shall be the President of the All India Congress Committee;

(b) The AICC shall arrange for the implementation of the programme of work laid down by the Congress and shall have powers to deal with matters and situations that may arise during its term of office;

(c) The AICC shall have power to frame rules, not inconsistent with this Constitution, for regulating all matters connected with the Congress which shall be binding on all subordinate Congress Committees;

(d) The AICC shall meet as often as required by the Working Committee, or on a joint requisition addressed to the Working Committee by not less than 50 members. Such requisition shall specify the purpose for which the requisitionists desire a meeting of the AICC. A requisitioned meeting shall be held within two months of the receipt of the requisition. At any requisitioned meeting, additional items of business may be brought up by the Working Committee for consideration;

(e) At all meetings of the AICC other than requisitioned meetings, as far as possible, 4 hours shall be allotted for consideration of propositions of which due notice has been given by the members of the AICC in accordance with the rules prescribed in that behalf;

(f) Seventy or one-fifth of the total number of members, whichever is less, shall form the quorum for a meeting of the AICC;

(g) Every member of the AICC shall pay an annual fee of Rs. 10/-. He shall receive a certificate duly signed by one of the Secretaries of the AICC to the effect that he is .a member. Members will not be permitted to take part in any meeting of the AICC, Subjects Committee or any Congress Session without paying the fees.

Article XIV

COMMITTEES SUBORDINATE TO THE DCC

The PCC may constitute Committees subordinate to the DCC and above and/or below the Block Congress Committees in the manner laid down in the Constitution of the PCC.

Article XV

SUBJECTS COMMITTEE

(a) The AICC shall meet as the Subjects Committee under the Chairmanship of the President at least two days prior to the Congress Session. The Working Committee, or in case a new President has been elected before the Session and there is no Working Committee appointed by him functioning, a Steering Committee appointed by the President, shall submit to the Subjects Committee the programme of work, including draft resolutions, for the Congress Session. While drafting the resolutions the Working Committee or the Steering Committee shall take into consideration the resolutions recommended by the Pradesh Congress Committees and resolutions given notice of by the members of the AICC.

(b) The Subjects Committee shall proceed to discuss the programme and shall frame resolutions for being moved in the Open Session. As far as possible, four hours shall be allotted for the consideration of propositions of which due notice has been given by the Pradesh Congress Committees or the members of the AICC.

Article XVI

ANNUAL CONGRESS SESSION

(a) A Session of the Congress shall ordinarily be held annually at the time and place decided upon by the AICC or the Working Committee.

(b) A Congress Session shall consist of the President of the Congress and all other delegates.

(c)   (i) A Congress Session shall consider resolutions recommended to it for adoption by the Subjects Committee in the first instance;

     (ii) Thereafter the Session shall take up any substantive motion not included in (i) above, but which 40 delegates have, before the commencement of the day's sitting, requested the President in writing to allow them to place before the Congress, provided, however, that no such motion shall be allowed unless it has been previously discussed at a meeting of the Subjects Committee, and received the support of at least a third of the members then present at the Subjects Committee meeting.

(d) The Pradesh Congress Committee, in whose jurisdiction the Congress Session is held, shall make such arrangements for holding the Congress Session as may be deemed necessary and, for this purpose, shall form a Reception Committee which shall work under its general guidance and which may include therein persons who are not its members.

Appendices

(e) The Reception Committee shall elect its Chairman and other office-bearers from amongst its own members.

(f) The Reception Committee shall collect funds for the expenses of the Session and shall make all necessary arrangements for the reception and accommodation of delegates. It may also make necessary arrangements for the visitors.

(g) The receipts and disbursements of the Reception Committee shall be audited by an auditor or auditors, appointed by the Pradesh Congress Committee concerned, and the Statement of Accounts together with the audit report shall be submitted by the Pradesh Congress Committee to the Working Committee within six months of the conclusion of the Congress Session. Any surplus funds remaining with the Reception Committee shall be divided equally between the AICC and the PCC.

Article XVII

SPECIAL SESSION

(a) A Special Session of the Congress shall be held in case the AICC so decides or if a majority of PCCs, through their resolutions, request the President of the Congress to convene such a Special Session.

(b) Such a Session shall be organized by the PCC of the Pradesh selected for holding the Session.

Article XVIII

ELECTION OF THE PRESIDENT

(a) The Working Committee shall appoint one of the General Secretaries of the AICC to work as Returning Officer for the election of the President:

Provided that no General Secretary, who is a candidate for Presidentship, shall be appointed, and that if all the General Secretaries are such candidates, the Working Committee shall appoint some one else to work as the Returning Officer.

(b) Any ten delegates may jointly propose the name of any delegate for the election as President of the Congress. Such proposals must reach the Returning Officer on or before the date fixed by the Working Committee.

(c) The Returning Officer shall publish the names of all persons so proposed and it shall be open to any person whose name has been so proposed to withdraw his candidature within seven days of the publication of the proposed names by writing to the Returning Officer to that effect.

(d) After eliminating the names of those who have withdrawn, the Returning Officer shall immediately publish the names of the remaining candidates and circulate them to the Pradesh Congress Committees. If, after elimination, there remains only one candidate, he shall be declared duly elected as President of the next Congress Session.

(e) On a date fixed by the Working Committee, which shall not ordinarily be less than seven days after the final publication of the names of contesting candidates, each delegate shall be entitled to record, for the election of a President, his vote in the following manner:

On the voting paper, which shall exhibit the names of the candidates, the delegate shall, if there are only two candidates, record his vote for one of them. If there are more than two candidates, the delegate shall record at least two preferences by writing the figures 1, 2, etc. against the names of the candidates voted for. In such a case, he may give more than two preferences if he wishes to do so but any voting paper showing less than two preferences will be regarded as invalid. The voting paper shall be deposited in a ballot-box provided for the purpose.

(f) The Pradesh Congress Committees shall immediately forward the ballot-boxes to the AICC.

(g) As soon as may be after the receipt of the ballot-boxes the Returning Officer shall count the votes or the first preferences recorded for each candidate. If a candidate secures more than 50 per cent of the votes of the first preferences, he shall be declared elected as President. If no candidate secures more than 50 per cent of the first preferences, the candidate who has secured the smallest number of first preferences shall be eliminated, and the second preferences, recorded by the voters who gave him the first preferences, shall be taken into account in counting the votes of the remaining candidates. In this counting the candidate who secures the smallest number of votes shall be eliminated. By this process of eliminating the candidates who secure the smallest number of votes in subsequent countings after the transfer of votes according to recorded preferences, the candidate who secures more than 50 per cent of the votes, shall be declared elected as President.

(h) In the event of any emergency arising by reason of any cause, such as the death or resignation of the President elected as above, the Working Committee shall forthwith fix a date for a fresh election by the delegates as prescribed above. In case such a procedure is not found possible by the Working Committee, it shall convene a meeting of the AICC to elect a President.

(i) The President shall preside over the Sessions of the Congress held after his election and during his term of office, and he shall exercise all the powers of the Working Committee when it is not in session.

Article XIX

WORKING COMMITTEE

(a) The Working Committee shall consist of the President of the Congress and twenty members, of whom seven members will be elected by the AICC as per rules prescribed by the Working Committee and the rest shall be appointed by the President. The President shall appoint a Treasurer and one or more General Secretaries from amongst the members elected by the AICC or appointed by the President. Ordinarily, members of the Working Committee will be appointed from amongst the members of the AICC but, in special cases, delegates, who are not members of the AICC, may be appointed; provided, however, that a delegate so appointed shall cease to be a member of the Working Committee if he is not elected as a member of the AICC within six months of his appointment.

(b) The quorum for a meeting of the Working Committee shall be seven.

(c) The Working Committee shall be the highest executive authority of the Congress and shall have the power to carry out the policies and programmes laid down by the Congress and by the AICC and shall be responsible to the AICC. It shall be the final authority in all matters regarding interpretation and application of the provisions of this Constitution.

(d) The Working Committee shall place before every meeting of the AICC a report of the proceedings of the previous meeting of the AICC and also an agenda of business for the meeting and shall allot time for non-official resolutions of which due notice may have been given by the members of the AICC in accordance with the rules prescribed in that behalf.

(e) The Working Committee may appoint one or more auditors or inspectors or other officers to examine the records, papers and account books of all Congress Committees and organisations. It shall be incumbent on all such Committees and organisations to furnish all the required information to the auditors, inspectors, or other officers and to give them access to all offices, accounts and other records.

(f) The Working Committee shall have the power,

  (i) to frame rules for the proper working of the organisation. Such rules shall, as early as possible, be placed for the consideration of the AICC;

 (ii) to issue instructions not inconsistent with this Constitution and frame rules in all matters not otherwise provided for;

(iii) to superintend, direct and control all Pradesh Congress Committees and subordinate Committees, as well as the Reception Committees;

(iv) to take such disciplinary action as it may deem fit against a Committee other than the AICC or any individual;

 (v) in special cases to relax application of provisions under Articles IV (a) (ii), IV (b), VII (a) and VII (b).

(g) The Working Committee shall have the accounts of the AICC audited annually by an auditor or auditors appointed by the AICC every year.

(h) The Working Committee shall fix the date by which the formation of Block, District, Pradesh and All India Congress Committees shall be completed.

(i) The Working Committee shall appoint a Board of Trustees for holding properties belonging to the All India Congress

Committee. The term of the Board shall be for three years and the Treasurer of the All India Congress Committee shall be an ex-officio member of the Board.

(j) To meet any special situation, the Working Committee shall have the power to take such action in the interest of the Congress as it may deem fit; provided, however, that if any action is taken which is beyond the powers of the Working Committee as defined in this Constitution, it shall be submitted as early as possible to the AICC for ratification.

Article XX

TREASURER

The Treasurer shall be in charge of the funds of the Congress and shall keep proper accounts of all investments, income and expenditure.

Article XXI

GENERAL SECRETARIES

(a) Subject to general control of the President the General Secretaries shall be in charge of the office of the AICC;

(b) The General Secretaries shall be responsible for the preparation and publication of a report of the proceedings of the Congress Session, including its audited accounts, as soon as possible after the Session;

(c) The General Secretaries shall prepare a report of the work of the AICC and the Working Committee, including an audited statement of Accounts, for the period since the last submission of such a report and submit the same to the first meeting of the AICC held before the annual session of the Congress.

Article XXII

SCRUTINY OF MEMBERSHIP

The Executives of the District Congress Committees and Pradesh Congress Committees shall arrange for periodical scrutiny and disposal of complaints regarding the enrolment of primary and active members in accordance with the rules prescribed by the Working Committee, but when complaints of a grave nature are reported to the Working Committee, it may enquire into such complaints and take such action as may be deemed necessary.

Article XXIII

ELECTION DISPUTES

The Executives of the District Congress Committees and Pradesh Congress Committees shall arrange for disposal of complaints regarding elections in accordance with the rules prescribed by the Working Committee, but when complaints of a grave nature are

466

reported to the Working Committee, it may enquire into such complaints and take such action as may be deemed necessary.

Article XXIV

ELECTION MACHINERY

(a) The PCC or TCC as the case may be, shall, within a period of two months from the beginning of its term, appoint by a majority of two-thirds of its members present and voting a Pradesh or Territorial Returning Officer, whose term will be coterminous with the term of the PCC or TCC.

(b) If any PCC or TCC fails to appoint a Pradesh or Territorial Returning Officer, the Working Committee shall appoint a Pradesh or Territorial Returning Officer.

(c) The Pradesh Returning Officer shall conduct all Congress elections in the Pradesh. He shall, in consultation with the Executive of the PCC or TCC and DCCs. appoint District Returning Officers and such other Officers as may be necessary for the proper conduct of elections in the Pradesh or Territory. He shall also perform such other functions as are allotted to him by the Working Committee from time to time.

(d) The Pradesh Returning Officer shall hold Office ordinarily for one term but he will continue to function till a new Pradesh Returning Officer is appointed or he is removed from Office in accordance with the rules framed in this behalf by the Working Committee.

Article XXV

FLAG

The flag of the Indian National Congress shall consist of three horizontal colours, saffron, white and green, with the picture of a Charkha in blue in the centre. It shall be made of hand-spun and hand-woven Khadi.

Article XXVI

(A) PARLIAMENTARY BOARD

The Working Committee shall set up a Parliamentary Board consisting of the Congress President and seven other members, with the Congress President as the Chairman, for the purpose of regulating and co-ordinating the Parliamentary activities of the Legislature Congress Parties and shall frame rules in that behalf.

(B) ELECTION COMMITTEES

(a) A Central Election Committee shall be set up consisting of members of the Parliamentary Board, the leader of the Congress

467

Party in Parliament and five other members elected by the AICC for the purpose of

    (i) making the final selection of the candidates for the State and Central Legislatures, and

    (ii) conducting election campaigns.

(b) The Pradesh Election Committee shall consist of the President of the PCC, the leader of the Congress Legislature Party and/or in case of Union Territories, the leader of the Congress Party in the Territorial Council and not more than ten and not less than four other members, who shall be elected by the general meeting of the PCC or TCC. If the members of the Committee to be elected, other than the PCC or TCC President and the leader of the Congress Legislature Party and/or in the case of Union Territories, leader of the Congress Party in the Territorial Council, are elected by a two-third majority of members present and voting, they shall be declared elected. The voting for such an election shall be by ballot and on each ballot paper the voter shall have to record as many votes as there are members to be elected to the Committee. In case a two-third majority is not secured by each of the members to be elected, there shall be a fresh election by the system of single transferable vote.

The President of the PCC or TCC shall be ex-officio Chairman of the Pradesh or Territorial Election Committee.

(c) The Pradesh or Territorial Election Committee, constituted in the above manner, shall recommend candidates for the Central and State Legislatures to the Central Election Committee.

(d) The Central Election Committee shall frame necessary rules to give guidance to the Pradesh Election Committees in regard to the selection of candidates and other matters relating to the conduct of elections.

Article XXVII

VACANCIES

(a) The Office of a delegate or a member of any Committee or Board constituted under this Constitution shall be vacated by resignation, removal or death.

(b) All vacancies shall, unless otherwise provided for, be filled in the same manner in which the vacated member was chosen and members so elected shall hold office for the unexpired term of the seat vacated.

(c) In the absence of any provision to the contrary, a Committee or Board, once it is properly constituted, shall not become invalid by reason of any vacancy on it.

Article XXVIII

MISCELLANEOUS

(a) No person shall be a member of any two parallel Committees provided that this provision shall not apply to associate members.

(b) A Committee may delegate any of its powers to a smaller committee or an individual.

(c) Population figures of the last available census shall be the basis for all Congress purposes.

(d) Where there is a question of the value of fractions, a fraction of one-half or more shall be treated as one, and less than half as zero.

(e) Wherever, in this Constitution, the word 'vote' or any of its inflections occurs, it means or refers to a valid vote.

(f) The Block, District and Pradesh Congress Committees shall elect from amongst its members the Presidents, Vice-Presidents and Treasurers.

District and Pradesh Congress Committees shall also elect members of their Executive Committees and from amongst the members of the Executive Committees, the Presidents of the respective Committees shall appoint their Secretaries.

(g) Any question or dispute arising under the Constitution with regard to provisions, contents, interpretations or the procedures laid down therein, between members and between members and Committees or between Committees *inter se*, shall be determined by the appropriate authority or authorities, indicated in this Constitution, and the decisions of such an authority shall be final and binding on all members and Committees of the Indian National Congress, and shall not be liable to question by any of them in a court of law.

Article XXIX

CHANGES IN THE CONSTITUTION

This Constitution can be amended, altered or added to only by a Session of the Congress. The AICC shall, however, have authority, except in regard to Article I, to amend, alter or add to the Constitution when the Congress is not in Session, if so desired by the Working Committee, provided that no such addition, alteration or amendment shall be made by the AICC except by a majority of two-thirds of the members present and voting at a meeting held specially for this purpose after due notice of the proposed changes has been given to each member at least one month prior to the date of such a meeting. The changes made by the AICC shall be placed before the next Session of the Congress for ratification, but they may come into operation even before ratification from such date as may be prescribed by the AICC.

Appendices

PRIMARY MEMBERSHIP FORM (A)

Under Article IV (a) of the Constitution

FORM NO. ....

I wish to be enrolled as a primary member of the Indian National Congress. I accept Article I of the Congress Constitution which is as follows:

"The object of the Indian National Congress is the well-being and advancement of the people of India and the establishment in India, by peaceful and constitutional means, of a Socialist State based on Parliamentary Democracy in which there is equality of opportunity and of political, economic and social rights and which aims at world peace and fellowship."

I am not a member of any other political party, communal or other, which has a separate membership, constitution and programme. I herewith deposit 25 paise as membership subscription.

Name ....

Father's or husband's name..

Permanent address..

Permanent place of residence or place of work......................

....

Age ....Occupation ....

Date.................................   ....

....
In case of thumb impression   Signature or thumb impression
signature of the attesting person   of the applicant

                                                 Date....................
....
Signature of the enroller

NOTE: Address should be given in full which should be traceable.

Appendices

The above application of...has
been received in this office with 25 paise as membership fee, which
has been deposited by the enroller Shri.......................................The
serial number in the Block/District Congress Committee Register
is.............................. ,

Signature of the Secretary,

Date............................   Block/District Congress Committee

---

RECEIPT TO BE GIVEN TO THE APPLICANT

RECEIPT NO. ....

Received from Shri...
his primary membership form along with the fee of twenty-five
(25) paise.

....
Signature of the Secretary

....   Block/District Congress Committee

Signature of enroller

Date............................

Appendices

ACTIVE MEMBERSHIP FORM(A)

Under Article IV (B) of the Constitution

FORM NO.....................

I wish to be enrolled as an active member of the Indian National Congress. I declare that

   (i) I am of the age of 21 or over;

  (ii) I am a habitual wearer of hand-spun and hand-woven Khadi;

 (iii) I abstain from alcoholic drinks;

 (iv) I do not observe or recognise untouchability in any shape or form;

  (v) I am a believer in communal unity and have respect for the faiths of others;

 (vi) I undertake to have the minimum training and to perform the minimum tasks as laid down from time to time by the Working Committee.

(vii) I have enrolled 50 primary members.

I desposit herewith Re. 1/- as the membership subscription and Rs. 12.50 as the subscription of 50 primary members.

Name ....

Father's or husband's name...

Permanent place of residence or place of work................................

....

Permanent address...

Age.. Occupation ....

Block Committee under which applicant is a member ....

....

....

In case of thumb impression   Signature or thumb impression

signature of the attesting person   of the applicant

Date................................

Signature of enroller .... Date ....

NOTE: Address should be given in full which should be traceable.

Appendices

1. Received on..

2. Serial number in the Register of active members...........................

Date........................   Signature of the Secretary,
Block/District Congress Committee

RECEIPT TO BE GIVEN TO THE APPLICANT

RECEIPT NO.....................

Received from...
(address) ....
on...the application for active membership
of the Indian National Congress along with Re. 1 as active membership subscription and Rs. 12.50 as subscription of 50 primary members.

....
Signature of the enroller   Signature of the Secretary,
Date.........................   Block/District Congress Committee

473

Appendices

ACTIVE MEMBERSHIP RENEWAL FORM (B)

FORM NO.....................

I am depositing herewith Rs......................for renewal of active membership as detailed below:

Re. 1/- towards active membership subscription.

Rs. 12.50 as subscription of 50 primary members enrolled by me.

Name ....

Father's or husband's name...

Permanent place residence or place of work...

Permanent address...

Age........................... Occupation..

Name of Block Committee under which the applicant is a member...............................

Serial number in the primary membership register.............................

Serial number in the active membership register.................................

Date........................... ....

In case of thumb impression   Signature or thumb impression
signature of the attesting person   of the applicant
....   Date......................
Signature of receiver

NOTE: Address should be given in full which should be traceable.

474

Appendices

The above active membership renewal form of.............................
has been received in this office with Rs..which
has been deposited by the receiver Shri...

The details of the amount received are given below:

Re. 1/- as active membership subscription.

Rs. 12.50/- as subscription of 50 primary members.

Date...........................
Signature of the Secretary,
Block/District Congress Committee

RECEIPT TO BE GIVEN TO THE APPLICANT

RECEIPT NO......................

Received from...
(address) ....
on...the renewal application for active
membership of the Indian National Congress along with Re. 1.00
as active membership subscription and Rs. 12.50 as subscription of
50 primary members.

....
Date...........................
Signature of the Secretary,
Block/District Congress Committee

475

bibliography

I. BOOKS

Andrews, C. F., and Mookerjee, G. *The Rise and Growth of the Congress in India.* London: G. Allen & Unwin, Ltd., 1938.

Ayer, Subbier Appadurai. *The Lone Sentinel: Glimpses of Morarji Desai.* Bombay: Popular Book Depot, 1960.

Azad, Maulana Abul Kalam. *India Wins Freedom: An Autobiographical Narrative.* Calcutta: Orient Longmans Private Ltd., 1959.

Bailey, Frederick George. *Politics and Social Change: Orissa in 1959.* Berkeley: University of California Press, 1963.

Bhattacharya, Bejoy Krishna. *A Short History of the Indian National Congress.* Calcutta: The Book Emporium Ltd., 1948.

Birla, G. D. *In the Shadow of the Mahatma.* Calcutta: Orient Longmans Private Ltd., 1948.

Bondurant, Joan. *Conquest of Violence: The Gandhian Philosophy of Conflict.* Princeton: Princeton University Press, 1958.

———— (ed.). *Regionalism Versus Provincialism: A Study in Problems of Indian National Unity.* Berkeley: University of California Press, 1958.

———— and Fisher, Margaret W. *The Indian Experience with Democratic Elections.* Berkeley: University of California Press, 1956.

Bose, D. R. (ed.). *New India Speaks.* Calcutta: A. Mukherjee and Co., 1947.

Brass, Paul. *Factional Politics in an Indian State: The Congress Party in Uttar Pradesh.* Berkeley: University of California Press, 1965.

Brecher, Michael. *Nehru: A Political Biography*. London: Oxford University Press, 1959.

———. *Nehru's Mantle: The Politics of Succession in India*. New York: Frederick A. Praeger, 1966.

Bright, J. S. (ed.). *Before and After Independence*. New Delhi: Indian Printing Works, 1950.

———. *President Kripalani and His Ideas*. New Delhi: Indian Printing Works, 1947.

Coupland, Sir Reginald. *The Indian Problem: Report on the Constitutional Problem in India*. London: Oxford University Press, 1944.

Dastur, Aloo J., and Mehta, Usha. *Congress Rule in Bombay, 1952 to 1956*. Bombay: Popular Book Depot, 1958.

Davis, Kingsley. *The Population of India and Pakistan*. Princeton: Princeton University Press, 1951.

Democratic Research Service. *Co-operative Farming: The Great Debate*. Bombay: Democratic Research Service, 1959.

Desai, A. R. *Recent Trends in Indian Nationalism*. Bombay: Popular Book Depot, 1960.

———. *Social Background of Indian Nationalism*. Bombay: Popular Book Depot, 1954.

Desai, Mahadev. *Maulana Abul Kalam Azad: The President of the Indian National Congress*. Agra: Shiva Lal Agarwala Ltd., 1946.

Duverger, Maurice. *Political Parties: Their Organization and Activities in the Modern State*. London: Methuen & Co., 1955.

Eldersveld, Samuel J. *Political Parties*. Chicago: Rand-McNally & Co., 1964.

Fischer, Louis. *The Life of Mahatma Gandhi*. Bombay: Bharatiya Vidya Bhavan, 1951.

Gandhi, M. K. *Congress and Its Future*. Ahmedabad: Navajivan Publishing House, 1960.

———. *Letters to Sardar Vallabhbhai Patel*. Ahmedabad: Navajivan Publishing House, 1957.

Bibliography

Ghosh, Dr. P. C. *The Development of the Indian National Congress, 1892-1909.* Calcutta: Firma K. L. Mukhopadhyay, 1960.

Griffiths, Sir Percival. *Modern India.* New York: Frederick A. Praeger, 1962.

Hangen, Wells. *After Nehru, Who?* New York: Harcourt, Brace & World, Inc., 1963.

Hanson, A. H. *The Process of Planning.* London: Oxford University Press, 1966.

Harrison, Selig B. *India: The Most Dangerous Decades.* Princeton: Princeton University Press, 1960.

Heda, H. C. *On the High Seas: Reflections on the Congress.* New Delhi: The Institute of National Affairs, 1958.

Isaacs, Harold R. *India's Ex-Untouchables.* New York: John Day & Co., 1964.

Jain, Ajit Prasad. *Rafi Ahmad Kidwai: A Memoir of His Life and Times.* New York: Asia Publishing House, 1965.

Kogekar, S. V., and Park, Richard (eds.). *Report on the Indian General Elections, 1951-1952.* Bombay: Popular Book Depot, 1956.

Kripalani, J. B. *Fateful Year.* Bombay: Vora & Co., 1948.

——. *The Future of the Congress.* Bombay: Hind Kitab Ltd., 1946.

——. *The Indian National Congress.* Bombay: Vora & Co., 1946.

——. *Presidential Address, First Annual Convention, Praja Socialist Party, Allahabad.* Lucknow: Jana Sahitya Press, 1953.

——. *Toward Sarvodaya.* New Delhi: Kisan Mazdoor Praja Party, 1951.

Lasswell, Harold D., and Lerner, Daniel. *World Revolutionary Elites.* Cambridge: Massachusetts Institute of Technology Press, 1965.

McCully, Bruce Tiebout. *English Education and the Origins of Indian Nationalism.* New York: Columbia University Press, 1940.

479

McKenzie, R. T. *British Political Parties: The Distribution of Power within the Conservative and Labour Parties*. New York: Frederick A. Praeger, 1963.

Malenbaum, Wilfred. *Prospects for Indian Development*. London: George Allen & Unwin, Ltd., 1962.

Malkani, K. R. *The Rise and Fall of the Congress*. Delhi: Vijey Pustak Bhandar, 1951.

Matthews, Donald R. *The Social Background of Political Decision-Makers*. New York: Random House, 1954.

Michels, Robert. *Political Parties*. Glencoe, Ill.: The Free Press, 1949.

Misra, B. B. *The Indian Middle Class*. London: Oxford University Press, 1961.

Mitra, N. N. *Indian Annual Register, 1936-1939*. Bombay: yearly 1920-1947.

Moon, Penderel. *Divide and Quit*. London: Chatto & Windus, 1961.

Moraes, Frank. *Jawaharlal Nehru*. Bombay: Jaico Publishing House, 1959.

————. *India Today*. New York: The Macmillan Company, 1960.

Morris-Jones, W. H. *The Government and Politics of India*. London: Hutchinson University Library, 1964.

————. *Parliament in India*. Philadelphia: University of Pennsylvania Press, 1957.

Nanda, B. R. *Mahatma Gandhi: A Biography*. London: George Allen & Unwin, Ltd., 1958.

Nayar, Baldev Raj. *Minority Politics in the Punjab*. Princeton: Princeton University Press, 1966.

Neale, W. C. *India: The Search for Unity, Democracy and Progress*. Princeton: D. Van Nostrand, 1965.

Nehru, Jawaharlal. *A Bunch of Old Letters*. Bombay: Asia Publishing House, 1958.

————. *Co-operative Farming*. New Delhi: Lok Sabha Secretariat, 1958.

————. *Discovery of India*. New York: John Day, 1946.

————. *Independence and After*. Delhi: Publications Division, Ministry of Information and Broadcasting, Government of India, 1949.

―――. *Jawaharlal Nehru's Speeches*, Vol. 3, March 1952-August 1957. New Delhi: Publications Division, Ministry of Information and Broadcasting, Government of India, 1958.

―――. *Toward Freedom*. New York: John Day, 1941.

Panjabi, Kewal L. *Rajendra Prasad*. Bombay: The Macmillan Co., 1960.

Parikh, Narhari D. *Sardar Vallabhbhai Patel*. Ahmedabad: Navajivan Publishing House, 1953.

Park, Richard L., and Tinker, Irene (eds.). *Leadership and Political Institutions in India*. Madras: Oxford University Press, 1960.

Patel, Maniben. *Letters to Sardar Patel*. Ahmedabad: Navajivan Publishing House, 1950.

Patel, Vallabhbhai. *Said the Sardar*. Bombay: National Information and Publications, Ltd., 1950.

Patil, S. K. *The Indian National Congress: A Case for Its Reorganisation*. Aundh: Aundh Publishing Trust, 1945.

Patwardhan, M. V. *Nehru, Tandon Reconciled; or, A Solution to the Communal Problem of India*. Poona: The Author, 1952.

Planning Commission, Government of India. *The New India: Progress Through Democracy*. New York: The Macmillan Co., 1958.

Potter, David C. *Government in Rural India*. London: G. Bell & Sons, 1964.

Praja Socialist Party. *Nehru-Jayaprakash Talks*. Bombay: Praja Socialist Party, 1954.

Pyarelal. *Mahatma Gandhi: The Last Phase*. Ahmedabad: Navajivan Publishing House, 1958.

Pylee, M. V. *India's Constitution*. New York: Asia Publishing House, 1962.

Rao, M. V. Ramana. *A Short History of the Indian National Congress*. New Delhi: S. Chand & Co., 1959.

Rosen, George. *Democracy and Economic Change in India.* Berkeley: University of California Press, 1966.

Rudolph, Susanne H. *The Action Arm of the Indian National Congress: The Pradesh Congress Committee.* Cambridge: Center for International Studies, Massachusetts Institute of Technology, 1955.

————. *Some Aspects of Congress Land Reform Policy.* Cambridge: Center for International Studies, Massachusetts Institute of Technology, 1957.

Saksena, Shibban Lal. *Why Have I Resigned from the Congress?* Delhi: Delhi Directory Press, 1951.

Sampurnanand. *Memoires and Reflections.* Bombay: Asia Publishing House, 1962.

Satabhisha. *Rashtrapathi Dr. Pattabhi.* Madras: Jayeeya Jnana Mandir, 1948.

Schattschneider, E. E. *Party Government.* New York: Rinehart & Company, Inc., 1942.

Schuster, Sir George Ernest, and Wint, Guy. *India and Democracy.* Toronto: The Macmillan Co., 1941.

Sharma, Bodh Raj. *Report on Elections in the Punjab, 1951-1952.* Jullundur City: Khanna Book Depot, 1952.

Shukla, C. (ed.). *Reminiscences of Gandhiji.* Bombay: Vora & Co., 1951.

Singer, Marshall R. *The Emerging Elite: A Study of Political Leadership in Ceylon.* Cambridge: Massachusetts Institute of Technology Press, 1964.

Sirsikar, V. M. *Political Behavior in India.* Bombay: P. C. Manaktala and Sons, 1965.

Sitaramayya, Dr. B. Pattabhi. *Current History in Questions and Answers.* Calcutta: Automatic Printers Ltd., 1948.

————. *The History of the Indian National Congress.* 2 vols. Bombay: Padma Publications, 1946-1947.

————. *60 Years of Congress.* Bombay: Indian National Congress, 1945.

————. *Some Fundamentals of the Indian Problem.* Bombay: Vora & Co., 1946.

————. *Speeches Delivered by Dr. B. Pattabhi Sitaramayya,*

Bibliography

Governor, Madhya Pradesh. Nagpur: Government Printers, Madhya Pradesh, 1956.

——. *Why Vote Congress.* Bombay: Hind Kitab, 1945.

Smith, Donald. *Nehru & Democracy.* Calcutta: Orient Longmans Private Ltd., 1958.

Srinivas, M. N. *Caste in Modern India and Other Essays.* Bombay: Asia Publishing House, 1962.

Talbot, P. *The Second General Elections: Some Impressions.* New York: American Universities Field Studies Service, 1957.

——. *The Second General Elections: Voting in the States.* New York: American Universities Field Studies Service, 1957.

Tendulkar, D. G. *Mahatma: Life of Mohandas Karamchand Gandhi.* 8 vols. Bombay: Vithalbhai K. Jhaveri & D. G. Tendulkar, 1951-1954.

Tinker, Hugh. *India and Pakistan: A Political Analysis.* New York: Frederick A. Praeger, 1962.

Weiner, Myron. *Congress Party Elites.* The Carnegie Seminar on Political and Administrative Development, University of Indiana, Bloomington, Indiana, 1966.

—— and Kothari, Rajni. *Indian Voting Behavior.* Calcutta: Firma K. L. Mukhopadhyay, 1965.

——. *Party-Building in a New Nation: The Indian National Congress.* Chicago: University of Chicago Press, 1967.

——. *Party Politics in India.* Princeton: Princeton University Press, 1957.

——. *Political Change in South Asia.* Calcutta: Firma K. L. Mukhopadhyay, 1963.

——. *The Politics of Scarcity.* Chicago: University of Chicago Press, 1962.

—— (ed.). *State Politics in India.* Princeton: Princeton University Press, 1967.

Wriggins, W. H. *Ceylon: Dilemmas of a New Nation.* Princeton: Princeton University Press, 1960.

Zinkin, Taya. *India Changes*. London: Chatto & Windus, 1958.

————. *Reporting India*. London: Chatto & Windus, 1962.

Zolberg, Aristide R. *Creating Political Order: The Party-States of West Africa*. Chicago: Rand-McNally & Co., 1966.

II. PERIODICALS

Baily, F. G. "Politics in Orissa I: Congress Loses Majority," *The Economic Weekly*, XI (August 29, 1959), 1203-8.

————. "Politics in Orissa II: Voting Pattern in Hill and Coast," *The Economic Weekly*, XI (September 12, 1959), 1271-76.

————. "Politics in Orissa III: The Feudatory States," *The Economic Weekly*, XI (September 19, 1959), 1297-1302.

————. "Politics in Orissa IV: The Oriya Movement," *The Economic Weekly,* XI (September 26, 1959), 1331-38.

————. "Politics in Orissa VI: The Independence Movement," *The Economic Weekly*, XI (October 10, 1959), 1403-8.

————. "Politics in Orissa VII: The Party in Power," *The Economic Weekly*, XI (October 17, 1959), 1433-40.

————. "Politics in Orissa VIII: The Ganatantra Parishad," *The Economic Weekly*, XI (November 7, 1959), 1469-76.

————. "Politics in Orissa IX: The Congress Since 1947," *The Economic Weekly,* XI (November 7, 1959), 1503-10.

Bendix, Reinhard. "Public Authority in a Developing Political Community: The Case of India," *Archives of European Sociology*, 4 (1963), pp. 39-85.

Beteille, Andre. "Politics and Social Structure in Tamilnad," *The Economic Weekly*, XV (July 1963), 1161-67.

Bhambhri, C. P. "Pattern of Cabinet Making in Indian States," *The Political Science Review*, II (1963), 69-80.

Broomfield, J. H. "A Plea for the Study of the Indian Provincial Legislatures," *Parliamentary Affairs*, 14 (Winter 1960/61), pp. 26-38.

Bibliography

Chakraverti, P. R. "Amended Congress Constitution—The Malady Persists," *A.I.C.C. Economic Review*, XVI (July 10, 1964), 7-9.

———. "Malady—Organisational or Attitudinal," *A.I.C.C. Economic Review*, XII (June 1, 1960), 13-19.

———. "Party, Parliamentary Group and Power," *Modern Review*, CIX (February 1961), 195-200.

Delal, B. A. "Organizational and Legislative Wings of a Party," *Civic Journal*, August 1957, pp. 27-28, 42.

Dhebar, U. N. "The Language Issue and the Congress Working Committee's Resolution," *A.I.C.C. Economic Review*, XVII (August 15, 1965), 11-12.

———. "Role of Parliamentary Wing in the New Congress," *A.I.C.C. Economic Review*, IX (April 1, 1958), 3-7.

Franda, Marcus. "The Organizational Development of India's Congress Party," *Pacific Affairs*, 35 (Fall 1962), pp. 249-260.

Gadgil, N. V. "Democratic System and Parties," *A.I.C.C. Economic Review*, VII (June 15, 1955), 5-8.

———. "Government and the Party," *Indian Journal of Public Administration*, III (October-December 1957), 346-356.

Goyal, O. P., and Wallace, Paul. "The Congress Party—A Conceptual Study," *India Quarterly*, XX, No. 2 (April-June 1964), 180-201.

Gupta, Sisir. "The Avadi Resolution," *Indian Affairs Record*, I (May 1955), 6-9.

———. "Competing Elites," *Seminar*, 51 (November 1963), pp. 41-46.

———. "Live Issues in Indian Politics," *The Economic Weekly*, X (July 1958), 941-943.

———. "State of the Congress," *The Economic Weekly*, IX (January 1957), 171-172.

Guttsman, W. L. "The Changing Social Structure of the British Political Elite," *British Journal of Sociology*, II (1951), 122-134.

Harrison, Selig S. "Caste and the Andhra Communists," *American Political Science Review*, L (June 1956), 378-404.

————. "The Challenge to Indian Nationalism," *Foreign Affairs*, 34 (July 1956), pp. 620-624.

Huntington, Samuel P. "Political Development and Political Decay," *World Politics*, XXVII (April 1965), 386-430.

"India: After the Kamaraj Plan," *Round Table*, 54 (December 1963), pp. 82-86.

Kabir, Humayun. "Congress Ideology: A Statement," *India Quarterly*, XVI (January-March 1960), 3-23.

————. "Reorganization of the Congress," *Hindustan Times* (New Delhi), May 29, 1960.

Kamaraj, K. "The Food Crisis," *A.I.C.C. Economic Review*, XVII (February 10, 1966), 37-38.

"Kamaraj Plan," *Indian Recorder and Digest*, IX (September-October, 1963), 2-5.

"Keep the Flame Alive," *Indian Affairs Record*, 3 (January 1958), pp. 267-269.

Kochanek, Stanley. "Post Nehru India: The Emergence of the New Leadership," *Asian Survey*, VI (May 1966), 288-299.

Kothari, Rajni. "The Congress 'System' in India," *Asian Survey*, IV, 2 (December 1964), 1161-73.

————. "India: The Congress System on Trial," *Asian Survey*, VII (February 1967), 83-96.

————. "Three Bye-Elections," *The Economic Weekly*, XVII (May 22, May 29, and June 19, 1965), 845-858, 893-902, 987-1000.

Krishna, Gopal. "The Development of the Indian National Congress as a Mass Organization, 1918-1923," *The Journal of Asian Studies,* XXV (May 1966), 413-430.

————. "One Party Dominance—Development and Trends," *Perspectives*, Supplement to the *Indian Journal of Public Administration*, 12 (1966), pp. 1-65.

Lukas, J. Anthony. "Nehru's 'Munshi' Comes out of Nehru's

Shadow," *New York Times Magazine,* November 28, 1965, pp. 54, 161-171.

————. "Political Python of India," *New York Times Magazine,* February 20, 1966, pp. 27, 49-57.

Martin, Kingsley. "Ten Years of Nehru's India," *New Statesman,* 55 (April 12, 1958), pp. 467-468, 470-473.

Mehta, Asoka. "The P. S. P. Cadre: A Sample Survey," *Janata,* xvi (December 27, 1957), 7-11.

Meynaud, J. "The Parliamentary Profession," *International Social Science Journal,* xiii (1961), 513-543.

Morris-Jones, W. H. "Dominance and Dissent," *Government and Opposition,* i, 4 (July-September 1966), 451-466.

————. "Experience of Independence: India and Pakistan," *Political Quarterly,* 29 (July-September 1958), pp. 224-237.

————. "The Indian Congress Party: A Dilemma of Dominance," *Modern Asian Studies,* i (April 1967), 109-132.

————. "Recent Political Developments in India," *Parliamentary Affairs,* 11 (Autumn 1958), pp. 475-483.

Nanda, Gulzarilal. "Future Role of Indian National Congress," *Amrita Bazar Patrika,* May 11, 1947.

Patterson, M.L.P. "Caste and Political Leadership in Maharashtra," *The Economic Weekly,* vi (September 25, 1954), 1066-67.

"Profile of a Southern State—Mysore," *The Economic Weekly,* viii (July 21, 1956), 943, 1005-1006.

Rao, M.V.R. "No Crisis in Congress," *A.I.C.C. Economic Review,* 10 (August 15, 1958), pp. 25-28.

Ray, Renuka. "Background of the Hindu Code Bill," *Pacific Affairs,* xxv (September 1952), 268-277.

Rothermund, Dietmar. "Constitutional versus National Agitation in India, 1900-1950," *The Journal of Asian Studies,* xxi (August 1962), 505-522.

Roy, Ramashray. "Intra-Party Conflict in the Bihar Congress," *Asian Survey,* 6 (December 1966), pp. 706-715.

————. "Selection of Congress Candidates," *Economic and Political Weekly,* i (December 31, 1966), 833-840; ii

(January 7, 14, and February 11, 18, 1967), 17-23, 61-76, 371-376, and 407-416.

Rudolph, Lloyd I., and Rudolph, Susanne Hoeber. "The Political Role of India's Caste Associations," *Pacific Affairs,* XXXIII (March 1960), 5-22.

Rusch, Thomas A. "Decision-making in Underdeveloped Countries of Asia: India, A Case Study" (Abstract), *Western Political Quarterly,* 10 (July 1957), pp. 456-457.

Santhanam, K. "Guarantee for the Future," *Seminar,* 66 (February 1965), pp. 21-24.

Sarkar, S. C. "Congress and the Kuomintang," *The Economic Weekly,* IX (March 30, 1957), 443-446.

Shea, Thomas. "Agrarian Unrest and Reform in South India," *Far Eastern Survey,* XXIII (June 1954), 81-88.

————. "Implementing Land Reform in India," *Far Eastern Survey,* XXV (January 1956), 1-8.

Shriman Narayan. "Organization and Ideology," *Indian Review,* 58 (October 1957), pp. 436-437.

Singer, Milton, Hart, Henry C., Weiner, Myron, and Rudolph, Lloyd. "Urban Politics in a Plural Society: A Symposium," *The Journal of Asian Studies,* XX (May 1961), 265-297.

Sirsikar, V. M. "Leadership Patterns in Rural Maharashtra," *Asian Survey,* IV (July 1964), 929-939.

Sisson, J. Richard. "Institutionalization and Style in Rajasthan Politics," *Asian Survey,* VI (November 1966), 605-613.

Srinivas, M. N. "Caste in Modern India," *The Journal of Asian Studies,* XVI (August 1957), 529-548.

————. "A Note on Sanskritization and Westernization," *Far Eastern Quarterly,* XV (August 1956), 481-496.

Suda, J. P. "Origins and Significance of the National Movement in India," *Indian Journal of Political Science,* 19 (April-June 1958), pp. 134-141.

Suri, Surindar. "Pattern of Membership," *Seminar,* 66 (February 1965). 14-20.

Tangri, Shanti. "Intellectuals and Society in Nineteenth Cen-

tury India," *Comparative Studies in Society and History,* 3
(July 1961), pp. 368-394.

Tinker, Irene. "India's One Party Democracy," *Pacific Affairs*, XXIX (September 1956), 265-268.

Weiner, Myron. "Changing Patterns of Political Leadership in
West Bengal," *Pacific Affairs,* XXXII (September 1959),
277-287.

――――. "India's Political Problems: The Longer View,"
Western Political Quarterly, IX (June 1956), 283-292.

――――. "Prospect for India's Congress Party," *Far Eastern
Survey*, XXIII (December 1954), 182-188.

――――. "Struggle Against Power: Notes on Indian Political
Behavior," *World Politics*, VIII (April 1956), 392-403.

――――. "Traditional Role Performance and the Development of Modern Political Parties: The Indian Case," *Journal of Politics*, XXVI (November 1964), 830-849.

Windmiller, Marshall. "Linguistic Regionalism in India,"
Pacific Affairs, XXVII (December 1954), 291-318.

――――. "Politics of States Reorganization in India: The
Case of Bombay," *Far Eastern Survey*, XXV (September
1956), 129-143.

Wright, Theodore P., Jr. "Muslim Legislators in India: Profile of a Minority Elite," *The Journal of Asian Studies*,
XXIII (February 1964), 253-267.

Public Documents: Government of India

The Constitution of India (as modified up to July 1, 1960).
New Delhi: Manager of Publications, 1960.

Ministry of Home Affairs. *Report of the States Reorganization Commission*. New Delhi, 1955.

Planning Commission. *The First Five Year Plan*. New Delhi,
1952.

――――. *Second Five Year Plan, The Framework*. New Delhi,
1953.

――――. *Second Five Year Plan*. New Delhi, 1956.

――――. *Third Five Year Plan, A Draft Outline*. New Delhi,
1960.

Bibliography

Planning Commission. *Towards a Self-Reliant Economy: India's Third Plan 1961-1966*. New Delhi, 1961.
————. *Reports of the Committee of the Panel on Land Reforms*. New Delhi, 1958.

III. PUBLICATIONS OF THE INDIAN NATIONAL CONGRESS

A. Serial Publications

A.I.C.C. Economic Review. Bimonthly. New Delhi, 1948—1967.
Congress Bulletin. Allahabad and New Delhi, 1946—1967.
Report of the General Secretaries. Allahabad and New Delhi, 1937—1967.

B. Signed Pamphlets

Ali, Sadiq. *The Congress Ideology and Programme*. New Delhi, 1958.
————. *The General Elections 1957: A Survey*. New Delhi, 1959.
Barlingay, W. S. *Hindu Law of Succession for the Lay Man*. New Delhi, 1957.
Deo, Shankarrao. *The New Congress*. New Delhi, 1949.
Dhebar, U. N. *Presidential Address, The Indian National Congress, Sixtieth Session*. New Delhi, 1955.
————. *Presidential Address, The Indian National Congress, Sixty-first Session*. New Delhi, 1956.
————. *Presidential Address, The Indian National Congress, Sixty-second Session*. New Delhi, 1957.
————. *Presidential Address, The Indian National Congress, Sixty-third Session*. New Delhi, 1958.
————. *Presidential Address, The Indian National Congress, Sixty-fourth Session*. New Delhi, 1959.
————. *Review to All Indian Congress Committee, Berhampur*. New Delhi, 1955.
————. *The Role of Panchayats in New India*. New Delhi, 1957.
————. *Towards Constructive Revolution*. New Delhi, 1956.

490

————. *Towards a Socialist Co-operative Commonwealth.* New Delhi, 1957.

Hanumanthaiya, K. *Report on the Congress Constitution.* New Delhi, 1960.

Iyengar, G. *The Message and Mission of the Indian National Congress.* Bangalore, 1960.

Kamaraj, K. *Presidential Address, The Indian National Congress, Sixty-eighth Session.* New Delhi, 1964.

————. *Presidential Address, The Indian National Congress, Sixty-ninth Session.* New Delhi, 1965.

————. *Presidential Address, The Indian National Congress, Seventieth Session.* New Delhi, 1966.

Kripalani, J. B. *Presidential Address, Indian National Congress, Fifty-fourth Session.* Allahabad, 1946.

Malaviya, H. D. *Insurance Business in India.* New Delhi, 1956.

————. *Land Reforms in India.* New Delhi, 1955.

Mehta, V. L. *Co-operation.* New Delhi, 1959.

Nanda, G. L. *Progress of Land Reforms in India.* New Delhi, 1957.

Nehru, Jawaharlal. *India on the March.* New Delhi, 1957.

————. *Letters to the PCC Presidents.* New Delhi, 1955.

————. *Presidential Address, The Indian National Congress, Fifty-seventh Session.* New Delhi, 1951.

————. *Presidential Address, The Indian National Congress, Fifty-eighth Session.* New Delhi, 1953.

————. *Presidential Address, The Indian National Congress, Fifty-ninth Session.* New Delhi, 1954.

————. *Report to the All-India Congress Committee, Bangalore, 1951.* New Delhi, 1951.

————. *Report to the All-India Congress Committee, Avadi.* New Delhi, 1955.

————. *Towards a Socialistic Order.* New Delhi, 1956.

Prakasa, S. *Personal Behavior.* New Delhi, 1956.

Rajkumar, N. V. *Development of the Congress Constitution.* New Delhi, 1949.

———— (ed.). *The Pilgrimage and After.* New Delhi, 1952.

Bibliography

Rao, M. V. Ramana. *Development of the Congress Constitution.* New Delhi, 1958.

Reddy, N. Sanjiva, *Presidential Address, The Indian National Congress, Sixty-fifth Session.* New Delhi, 1960.

————. *Presidential Address, The Indian National Congress, Sixty-sixth Session.* New Delhi, 1961.

————. *Presidential Address, The Indian National Congress, Sixty-seventh Session.* New Delhi, 1962.

Sharma, J. S. *A.I.C.C. Circulars: A Descriptive Bibliography.* New Delhi, 1956.

Shriman Narayan (Agarwal). *Constructive Programme for Congressmen.* New Delhi, 1953.

————. *India and China.* New Delhi, 1956.

————. *India's Current Problems.* New Delhi, n.d.

————. *A Plea for Ideological Clarity.* New Delhi, 1957.

————. *Socialistic Pattern of Society.* New Delhi, 1957.

————. *Towards a Socialist Economy.* New Delhi, 1956.

Sitaramayya, Dr. B. Pattabhi. *Presidential Address, The Indian National Congress, Fifty-fifth Session.* New Delhi, 1948.

Tandon, P. D. *English Rendering of President's Hindi Address, The Indian National Congress, Fifty-sixth Session.* Bombay, 1950.

C. Anonymous Pamphlets

Annual Report of the Fourth All-India Convention of the Youth Congress. New Delhi, 1960.

The Chief Ministers Speak. New Delhi, 1951.

Congress Planning Sub-Committee: Ooty Seminar Papers. New Delhi, 1959.

Congress Planning Sub-Committee: Report on the Ooty Seminar. New Delhi, 1959.

Congress and the Problem of Minorities: Resolutions Adopted by the Congress, the Working Committee and the AICC since 1885 and Connected Matters. New Delhi, 1947.

Congress and the Second General Elections. New Delhi, 1957.

Bibliography

Congress Seva Dal: Information Series. New Delhi, 1960.

Constitution of the Indian National Congress. New Delhi, 1964.

Constructive Programme for Women: A Handbook. New Delhi, 1956.

Constructive Work: A Handbook for Congressmen. New Delhi, 1955.

The Country Votes Congress: An Analysis of the Results of the Central Assembly Elections, 1945-1946. Bombay, n.d.

Draft Outline of the Third Five Year Plan: A Symposium. New Delhi, 1960.

Election Manifesto 1957. New Delhi, 1957.

Handbook (Congress). Allahabad, 1946.

Handbook for Congressmen. New Delhi, 1951.

Handbook for Congressmen. New Delhi, 1957.

The Hindu Marriage Act: Passed by Parliament on May 5, 1955. New Delhi, 1956.

The Kerala Situation. New Delhi, 1959.

Memorandum of Association and Rules and Regulations of the Akhil Bharatiya Congress Rachanatmak Karya Samiti. New Delhi, 1957.

Our Immediate Programme. New Delhi, 1950.

Padayatra: A Report. New Delhi, 1960.

The Proceedings of the Allahabad Conference of the Presidents and Secretaries of the PCCs. New Delhi. 1947.

Proceedings of the Conference of the Conveners of the Women's Departments of the Pradesh Congress Committees. New Delhi, 1955.

Proceedings of the Meetings of the Presidents and Secretaries of the Pradesh Congress Committees. New Delhi, 1955.

Programme for Constructive Work. New Delhi, 1956.

Report of the Agricultural Production Sub-Committee. New Delhi, 1958.

Report of the Committee of the Congress Party in Parliament. New Delhi, 1960.

493

Bibliography

Report of the Congress Agrarian Reforms Committee, New Delhi, 1951.

Report of the Congress Planning Sub-Committee. New Delhi, 1959.

Report of the Congress Small Savings Committee. New Delhi, 1956.

Report of the Congress Village Panchayat Committee. New Delhi, 1954.

Report of the Constructive Work Committee. New Delhi, 1955.

Report of the Constructive Workers' Conference. New Delhi, 1956.

Report of the Economic Programme Committee. New Delhi, 1948.

Report of the Linguistic Provinces Committee. New Delhi, 1949.

Report of the Sub-Committee Appointed by the Executive Committee of the Gujarat Pradesh Congress Committee to Enquire into the Working of the Congress Organisation in Gujarat. New Delhi, 1957.

Report of the Sub-Committee on Democracy and Socialism. New Delhi, 1964.

Resolutions on Economic Policy and Programme, 1924-1954. New Delhi, 1954.

Resolutions on Economic Policy and Programme, 1955-1956. New Delhi, 1956.

Resolutions on Foreign Policy, 1947-1957. New Delhi, 1957.

Resolutions on Goa. New Delhi, 1956.

Resolutions on Language Policy (1949-1957). New Delhi, 1957.

Resolutions on States Reorganisation, 1920-1956. New Delhi, 1956.

Rules Framed Under Article XX (f), (i) and Other Articles of the Constitution. New Delhi, 1949.

The Socialistic Pattern: In Terms of the Congress Resolutions. New Delhi, 1956.

Bibliography

Training and Education Scheme for Congress Workers. New Delhi, 1960.

Vision of Young India: The Third All-India Convention of Youth Congress. New Delhi, 1959.

Volunteer Organisation: Being a Collection of Resolutions Passed by the Congress A.I.C.C. and Working Committee Since 1917 and Connected Matters. New Delhi, 1951.

Women and the Elections. New Delhi, 1957.

Women's Wing of the Congress. New Delhi, 1958.

Youth and Nation Building. New Delhi, 1955.

IV. JOURNALS AND NEWSPAPERS

Amrita Bazar Patrika (Calcutta).
Assam Tribune (Gauhati).
Bombay Chronicle.
Christian Science Monitor (Boston).
The Congress Socialist.
Deccan Herald (Bangalore).
Free Press Journal (Bombay).
The Hindu (Madras).
The Hindu Weekly Review (Madras).
Hindustan Standard (Calcutta).
Hindustan Times (New Delhi).
Hitavada (Nagpur).
The Indian Express (Bombay and New Delhi).
Indian Nation (Patna).
Leader (Allahabad).
Link (New Delhi).
Mail (Madras).
Manchester Guardian.
National Herald (Lucknow).
New York Times.
The Observer (London).
The Pioneer (Lucknow).
The Searchlight (Patna).
The Statesman (Calcutta and New Delhi).

Bibliography

The Times (London).
Times of India (Bombay and New Delhi).
Tribune (Ambala).
The Washington Post (Washington).

V. UNPUBLISHED MATERIALS

Congress Party in Parliament. Minutes of the Executive Committee, 1949-1960.

————. Minutes of the General Body, 1949-1960.

Elliott, Carolyn M. "Caste and Faction in Andhra Pradesh." Unpublished paper prepared for the Association of Asian Studies meeting, New York, April 1966.

Irschick, Eugene. "The Brahmin-Non-Brahmin Struggle for Power in Madras." Unpublished paper prepared for the Association for Asian Studies Conference, San Francisco, 1965.

————. "Politics and Social Conflict in South India: The Non-Brahmin Movement and Tamil Separatism, 1916-1929." Unpublished Ph.D. dissertation, University of Chicago, 1964.

Patterson, Maureen. "A Preliminary Study of the Brahmin vs. Non-Brahmin Conflict in Maharashtra." Unpublished M.A. thesis, University of Pennsylvania, 1952.

Prasad, Rajendra. Private papers. 1945-1950.

Retzlaff, Ralph Herbert. "The Constituent Assembly of India and the Problem of Indian Unity." Unpublished Ph.D. dissertation, Cornell University, 1960.

Roy, Ramashray. "A Study of the Bihar Pradesh Congress Committee." Unpublished Ph.D. dissertation, University of California, Berkeley, 1965.

Rudolph, Susanne H. "Congress in Power, A Study of Party in the Context of Asian Democracy," Unpublished Ph.D. dissertation, Radcliffe College, 1955.

Shrader, Lawrence L. "Politics in Rajasthan: A Study of the Members of the Legislative Assembly and the Development of the State's Political System." Unpublished Ph.D. dissertation. University of California, Berkeley, 1965.

Bibliography

Shukla, R. S., former Chief Minister of Madhya Pradesh. Private papers.

Sitaramayya, Dr. B. Pattabhi. "Autobiography."

————. Private letters.

VI. BIBLIOGRAPHIES

Sharma, Jagdish Saran. *Indian National Congress: A Descriptive Bibliography of India's Struggle for Freedom.* New Delhi: S. Chand & Co., 1959.

————. *Jawaharlal Nehru: A Descriptive Bibliography.* New Delhi: S. Chand & Co., 1955.

————. *Mahatma Gandhi: A Descriptive Bibliography.* New Delhi: S. Chand & Co., 1955.

VII. BIOGRAPHIES

Bombay Legislative Congress Party: *Directory of the Bombay Legislature, 1946-1947.* Bombay: Bombay Legislative Congress Party, n.d.

————. *Bombay Legislative Congress Party Directory, 1958.* Bombay: Bombay Legislative Congress Party, 1958.

Indian National Congress. *Delegates Directory, 1956.* New Delhi, 1956.

Government of Madras. *Madras Legislative Council, Who's Who, 1961.* Madras: Legislative Assembly Department, n.d.

————. *Madras Legislative Assembly, Third Who's Who, 1962.* Madras: Legislative Assembly Department, n.d.

Government of Mysore. *Almanac for Mysore and Who's Who, 1958.* Bangalore: Director of Printing, n.d.

————. *Mysore Legislative Assembly, Who's Who, 1959.* Bangalore: Director of Printing, n.d.

————. *Mysore Legislative Assembly, Who's Who.* Bangalore, 1963.

Madras Legislative Congress Party. *Directory of the Madras Legislature, 1950.* Madras: Madras Legislative Congress Party, n.d.

497

Parliament of India. *Who's Who, 1950.* New Delhi: Manager of Government of India Publications, 1950.

————. *Council of States, Who's Who, 1952.* New Delhi: Council of States Secretariat, 1953.

————. *House of the People, Who's Who, 1952.* New Delhi: Parliament Secretariat, 1952.

————. *Lok Sabha Who's Who, Supplement.* New Delhi: Lok Sabha Secretariat, 1959.

————. *Rajya Sabha, Who's Who, 1962.* New Delhi: Rajya Sabha Secretariat, 1962.

————. *Third Lok Sabha, Who's Who, 1962.* New Delhi: Lok Sabha Secretariat, 1962.

Singh, Trilochan (ed.). *Indian Parliament, 1952-1957.* New Delhi: Arunam & Sheel, n.d.

Sud, S. P. Singh, and Sud, Ajit Singh. *Indian Elections and Legislators.* Ludhiana: All-Indian Publications, 1953.

Taleyarkhan, Homi J. H. (ed.). *Bombay Legislative Directory, 1953.* Bombay Legislative Congress Party.

The Times of India. *Directory and Year Book including Who's Who* (volumes for 1947-1966).

Index

Avadi resolution (1955), 175-176. *See also* socialist pattern of society

Avadi Session (1955), 175-176

Azad, Maulana Abul Kalam, 17, 21, 33, 37-38, 40, 61, 123, 234, 236, 245, 256, 298, 402; opposes Pant resolution, 117-118; opposes elective element in Working Committee, 127-128; resists zamindari abolition, 192; role in West Bengal, 252-253; role in candidate selection, 282-283

Babu politicians, 325

backward classes and Congress, 352

Bakshi, Ghulam Mohammed, 80

balkanization in Congress, 438, 441. *See also* authority structure

Bangalore A.I.C.C. (1951), 34, 41-43, 44, 46, 51

Bangalore A.I.C.C. (July 1965), 95, 144, 209

Bangalore Report, 41

Bangalore Session (1960), 72

Bangalore Unity Resolution, 42-43

banyan tree metaphor, 96

Belgaum District Congress, 350-351, 359

Bengal-Bihar border dispute, 151-155

Berhampur A.I.C.C. (1955), 178-179

Betinck's Order in Council, 321

Bhaktavatsalam, M., 204, 411

Bharatiya Kranti Dal (B.K.D.), 440

Bhargava, Dr. Gopi Chand, 255-258

Bhave, Vinoba, 169

Bhavnagar Session (1961), 313-332

Bhoodan Movement, 169-170

Bhubaneshwar Session (1964), 85, 90, 132

Bihar, 64-65, 238, 291, 293, 372, 396; factionalism in, 264, 279-280, 443; role of C.E.C. in, 279-280; caste in, 379

Bihar-West Bengal merger proposal, 153

Bikaner, 293

Birla, G.D., 21; family, 192

bogus membership, 213, 222, 297

Bombay A.I.C.C. (1945), 216

Bombay A.I.C.C. (1948), 119, 120, 128

Bombay A.I.C.C. (1966), 287-288

Bombay bifurcation, 181, 183, 283, 356

Bombay Congress, language groups, 356

Bombay constitution sub-committee (1945), 217, 225

Bombay sales tax, 55-56

Bombay Session (1885), 322-323

Bose, Subhas Chandra, 15, 22

bossism, 64-65, 313

Brahmins, 321, 324, 331, 355, 356, 371, 379, 386-391; in Cabinet, 386. *See also* caste.

Brass, Paul, 212, 229, 347, 348

Brecher, Michael, 77, 82, 99

British Conservative Party, 237, 428

British elite, 377

British Labour Party, 58

brokers, 229

Buddhists, 355

business community, 143

businessmen in Congress, among active members, 349, 360; as members of Lok Sabha, 381-382; and father's occupations, 391-392. *See also* occupation

by-elections (May (1963), 76-77, 78, 212

Cabinet, *see* Indian Cabinet

cabinet formation in the states (1962), 261-265; (1967), 424-427

Cabinet Mission proposals, 6

Index

Suba, 184; criticizes devaluation decision, 184-185; and role in Bihar candidate selection, 279; and role in Gujarat politics, 283-284; and dissident group in C.E.C. elections, 287-288; becomes Deputy Prime Minister, 412

Deshlehra, M.C., 263, 281

Deshmukh, C.D., 172, 179

Dev, Narendra Acharya, 12

devaluation, 184-185

devolution of power in Congress, xx, 297-298, 312-313. *See also* authority structure

Dhebar, U.N., 67-68, 71, 73, 104, 201, 244, 263, 298, 417; views party-government relations, 59-60, 62, 180-181, 244; selected as Congress President, 60-61; relationship with Nehru of, 61-63; role in party reorganization of, 63, 229, 231; reasons for resigning from Congress presidency of, 63-65; criticizes Nehru, 65; role in selection of Mrs. Gandhi as Congress President of, 67-68; role in Bengal-Bihar border dispute of, 152-155; gives pros and cons of Gandhian economics, 171-172; role in Avadi Resolution of, 176; views language policy, 207-208; and yarn franchise, 228; influence on distribution of power in the Congress, 428-437. *See also* party-government relations

divergence, period of, xxiv, 299, 429; party-government relations during, 77-103, 105-107, 181-187, 314-315; survey of, 312-316; characteristics of, 312

Dravida Munnetra Kazhagam (D.M.K.), 77, 446, 447

dual leadership of party and government, 129, 240-244, 258-259, 431; Nehru on, 4-5, 30, 51, 54-55, 56, 243, 311. *See also* party-government relations

Dufferin, Lord, 325

Duke of Windsor, 25

Durgapur Session (1965), 132n, 150

East India Company, 320

economic policy, 168-181, 302-303, 308-309

Economic Programme Committee Report, 164-167; compared to Industrial Policy Resolution, 165-166

education, of Congress members of Lok Sabha by age groups, 339; of Working Committee and A.I.C.C. members, 366-367; of Congress members of Lok Sabha (1952-1962), 398-399; of Uttar Pradesh Congress legislators, 399

education, expansion under British, 320, 321, 327-328

educators in the Congress, 348, 374-375

effective members, 220, 222

election tribunals, 218, 221, 222, 226, 230-231

elective element in the Working Committee, 127-132, 144-145; Bhavnagar Session (1961), 131-132; Bhubaneshwar (1964), 85, 132; Durgapur (1965), 132n; Hyderabad (1968), 133n

electorate, attitude toward skill levels of leadership, 401

Elliott, Carolyn M., 212, 351, 400

emergency powers of the Working Committee, 226

English-educated elite, 320, 322, 324-325

English, status of, 203, 204, 205-206

examination for the all-India services, 206, 404

Index

Gandhian group (West Bengal), 251, 252

Gandhianism and Kamaraj Plan, 81-82

Gandhians, 11, 14, 21, 28, 125, 140, 169, 170, 308; role in election of Congress President of (1948), 14-23; role in election of Congress President of (1950), 30; secede from Congress, 39, 169; demand role for village and cottage industries, 169-170, 172-174; demand demarcation of spheres of production, 170-171; pros and cons of economic position of, 171-172; and Ajmer Resolution, 174; reaction to socialist pattern of society of, 177-178; at Berhampur A.I.C.C., 178-179; and Second Plan, 179-181

generational revolution, 411

Ghose, S.M., 252

Ghosh, Atulya, 83, 84, 124, 125, 264, 276, 295, 348, 368, 411. *See also* Syndicate

Ghosh, Dr. P.C., 14, 19, 21, 22, 39, 200, 201, 251

Go Seva Sangh, 159

Government of India Act of 1935, 252

Govind Das (Seth), 38, 131, 160

Gujarat, 293, 354, 356, 396; composition of Congress in, 347-357; factionalism in, 283-284

Gupta, C.B., 80, 85, 101, 281, 285, 287, 288, 295, 417, 426

Gupta, Ram Ratan, 285-286

Gupta, Sisir, 401

Gurdwara elections, 278

Guttsman, W.L., 377

Hanumanthaiya, K., 55, 70, 128, 131, 246, 277; prepares note on reorganization of party, 240-241

Harijan, 31

Harijans, 22, 356, 381, 382-383, 386, 388, 391, 400

Haryana, 440, 447; factionalism in, 425-426

Hindi, designated the official language of the Union, 203

Hindu Code Bill, 50

Hindu elite, 321, 324

Hindu Mahasabha, 332

Hindu-Muslim relationship, 326, 330. *See also* communalism

Hindu revivalism, 325, 326

Hindustan Times, 18, 29

Home Ministry communiqué of Jan. 15, 1956, 152-153

Hooghly group (West Bengal), 251-252

Huntington, S.P., xxiii

Husain, Dr. Zakir, 413

Hyderabad A.I.C.C. (1958), 65

Hyderabad resolution (1958), one-term limit on office holding, 65, 94-95, 107

Hyderabad Session (1953), 56, 169-170, 197, 259

Hyderabad Session (1968), 133n

income, of Congress members of Second Lok Sabha, 383-385; by age groups, 338-339

Indian Cabinet, *see* party-government relations

Indian Constitution, 203, 254, 299

Indian decision-makers, summary analysis of, 399-404

Indian National Congress, factors contributing to success of, xix-xx; as parallel government, xx-xxiii; adaptability of, xxiii-xxiv, xix; creation of, 322; first session of, 322-323; early demands of, 323; distribution of power in, 428-437; authority structure in, 437-441; social composition of, 441-445; loss of hegemony by, 445-447; Constitution of (1947), 454-475; structure and composition of the national decision-mak-

284, 312, 429, 435; origins of, 77-78; Nehru's reaction to, 78; list of retirees under, 79-80; Nehru's motives in supporting, 80-83; and party-government relations, 80-81; impact on succession, 85-87

Kanpur, Congress membership, 347, 349, 350

Kappan, C.J., 271

Kashmir, 10, 258

Katju, K.N., 263, 281

Kayasthas, 378, 386, 387. *See also* caste

Kerala, 293, 296, 443-444

Kher, B.G., 60, 333

Khilafat Movement, 330

Kidwai, Rafi Ahmad, 21, 41-42, 123; and role in 1950 election of Congress President, 29-30; demands special session of A.I.C.C., 39-40; resigns from Cabinet, 44, 45; criticizes Tandon, 44-45

Kisan Mazdoor Praja Party (K.M.P.P.), 39, 52

Kishore, Jugal, 19, 220

Kitchen Cabinet, 99, 415

Kothari, Rajni, 101

Kottayam, 271

Kripalani, Acharya J.B., 7, 25, 61, 77, 79, 92, 121, 158, 218, 330; selected Congress President, 5; effect on party-government relations of, 5-12, 25-26; resigns, 10-11; offered governorship of Bihar, 11; as candidate for Congress President (1948), 17-18; as candidate for Congress President (1950), 28-32; criticizes 1950 organizational elections, 35-36; resigns from Congress, 39; applies one-third rule to Working Committee, 118-119

Kripalani, Sucheta, 69, 126

Krishnamachari, T.T., 86, 185

Kshatriyas, 386, 388. *See also* caste

land ceilings, role of Working Committee, 195-199

landholdings, of Congress members of Second Lok Sabha, 383-386; by age groups, 337-338

land policy, role of Working Committee, 195-196

land reforms, *see* Congress land policy

language policy, 199-210, 403

language riots (1965), 204

lawyers in Congress, 324, 330-331, 358, 377-378. *See also* occupation

leadership change, 401-404

legislative party leaders, in Working Committee, 122, 433n; annual election of, 250-251. *See also* Chief Ministers

Lingayats, 340, 356, 386

linguistic makeup of active membership, 355

linguistic minorities, 200-203

Linguistic Provinces Commission, *see* Dar Commission

linguistic states, xxi, 18, 161-164, 302

Lohia, Dr. Ram Manohar, 77

Lok Sabha, 294, 360; Congress members, 1952-1962, occupation of, 379-383; age of, 394-397; education of, 398-399; Congress position in (1952-1967), 408. *See also* Second *and* Third Lok Sabha

Lok Sevak Sangh (Bengali-speaking Congress Gandhians in Bihar), 200

Lok Sevak Sangh (Gandhian social service organization), 81, 220, 221, 304

Macaulay memo, 321

Madhya Pradesh, 49-51, 281, 293, 427; factionalism, 263-264, 281-282

Madras, 245, 248, 250, 332, 396; caste, 332-333, 379

Index

Mahajans, 379

Mahalanobis, P.C., 178; Mahalanobis Plan Frame, 178, 308

Maharashtra, 162, 332, 347-357, 378, 396, 442-443; caste, 270, 332-333, 443; panchayati raj, 371

Mahtab, H.K., 131

Malaviya, K.D., 101, 288, 417

Malenbaum, Wilfred, 178

Malliah, U.S., 54

Mandaloi, B.A., 80, 263

Manipur, 150

manual workers and Congress, 371-372

Marathas, 340, 355, 378, 386, 443. *See also* caste

Masani, M.R., 77

Mass Contacts Committee, 214

mass franchise, xxiii, 402, 441, 446

Mathai, M.O., 271

medium of examination, 208

Meerut constitution sub-committee (1946), 217

Meerut Session (Nov. 1946), 6, 216

Mehta, Asoka, 99, 367, 417

Mehta, Balvantrai, 54

Mehta, Jivraj, 283-284

membership enrollment (1949), 222, 343

membership in other political parties, 217-218

Menon, V.K. Krishna, 86, 91, 185, 294-295, 297, 417n

Meynaud, J., 359, 383, 394

middle peasantry, 350-351, 355, 360, 386

mid-term polls, 445

minorities and candidate selection, 269

Mishra, Pandit D.P., 44, 49-51, 101, 288

Mishra, S.N., 101

Misra, Mahesh Dutta, 239

moderates, period of (1885-1900), 225, 319, 320-324

modernized elite, 168, 169, 180, 308, 320, 369, 370, 387, 392, 394, 404

Moraes, Frank, 57

Morris-Jones, W.H., 356, 402

multi-partyism, 427

Musafir, G.S., 411

Muslim League, 6, 272

Muslims, 22, 131, 132, 271, 321n, 324, 366, 413

Mysore, 162; factionalism in, 263; caste in, 270, 379

Nagaland, 100, 150. *See also* Nagas

Nagas, 100, 150

Nagpur Session (1959), 65-68, 70

Nair, K.P.M., 68

Nanda, G.L., 86, 124, 139, 207; designated acting Prime Minister, 88, 97; removed as Home Minister, 98-99, 102; as invitee to Working Committee, 138; and draft resolution on Planning Commission, 140-143; and Ten Point Program, 417; as mediator in Haryana, 425-426

Narayan, J.P., 81-82

Narayan, Shriman, 172-173, 177

Nasik Session (1950), 28, 32-33, 41, 225

National Development Council, 175, 178, 190, 309, 310

National Integration Conference, 206

national language controversy (1965), 93

national language policy, 189, 203-208

nationalist movements of Asia and Africa, xix, 214, 217, 341

nationalization of general insurance, *see* Ten Point Program

Neale, W.C., 198-199

Nehru, Jawaharlal, 29, 61, 71, 123, 172, 256, 330, 367, 368, 387, 398, 402; as arbitrator,

Index

281-282, 282-283, 278, 286; assurances on language of, 204, 208; attempts to resign from prime ministership, 56, 65-66, 79; from Working Committee, 45; from Parliamentary Board, 251; on Bengal, 253; charisma of, xix, 428; as Congress President, 4-5, 54-57; consensus approach of, 42-43, 174-175, 300-304; death of, 87, 204; and disavowal of Congress Economic Programme Committee Report, 166-167; on dual leadership, 4-5, 30, 51, 54-55, 56, 243, 311; on elective element in Working Committee, 130; impact on composition of Working Committee of, 121-122, 167-168; as invitee to Working Committee, 138; on party-government relations, 7-8, 57-59, 75-76, 102, 147-148, 158, 163, 239-240, 300-304; and Pattabhi's election, 14, 16-17, 20-23; and Prasad's selection as Congress President, 12, 14; reaction to Mrs. Gandhi's becoming Congress President of, 67-68; relation to Dhebar of, 60-61, 61-63; relation to Patel of, 13, 27, 28, 34; role in party before Patel's death of, 34; role in selection of Congress Presidents of, 59-60; suffers stroke, 85-86; and Tandon controversy, 27-53, 144, 163, 167, 240, 268, 297; and zamindari abolition, 194

Nehru, Motilal, 81, 330

Nijalingappa, S., 68, 84, 123, 163, 263, 277, 386; mentioned as possible Congress President, 66, 70; elected President, 413-415. *See also* Syndicate

Nizam of Hyderabad, 10

no-confidence motion, 79, 250

non-Brahmins, 332-333, 355, 400

non-Congressism, 410, 444

non-cooperation, 235, 330

non-planning issues, role of working Committee, 199-210, 310

North India, Congress Party and social change in, 425-427, 443

notables, 351

nuclear weapons, 435

occupation, of Congress members of Second Lok Sabha, 359; by age groups, 335-336; of Congress members of Lok Sabha (1952-1962), 379-383; of Congress delegates (1892-1909), 324; of active members, 347-352; of A.I.C.C. and Working Committee members, 358-361; of active members, A.I.C.C. and Working Committee, compared, 358; of A.I.C.C. members by age groups, 363-365; of A.I.C.C. members in 1919-1923 and 1956, compared, 264-265; of members of Uttar Pradesh assembly, 373-375; of Congress members Council of Ministers in eight selected states, 376-378; by age groups, 377-378; of Indian Council of Ministers (1962), 378

Official Language Act, 204, 205

official resolutions, role of, 139, 433-434

oligarchic tendencies in Congress, checks on, xx, 434-437

one-party dominance, xix, 407, 427, 432, 443

one-term ban on office holding, Hyderabad resolution (1958), 65, 94-95, 107; Bangalore resolution (1965), 95, 144, 209

one-third retirement policy for legislators, 353, 394, 395, 396

organizational development, from 1946 to First General Elections, 216-226

organizational elections, in 1950,

509

Index

27-28; Kripalani's criticism of, 35-36; in 1967, 422, 445
orientalists, 321
Orissa, 446, 447
overlapping membership, in Working Committee, 118-127; in A.I.C.C., 436-437

Pakistan, 10, 27, 32, 50
panchayati raj, xxi, 370-371, 421
Pant, G.B., 47, 59, 67-68, 71, 123, 264, 278, 286, 368
Pant resolution, 117-118, 145
Parliamentary Board, 13, 111, 114, 147, 149, 156, 193, 437; origins of, 233-234, 236-237; composition of, 234; orders Congress ministers to resign (1939), 236; role from 1946 to 1949 of, 246-251; development of umpire role of (1949-1952), 251-259; role from 1952 to 1963 of, 259-266; post-1967 election role of, 423-427
Parsis, 324
partition, 255, 299
partition of Bengal (1905), 326
party bureaucrats, 401-404, 442
party-government relations, xxii, 8-9, 20, 403, 428-429, 435; under Kripalani, 5-12, 30; under Pattabhi, 16-17, 24-26; under Tandon, 31, 45, 48, 159-161; at Indore A.I.C.C., 55-56; under Dhebar, 59-60, 62, 180-181, 244; and Nehru, 7-8, 57-59, 75-76, 102, 147-148, 158, 163, 239-240, 300-304; and Deo, 166-167; and Shastri, 181; and composition of Working Committee, 121-127; over Vanaspati, 159-161; over linguistic states, 161-164; over Economic Programme Committee, 164-167; over Punjabi Suba, 181-184; over devaluation, 184-185; as camouflage

for group conflict, 186-187, 416; origins and development of issue of, 235-244; during post-1967 election period, 416-421; and coordination machinery, 419-421, 434; used to check Mrs. Gandhi, 415; during Gandhian era, 428-429. *See also* dual leadership, relationship of Prime Minister to Congress President, *and* Working Committee
party-government relations in the states, role of Parliamentary Board, 233-234, 244-248; origin and development of controversy over, 235-244; role of factionalism in, 248-250; and attempts to strengthen ministries, 249-251; and development of consultation machinery, 246-248, 259-261. *See also* Working Committee
party politics in India, disillusionment with, 446-447
Patel, Vallabhbhai, 7, 10, 17, 18-19, 50, 123, 167, 236, 245, 330; asks Prasad to become Congress President, 12, 14; relation to Nehru, 13, 27, 28, 34; and role in election of Congress President (1948), 14, 19-20; and role in election of Congress President (1950), 21; dies, 34
Pathak, G.S., 99
Patiala ministry, 18
patidars, 356
Patil, S.K., 38, 55, 66-67, 79, 80, 81, 82, 84, 123, 224, 234, 294, 295, 368, 411, 413. *See also* Syndicate
Patna convention, 40, 41, 42
Patnaik, Biju, 77, 80, 91, 124, 185
patronage, 230
pattern of leadership selection in the states, 261-265, 423-424

510

Index

peasant leagues, 214

planned economic growth, basic strategy, 168-181, 302-303, 308-309

planning, role of Working Committee in, 189-199

Planning Commission, 189, 196; role of Working Committee in decision-making of, a case study, 139-143

polarization of Congress, 444-445

policy-making and Congress composition, 403-404

political fasts, 102

polycentric pattern of decision-making, 429

Poona A.I.C.C. (1960), 129-130, 145, 240-244

Poona Pact, 388

post-Nehru leadership, failure of, 410

Potter, David, 370

Praja Socialist Party (P.S.P.), 277

Prakasam, T., 223

Prasad, Rajendra, 7, 18, 22, 25, 61, 123, 191, 234, 236, 245, 248, 253, 330, 368; as Congress President, 12-13; supports Pattabhi for Congress President, 16-17, 19-23; opposes Kripalani's bid for Congress President, 17-18; compared to Kamaraj, 93-94; and ministerial element in Working Committee, 119; and role in zamindari abolition, 191-194; drafts language resolution, 201-202; and Standards of Public Conduct resolution, 239

Presidential Rule (Article 356), 254, 256, 257, 258, 265, 440

President of the Indian National Congress, selection of, xxii, 59-60, 106-107; and proposals for reform, 4, 54-55; as Rashtrapathi, 25, 241, 432; relation to Prime Minister of, 103-107, 427-433; Nehru as, 4-5, 54-57; Kripalani as, 5-11; Prasad as, 12-13; Pattabhi as, 14-26; Tandon as, 28-49; Dhebar as, 60-65; Mrs. Gandhi as, 66-70; Sanjiva Reddy as, 70-73; D. Sanjivayya as, 72-73; Kamaraj as, 84-103, 412-415; S. Nijalingappa as, 413-415. *See also* party-government relations

price floors for agricultural commodities, 144

primary membership, 220; from 1949 to 1967, 342-344. *See also* four anna membership

Prime Minister, relation to Congress President of, 103-107, 427-433; role in selecting Congress Presidents of, 106-107; role in determining Working Committee agenda of, 135; acceptability to opposition of, 432; and election of Shastri, 87-92; of Mrs. Gandhi (1964), 83, 97-98; of Mrs. Gandhi (1967), 411-412. *See also* party-government relations

princes, role in politics of, 271-272

privy purses, *see* Ten Point Program

pro-changers and no-changers, 40

professional politicians, 391. *See also* public workers

professions, among active members, 349; among Congress members of Lok Sabha, 380. *See also* occupation

provincial returning officers, 228, 229, 230, 422

public workers, 349-350, 365, 381. *See also* constructive workers

Punjab, 65, 248, 292, 396, 424; factionalism in, 255-258; caste in, 270, 379; role of Parliamentary Board in, 255-258

Index

Punjabi Suba, 100, 144, 181-184, 314

qualifications for membership, 216-217, 228
qualified member, 220, 222
Quit India Movement (1942), 213, 304, 335, 353
quotas for services, 206

Radhakrishnan, S., 88, 413
Raipur A.I.C.C. (1960), 128-130
Raipur resolution, 128-131
Rajagopalachari, C., 7, 33, 70, 124, 256, 330, 402
Rajagopalan, G., 131, 132n
Rajasthan, 293, 388, 396; caste in, 270, 379; factionalism in, 282-283, 293, 403; panchayati raj in, 370-371; social composition of Congress in, 442
Rajasthan Kshatriya Mahasabha, 270
Rajmata Vijaya Raje Scindia of Gwalior, 271
Rajputs, 270, 379
Raju, A.S., 72
Raju, V.B., 131
Ram, Jagjivan, 22, 80, 91, 123, 368
Ranga, N.G., 223
Rann of Kutch, 93, 150
Rao, J. Rameshwar, 242-243
Rao, Kala Venkata, 32, 193, 222, 245-246, 253
recruitment in Congress, xxiii, 401; pattern of, 1967 and 1951 compared, 296-297; trend since 1920 of, 335; trend since independence of, 352-354; and impact on social composition, 372-373, 385
Reddi, B. Gopala, 80, 82
Reddis, 340, 386; of Warangal, 351
Reddy, N. Sanjiva, 70-71, 71-73, 84, 104, 123, 223, 243-244, 262, 283, 288, 290, 291, 367, 402. *See also* Syndicate

Reddy, Subba, 291
refugees, 27, 254, 255
regional factors, in candidate selection, 269; in 1967 elections, 411
regional language elite, 361, 403-404, 441
religion, 323, 355; plays role in selection of candidates, 270-271; of active members, 355; of Working Committee and A.I.C.C., 365-366
reorganization, Working Committee sub-committee on, 129
Report of the Congress Agrarian Reforms Committee (1949), 191, 195-196; definition of an economic holding, 195n
Report of the General Secretary for 1938-40, 215
revolution and leadership change, 401-402
Rosen, George, 314, 404
Rowlatt Bills, 330
Roy, B.C., 47, 123, 253, 257, 262, 276
Roy, Kiron Shankar, 252
Roy, Ramashray, 439

sabotage and elections, 284-286, 297, 410
Sachar, Bhim Sen, 182, 255-258
Sadiq, G.M., 101
Sahay, K.B., 264, 280, 411
Sanjivayya, D., 72-73, 104, 124, 290
sarvodaya, 169, 179-180, 221; sarvodaya economic plan, 139
satyagraha, 330; salt satyagraha, 331-332
Saurashtra, 293
Schattschneider, E.E., 298
scrutiny committees, 229, 231
second civil disobedience movement, 214, 331-332, 332-334, 335, 353, 363
Second General Elections, 63
Second Lok Sabha, Congress members of, analysis by age

Index

groups, 334-341; background of, 383-399. *See also* Lok Sabha

Second Plan, 198

secrecy, of Working Committee deliberations, 6-7, 134

Sen, P.C., 411

seniority and succession, 83

Seventh Amendment to Indian Constitution, 202

Shah, Manubhai, 417

Sharma, Bhagwat Dayal, 425

Shastri, Lal Bahadur, 59, 73, 80, 123-124, 367, 387; as candidate for Congress President (1963), 84-85; recalled to Cabinet, 86-87; elected Prime Minister, 87-92, 430; and re-election of Kamaraj as Congress President, 94-96; dies, 97; as invitee to Working Committee, 138; evolves pattern of party-government coordination, 181; as arbitrator, 275, 281, 286

Shea, Thomas, 198

Shrader, Lawrence L., 403

Shrimali, K.L., 80, 82

Sikhs, 22, 271, 278, 355, 366

Singh, Charan, 426

Singh, Darbara, 124, 131, 132n, 184, 292

Singh, Dr. Ram Subhag, 124, 131-132, 185, 288, 295

Singh, Sant Fateh, 182

Singh, Swarah, 280, 417

Singh, Tara, 182, 278, 279

Sinha, S.K., 44, 64

Sino-Indian border dispute, 76

Sirsikar, V.M., 371, 378

Sitaramayya, Dr. B. Pattabhi, 26, 27, 30, 61, 124, 223; as candidate for Congress President, 5; elected (1948), 14-23; views party-government relations, 16-17, 24-26; describes role of Congress President, 23-25; describes state of Congress organization in 1950, 222-223

skill levels of legislators, decline of, 400-401

social composition of the Congress, xxiv-xxv, 114, 199, 322, 325, 442; and land reform policy, 198-199, 403; impact on recruitment patterns of, 372-373; before independence, 319-341; in mass organization, 342-369; in parliamentary wing, 370-404; changes in, 441-444; relations to state social structure of, 441-442; and social changes in North India, 443

social control of banks, *see* Ten Point Program

socialist pattern of society, 175-177

social mobility, 389-390

social origin of Congress members of Lok Sabha, 390-391

social stratification, role of caste, 378-379, 385-388; role of occupation, 370-378

Standards of Public Conduct resolution, 239-240

state assemblies, Congress position (1952-1967), 408; Congress position by state (1952-1967), 409

state Congress elite, 371-375

state revenue ministers, meeting of, 191

States Reorganization Commission (S.R.C.), 151-155, 181, 202; Working Committee in relation to, 152

Subramaniam, C., 66, 70, 99, 204, 205, 207, 367, 417

sudra castes, 386, 388. *See also* caste

Sukhadia, M.L., 85, 101, 124, 282, 367

swadeshi, 326

Swarajists, 235

Swatantra Party, 70, 124, 271, 382

Index

verifying party electoral rolls, problems of, 228-230

village and cottage industries, 168-174, 177-181. *See also* sarvodaya

voting rights of primary members, 227-228

Vyas, J.N., 283

Weiner, Myron, 229, 351, 352, 359, 372, 404

West Bengal, 238, 245, 248, 293, 396, 422; Parliamentary Board's role in, 251-255; and South Calcutta by-election, 252; factionalism in, 251-255; organizational elections in, 254; membership, 347-357

West Bengal-Bihar Transfer of Territories Act, 153-155

westernized elite, passing of, 404. *See also* modernized elite

white-collar workers and Congress, 349, 371

women, in Working Committee, 125-126

Working Committee, xxii; analysis of agenda of, 145-149; preparation of agenda of, 135; and Bangalore resolution, 144; breakdown of collective responsibility in, 95-96, 144, 184; collective responsibility in, 134; consensus building in, 139-145, 202; duration of meetings of, 136-137; elective element in, 85, 127-132; format of discussions by, 143; frequency of meetings of, 136; functions of, 111-112; functions before independence of, 112; impact of 1967 General Elections on composition of, 415; issue of autonomy of, 115-122; May 1967 meeting, special features of, 416-417; and members defeated in 1967 elections, 414n; membership analyzed, 122-127; one-third rule in, 118-122;

preparation of notes for, 135-136; problems of formal composition of, 115-121, 127-132; provision for free discussion in, 116-118, 149-151; resolutions, nature of, 139; role of informal contacts in, 151-155; role of invitees, 122, 137-138; secrecy of deliberations of, 6-7, 134; size increased, 119-121; social composition of, 358-367; role in succession of, 89-90, 137

chief policy-maker: 111, 433-434; foreign policy role of, 8-10, 150-151; traditional policy-making function of, 112-114; and vanaspati, 159, 161; and linguistic states, 161-164; and Economic Programme Committee, 164-167; and strategy for planning, 169-181; and Punjabi Suba, 181-184; and devaluation, 184-185; provides camouflage for group conflict, 186-187, 416. *See also* party-government relations

all-India policymaking: relationship to state governments of, 113-114, 403, 421-422; and planning issues, 189-199; and zamindari abolition, 191-194; and ceilings, 194-199; non-planning issues, 199-210; language policy, 199-210; linguistic minorities, 200-203; national language, 203-208; settlement of interstate disputes, 209; used to prod states, 200-203. *See also* center-state relations

chief executive of the party: 114, 231-232, 422-423; formal powers of, 211, 437; factionalism in, 212-213; organizational problems before independence of, 214-216; delays in reorganization of, 216; problems of reorganization of,